BRINGING BACK
===== *the* =====
Black Robed
Regiment

Bob & JoAnna,

"Fight the good fight!"

Dan Fisher

BRINGING BACK

the

Black Robed Regiment

*How the 18th century church stood for
liberty and why it must do so again*

Second Edition

DAN FISHER

TATE PUBLISHING
AND ENTERPRISES, LLC

Published by Tate Publishing & Enterprises, LLC
127 E. Trade Center Terrace | Mustang, Oklahoma 73064 USA
1.888.361.9473 | www.tatepublishing.com

Tate Publishing is committed to excellence in the publishing industry. The company reflects the philosophy established by the founders, based on Psalm 68:11,
"The Lord gave the word and great was the company of those who published it."

Book design copyright © 2015 by Tate Publishing, LLC. All rights reserved.
Cover design by Jim Villaflores
Interior design by Richell Balansag

Published in the United States of America

ISBN: 978-1-68270-655-8
1. Religion / Church & State
2. Religion / Religion, Politics & State
15.09.21

Contents

Introduction

"THERE WAS A TIME IN AMERICA"

W hen the Christian Church believed in liberty so strongly that some of her preachers, "patriot preachers" as they are called, were willing to stand in their pulpits and boldly proclaim the biblical principles of liberty and just government; all while emphatically denouncing perceived tyrants and apparent tyranny.

> "... it will appear that we are in the way of our duty in opposing the tyranny of Great Britain; for, if unlimited submission is not due to any human power, if we have an undoubted right to oppose and resist a set of tyrants that are subverting our just rights and privileges, there cannot remain a doubt in any man, that will calmly attend to reason, whether we have a right to resist and oppose the arbitrary measures of the King and Parliament; ... they are robbing us of the inalienable rights that the God of nature has given us as men and rational beings, and has confirmed to us in his written word as Christians."[1]
>
> Pastor Samuel West, 1776

> "Liberty is the grand fountain, under God, of every temporal blessing, and what is infinitely more important, it is favorable to the propagation of unadulterated Christianity. Liberty is the parent of truth, justice, virtue, patriotism, benevolence, and every generous and noble

purpose of the soul. ... How inestimable a blessing then must liberty be, and how inconceivably great its loss! ... certainly tyranny & oppression are the cause of the devil, the cause which God's soul hates."[2]

Pastor Abraham Keteltas, 1777

"When a constitutional government is converted into tyranny, and the laws, rights and properties of a free people are openly invaded, there ought not to be the least doubt but that a remedy ... is provided in the laws of God and reason, for their preservation; nor ought resistance in such case to be called rebellion."[3]

Pastor Elizur Goodrich, 1787

"THERE WAS A TIME IN AMERICA"

... when many of these patriot preachers felt that tyranny was so *conscripting* them and liberty was so *compelling* them that they led the men of their congregations off to distant battlefields to defeat that tyranny and to defend those liberties.

"Our late happy government is changed into the terrors of military execution. Our firm opposition to the establishment of an arbitrary system is called *rebellion,* and we are to expect no mercy but by yielding property and life at discretion. This we are resolved at all events not to do; and therefore, we have taken arms in our own defense, and all the colonies are united in the great cause of liberty."[4]

Samuel Langdon, Pres. Of Harvard, 1775

"We are not fighting against the name of a king, but the tyranny; and if we sailor that tyranny under another name, we only change our master without getting rid of our slavery. ... Now is the golden opportunity for banishing tyranny as well as royalty out of the American states, and sending them back to Europe, from whence they were imported."[5]

Pastor William Gordon, 1777

"Peace, peace, we ardently wish; but not upon terms dishonorable to ourselves, or dangerous to our liberties; and our enemies seem not yet prepared to allow it upon any other. At present the voice of providence, the call of our still invaded country, and the cry of every thing dear to us, all unite to rouse us to prosecute the war with redoubled vigor; upon the success of which all our free constitutions, all our hopes depend."[6]

Pastor Samuel Cooper, 1780

JOAB TROUT ... THE BLACK ROBED REGIMENT

... On September 10, 1777, the sun was preparing to dip beneath the horizon and darkness was beginning to overtake the countryside just outside of Philadelphia, Pennsylvania. A young Lutheran preacher in his mid-twenties, himself a native of Pennsylvania, stood before his fellow patriots on the bank of Brandywine Creek to offer a few words of challenge and encouragement on the eve of the Battle of Brandywine. Looking out over a portion of the American troops, including Generals George Washington, Anthony Wayne, Peter Muhlenberg, and other officers,[7] Chaplain Joab Trout began to speak:

> "Soldiers and Countrymen: We have met this evening perhaps for the last time. We have shared the toil of march, the peril of flight, and the dismay of the retreat; alike we have endured the cold and hunger, the contumely

of the internal foe and the courage of foreign oppression. We have sat, night after night, beside the campfire; we have together heard the roll of the reveille which called us to duty, or the beat of the tattoo which gave the signal for the hardy sleep of the soldier with the earth for his bed and knapsack for his pillow.

And now, soldiers and brethren, we have met in the peaceful valley on the eve of battle while the sunlight is dying away behind yonder heights, the sunlight that, tomorrow morn, will glimmer on scenes of blood. We have met amid the whitening tents of our encampment, in time of terror and gloom, have gathered together, God grant it may not be the last time. ...'They that take the sword shall perish by the sword.' And have they not taken the sword? Let the desolated plain, the blood-trodden valley, the burned farmhouse, the sacked village and the ravaged town answer ... They may conquer us tomorrow; might and wrong may prevail, and we may be driven from this field – but the hour of God's own vengeance will come. ...

You have taken the sword, but not in the spirit of wrong and ravage. You have taken the sword for your homes, your wives, your little ones; for truth, for justice and right, and to you the promise is: Be of good cheer, your foes have taken the sword in defiance of all that man holds dear; they shall perish by the sword.

Tomorrow morning we will go forth to battle, for I need not tell you that your unworthy minister will march with you, invoking God's aid in the fight – we will march forth to battle! Need I exhort you to fight the good fight, to fight for your homesteads, for your wives and children? I might urge you by galling memories of British wrongs; I might paint all this again in the vivid colors of the terrible reality, if I thought your courage needed such wild excitement. But I know you are strong in the might of the Lord. You will march forth to battle on the morrow with light hearts and determined spirits, ... And in the hour of battle, when all around is lit by the lurid cannonade-glare, and the piercing musket-flash, when the wounded strew the ground, and the dead litter your path, then remember that God is with you; God the awful and infinite fights for you and will triumph.

And now farewell! Many of us may fall tomorrow. God rest the souls of the fallen! Many of us may live to tell the story, and in the memory of all will ever linger the quiet scene of this autumnal night. ... When we meet again, may the shadows of twilight be flung over a peaceful land. God in Heaven grant it. Let us pray.

Great Father, we bow before thee, we invoke thy blessing, we deprecate thy wrath, we thee return thanks for the past, we ask thy aid for the future; for we are in times of trouble, O Lord, and sore beset by foes, merciless and unpitying. The sword gleams over our land, the dust of the sod is dampened with the blood of our neighbors and friends. O God of mercy, we pray thy blessing upon the American arms. ... Visit the tents of our host, comfort the soldier in his wounds and afflictions; nerve him for the fight and prepare him for the hour of death.

And in the hour of defeat, O God of hosts, do thou be our stay, and in the hour of triumph be thou our guide. Teach us to be merciful. ... In the hour of death do thou guide us to the abode prepared for the blest. So shall we return thanks to thee through Christ our Redeemer. God prosper the cause. Amen."

The next day, September 11, 1777, Joab Trout died[8] defending what I'm certain he believed to be his God-given right to liberty – especially religious liberty. (The above transcription of Trout's sermon was found in the mid 1800's among the papers of John Jacob Schaefmyer, Major in the Continental Army.)

"THERE WAS A TIME IN AMERICA"

... when we understood the significant role the patriot preachers and their congregations played in helping to secure America's independence from Great Britain. For example, in 1864, journalist/historian Joel Headley emphasized the importance of the patriot preachers:

> "It is unquestionably true that, if the clergy of New England had from the outset taken the decided and determined stand against the cause of the colonies, which they did for it, the result would have been totally different."[9]

In 1860, John Wingate Thornton summed up the vital contribution these preachers made:

> "Thus is manifest, in the spirit of our history, in our annals, and by the general voice of the fathers of the republic, that, in a very great degree – to the pulpit, the Puritan pulpit, we owe the moral force which won our independence."[10]

WHO WAS THE BLACK ROBED REGIMENT?

Sadly, when most Christians hear of the Black Robed Regiment today, they probably envision judges wearing their black robes as they sit behind the bench. Little do they know that the "men in black" of the Revolution era were actually preachers – preachers who normally wore black robes as they stood before their congregations each Sunday. These "patriot preachers," as some have called them, were so committed to religious liberty that they proclaimed from their pulpits the biblical principles of government and liberty (as they understood them); and when the time came, some bravely led the men of their congregations to actually fight on the battlefield to defend those principles.

It is important to understand that the "Black Regiment" was not an actual regiment in the Colonial/American Army. These "pro-independence" preachers never organized themselves into any type of "official" group or organization. In fact, most of these preachers were probably not even familiar with the term. They would never have imagined introducing themselves by saying, "Hello, I'm pastor Caldwell and I'm a member of the Black Robed Regiment."

The Tory, Peter Oliver, Chief Justice of the Superior Court of Massachusetts, used the title, "Black Regiment" as he referred to the pro-independence preachers who were standing with the patriot James Otis.[11] Oliver was particularly upset at these preachers for their outcries against the British Regulars who had fired upon the citizens in the Boston Massacre and he claimed that the "pulpits rang their chimes upon blood guiltiness, in order to incite the people."[12] Then when the trials of the British soldiers had concluded and the pastors, who passionately disagreed with the verdict of the court, loudly voiced their disapproval, Oliver lamented that the pulpits "rang their peals of malice against the courts of justice."[13] Oliver penned his actual opinion of the patriot preachers in his book, *The Origin and Progress of the American Rebellion*:

> "Mr. Otis, ye. Son, understanding the Foibles of human Nature, … advanced one shrewd Position … that it was necessary to secure the black Regiment, these were his Words, & his Meaning was to engage ye. Dissenting Clergy on his Side. … & this Order of Men might, in a literal Sense, be stiled such, for like their Predecessors of 1641 they have been unceasingly sounding the Yell of Rebellion in the Ears of an ignorant & deluded People. … Mr. Otis's black Regiment, the dissenting Clergy, were also set to Work, to preach up Manufactures instead of Gospel. They preached about it & about it, until the Women & Children, both within Doors & without, set

their Spinning Wheel a whirling in Defiance of Great Britain. The female Spinners kept on spinning for 6 Days of the Week; & on the seventh, the Parsons took their Turns, & spun out their Prayers & Sermons to a long Thread of Politicks, & to much better Profit than the other Spinners; for they generally clothed the Parson and his Family with the Produce of their Labor: This was a new Species of Enthusiasm, & might be justly termed, the Enthusiasm of the Spinning Wheel."[14]

If any of the preachers of the Black Regiment ever knew the irritation and concern they had caused King George, the Parliament, and the Tories, no doubt they were probably quite pleased. As we will see, it seems that many British leaders feared this "regiment" almost as much as they did the actual regiments of the Colonial Army. Journalist/Historian Joel Headley wrote, "every such rebel parson was more dangerous to the cause of the King than a whole regiment of militia."[15]

Even though Peter Oliver obviously meant the title to be a term of derision, today it is recognized by many as a badge of honor – at least by those who believe the patriot preachers were correct in what they did. So, for our purposes in this book, the "Black Robed Regiment" or the shorter "Black Regiment" will be used to refer to those patriot preachers who were pro-independence and stood against King George and the British Parliament.

WHY WRITE THIS BOOK?

On July 24, 1766, in a sermon celebrating the repeal of the Stamp Act, Pastor Joseph Emerson declared:

"And what is the great, the mighty deliverance we have experienced? Does it deserve a commemoration? Yes, if anything great and good ever did. Is it worthy to be handed down to posterity? Yes, to be printed in a book and preserved with sacred care as long as time shall last.

Is it of such value as to demand a whole day to be spent in praising God for it? Yes, our lives – yea, eternity – as it is what our Savior purchased for us, and as there are such glorious things, of a spiritual nature, connected with it. And what is it? A deliverance from slavery – nothing less than from vile ignominious slavery."[16]

Whether or not the repeal of the Stamp Act was as worthy of the "great commemoration" Emerson believed it was, I am convinced that the performance of the patriot preachers in helping secure America's independence is.

This book is my attempt to do just that – offer a modern "commemoration" of the patriot preachers of our War for Independence who, as preacher Emerson claimed, helped free the American colonists from what they believed was the "ignominious slavery" of the British. To be sure, others in the past have attempted to chronicle the story of these sincere and determined men. But, I believe their story must be retold to the modern church in a relevant way. Their courage and commitment to liberty, especially religious liberty (as they understood it in their time), should inspire 21st century Christians to reconsider the role today's church should play in the defense of liberty, as we understand it. In retelling their story of a long ago era, we're obligated to ask fundamental questions about ourselves here in the 21st Century.

A WORD OF WARNING

It must be remembered that the patriot preachers of the Black Robed Regiment lived in 18th century America – not the 21st century. Things were very different in their day than they are in ours. Obviously, over two centuries of inventions, innovation, and learning have created a very different world than the one they knew. Sadly the most significant changes have occurred with the great downward shift in our philosophy and morality of our culture. The patriot preachers who marched off to fight for religious liberty over two hundred and thirty years ago would probably see us as a modern day Sodom and Gomorrah.

Although it would be insane to claim that every American colonist in the 18th century was a born again Christian or even claimed to be a Christian, it is an undeniable fact that the culture of the Revolution era was highly religious and that Protestant Christianity was the dominant faith. Even among those who did not claim to be Christian, there was still a healthy respect for, and even belief in, at some level, the Bible, its teachings, and the claims of Christ. Most people of that day, including most of the Founders, viewed the world, including politics and law, through lenses significantly tinted by biblical principles.

Obviously, the world in which we live today is a very different place. Even though the Judeo/Christian perspective remains the dominant view of the majority of Americans, there is no denying the fact that we live in a truly pluralistic society. Unfortunately for Christians, the Bible no longer holds sway over the American mind as it did in the day of the Black Regiment.

Therefore, it would be a huge mistake to conflate the time of the patriot preachers with our time. Although I believe there is much we can learn from these preachers in how they impacted their culture, especially in regard to religious liberty, we in the 21st cannot simply copy their strategy and assume we will have the same results. If we want to defend liberty as they did, we must take the eternal principles they employed and then enlist them in a way that is relevant to our day.

DEFINING TERMS

As you read this book, you will often encounter common phrases. For example, you will read the words, "as they understood it," especially as it relates to the term "liberty." I use this phrase intentionally to describe how *they defined* liberty and how *they believed* that their liberties were under attack from King George and the Parliament. When I refer to their liberty being under attack, I generally mean that the American Colonists longed to govern themselves and no longer wanted the King or Parliament making governmental policies for them – especially when they had little or no say in the matter. It must be understood that this was both an evolutionary and revolutionary idea. From the development of settlements in the 1600's under Charters from the King, the colonists considered themselves Englishmen. Consequently, they were in no hurry to separate themselves from the traditions or the economic and physical protections of Britain. But eventually, with increased governmental abuse by Great Britain and because of the success of "political agitators" like Sam Adams, Thomas Paine, John Adams, and a whole host of others, including the preachers of the Black Regiment, the idea of independence gained acceptance in the mid 1700's, eventually leading, of course, to the War for Independence. But as we consider their story, we must be careful to understand their passion for liberty within *their* context and *their* time. Their situation and understanding was unique to *them* – just as our situation and understanding of liberty are unique to our time.

Therefore, when I use the term "liberty," as it relates to our time, first, I generally mean the right of the people to live free from the harassment and overregulation of government – local, state, and federal. Second, while I do not believe government should be overbearing, I also do not believe anarchy is a viable alternative. Just government is an institution of God and is essential for establishing and maintaining a civil society. Last, I believe government should be as small and have as little control over our lives as is possible. Government's primary purpose should be the securing of our unalienable rights and responding to the "consent of the governed" – not micro-managing every aspect of our lives and robbing from us through unlawful taxation to support endless social programs to support those who could, but choose not to provide for themselves.

In this regard, I believe "federalism" where the greatest governmental power is held closest to the people, i.e., the state and local governments, holds the greatest promise to provide an environment where true liberty can flourish. Although the purpose of this book is not to offer a detailed discussion of federalism, suffice it for now to say that law-abiding men and women require and request minimal government. Unfortunately, right now, government, especially the federal government, has far too much power over our lives and is expected to provide way too much for its citizens. Smaller, more manageable, and closer government is far more accountable to the citizens it serves and is therefore much easier to affect for good. Sadly, with the exponential growth of our federal government, state governments are being marginalized and minimalized and thus, true representative government is in danger of extinction in America today.

For all practical purposes, this is the very problem the patriot preachers were preaching and fighting against over two hundred and thirty years ago. In a strange twist of irony, it appears that our history has circled back around and, many of us believe our liberties are once again under attack by an overreaching government just as theirs were in the 18th century. Only today, instead of being threatened by an overbearing king three thousand miles away in England, our liberties are now being assaulted by an overbearing federal government one to two thousand miles away in Washington D.C. If Paul Revere were to make his "midnight ride" today, rather than crying, "The regulars are coming," he'd probably be shouting, "The feds are coming!" By analyzing the Black Regiment's response to their crisis of liberty in their day, perhaps we can shed some light on how we should respond to the crisis of liberty in our generation.

GETTING THE STORY STRAIGHT

Retelling a story like that of the Black Robed Regiment is a daunting task – especially for one like myself who is not a credentialed historian, yet still is a passionate "student" and lover of history. But because I believe the story of the patriot preachers is so critical to the modern church, I have endeavored to retell it as accurately and compellingly as I can.

But before plunging headlong into their amazing story, I believe it is important to remember that the men who made up "the Regiment" were as human and fallen as the rest of us. No doubt, they attempted to live as Christ-like as they could, but like all men, they were fallible and inconsistent at best. In telling their story, we must refrain from allowing our patriotic passion to cause us to embellish the facts. In this regard, historian Dr. John Fea offers good advice:

> "The past is messy. ... human experience is often too complex to categorize in easily identifiable boxes. The study of the past reminds us that when we put our confidence in people – whether they are in the past (such as the founding fathers) or the present – we are likely to be inspired by them, but we are just as likely to be disappointed by them. Sometimes great defenders of liberty held slaves, and political leaders who defended a moral republic rejected a belief in the resurrection of Jesus Christ or the inspiration of the Bible. Historians do their work amid the messiness of the past. Though they make efforts to simplify the mess, they are often left with irony, paradox, and mystery."[17]

Therefore, in telling the amazing stories of the Black Robed Regiment, I have attempted to refrain from the Christian Right's all too common tactic of playing fast and loose with the facts in order to create a group of men who were bigger than life and thus, end up with a story that is as much fiction as it is fact. As a follower of Christ, I believe we have a mandate from God to stay true to the facts. There is no place in Christianity for embellishing the story in order to satisfy some presupposed narrative. As Christians, we should demand an honest handling of the facts. What's more, the story of the patriot preachers is so compelling, there is no reason to embellish it – even if one is so inclined.

That said, finding original source material for some of the stories has been a herculean task, and in some instances, practically impossible. For one thing, since those who bore the title "historian" in the late 18th and early 19th centuries were not required to meet the stringent standards as the credentialed historians of our day, the accuracy of their accounts is sometimes in question. Thankfully, new scholarship is growing and more and more will be understood about the involvement of these preachers as time goes on. In addition, many of the stories of the Revolution era were not actually written down until years later and many of those accounts were compiled by family members or adoring fans whose retelling of the story sometimes seems to lean toward embellishment. When I have chosen to use any "disputed" source, I have either noted this in the text or have sought to corroborate the story by using other sources in order to follow, as best I could, Jesus' admonition, "that by the mouth of two or three witnesses every word may be established." (Matthew 18:16) Although I have confidence in my sources, I am constantly in the quest to find more or even better sources, and when I do, I always make the necessary corrections or update my work.

In writing this book, I have tried to use as many examples from as many preachers and sermons as possible. Even though there were many others that could have been discussed, there are obvious limits to how much material can be gathered, collated, and then written down in a coherent fashion. I have chosen to use material from some of the better known preachers of the period with the unique understanding that others were equally worthy of mention, had space allowed. Additionally, the choice of which preachers and sermons were used was aided by the mere accessibility of the material. Though many of the stories and sermons of this era have regrettably been lost to time, a surprisingly large number have survived and are still available for analysis.

I do believe the relatively large sampling of sermons cited in this work offers a fair representation of what most of the patriot preachers of that time believed, preached, and did. Because the sermons of that era were relatively lengthy and covered a wide range of topics, I have used multiple excerpts from the same sermon in numerous places in this book. Each of the excerpts have been categorized according to subject and will serve as a window into the thinking of the patriot preachers who believed they were fighting to defend their unalienable rights and to create a country in which those rights would be successfully preserved for posterity.

Given the fact that these sermons were written and delivered over two centuries ago, I have made minor adjustments in spelling to improve readability for a modern audience. Even so, I have chosen to present most of the material as it was written. Because the grammar practices of that time were somewhat different from modern usage, the reader will encounter sentence fragments, spelling, capitalizations, and italics that are awkward, but were left mostly untouched to preserve the authentic "feel" of the text.

"CHRISTIAN NATIONALISM"

Before beginning the compelling stories of these preachers, I feel that I must address one other issue: "Christian nationalism," as it is often called. Even though we American Christians are, for the most part, honest and patriotic people who want to protect liberty, if we are not careful, we can often allow our patriotism to overwhelm our judgment and lead us to overstate the facts. Although most would never do this on purpose, our desire to buttress our own beliefs can sometimes lead us to "color" the story so it better fits our narrative. Sometimes in our attempt to make our Founders more Christian than they may have actually been, some historians have either neglected to tell the whole story, have "cherry picked" certain quotes, or have actually embellished the story.

I fear that the end result has too often been a historical narrative that is not really true to the facts, but fits well within our own biblical/political/patriotic framework. This, I believe, has led many to almost deify some of the Founders, to see the U.S. Constitution as a practically God-inspired document almost on the level of Scripture, or to unknowingly break the first and second commandments that warn us against idolatry by elevating America to idol status. If you're like me and grew up in a red-blooded, patriotic, America-loving family, it's pretty easy to practically worship some of the heroes of our past and become prideful over our great "national" accomplishments, somehow thinking we're better than everyone else. It is true that America was founded in a very "Christian" culture and many of our Founders were indeed committed followers of Christ. It is also true that Americans have accomplished great things and have helped millions to experience greater liberty and a better way of life, but that doesn't mean America is infallible. Being proud of one's heritage and country is one thing, but idolatry is another.

Unfortunately, there continues to be a great deal of controversy created by some of my fellow believers who continue to claim that America was/is/should be a "Christian nation." The idea that the United States is, or ever was, a monolithic "nation," as Israel was a "nation" with borders and various systems that supported a national government (a theocracy with God as King and then later a monarchy) is simply not supported by the facts. Certainly, there is plentiful evidence in Scripture that God *directly established* the nation of Israel, but Scripture offers no evidence, of course, that God *directly established* the United States of America. There is plentiful evidence that the Church, and Christians in particular, had a significant impact on the founding of the colonies and later, the United States, but there is no empirical evidence that God *directly established* the United States as a "Christian nation." It is clear that in the sovereign, permissive will of God, He allowed, and maybe even assisted, the establishment of a representative republic in North America in the years between 1776-1789 – one that was heavily influenced by Christian principles. But the United States of America was never a "nation" in the sense that Israel was/is a "nation."

Most of our Founders never intended for the United States to be one, monolithic "nation," governed by one, all-powerful federal government. Instead, they intended it to be a compact/union of multiple, sovereign states. In many ways, this system of government is similar to the one Israel implemented during the period of the Judges in the Old Testament. During this time, essentially, the Israelites functioned as a confederation of 12 tribes without any real central authority. But, this experiment in representative government also teaches us that if close attention is not paid to the administration of a confederation (in our terms, a Union), it can quickly devolve into a monarchy where the people allow/demand a king – just as the Israelites did in 1 Samuel 8. Ironically, this almost parallels our experience in America today because we have all but transitioned from a confederation of 50 states, to one, huge, monolithic "nation" ruled by a new kind of "king" in Washington DC.

The United States is, and has always been, just that – states that are united. The preamble to the U.S. Constitution begins with the words, "In order to form a more perfect Union." Notice that it does not say "nation" – it says "union." America is a union/compact of fifty (originally thirteen) sovereign states who voluntarily joined into a compact in which they surrendered a limited amount of their state sovereignty to a limited, central government whose powers are "enumerated" in Article I, Section 8 of the U.S. Constitution. Most of the Founders would have never envisioned themselves, certainly at the beginning, to be surrendering their state's complete sovereignty as they joined the union called the United States of America. Had they understood themselves to be doing that, no doubt, many of them would have been against the compact in the first place.

So, as I refer to America in this book, I am referring to a union of fifty sovereign states that work together to form a working compact; a form of government called federalism – and when it comes to providing for individual liberty, federalism is about as good as it gets this side of heaven. When I speak of the church taking its proper role, I do not mean that it should "take over" and force people to live under Mosaic Law; I mean that Christians should be "salt and light" and do their best, using the biblical principles they believe, to influence government and policy just as other groups/people do. I do not believe that the goal of the Church should be to establish a theocracy in America. We have a republican form of government expressed in a representative republic and this form of government, I believe, offers the very best insurance that all citizens' civil and religious liberties will be protected.

TO MY FELLOW CHRISTIANS

This account of the Black Robed Regiment is a story of courage and conviction that will shed new light on what and how some in the 1770's understood what it meant to live and think "Christianly" in their day. The patriot preachers showcased in this book provide a little known perspective of the founding era and what part the church played in the success of the War for Independence.

To be sure and to be fair to history, there were many other preachers who opposed separating from the King, John Wesley being one of the more prominent figures in this regard. But this book isn't about those who opposed separating from England, it's about those who felt a moral, political, and theological obligation to separate.

It is my prayer that this book will play some small part in helping to revive the story of the amazing patriot preachers and begin a similar modern day revival among today's preachers and Christians. If ever we needed to understand the ministry of these men and their commitment to our founding principles, it is today. Quoting historian, Dr. John Fea again,

> "The past has the power to stimulate us, fill us with emotion, and arouse our deepest convictions about what is good and right. When we study inspirational figures of the past, we often connect with them through time and leave the encounter wanting to be better people or perhaps even continue their legacy of reform, justice, patriotism, or heroism."[18]

TO MY FELLOW PREACHERS/PASTORS:

Having served as a preacher/pastor for over thirty-one years, I understand what a high and holy calling it is to be led by God into the preaching ministry. I, like many of you, believe the Bible to be the inspired, inerrant Word of God and am consistently overwhelmed with the enormous honor and responsibility of having been chosen to proclaim God's Word to His people. It is a sacred trust that I take quite seriously – one I endeavor to fulfill with all of the strength the Holy Spirit supplies. As Paul admonished, I always desire to "skillfully handle the Word of God" and never be guilty of John's warning against "adding to or taking away" from its holy message. Therefore I am extremely careful when handling the biblical text. Preaching the Gospel of Jesus Christ so that lost men can be saved and saved men can be sanctified is the greatest of all responsibilities.

But just as we are responsible to handle the Scriptures with great care, we are also equally responsible to preach the "whole counsel" of God – not just the parts we like the best or that our people want to hear. Paul warned Timothy:

"Preach the word; be instant in season, out of season; reprove, rebuke, exhort with all longsuffering and doctrine. ³For the time will come when they will not endure sound doctrine; but after their own lusts shall they heap to themselves teachers, having itching ears; ⁴And they shall turn away their ears from the truth, and shall be turned unto fables. ⁵But watch thou in all things, endure afflictions, do the work of an evangelist, make full proof of thy ministry." 2 Timothy 4:2-5

The many preachers discussed and quoted in this book came from divergent doctrinal backgrounds and did not agree on many subjects. Honestly, most of us who consider ourselves to be evangelical Christians would probably take issue with a number of their doctrinal positions. For example, some were extreme Calvinists, while I, though embracing some Calvinist positions, do not consider myself a Calvinist to their degree. Additionally, a number of them believed America was the "new Israel" and carried the direct blessing of God. While I do believe they, by virtue of being true Christians, were part of God's family and plan, I do not believe they had become the new Israel. That being said, there is still much we can learn today from these intriguing Christian preachers of the Revolution era.

It is also important to understand that the War was indeed a Presbyterian war buttressed by Calvinistic theological concepts (although representatives of most other denominations would eventually engage). In his book, *Presbyterians and American Culture: A History,* Professor Bradley J. Longfield, in writing about John Witherspoon, a leading member of the Black Regiment, made this point when he wrote, "Witherspoon's combination of Calvinist theology, Scottish Philosophy [particularly Francis Hutchenson], and Real Whig ideology compelled him to throw himself into the Revolutional cause with force and energy."[19] Witherspoon's Calvinist theology, seasoned with Scottish Enlightenment philosophy, along with a dose of Whig political ideology, collided together in his mind, compelling him to engage in the struggle intensely. (I highlight his contribution to the War for Independence in Chapter 11) This was the mindset of many of the preachers who made up the Black Regiment.

But to be fair to the story of this period, there were also well known Christians who supported the King and his right to rule the colonies. For example, as I mentioned earlier, the famous Methodist preacher John Wesley did not support American independence. It would, therefore, be misleading to suggest that support for revolution against England among American Christians in the 1770's was unanimous.

But when it came to their understanding of the principles of just government and the need for men to defend their God-given rights, the patriot preachers were in agreement. For the sake of liberty, they willingly set aside their doctrinal differences, linked arms, stood up, spoke out, and at times, marched off to fight. They knew that if they won the war, there would be plenty of time for doctrinal debate later. But they also understood that if they lost the war, doctrinal disagreement would be the least of their concerns.

So as they set aside their doctrinal differences for the bigger struggle of liberty, they generally did so under the umbrella of Whig political philosophy. A product of the Enlightment period, Whig political philosophy of that time stressed the constitutional rule of law and individual sovereignty under that law. What made these preachers so valuable to the "cause" was their remarkable ability to defend this political philosophy with strong biblical arguments. They effectively preached sermons (though perhaps straining the text at times) about the biblical underpinnings of liberty, self-governance, and the need for Christians to resist unlawful, unjust government. Insisting that the colonists had a "biblical" right to revolt, many of the preachers who supported the War forcefully advocated for the conflict.

Admittedly, this creates a bit of a conundrum for the modern preacher, which, I believe, is the reason why so many are unwilling to speak out against the overreach of federal bureaucracy today. Fundamentally, the War for Independence forces us to confront the issue of whether or not Christians had a biblical right to revolt against the King of England then, and if Christians have a right to challenge governmental abuse of authority today. This is the philosophical question the patriot preachers faced in the 1760s and 70s. In many ways, it is the very same question we face today.

For me personally, while I do not see an explicit command in the Scriptures *for* revolution of the type they successfully executed in 1776-1783, neither do I see in them an explicit command *against* it. I am convinced that the issue of whether or not a people have biblical justification to revolt against what they perceive to be an unjust government will never be settled by an explicit Biblical argument. Rather, those involved in this debate must learn to make cogent, forceful arguments defending their positions, just as many in the Black Regiment did.

So, the premise of this book is simple: in the period shortly after the First Great Awakening, a movement emerged that challenged the right of the King and Parliament to rule the colonies. This movement was made up of political agitators, rugged individualists, men of ambition, and men of the cloth referred to as the Black Regiment. This book is written to reacquaint the 21st century church with their story in the hope that their experience may help us find solutions to the even greater problems we face today.

Just as it did for them, the time has come, I believe, for us to follow the example of our patriot preacher ancestors, set aside our doctrinal differences, link arms, and stand up for liberty, as we understand it here in the 21st century. If we win the day, there will be plenty of time later for doctrinal debate – if not, we have much greater problems. I am convinced that if we fail in this task, the freedoms the patriot preachers fought and died for could be lost – maybe forever. The future survival of our once great republic may well depend on whether or not today's generation of preachers is up to the challenge. Can we rediscover the spirit of our patriot preacher ancestors and find the courage to stand up against today's tyranny as they did more than two centuries ago?

If we agree that the most important thing is the preaching of the Gospel of Jesus Christ, then surely *we must also agree* that the second most important thing is the preservation of the freedom to do the most important thing. How can we preachers/pastors of today do less for liberty than our patriot preacher forefathers? My prayer and my passion is that God will fill today's preachers/pastors with the spirit of the Black Robed Regiment of old so that they will rise up and fully engage in the defense of liberty in the 21st century. To this end, I dedicate this book.

Dan Fisher, June 1, 2015

Section I:

How they fought

Chapter 1

"IN NEED OF OUR MOST EXPERIENCED PATRIOTS"

On October 24, 1780, in a letter to James Warren, President of the Massachusetts Provincial Congress, Samuel Adams wrote:

> "If ever a time should come, when vain and aspiring men shall possess the highest seats in Government, our country will stand in need of its experienced patriots to prevent its ruin."[20]

Adams' 18th century "prophecy" has eerily come to pass here in the 21st century. Just as some in the church stood for liberty then led by their patriot preachers, so it must take its stand again today if we are to, as Adams said, "prevent our country's ruin."

Who was the Black Robed Regiment? It was John Treadwell …

Expecting a war with the British to break out at any moment, John Treadwell, pastor of the First Church of Lynn, Massachusetts, kept his loaded flintlock musket with him in the pulpit. It is said that he would approach the pulpit with his sermon under one arm and his cartridge box under the other.[21]

Who was the Black Robed Regiment? It was Joab Houghton …

On April 23, 1775, as the news of the battles of Lexington and Concord reached New Jersey, Joab Houghton, pastor of the First Baptist Church in Hopewell, New Jersey, called his congregation together and delivered this impassioned call to arms: "Men of New Jersey, the red coats are murdering our brethren of New England! Who follows me to Boston?" Every man in his congregation stepped forward and followed their pastor to Boston to fight for liberty.[22]

Who was the Black Robed Regiment? It was John Rosbrugh ...

> "It was hardly possible, in a war in which clergymen often exposed themselves like the meanest soldier, and rendered themselves so obnoxious to the enemy by the leading part they took in the rebellion, that some should not have fallen on the battlefield, or otherwise suffered a violent death from the hands of their foes. The Revolution would have been less sacred, if their blood had not mingled in the costly sacrifice that was laid on the altar of freedom. John Rosbrugh was one of these, giving his life to the cause to which he had already given his heart."[23]

This is how journalist/historian Joel Headley began his short biography of John Rosbrugh in 1864. Scots-Irish by birth, John entered this world in 1714. He and his older brother William immigrated to America sometime around 1730 and at the age of nineteen, he married his first wife, Sarah (her maiden name has been lost to history). Tragically, Sarah died giving birth to their first child, a son, who died also. Profoundly affected by this experience, John's deep and heavy grief drove him to the Lord. In Christ he found not only the healing he so desperately needed, but a new calling for his life as well – the ministry. Though of extremely modest means, John, with the financial aid of donors, immediately began preparing himself for the pastoral ministry by attending Princeton. Graduating in 1761, he was licensed to preach in 1763 and ordained into the ministry on December 11, 1764. He began his pastoral ministry preaching to the congregations of Greenwich, Oxford, and Mansfield Woodhouse – all located in the Musconetcong River valley in Warren County in the northwest section of New Jersey just east of the Pennsylvania border.

In 1769, John Rosbrugh was called to be the pastor of Allen Township Presbyterian Church and he and his family made their new home at the "Forks of the Delaware" in Pennsylvania. It was from this pulpit that Rosbrugh, already well known as a strong preacher of the Gospel, also became known as an outspoken patriot of American liberty and independence.[24]

On May 20, 1775, with war imminent, the Presbyterian Synod of New York and Philadelphia, of which Rosbrugh was a member, sent a letter to all of its pastors. The letter read in part:

> "... exhort especially the young and vigorous, by assuring them that there is no soldier so undaunted as the pious man; no army so formidable as those who are superior to the fear of death. ... Let therefore, every one, who from generosity of spirit, or benevolence of heart, offer himself as a champion in his country's cause, be persuaded to reverence the name, and walk in the fear of the Prince of the kings of the earth, and that he may, with the most unshaken firmness, expect the issue either in victory or death."[25]

Historian and Pastor John C. Clyde described Rosbrugh's response to the Synod's letter this way: "Thus Mr. Rosbrugh would feel that he was under moral obligation, with all Presbyterians, to lend his aid to repel what seemed to him an unjust demand on the part of the Mother Country."[26] Just as John had refused to accept the yoke of tyranny in his native home of Ireland, he was just as unwilling to accept it in his new home of America. Not long after receiving the afore-mentioned letter, John's passions were intensified even more when members of his own family and community began joining the Colonial army and marching off to war.

When Fort Washington, situated on Manhattan Island, fell to the British on November 16, 1776, calls began going forth from Congress and Committees of Safety across New England for the militia to rally to the defense of their country. On December 7, 1776, the Pennsylvania Council of Safety resolved,

> "Whereas, The safety and security of every state depends on the virtuous exertions of individuals in its defense, and as such exertions can never be more reasonable and necessary than when a people are wantonly invaded by a powerful army, for the avowed purpose of enslaving them, which is at present the unhappy situation of our neighboring states, and which may hourly be expected in this, therefore, *Resolved*, That no excuse ought to be admitted or deemed sufficient against marching of the militia at this time, except sickness, infirmity of body, age, religious scruples or an absolute order from authority of this State. *Resolved*, That it is the opinion of this board that every person who is so void of honor, virtue and love of his country, as to refuse his assistance at this time of imminent public danger, may justly be suspected of designs inimical to the freedom of America; and where such designs are very apparent from the conduct of particular persons, such persons ought to be confined during the absence of the militia, and the officers of this State to have particular regard to the above resolve and act accordingly, with vigor, prudence and discretion, reserving appeals to this Council, or a committee thereof, where the same is requested."[27]

On the next day, December 8, it was learned that General Howe and his Redcoats were on the move with the assumed objective of the American capitol in Philadelphia. General Washington issued a call to the Pennsylvania militia to make all haste and spare no sacrifice to join his army in the defense of the capitol.

Invigorated by General Washington's call to defend Philadelphia due to the urgency of the moment, Pastor Rosbrugh called his congregation together and read Washington's desperate plea for reinforcements from his pulpit. Then he read Judges 5:23, "Curse ye Meroz, saith the angel of the Lord; curse ye bitterly the inhabitants thereof; because they came not to the help of the Lord, to the help of the Lord against the mighty." He then delivered his own impassioned plea, declaring that he was ready to accompany the men of his church to battle as their chaplain and, if need be, die in the process. With that he challenged his men to join him in marching to the aid of Gen. Washington. The churchmen agreed to go on one condition – if their pastor would be their commander.

Rosbrugh requested time to retire to his home to discuss and to, no doubt, pray over the matter with Jane. After spending what was most likely a long night of intense discussion, prayer, and tears, the Rosbroughs apparently came to the conclusion that God was calling John to lead the men of his church off to war.[28] As evidence of his understanding of the dangers he was about to face and a belief that he might not see his family again, John penned his Last Will & Testament. The document said in part:

"In the name of God, Amen. December ye 18th, 1776 – I, John Rosbrugh, of Allen township, Northampton county, and Province of Pennsylvania, being in perfect health, sound judgment and memory, through ye great and tender mercy of God, but calling to mind that my dissolution may be near at hand, and that it is appointed for all men once to die, therefore I constitute, ordain and appoint this to be my last will and testament, in ye form and manner following: In ye first place, having received many and singular blessings from Almighty God, in this the land of my pilgrimage, more especially a loving and faithful wife and five promising children, I do leave and bequeath them all to ye protection, mercy and grace of God, from whom I have received them, being encouraged thereto by God's gracious direction and faithful promise, Jer. 49:11 'Leave thy fatherless children, I will preserve them alive; and let thy widows trust in me.'"[29]

In a touching recollection by Mrs. Lettice Ralston in a letter dated December 28, 1850, she recalls that the following morning, John Rosbrugh bid an extremely emotional farewell to his family; so much so, that his wife, overcome with grief, clung to him so tightly that he had to forcibly extricate himself from her embrace.[30] Turning away to conceal his own emotions, the great patriot pastor marched away with James, his nine-year-old son, riding their gray horse by his side. Once they had reached the church, Pastor Rosbrugh gave the men one last spirited address and then, releasing from obligation any who felt they simply could not abandon their families, shouldered his musket and, calling all who would to follow him to the preservation of his country, marched away to war. After going a good distance further, Rosbrugh took his son from the horse, lovingly kissed him, and then sent him back home to take care of his mother. How little did father and son know that this would be the last time they would see each other in this life.[31]

Then, pastor and parishioner took up their march and headed down the old "Bethlehem road," reaching Philadelphia sometime around the 24th of December.[32] In just over two weeks after having heard Gen. Washington's call to arms, Rosburgh and his men had made the necessary preparations to leave their families and homes and had marched to the camp of Washington's army, ready for battle. On Christmas Day 1776, Rosbrugh wrote to his wife:

"My Dearest Companion: I gladly embrace ye opportunity of telling you that I am still yours, and also in a tolerable state of health, thro' ye tender mercy of our dear Lord.

The important crisis seems to draw near, which I trust may decide the query whether Americans shall be slaves or free men. May God grant ye latter, however dear it may cost. An engagement is expected in a few days. All our Company are in Philadelphia in health and in good spirits. … My dearest creature, ye throne of Grace is free and open; I trust you have an interest there; it will be to your interest and happiness to live near ye Throne; you will find ye way of duty ye only way of safety. Farewell for a while. … Praying that God may pour out his blessing upon you all, this from your truly affectionate husband …"[33]

On December 26, 1776, Pastor Rosbrugh understood that he was more valuable to the Pennsylvania troops as chaplain than commander and surrendered his command and requested that a military man be placed at its head.[34] The Council of Safety commissioned him as the official chaplain of the Northampton County Militia and soon afterwards, John wrote Jane this short note informing her of this change in his responsibilities:

"I have received this afternoon a commission sent me by the Council of Safety, to act as Chaplain of Northampton county militia, and am now entered upon the duties of my office. Oh! That God would enable me to be faithful."[35]

As Rosbrugh and his fellow soldiers helped to guard Philadelphia from an attack by the British, Gen. Washington led a portion of his army in a surprise attack on the Hessian mercenaries encamped at Trenton, New Jersey. After routing the Hessians, Washington began massing his troops around Trenton to repulse an expected counter attack by the British. Rosbrugh and his compatriots were ordered to quickly link up with the main body of the army and in doing so they arrived at Bristol Ferry, New Jersey on December 27. On that evening, Pastor Rosbrugh wrote his wife a hastily composed letter, apparently on horseback as historian John Clyde observed, since his pen kept pushing through the paper in numerous places (denoted by brackets):

"[Friday] morning, 10 o'clock at Bristol Ferry, Decem[ber 27, 1776.] I am still yours [but] I haven't a minute to tell yo[u that by god's grace our] company, are all well. We are going over to N[ew Jerse]y. You would think it strange to see your Husband, an old man, riding with a French fusee slung at his back. This may be ye la[st letter] ye shall ever receive from your Husband. I have counted myself you[rs and have been en]larged of our mutual love to God. As I am out of doors [I cannot at present] write more. I send my compliments to you, my dear, and children. Friends pray for us. From your loving Husband, John Rosbrugh"[36]

In a few days, Rosbrugh and his fellow soldiers made it to Trenton where Gen. Washington and the rest his army were preparing for another battle. Desperate to regain what had been lost in the first battle at Trenton on December 26, Cornwallis sent between four and five thousand Redcoats against Washington on January 2, 1777 in what would be called the Second Battle of Trenton. Though overlooked by most historians, second Trenton, a battle the British thought would be an easy victory, turned out to be one of their most costly and bloody clashes of the war. Charging over and over again against the well-defended American position, the British were brutally repulsed each time, incurring a large number of casualties. Darkness mercifully brought an end to the carnage and death.

When the day was done, numbered among the casualties on the American side was none other than Chaplain John Rosbrugh. Captain John Hays, commander of Rosbrugh's company and the one who found and buried his body, relayed the following story of what happened to the chaplain.

When Gen. Washington hurriedly crossed his men over to the south side of the Assunpink River in preparation to engage

Cornwallis's Redcoats, during the confusion of this speedy maneuver, Pastor Rosbrugh was trapped on the Trenton side of the river and was forced to spend the day evading capture by the British. Once nightfall ended most of the fighting, a hungry John Rosbrugh rode to a nearby tavern to get something to eat. Tying his horse outside under a shed, he went inside and was eating when someone cried out that the Hessians were coming. Rosbrugh hurried outside to get his horse only to discover that it had been stolen. Working his way along the bank of the river, he frantically looked for a place to cross over to the American army and safety. As he pushed through a grove of trees, he suddenly found himself surrounded by a group of Hessian soldiers commanded by a British officer.[37]

(Although there are a number of versions of what happened next, the version below is excerpted from John Cunningham Clyde's *Rosbrugh, a tale of the Revolution*.)

Realizing that escape was impossible, Pastor Rosbrugh appealed to his captors' decency and mercy, pleading with them to spare his life and take him as their prisoner. Offering them his gold watch and money, Rosbrugh explained that he had a wife and young children at home who needed him desperately. The only response his enemies gave was a cruel laugh. Knowing that his entreaties were wasted on ruthless men bent on killing him, regardless of his appeals for mercy, Rosbrugh asked if they would grant him some time for prayer to prepare himself for death.

As he knelt there on the ground, he prayed aloud for his own soul about to make its way to God and for his wife and children whom he would be leaving behind. Then to the Hessians' astonishment, the saintly patriot asked God to forgive his murderers and to absolve them from the guilt of his death. As his prayer ended, the bloodthirsty Hessians jumped upon him and began stabbing him with their bayonets.[38] Altogether, he received three saber gashes to his head and seventeen bayonet wounds – with one of the bayonets left broken off in his body.[39] As his corpse lay on the ground in a pool of its own blood, the merciless savages rifled through his belongings stealing anything of value. (Some have claimed that Rosbrugh's body was so disgracefully and viciously mutilated that days later, Mrs. Rosbrugh could barely recognize it as that of her husband.) Abandoning the chaplain's body on the damp ground, the Hessians rushed off to celebrate their victory.

Captain John Hays, who was not only Rosbrugh's company commander but also a member of his church, found the body and gave his pastor a quick battlefield burial. When fellow Black Regiment preacher and army chaplain, Pastor George Duffield, heard of the death of his pastor friend, he insisted that the venerable patriot be disinterred and given a decent Christian burial. In the presence of Captain Hays, Mrs. Rosbrugh, and her brother, Pastor George Duffield preached his fallen compatriot's funeral and saw to it that his friend's body was honorably buried in a church cemetery near Trenton, where to this day, the exact spot is unknown.[40] In this way, the great patriot pastor met his earthly end and winged his way to his Heavenly Father.

According to Headley, Clyde, and Sprague, the Hessian who recounted the story to a woman in Trenton, barged into her hotel boasting that he had helped "kill a rebel minister" and waved Rosbrugh's watch around as proof. The murderer did have the decency to admit "it was too bad he should have been praying for them while they were killing him." When the woman condemned him for his dastardly deed, the crazed Hessian threatened to stab her with his sword and then ran off, with one account suggesting he ran off as if possessed. British officers standing nearby applauded him.[41]

Headley paid tribute to Rosbrugh's noble sacrifice by writing the following:

> "Let the scrupulous Christian of today condemn, if he can, this noble divine for fighting in defense of his country. He had no doubts of the righteousness of his

conduct, when passing with prayer on his lips into the presence of his God. Amiable, kind, and distinguished as a peacemaker, he had to overcome all his natural tendencies to war, to take up arms; but having settled it to be his duty, he had no after misgivings. In the turbulent scenes that followed his death, his grave was left unmarked, and no one, at this day, can tell where the sainted patriot sleeps."[42]

In just two short weeks after rallying the men of his church to defend liberty, Pastor John Rosbrugh was dead at the age of sixty-three; having given his life on the battlefield for the cause he had previously so vigorously defended from his pulpit. Reverend John Clyde wrote,

"John Rosbrugh tasted of that sweetness, and had the patriot's glory. His unmarked grave deserves a tribute of respect from every true American who is in the enjoyment of the liberties which he died to secure. His name and record are worthy of a place, not only in the archives of written history, but in the thankful remembrance of every lover of human liberty, along with the other Revolutionary patriots who died that a nation might be born and live."[43]

A pastor dying alone in the woods so others could stand in their pulpits and freely preach their own beliefs about the proper role of government without fearing the reprisals of the very government they were preaching about. ... This was the Black Robed Regiment.

Who was the Black Robed Regiment? They were sentinels of biblical truth and liberty, standing erect before their congregations – faithful watchmen at their posts. Wearing their black robes and preaching bands and tightly gripping their worn Bibles, they boomed out their messages. Their congregations, eager to hear the truth from their trusted pastors, weekly sat in their pews ready to receive answers from heaven – words that would help them make sense of the cataclysm of war breaking all around them. These patriot preachers boldly thundered out impassioned sermons that often, like lightning bolts, shot across their audiences, exploding with all of the fury of a raging storm. ... This was the patriot preacher.

When the destiny of the Thirteen Colonies was hanging in the balance, it was the patriot preachers of the Black Robed Regiment who were willing to stand in the gap and help lead the way to independence and liberty. On December 11, 1783, with the war over and the Colonies victorious and free, George Duffield, pastor of the Third Presbyterian Church in Philadelphia, himself a chaplain in the Continental Army, looked back to the beginning of the conflict and recalled how the patriot preachers had, without hesitation, boldly rallied to their country's defense:

"Quick as the flash of lightning glares from pole to pole; so sudden did a military spirit pervade those then limited colonies; but now, blessed be God, confederated, established states. The peaceful husbandman forsook his farm, the merchant relinquished his trade; the learned in the law dismissed their clients; the compassionate physician forgot his daily round; the mariner laid aside his compass and quadrant; the mechanic resigned his implements of employment; the sons of science ceased their philosophic pursuits, and even the miser half neglected, for a time, his gold and his gain; and the griping landlord his rents. All prepared for war, and eagerly flew to the field. The delicate female herself forgot her timidity, and, glowing with patriot zeal, prompted the tardy to arms; and despised and reproached the lingerer that meanly loitered behind. Nor were those of the sacred order wanting to their country, when her civil and religious liberties were all at stake. But, as became faithful watchmen, they blew the trumpet on the walls of our Zion, and sounded an alarm for defense."[44]

THEY LEARNED IT FROM THEIR PREACHERS

In the months leading up to the War of Independence, an American magistrate loyal to King George III, wrote a letter to the British Board of Trade in which he complained:

"If you ask an American who is his master? He will tell you he has none, nor any governor but Jesus Christ. I do believe it, and it is my firm opinion, that the opposition to the measures of the legislature of this country, is a determined prepossession of the idea of total independence."[45]

From whence did Americans most likely acquire the notion that they had "no master nor governor but Jesus Christ"? The answer seems clear – their preachers! But today, the pulpit is mostly silent about the proper role of government, even though, while you read this chapter, the federal government in Washington D.C. is growing like a cancerous malignancy. Modern preachers seem reluctant or refuse to address anything that can remotely be labeled as "political." But it was not always this way. In 1848, Nicholas Murray, pastor of the First Presbyterian Church of Elizabethtown, New Jersey, addressed the need for ministers to engage in politics and government:

"A question has arisen, and perhaps it will present itself to many minds, as to the propriety of a minister of the gospel taking such an active part in the secular affairs of the country. On a suitable occasion I should like to meet the man who would take the negative of the question. We owe the freedom of this country to the religious ministers of the country. If all the ministers of the country had taken boldly the ground assumed by some, that there could not be a state without a king, the lion and the unicorn guarding the crown would have been the emblem of our sovereignty until the present hour."[46]

Certainly, like preachers of every century, the patriot preachers of the eighteenth century regularly preached from God's Word about subjects such as heaven and hell, eternal salvation, and the judgment to come. But since they were committed to preaching the "whole counsel of God," they also addressed principles like the rights of men, the role of government, and the need for righteous men to stand against the evils of tyranny. In 1862, historian Frank Moore noted the pastors' willingness to engage every issue when he said, "The preachers of the Revolution did not hesitate to attack the great political and social evils of their day …"[47]

So, convinced that Scripture dealt with every area of life, the patriot preachers felt compelled to educate their congregations accordingly. Consequently, when the war came, both pastor and parishioner were poised and ready. This was the Black Robed Regiment. Author and Journalist James Adams wrote:

> "The Christian 'ministers of war' had done their job well, in fusing their congregants with the feeling they were first and foremost Christian soldiers marching as to war. … If God is for you, what does it matter that you are going out to do battle with the world's strongest army? … Equipped with the shield of faith and the sword of the Spirit, the poorly armed, ragtag American recruits set forth to do battle … In the process they would turn the world upside down."[48]

In conclusion, returning to Samuel Adams' warning to James Warren quoted earlier, many concerned Americans believe today that the time Adams warned of has now come. For those of us who believe it has, we are sounding out the desperate message that "our country stands in need of its most experienced patriots to prevent its ruin." Thankfully, our situation is different from that of the mid 1770s and no one is advocating armed conflict – we still have powerful political options available to us. But many of us do believe that it is time, actually well past time, to *Bring Back the Black Robed Regiment.*

Chapter 2

"PETER MUHLENBERG: THE PATRIOT PASTOR"

"There is a time to fight and that time has now come!"
Peter Muhlenberg to his congregation

What was Pastor Peter Muhlenberg feeling and what was he thinking when he realized that he had reached the point where he had to rally to the cause of independence and liberty? What were the members of his church and community feeling and thinking?

As a pastor who tries to live in the "spirit" of the Black Robed Regiment of the 18th Century, I have tried to imagine what that moment must have been like for Peter Muhlenberg. But as a student and writer of history as well, I know there is always the need to exercise great caution when writing about perceived heroes such as Muhlenberg and not read and write too much into their lives and thus create a narrative that does not align with the facts. After all, I wasn't there in the 1770's so I cannot know or communicate firsthand accounts; I can only read the firsthand accounts or accounts as close to the event as are available and then try to retell that story to the best of my ability to my contemporary audience.

However, there are times when our own personal experiences give us a "special feel" for the story and provide greater insight to what happened. For me, the story of Peter Muhlenberg is one of those cases. Because of what I know about the Revolution era and what I know about being a pastor with the obligation to preach the whole counsel of God, it is not very difficult for me to place myself into Muhlenberg's pulpit on January 21, 1776. The following is an extrapolation of events in Peter Muhlenberg's life that would impact a congregation, a town, and a war.

January 21, 1776 would become a day of destiny for Lutheran Pastor Peter Muhlenberg. This was the day Peter Muhlenberg burned all of his bridges. There would be no equivocating, no debating, no hesitating, no turning back – the time for words had passed and the time for actions had come!

Having served a number of congregations in the Virginia frontier for some five years, he had also represented those same folks in the Virginia House of Burgesses and Virginia's Provincial Convention. Keenly aware of the swirling winds of impending war all around him, Muhlenberg had been diligently preparing his people for the fight that was coming. With what was no doubt a heart heavy with conviction, Peter Muhlenberg had announced that he was going off to war and would preach his final sermon to his church on January 21, 1776. Although many have questioned what really happened that day, the only detailed account that exists is the one written in 1849 by Henry Augustus Muhlenberg, great nephew to Peter:

> "Upon his arrival at Woodstock, his different congregations, widely scattered along the frontier, were notified that upon the following Sabbath their beloved pastor would deliver his farewell sermon. ... The appointed day came. The rude country church was filled to overflowing with the hardy mountaineers of the frontier counties, among whom were collected one or more of the independent companies to which the forethought of the Convention had given birth. So great was the assemblage, that the quiet burial-place was filled

with crowds of stern, excited men, who had gathered together, believing that something, they knew not what, would be done in behalf of their suffering country. We may well imagine that the feelings which actuated the assembly were of no ordinary kind. The disturbances of the country, the gatherings of armed men, the universal feeling that liberty or slavery for themselves and their children hung upon the decision the Colonies then made, and the decided step taken by their pastor, all aroused the patriotic enthusiasm of the vast multitude, and rendered it a magazine of fiery passion, which needed but a spark to burst into an all-consuming flame.

In this spirit the people awaited the arrival of him whom they were now to hear for the last time. He came, and ascended the pulpit, his tall form arrayed in full uniform, over which his gown, the symbol of his holy calling, was thrown. He was a plain, straightforward speaker, whose native eloquence was well suited to the people among whom he labored. At all times capable of commanding the deepest attention, we may well conceive that upon this great occasion, when high, stern thoughts were burning for utterance, the people who heard him hung upon his fiery words with all the intensity of their souls. Of the matter of the sermon various accounts remain. All concur, however, in attributing to it great potency in arousing the military ardor of the people, and unite in describing its conclusion. After recapitulating, in words that aroused the coldest, the story of their sufferings and their wrongs, and telling them of the sacred character of the struggle in which he had unsheathed his sword, and for which he had left the altar he had vowed to serve, he said 'that, in the language of holy writ, there was a time for all things, a time to preach and a time to pray, but those times had passed away;' and in a voice that re-echoed through the church like a trumpet-blast, 'that there was a time to fight, and that time had now come!'

The sermon finished, he pronounced the benediction. A breathless stillness brooded over the congregation. Deliberately putting off the gown, which had thus far covered his martial figure, he stood before them a girded warrior and, descending from the pulpit, ordered the drums at the church door to beat for recruits. Then followed a scene to which even the American Revolution, rich as it is in bright examples of the patriotic devotion of the people, affords no parallel. His audience, excited in the highest degree by the impassioned words which had fallen from his lips, flocked around him, eager to be ranked among his followers. Old men were seen bringing forward their children, wives their husbands, and widowed mothers their sons, sending them under his paternal care to fight the battles of their country. It must have been a noble sight, and the cause thus supported could not fail. Nearly three hundred men of the frontier churches that day enlisted under his banner; and the gown then thrown off was worn for the last time. Hence forth his footsteps were destined for a new career."[49]

(Although Henry Muhlenberg's account has been disputed, it has never been refuted. Admittedly, the account was written long after the event, but given it was written by a family member who probably had access to the family records relating to the story and given the fact that no solid proof exists to invalidate the account, it seems worthy of inclusion into the historical record of this event and is probably the most authentic version of the story we will ever have.)

It has been said that, upon donning his uniform, Col. Muhlenberg cried out to the men of his church, "Who among you is with me?" – all while his congregation solemnly rose to their feet and began to sing Martin Luther's great hymn, "A

Mighty Fortress Is Our God." If so, that song must have been like a soothing balm to their troubled souls as the sound settled over the congregation like a warm blanket, covering the church as it rose heavenward.

As the men of Muhlenberg's church stood huddled around their courageous pastor, the drum continued to beat as the sound drifted across the January air. Those of the community heard its sound and came running to see what was happening. It was reported that one by one, most of the men of Muhlenberg's church and community boldly stepped up to sign their names under their pastor's as they joined the 8th Virginia Regiment and the War of Independence.[50] In the cold January air, the fires of liberty and patriotism were burning bright outside the little Lutheran church in Woodstock, Virginia.

In just hours, the Woodstock congregation and community watched their men ride off to war with their pastor, Colonel Peter Muhlenberg, riding in the lead. No doubt with tears of sorrow mingled with intense pride, family members waved goodbye to husbands, fathers, and sons until the 8th Virginia Regiment rode out of sight and into history – knowing not if they would ever see them again in this world – some never did.

Though there are debates among scholars about what precisely happened on that day, experience demonstrates that it is not beyond reason to imagine the day played out similar to the description by his great nephew, Augustus Muhlenberg coupled with my comments. What cannot be disputed is that Peter Muhlenberg was a remarkable man, a gifted leader, and servant of God who led an amazing life.

AN AMAZING LIFE

John Peter Gabriel Muhlenberg was an amazing man to say the least. He truly was the quintessential patriot pastor. His life and exploits, both on and off of the battlefield, are legendary. In almost any discussion of the preachers/pastors of the War for

Independence, the name of Peter Muhlenberg surfaces almost immediately. Today, one can visit the Capitol building in Washington D.C. and find his white marble statue still standing in reasoned defiance in the basement crypt once intended to be the burial place for George Washington, but now a place of honor for numerous patriots of liberty.

Peter Muhlenberg was descended from an illustrious Lutheran family that helped found the Lutheran church in Pennsylvania. He was born on October 1, 1747 in Trappe, Pennsylvania to Henry and Mary Muhlenberg. Peter's family was certain that he, the son and grandson of Lutheran preachers, was destined for the ministry as well. But young Peter was more interested in hunting and fishing than he was in preaching. Rather than entering the ministry, his plan was to join the military as soon as he was old enough. Unfortunately for him, his parents had other plans.

Convinced that he was cut out to be a preacher, his parents considered his education of utmost importance, so great care was taken to see to it that he received the best possible. Early on, Peter's father served as his teacher, but once the family moved to Philadelphia, Peter attended the Academy of Philadelphia (presently the University of Pennsylvania) and was placed under the tutelage of Dr. William Smith, the Provost of the school. In 1763, at the age of 16, before graduating from the Academy, Peter, along with his brothers Frederick and Henry Ernest, was sent to Halle, Germany to study for the ministry.

But the strict and almost cruel atmosphere of discipline at the University of Halle did not mesh well with Peter's fiery temperament. Having been insulted by one of his college instructors, Peter responded by hitting the teacher. Facing certain expulsion from the school, he ran away and joined a regiment of the English Dragoons. While in the military, his fierce spirit earned him the nickname "Devil Pete," a title his enemies would remember years later as they faced their old classmate on the field of battle.

But like Jonah of old, Peter could not run far enough or work hard enough to escape the call of God on his life. So finally in 1767, with his resistance worn down, he returned to Pennsylvania to study for the ministry in earnest. In 1769 he was licensed as a Lutheran minister, and for a time, assisted his father in ministering to the Lutheran congregations of New Jersey. The next year on November 6, 1770, Peter married Anna Meyer, the daughter of a successful potter, and together they had six children – four daughters and two sons.

In 1771, a Lutheran congregation in Woodstock, Virginia, a community situated in the Shenandoah Valley and settled mainly by German Lutherans from Pennsylvania, called him to be their pastor. But since Virginia laws required all ministers to be ordained by the Anglican Church, Peter was forced to travel to England to be ordained as an Anglican minister. In 1772, duly ordained as an Anglican preacher, Peter returned to Virginia and began his ministry in the very Lutheran church in Woodstock that had first issued him the call the year before.

Peter enjoyed a successful ministry in Woodstock and developed a reputation as a strong preacher, an ardent patriot, and an outspoken proponent of American independence. Effectively using his pulpit as a sounding board for truth and liberty, he contributed greatly to the debate and threw himself headlong into the struggle. In 1774 he was elected to the Virginia House of Burgesses where he became a colleague of George Washington and Patrick Henry. When the British loyalist, Lord Dunmore, dissolved the House of Burgesses, Peter gladly accepted the opportunity to defy Dunmore and the British Parliament by serving as a delegate to the Virginia Provincial Convention.

On June 16, 1774, because of his earlier military experience in Europe and the tremendous confidence and respect his fellow citizens had for him, Peter was selected as the leader of the Committee of Safety* for Dunmore County. Having been chosen to that position unanimously, he energetically led the effort organizing the military forces of Virginia in preparation for the war with Britain that seemed certain to come.

(*Committees of Safety were formed at the suggestion of the First Continental Congress in 1774 to monitor the greatly disliked and distrusted British government. These committees were an outgrowth of the "Sons of Liberty" groups that had been formed a decade earlier that discussed and promoted public awareness of the increasing untenable situation of the colonies under British rule. By 1775 the committees had all but replaced British authority in the colonies and had taken control of the local governments. They regulated the economy, politics, morality, and militias and also oversaw the critical task of selecting representatives who attended the county and colony level assemblies to discuss the abuse of the colonists' rights and the growing cry for independence. It is believed that some 7000-8000 patriots served on these committees. Ultimately, the committee members became the leaders of the American resistance to the British and largely determined the war effort to secure American independence.)

Peter Muhlenberg was not only an effective voice *for* the Lord, he was also a loud voice *against* the British. It was said of him:

> "He was the head and soul of the opposition in that whole region and so much did he possess the confidence of the people that they sent him to the House of Burgesses of the state. Ardent, fearless and patriotic he became so absorbed in the approaching struggle, that, when the news of the battle of Bunker Hill reached him, he resolved at once to throw off his profession, and enter the army. Having talked and preached for freedom, he determined now to strike for it."[51]

As it always does, a strong stand like the one Peter took drew a good amount of criticism – even from members of his own family. His father, Henry Melchior Muhlenberg, felt that ministers should not get involved in politics and war, and Peter's younger brother, Frederick, condemned his involvement as "trying to serve two masters." Deeply concerned that his brother was making a tragic mistake, Frederick had written a letter to the youngest of the Muhlenberg brothers, Henry Ernest, criticizing Peter's actions. Henry Ernest forwarded the letter to Peter which prompted a heated response from the latter on March 2, 1776. Historian Paul Wallace took Peter's and Frederick's correspondence and combined them into what he called a running "duel of quills":

Peter: "Thus far I had wrote, when I recd. Brother Henry's Letter from you to him, wherein you made some exceeding sensible Observations on my conduct in the present alarming Crisis, from what those Observations flowed, I'm at a Loss to conjecture. You say as a Clergyman nothing can excuse my Conduct, this excellent Doctrine is certainly a Production of that excellent City N.Y. which must be purged with Fire, before ever it is cleaned from Toryism; may there be none to pity it."

Frederick: "Purged with Fire – Toryism ... I am convinced the majority here are as strong for the American cause as the Virginians, if not stronger. ... None to pity it Good God! ... Brother, brother, the rough soldier peeps out from behind the black hat–... that is contrary to the teaching of Jesus, which you formerly preached. None to pity it ... Heathenish."

Peter: "I am a clergyman it is true, but I am a Member of Society as well as the poorest Layman, and my Liberty is as dear to me as to any Man, shall I then sit still and enjoy myself at Home when the best Blood of the Continent is spilling? Heaven forbid it."

Frederick: "Words, words, words."

Peter: "Seriously Brother, I am afraid you have imbibed bad Principles in N.Y."

Frederick: "How do you make that out? Because I think it wrong for you to be both preacher and soldier in one? Bad logic.

... You do not know me – I believe I have always been, and still am, as firm in our American cause as you are, even though I am not a colonel marching to the field."

Peter: "But even if you were on the opposite Side of the Question you MUST allow that I have in this last Step acted for the best. You know that from the Beginning of these Troubles, I have been compelled by Causes to you unknown to have a Hand in public Affairs. I have been Chairman to the Committee and Delegate for this County from the first, do you think then if America should be conquered I should be safe, on the contrary, and would you not sooner fight like a man than die the Death of a dog?"

Frederick: "Why must I admit it? Listen: Because from the beginning you have been the Committee Chairman and Delegate ... you would have acted for the best if you had kept out of this business from the beginning. You were impelled by causes to me unknown–... I think a needless self-love and ambition, a desire to appear the big man ... were the secret causes. ... The Convention could have gotten along whether you were a delegate or not. Die the Death of a Dog ... Whoever dies with Christ's image in his heart dies well."

Peter: "I am called by my country in its defense – the cause is just and noble – were I a Bishop, even a Lutheran one I should obey without Hesitation, and so far I am from thinking that I act wrong, I am convinced it is my Duty so to do a Duty I owe to God and my Country."

Frederick: "Sophistries. ... I must hasten to a close ... I now give you my thoughts in brief – I think you are wrong in trying to be both soldier and preacher together. Be either one or the other. No man can serve two masters. I have long had some doubts of my own. ... I recognize well my unfitness as a preacher. ... I incline to think a preacher can with good conscience resign his office and step into another calling. You think a man can be both preacher and colonel at the same time. How different are our ways of thinking! ... If anything I have said in this letter has offended you, look at it this way – as the text is, so is the sermon – your letter attacking me with the godforsaken name of Tory was just too much – but ... rest assured I shall always think of you in my prayers."[52]

But Peter Muhlenberg was not the only preacher who felt this way. A good number of ministers like Samuel Cooper, Jonathan Mayhew, George Whitefield, and John Witherspoon, among others, had been laying the groundwork for the revolution by preaching for years that believers could not separate their religious convictions from their political positions and actions. Without hesitation, fear, or apologies, the patriot preachers boldly called upon their congregations to stand and fight for liberty as they understood liberty in the 1770's. It was clear they saw no contradiction in mixing politics and religion.

On March 23, 1775, the Virginia Convention met in the St. John's Episcopal Church in Richmond, Virginia. Peter was present and, maybe providentially, had the opportunity to hear Patrick Henry deliver his historic "Give me liberty or give me death" speech. Henry's moving speech appears to have served only to galvanize Peter's resolve. No doubt his soul was stirred as he listened to the venerable Christian statesman declare:

> "Are fleets and armies necessary to a work of love and reconciliation? Have we shown ourselves so unwilling to be reconciled that force must be called in to win back our love? Let us not deceive ourselves, sir. These are the implements of war and subjugation; the last arguments to which kings resort. I ask gentlemen, sir, what means this martial array, if its purpose be not to force us to submission? Can gentlemen assign any other possible motive for it? Has Great Britain any enemy, in this quarter of the world, to call for all this accumulation of navies and armies? No, sir, she has none. They are meant for us: they can be meant for no other. They are sent over

to bind and rivet upon us those chains which the British ministry have been so long forging. And what have we to oppose to them? Shall we try argument? Sir, we have been trying that for the last ten years. Have we anything new to offer upon the subject? Nothing. We have held the subject up in every light of which it is capable; but it has been all in vain. Shall we resort to entreaty and humble supplication? What terms shall we find which have not been already exhausted? Let us not, I beseech you, sir, deceive ourselves. Sir, we have done everything that could be done to avert the storm which is now coming on. We have petitioned; we have remonstrated; we have supplicated; we have prostrated ourselves before the throne, and have implored its interposition to arrest the tyrannical hands of the ministry and Parliament. Our petitions have been slighted; our remonstrances have produced additional violence and insult; our supplications have been disregarded; and we have been spurned, with contempt, from the foot of the throne! In vain, after these things, may we indulge the fond hope of peace and reconciliation. There is no longer any room for hope. If we wish to be free— if we mean to preserve inviolate those inestimable privileges for which we have been so long contending—if we mean not basely to abandon the noble struggle in which we have been so long engaged, and which we have pledged ourselves never to abandon until the glorious object of our contest shall be obtained—we must fight! I repeat it, sir, we must fight! An appeal to arms and to the God of hosts is all that is left us!

They tell us, sir, that we are weak; unable to cope with so formidable an adversary. But when shall we be stronger? Will it be the next week, or the next year? Will it be when we are totally disarmed, and when a British guard shall be stationed in every house? Shall we gather strength by irresolution and inaction? Shall we acquire the means of effectual resistance by lying supinely on our backs and hugging the delusive phantom of hope, until our enemies shall have bound us hand and foot? Sir, we are not weak if we make a proper use of those means which the God of nature hath placed in our power. The millions of people, armed in the holy cause of liberty, and in such a country as that which we possess, are invincible by any force which our enemy can send against us. Besides, sir, we shall not fight our battles alone. There is a just God who presides over the destinies of nations, and who will raise up friends to fight our battles for us. The battle, sir, is not to the strong alone; it is to the vigilant, the active, the brave. Besides, sir, we have no election. If we were base enough to desire it, it is now too late to retire from the contest. There is no retreat but in submission and slavery! Our chains are forged! Their clanking may be heard on the plains of Boston! The war is inevitable— and let it come! I repeat it, sir, let it come.

It is in vain, sir, to extenuate the matter. Gentlemen may cry, Peace, Peace – but there is no peace. The war is actually begun! The next gale that sweeps from the north will bring to our ears the clash of resounding arms! Our brethren are already in the field! Why stand we here idle? What is it that gentlemen wish? What would they have? Is life so dear, or peace so sweet, as to be purchased at the price of chains and slavery? Forbid it, Almighty God! I know not what course others may take; but as for me, give me liberty or give me death!"[53]

In the months following, Muhlenberg continued his ministry to the people of the Woodstock area, but the swirling winds of impending war kept him equally busy preparing the people he represented for the conflict that seemed inevitable. Peter's opportunity came in December 1775 when Virginia voted to raise six more regiments for the Continental Army. On January 12, 1776, with the personal support of George Washington and Patrick Henry,[54] Peter Muhlenberg was appointed by the Virginia Convention as Colonel of the newly formed 8th Virginia regiment.[55]

OUT OF THE PULPIT AND ONTO THE BATTLEFIELD

Peter Muhlenberg proved to be just as bold and daring on the battlefield as he was in the pulpit. In fact, it is said that Gen. Anthony Wayne, himself so reckless in the heat of battle that his men called him "Mad Anthony," was a little uneasy at Muhlenberg's daring actions on the battlefield.[56]

After forming the 8th Virginia, Col. Muhlenberg immediately went about training his men and in just four short months had them ready to fight. They were so fit for battle that American Major General Charles Lee commented, "It was the strength and good condition of the regiment that influenced me to order it out of its own province in preference to any other. [It was] the best armed, clothed, and equipped for immediate service."[57]

Once they had received their orders from Gen. Lee, Muhlenberg and his men rode south and were "present and accounted for" at the Battle of Charleston, South Carolina on June 28, 1776. The British, who had superior firepower, attacked the small American force on Sullivan's Island at a fort later named Fort Moultrie after Colonel William Moultrie who helped to defend it. In that action, the 8th Virginia reinforced Col. Thompson's troops and fought valiantly to repulse British attempts to move around behind the fort and attack it from the rear. The stand Muhlenberg's men took was so instrumental to the success of the Continental Army that Gen. Lee claimed, "[they] made us very strong."[58]

The victory secured the port of Charleston for the Americans and dealt a major blow to British plans of invading the southern colonies. After the battle, Col. Thompson applauded the efforts of Muhlenberg's men by saying, "I know not which corps I have the greatest reason to be pleased with, Muhlenberg's Virginians or the North Carolina Troops; they are both equally alert, zealous, and spirited."[59]

Not long after the victory at Charleston, Muhlenberg was sent even further south to Savannah, Georgia to break up British efforts there. Unfortunately, it was during the season when sicknesses ran rampant in that part of the south, and the Virginians, unaccustomed to the climate, fell desperately ill. Col. Muhlenberg was among the sick and contracted a liver illness that plagued him for the rest of his life and that ultimately killed him some thirty-one years later.

BRIGADIER GEN. MUHLENBERG

Because of his bold and skillful leadership of the 8th Virginia, the Continental Congress took note of Col. Muhlenberg's performance and promoted him to the rank of brigadier general on February 21, 1777. General Muhlenberg would now be serving under the Commander and Chief of the Continental Army, General George Washington and, during numerous engagements in Pennsylvania, under the command of General Nathaniel Greene. Time was beginning to show that, in addition to being a well-trained and effective pastor, Peter Muhlenberg was turning out to be a pretty fair commander in the field as well. This is clearly evident in his actions at the famous Battle of Brandywine on September 11, 1777.

The Battle of Brandywine was a fierce but pivotal fight where Gen. Peter Muhlenberg and his men, serving under the command of Gen. Nathaniel Greene, fought courageously and valiantly. It was at Brandywine that Muhlenberg was reacquainted with his old German enemies he had made in his teens while serving in the

English Dragoons – General Baron von Wilhelm Knyphausen's dreaded Hessian soldiers. The Hessians, brutal mercenaries from Germany, were fierce and merciless warriors – a fact attested to by author Jim Ryun: "Feared and loathed in the same breath, the mercenaries from the German province of Hesse had been hired by George III to augment his troops in North America. With their tall hats, waxed mustaches, and ponytails, the Hessians' reputation was for giving – and expecting – no mercy. … it was the Hessians who would lead the charge of the British at the Battle of Long Island, bayoneting surrendering American troops without mercy."[60]

When their cannons opened fire, the Hessian warriors charged across the creek with drums beating and bayonets fixed. Spotting Muhlenberg through the fog mounted on his horse, the Germans recognizing their old classmate, cried out, "Hier kommt Teufel Piet: Here comes Devil Pete."[61]

As the battle raged on, Washington's right flank began to crumble under a withering attack by British General Cornwallis. The American lines began to give way under the fire of Cornwallis' well-trained troops, and suddenly, the Americans turned and started running for the rear in full retreat. Tensions ran high as it became clear to many of the American commanders that they might be witnessing the complete rout of their army. A desperate Washington called Gen. Greene's Division out of reserve and ordered the General to throw everything he had at the advancing Redcoats. Thankfully for the Americans and the cause of liberty, bravery was the order of the day for Greene's troops, including Muhlenberg and his men. The determined soldiers quickly moved out and set up a defensive line, allowing the battered and battle weary troops of commanders Sullivan, Sterling and Stephen to withdraw from the engagement and move into reserve for a much deserved rest. Gen. Muhlenberg and his men became a safe haven for the retreating Americans as they moved beyond the reach of the British muskets and bayonets. One can only imagine what relief the retreating soldiers must have felt as they saw ole' "Devil Pete" waving them into safety as his troops fired volley after volley into the pursuing Redcoats.[62]

The Black Robe preacher named Peter Muhlenberg conducted himself with gallantry and bravery that day at Brandywine. In fact, had certain defensive actions taken by Muhlenberg and fellow commanders like General Weedon not been as successful as they were, it's quite possible that Brandywine would have been Peter Muhlenberg's last engagement and the Colonial Army could very well have been destroyed and the War for Independence probably would have ended that day right there at Brandywine.

The day after the clash on Brandywine Creek, Thomas Paine published the fourth installment of his *The American Crisis*. On the heels of the courageous, but losing effort of the Continental Army at Brandywine, Paine perfectly summed up the situation for the Americans at that moment:

> "Those who expect to reap the blessings of freedom, must, like men, undergo the fatigue of supporting it. The event of yesterday is one of those kind of alarms which is just sufficient to rouse us to duty, without being of consequence enough to depress our fortitude. It is not a field of a few acres of ground, but a cause that we are defending, and whether we defeat the enemy in one battle, or by degrees, the consequence will be the same."[63]

After Brandywine, Muhlenberg and his men had little time to rest and in days, they were called upon again to help Gen. Washington launch another attack on the British – this time to free Philadelphia from occupation by the British. The fight that ensued occurred just outside of Philadelphia in Germantown, an outlying suburb in 1777. There the Continental Army slammed into the British in the heavy morning fog of October 4, 1777. In the fog, the battle became a confusing affair preventing the different wings of Washington's army from coordinating their attacks and causing some of the Americans to actually fire upon each other. Still, some of the American units had amazing success; among those were Muhlenberg and his men. Unfortunately, on other parts of the field the Americans did not fare as well. Unable to exploit their breakthrough, Muhlenberg and the rest of the army were forced to pull back, leaving the field still in the hands of their enemy. Nevertheless, Gen. Washington and the other commanders were impressed by their initial successes in the battle and took comfort that their Army, while not successful in freeing Philadelphia, was gaining the necessary experience it needed in order to develop into a formidable fighting force. But more importantly, the French were impressed. With the added attraction of Gen. Horatio Gates's defeat of British General Burgoyne at Saratoga, New York three days later on October 7 and his eventual surrender on Oct. 17, the French decided to increase their support for American independence – a development that would ultimately play a pivotal role in securing victory for America.

Some two months after the Battle of Germantown, Muhlenberg and his Virginians marched with Gen. Washington to winter quarters at Valley Forge. It was during that terrible time of cold and privation that Muhlenberg proved that the battlefield was not the only place where his services could be of great value. During that trying winter, Peter Muhlenberg showed himself to be of great value to General Washington and the cause.

But a lingering burden continued to weigh upon Peter Muhlenberg – his father's disapproval of his participation in politics and the military. As far as Henry Melchior Muhlenberg was concerned, it was just not right for a minister, and in this case, his own son, to run for office or take up arms. Thankfully for both men, the time of suffering at Valley Forge became a time of healing as well. Historian Paul Wallace wrote,

> "Even though the elder Muhlenberg was proud of his son, a brigadier general at the age of thirty, he had not yet quite forgiven him for throwing off his ministerial gown

on that memorable Sunday morning at Woodstock in January of '76. ... The reconciliation of father and son, toward the end of the Valley Forge winter, at a rendezvous back in the country, is one of the beautiful incidents in the history of the Muhlenberg family; for there Henry Melchior was finally convinced that a revolution sanctioned by George Washington and supported by Brigadier General the Reverend Peter Muhlenberg and his friends could not be running counter to religion."[64]

The following spring and summer, Peter Muhlenberg again distinguished himself as an exceptional field commander at contests such as the Battle of Monmouth Courthouse, New Jersey fought on June 28, 1778. During the battle, Maj. Gen. Charles Lee (who would later be court martialed for his actions during the battle) bungled that battle and his troops were running from the field with the British hot on their heels, an enraged Gen. Washington bravely charged into the melee on his horse. Seizing command from Lee, Washington succeeded in rallying the faltering troops who were just moments from destruction and were now in full retreat. Eventually, after deploying his own forces to regain control of the battle, General Washington ordered Lee and his troops back to Englishtown to act as reserve. General Muhlenberg once again was on the field and as the battle seesawed throughout the day, in the end, it was the British, not the Americans, who surrendered the field. As usual, Muhlenberg, the Lutheran preacher turned soldier, was in the thick of the fight. After the battle, which many considered an American victory, Muhlenberg wrote that it was at Monmouth that he "... lost two fine officers by their cannon, Major Dickinson and Capt. Fauntlroy, who was killed very near me."[65]

MUHLENBERG BUTTRESSES VIRGINIA

With major conflicts over in the north and a general stalemate ensuing, the attention of the American forces necessarily turned to the south. Cornwallis, and later Benedict Arnold, were making gains there and British General Clinton saw that, while stalemated by General Washington in the north, gains could be made in the south. Recognizing this, General Muhlenberg was dispatched back to Virginia in the early weeks of 1780 tasked with the responsibility of raising additional troops to send to other operational theaters, mainly the Carolinas and Georgia, and to raise troops to defend Virginia. This was a daunting task for anyone, including the native Virginian, Peter Muhlenberg. What made the assignment so difficult was the fact that the Virginia government was essentially out of money, thus making recruiting new soldiers virtually impossible. One historian, Edward W. Hocker, recorded that things were so bad during this time that Muhlenberg "himself had to pay $20,000 for a horse, the payment being in greatly depreciated Continental currency."[66] But these difficulties did not dissuade the "fighting parson" and he set upon his task with measured success.

By the summer of 1780 the Continental Army was about to face its greatest challenge. With desertions on the rise, a generally worthless currency, declining morale after another harsh winter in New Jersey, things looked bleak. Roughly 6000 French soldiers were blockaded in Rhode Island and General Cornwallis was dominating in the southern theater. With the British in charge of Charleston and their huge fleet anchored in the harbor, it is safe to say that the hope for American independence was beginning to look pretty bleak.

In early summer, Muhlenberg reported to Washington that, although he was proceeding fairly well with recruiting, the new recruits had little or no provisions, weapons, or ammunitions. Gen. Washington responded to General Muhlenberg on July 18, 1780, writing:

"I have now only to entreat that you will use every possible exertion to collect and form the Drafts and to have them disciplined. I entreat this; I expect it of all the Officers. They will remember that the forming of a New Army or at least of a whole State Line and fitting it for the Field, devolves in a great measure upon them, and as it shall act, so in a degree will be their reputation. They have a glorious opportunity to signalize themselves, and I doubt not they will avail themselves of the occasion. The crisis is a most interesting One, and on your and their exertions, and discipline and bravery of the Troops, great and early events much depend."[67]

Thomas Jefferson, the governor of Virginia, had communicated the same when he wrote to Gen. Washington, "I have entreated Genl Muhlenberg ... to use every possible exertion to collect and discipline the Men."[68]

In typical fashion, Muhlenberg rose to the occasion and continued to recruit under incredibly challenging circumstances and, fortunately for the War effort, his efforts enjoyed increasing success. But still there were few provisions. Writing to Gen. Washington on August 24, 1780 about the lack of provisions for his soldiers, Gen. Muhlenberg said, "In what manner they are to be equipped for the Field is at present a mystery to me."[69] Again, on September 29 Muhlenberg wrote, "The New Levies of the lower Counties are nearly collected and are forming into Battalions but we are totally destitute of every Article necessary to fit them for the Field."[70]

But General Gates was in desperate need of new troops and since Muhlenberg's recruits were his only source, Gates insisted that Muhlenberg keep sending him men, claiming that even if they did show up wearing only "hunting shirts, overalls, and shoes,"[71] they could be put to good service immediately. Muhlenberg was in a "no win" situation and even when he complied with Gates' requests, the general then complained that the troops he was sending were ill equipped having "neither clothes, blankets, arms, nor accouterments"[72] and only served to increase the burden on his already over-burdened army. Even though the situation must have been incredibly frustrating and demoralizing to Muhlenberg, he labored on.

With time and tenacity, Peter Muhlenberg's situation finally began to improve. Then, things suddenly broke decidedly in Peter Muhlenberg's favor when British General Alexander Leslie began moving out of Portsmouth with some three thousand troops – the British invasion of the mainland of Virginia had begun! Now Peter could do what he did best – fight Redcoats!

In what would later be called the Tidewater Campaign, Gen. Muhlenberg, with few supplies and a small force of some eight hundred regular soldiers, moved to check Leslie's advance. Though outnumbered almost four to one, the American forces kept the British checked without a major clash of arms.

Muhlenberg, along with reinforcements from militia General Lawson with 800 volunteers and 1000 men each from generals Weedon and Nelson, together held Gen. Leslie at bay. This effectively led to British General Leslie deciding against further encroachment into Virginia and on November 25, 1780, Leslie abandoned camp and withdrew southward to link up with Cornwallis in the Carolinas. [73] Muhlenberg's tactical decisions on the battlefield shored up the tide that was beginning to tilt in favor of the American forces though they certainly did not know it at that time.

Then, beginning in December, British General Clinton sent traitor Benedict Arnold up the James River with some sixteen hundred soldiers to invade Virginia, destroy the Continental Army's supplies and supply lines, and block troop reinforcements to General Greene in the Carolina's. With the Virginia government having moved from Williamsburg to Richmond, Arnold decided upon an invasion of Richmond and spent roughly twenty-four hours burning buildings and taking supplies. Governor Jefferson was roundly criticized for not being prepared to defend the Virginia Capitol and was nearly trapped himself.[74]

Gen. Baron von Steuben, now in charge of all Virginia forces, maneuvered the few forces he had to try and defend Richmond, to no avail. Once Arnold's raiding party had completed its mission, it returned to the James River, setting sail for Portsmouth. Von Steuben called upon Muhlenberg now in command of all forces south of the James River to take whatever troops he had and move along the south side of the river with General Lawson stalking Arnold's movements on the north side. Their objective was to keep Arnold's forces "within their lines" without bringing on an actual engagement.[75] British General Arnold knew that he did not have the forces to invade again now that Muhlenberg and Lawson tailed him back to Portsmouth so he called for reinforcements and General Clinton answered sending General Phillips to meet up with Arnold and harass the Virginia forces and supply/communication lines. With Generals Phillips and Arnold preparing to re-invade Virginia, it fell to Maj. General Von Steuben and Brigadier General Muhlenberg to intervene. With their forces significantly outnumbered, they held their own against Phillips and Arnold eventually retreating across the Pocahontas Bridge, near Blandford, Virginia.[76] But they had made their point, Virginia was developing forces and was about to put up a fight – due in no small part to the actions and leadership of Peter Muhlenberg. The day after the battle at Blandford, Peter wrote to his brother Frederick:

> "Yesterday, about one o'clock, p.m., the enemy approached the town in two columns, and were met by our light infantry about a mile from the town, where the skirmish commenced, and every inch of ground to the bridge was warmly disputed. The dispute was very hot at the bridge for some time; but at length they cannonaded us so severely, that we broke up the bridge and retreated in the greatest regularity, after maintaining the fight for

nearly two hours. I have the pleasure to assure you that the militia behaved with a spirit and resolution which would have done honor to veterans."[77]

Peter Muhlenberg received high praise from his superiors. Maj. Gen. Von Steuben was elated with the job Muhlenberg had done in Virginia and gave him his highest praise in his General Orders: "He [Steuben] begs General Muhlenberg to accept his very particular thanks for his gallantry and good dispatches."[78] Reporting to Congress, Gen. Steuben added, "General Muhlenberg merits my particular acknowledgements for the good disposition he made, and the great gallantry with which he executed it."[79] General Greene, upon receiving Steuben's report, responded, "Your report of the good conduct of General Muhlenberg, and the troops under his command, affords me great pleasure, and claims my entire approbation. This spirited opposition will have a most happy effect upon their future operations."[80] Muhlenberg's efforts in Virginia had succeeded; the war might not be lost after all – at least not in Virginia!

YORKTOWN AND THE END

For weeks Gen. Washington had been working on setting a trap for Cornwallis and everything had gone as planned. Now, the British were cornered in Yorktown, Virginia with their backs against the sea. With the French fleet blocking the British navy from coming to Cornwallis's rescue, the Redcoats had no way to escape. All that was left for the Americans to do was fight through the British defenses and the war would be all but over. The siege of Yorktown officially began on September 28, 1781 and as the American lines crept ever closer to the main body of the British army, so did an American victory. Finally, the only hurdles that stood between the Americans and the British main body were defensive positions known as Redoubts 9 and 10.

On October 14, 1781, the attack on Redoubts 9 and 10 commenced. Muhlenberg and his men were among those who fought courageously, and when the day was over, the Americans controlled both redoubts. With the last British redoubt in American hands, the way was now open to the main body of the enemy, the ultimate surrender of Cornwallis, and the end of the war.

What poetic justice that Peter Muhlenberg, the man who had labored so long and hard to rebuild the army in Virginia, was there at Yorktown, Virginia to participate in the final moments of the war. Today, Major General Peter Muhlenberg can be seen sitting astride his horse in John Trumbull's famous 1819 painting that hangs in the Capitol rotunda in Washington D.C. of the October 19, 1781 surrender ceremony of Cornwallis.

In his 1824 *Remembrance of the Departed Heroes, Sages, and Statesmen of America*, Thomas J. Rogers wrote of Muhlenberg and his performance at Yorktown:

> "General Muhlenberg was a particular favorite of the Commander-in-chief, and he was one of those brave men in whose coolness, decision of character, and undaunted resolution, he could ever rely. … It is, however, a well-known fact, that he acted a distinguished and brave part at that siege [Yorktown]."[81]

THE OLD SOLDIER

Peter Muhlenberg returned home a war hero but because he had served as a soldier, he considered himself no longer qualified for the ministry (had I been around in those days, I would have attempted to convince him otherwise). Faced with the task of finding a new career, he determined to serve the people of Pennsylvania by assisting in their new state government. In 1784 he was elected as Montgomery County's representative to the Pennsylvania Supreme Executive Council

– Pennsylvania's governing body under its first state constitution. In 1785, when Benjamin Franklin was elected Pennsylvania's President (governor), Peter was elected vice-president, a position equivalent to Lt. Governor. As Vice President, he worked to urge Pennsylvania's early ratification of the U.S. Constitution. He served as an ex-officio member of the board of trustees of the University of Pennsylvania and in 1789 was elected to represent Pennsylvania in the first U.S. Congress. There he served with his brother, Frederick, who became the first Speaker of the House (more about Frederick's change of heart about politics in chapter 17). In 1793, Peter was sent back to Congress by the citizens of Pennsylvania to serve in the 3rd Congress and in 1799, he was elected to serve a third and last term.

Peter was active in Pennsylvania politics and helped elect Thomas McKean as governor. He also campaigned for Thomas Jefferson in his run to become the third president of the United States. In late 1801, Muhlenberg was elected to a fourth term in Congress but chose, instead, to accept an appointment by President Jefferson to the position of Supervisor of Revenue for Pennsylvania. Then in 1803, President Jefferson appointed Muhlenberg as Customs Collector for Philadelphia – a position he held until his death in 1807.

In the fall of 1806, Peter's wife, Anna, became ill. For two months, he never left her side as Anna's health continued to deteriorate. On October 28, 1806, Hannah Muhlenberg succumbed to her illness. She was buried in Trappe Pennsylvania in the Muhlenberg burial plot.

In 1804, the *Aurora General Advertiser* celebrated Peter Muhlenberg's distinguished service by saying,

> "Among the Germans, the man most celebrated was General Peter Muhlenberg, who had distinguished revolutionary services to be proud of, but who has been the last ever to name, and the most reluctant to hear them spoken of. General Muhlenberg, now in the advance of

life, with the resolution of a lion when in danger, and with a highly cultivated mind, displays the simplicity of one unacquainted with human affairs, and unsuspecting of human infirmities."[82]

Peter remained a faithful Christian layman in the Lutheran church until his death. By all accounts, he lived an exemplary Christian life and was known for his sincerity and amiability and was greatly respected by all who knew him. He passed from this life on October 1, 1807 on his sixtieth birthday at his home in Gray's Ferry, Pennsylvania. He died from the very liver disease he had contracted so many years before in Savannah, Georgia in 1776.

Peter Muhlenberg was buried beside his beloved Hannah in a small burial plot behind the Augustus Lutheran Church in Trappe, Pennsylvania where his father, Henry, served as pastor. Inscribed on his tombstone are these words:

"He was Brave in the field, Faithful in the Cabinet, Honorable in all his transactions, a Sincere Friend and an Honest Man."

His native state of Pennsylvania chose Peter as one of two Pennsylvanians to be honored by having their statues placed in Statuary Hall in Washington D.C. The quintessential patriot preacher stands there resolute, immortal, in white marble, holding his sheathed sword in his left hand; with his clerical robe he removed to fight for liberty, flowing over his right arm and behind him.

This is the cloth from which the "Black Robed Regiment" was cut. Of such was the true patriot preacher.

Chapter 3

THE BIBLE IN ONE HAND AND A MUSKET IN THE OTHER

On April 26, 1777, ten months after urging separation from Great Britain with the adoption of the Declaration of Independence and with almost two years of armed conflict already behind them, John Adams wrote a letter to his wife, Abigail, pointing out to future generations the cost his generation was paying for their liberty:

> "Posterity, you will never know how much it cost the present generation to preserve your freedom. I hope you will make good use of it. If you do not, I shall repent in heaven that ever I took half the pains to preserve it."[83]

Their posterity may have never fully grasped the cost of their freedom, but the preachers and congregations of Adams's generation certainly did. In 1864, the Historian, B. F. Morris wrote,

> "The ministers of the Revolution were, like their Puritan predecessors, bold and fearless in the cause of their country. No class of men contributed more to carry forward the Revolution and to achieve our independence than did the ministers. ... [B]y their prayers, patriotic sermons, and services [they] rendered the highest assistance to the civil government, the army, and the country."[84]

The American Quarterly Register wrote in 1833 about the Black Regiment:

"As a body of men, the clergy were preeminent in their attachment to liberty. The pulpits of the land rang with the notes of freedom."[85]

Pastor Samuel West, a colleague of John Hancock and James Otis, both leaders in the cause for American independence, certainly understood the cost of liberty and what was at stake. On May 29, 1776, just as the war was beginning to gain momentum, West cried out to the Massachusetts legislators in that year's election sermon:

"It is an indispensable duty, my brethren, which we owe to God and our country, to rouse up and bestir ourselves; and being animated with a noble zeal for the sacred cause of liberty, to defend our lives and fortunes to the shedding of the last drop of blood. The love of our country, the tender affection that we have for our wives and children, and the regard that we ought to have for unborn posterity, yea, every thing that is dear and sacred, do now loudly call on us to use our best endeavors to save our country. We must turn our plowshares into swords, and our pruning hooks into spears, and learn the art of self-defense against our enemies. To be careless and remiss, or to neglect the cause of our country through the base motives of avarice or self-interest, will expose us, not only to the resentments of our fellow-creatures, but to the displeasure of God Almighty. ... [T]o save our country from the hands of our oppressors ought to be dearer to us than our lives, and next to the eternal salvation of our souls, the thing of greatest importance – a duty so sacred that it can not be dispensed with for the sake of our secular concerns. Doubtless for this reason God has manifested His anger against those who have refused to assist their country against its cruel oppressors. ... [W] hat a dreadful doom are those exposed to, who have not only refused to assist their country in this time of distress, but have, through motives of interest or ambition, shown themselves enemies to their country, by opposing us in the measures we have taken ... He, that is so lost to humanity as to be willing to sacrifice his country for the sake of avarice or ambition, has arrived at the highest stage of wickedness that human nature is capable of, and deserves a much worse name than I, at present, care to give him; but I think I may with propriety say that such a person has forfeited his right to human society,"[86]

Sermons like Pastor West's were effective communication tools in the churches during the period leading up to the war for independence. There is ample evidence in the historical record to prove that not only did the pastors preach these sermons, but they acted upon them as well. In fact, in a number of instances, it was the pastors themselves who recruited the men from their churches and then led them off to war.

In the fall of 1774, even before the war had begun, news of a likely clash between the British and the colonists in Boston had spread throughout the countryside. On many Sundays, handbills describing the events were read throughout the churches of Connecticut. The following are just a few of the preachers who sprang into action for liberty early on:

- Jonathan Todd of East Guilford, Connecticut marched to Boston with eighty-three of the men from his church.[87]

- Eleazer May of Haddam, Connecticut marched to Boston with one hundred of his men.[88]

- Benjamin Boardman of Chatham, Connecticut also marched to Boston with one hundred men.[89]

Throughout the winter of 1774, the "pro-independence" pastors were busy helping the colonists prepare for the conflict they were certain was to come. Some of the pastors served as officers of army companies, some served as clerks, others kept watch over alarm lists in the event of a British attack, and some even led foraging expeditions to collect military supplies such as gunpowder and arms.

John Adams of Durham, New Hampshire, along with other patriots, traveled to the fort at Newcastle, New Hampshire to move the supplies stored there to a more secure and accessible place in the event of a British attack. It is believed that Rev. Adams stored the gunpowder taken from the fort under his pulpit. So ironically, each Sunday he blazed forth his powerful sermons on truth and liberty while standing above huge stores of gunpowder![90]

When Paul Revere rode through Lexington, Massachusetts on the night of April 18, 1775 crying, "The Regulars are coming," he was headed to the house of Rev. Jonas Clark, the pastor at Lexington. Pastor Clark, with the help of Captain John Parker, a deacon and a veteran of the French Indian War, had been training the men of his church and other citizens in Lexington how to fight as a military unit in the event of a British invasion. On the morning of April 19, 1775, Jonas Clark and Captain John Parker led the Lexington Minutemen (a number of whom were Clark's own church members) out to face the British. It was there on the church green that the first shot of the Revolution was fired – the "shot heard around the world" was fired in Pastor Jonas Clark's churchyard.[91] (Jonas Clark's bio is found in chapter 6)

As word of the fighting at Lexington and Concord began to spread, pastors from all over the area gathered their men together and marched toward the fighting to defend their fellow Americans. From towns and communities all around Lexington and Concord, groups of minutemen, many led by their pastors, prepared a warm reception for the British at Concord. As the fighting in Concord continued, the British found themselves practically surrounded by the patriots. Outnumbered and outgunned, the Redcoats began to retreat back toward Boston, but as they moved down the road, they found it lined with more minutemen. By then, additional militia, totaling perhaps 19,000, including pastors, had arrived and began to engage the British all along the road. From the cover of rock walls, fences, rocks, and trees, the colonists showered the British troops with a withering fire that thinned their ranks significantly.[92] Both sides suffered casualties, the patriots lost ninety-four and the British nearly three hundred.

Once they had heard about the fighting at Lexington and Concord, numbers of pastors began to take aggressive actions to check British military operations. Among them were:

- Phillips Payson of Chelsea, Massachusetts (who had initially been against fighting the British) and Benjamin Balch of Danvers, Massachusetts were among the pastors who, once they learned that their fellow Americans had been fired upon at Lexington, took up their own arms and led the men of their congregations to ambush the British along the road leading back to Boston (called Battle Road today).[93]

- Benjamin Balch served as Lieutenant of the third alarm list in Danvers and also as chaplain in the army and navy. His bravery won him the title, "The Fighting Parson."[94]

- Samuel Haven of Portsmouth, New Hampshire, after hearing of the battles at Lexington and Concord, immediately went to work making bullets for the troops. He also organized and led a large effort manufacturing saltpeter to assist in supplying the American soldiers with precious gunpowder. He became so successful in this task that the *New Hampshire Gazette*, which opposed American independence, took note of his efforts on January 9, 1776. The author of the *Gazette* article which had predicted that the colonists would lose the effort, if for no other reason, for lack of gunpowder, wrote, "The making of Salt Petre has made such rapid progress, especially at Portsmouth, where both clergy and laity are employed six days in the week and the Seventh is seasoned with it, that I beg leave to subtract that (the colonists will lose for lack of powder)."[95]

Eventually, pastors farther away from Lexington and Concord began to hear of the British attack on their countrymen. Many gathered the men of their churches together and marched to Boston and eventually participated in the Battle of Breed's/ Bunker Hill. Some who did so included:

- Joab Houghton, pastor of the First Baptist Church, Hopewell, New Jersey, when the news of the battles of Lexington and Concord finally reached him on April 23, 1775, called his congregation together and said, "Men of New Jersey, the red coats are murdering our brethren of New England! Who follows me to Boston?" Every man in his congregation stepped forward and followed their pastor to Boston to fight for liberty.[96]

- David Avery of Gageborough (Windsor), Vermont, as soon as the news of Lexington and Concord reached Vermont, preached a farewell sermon and then marched away toward Boston with twenty of his men. As Avery and his men marched, he preached and recruited additional troops all along the way.[97]

- Stephen Farrar of New Ipswich, New Hampshire marched to Boston on April 30, 1775 leading ninety-seven men from his church.[98]

- Joseph Willard of Beverly, Massachusetts marched with two companies of men whom he had helped to recruit.[99]

Lexington and Concord served to light the fuse to the "keg of resistance" that had been waiting for just such a spark.

With American blood now spilled on the ground, the clergy entered the fray. When pastors from all over were gathered at the Annual Convention of Congregational Ministers held by special invitation of the Provincial Congress at Watertown, Massachusetts on June 1, 1775, just two months after Lexington/Concord and two weeks before the Battle of Bunker Hill, their moderator, Samuel Langdon, president of Harvard, signed this letter from the ministers in attendance:

> "To the Hon. Joseph Warren, Esq., President of the Provincial Congress of the Colony of the Massachusetts Bay, etc.,
>
> Sir, We, the pastors of the Congregational churches of the Colony of the Massachusetts Bay, in our present annual convention," at Watertown, June 1, 1775, gratefully beg leave to express the sense we have of the regard shown by the Honorable Provincial Congress to us, and the encouragement they have been pleased to afford to our assembling as a body this day. Deeply impressed with sympathy for the distresses of our much-injured and oppressed country, we are not a little relieved in beholding the representatives of this people, chosen by their free and unbiased suffrages, now met to concert measures for their relief and defense, in whose wisdom and integrity, under the smiles of Divine Providence, we cannot but express our entire confidence.
>
> As it has been found necessary to raise an army for the common safety, and our brave countrymen have so willingly offered themselves to this hazardous service, we are not insensible of the vast burden that their necessary maintenance must devolve upon the people.
>
> We therefore cannot forbear, upon this occasion, to offer our services to the public, and to signify our readiness, with the consent of our several congregations, to officiate, by rotation, as chaplains to the array.

We devoutly commend the Congress, and our brethren in arms, to the guidance and protection of that Providence which, from the first settlement of this country, has so remarkably appeared for the preservation of its civil and religious rights. Samuel Langdon, Moderator"[100]

By the time the Battle of Bunker Hill was fought on June 17, 1775, pastors and men from their congregations from all over New England had rallied to the cause, having marched to Boston, and were, along with the rest of the American militia, dug in and ready for a fight. Among the many pastors who fought at Bunker Hill were:

- Samuel McClintock of Greenland, New Hampshire. McClintock and his family were so committed to liberty that three of their four sons died during the war defending it.[101]

- David Avery of Gageborough (Windsor), Vermont who, having become chaplain and captain of the men from his church, marched to Boston and was present for duty during the battle and was a significant encouragement to the troops as he was seen conspicuously praying for victory. Avery also spent the weary winter of 1777-78 with Gen. Washington and his soldiers.[102]

- David Grosvenor of Grafton, Massachusetts, as soon as he heard that the Americans were fighting the British at Bunker Hill, abandoned his pulpit, and taking his flintlock musket, immediately marched off to join the fight.[103]

- Jonathan French of Andover, Massachusetts, when he heard of the battle at Bunker Hill, marched to war carrying both his medical case and his musket. He served as a drummer during the war and fought at Castle William in Boston Harbor.[104]

As the war progressed, other pastors joined the ranks of the Continental Army, most often as chaplains with the rank of Captain:

- Samuel Eells of Bradford, Connecticut, in 1777, when he heard that General George Washington and his troops were in dire need of assistance, read the notice from his pulpit and then he and his men formed a company of which he was made the captain.[105]

- Ablel Leonard of Woodstock, Connecticut, was considered so crucial to the war effort by Generals George Washington and Israel Putnam that in March 1776, they wrote to his congregation requesting they "loan" him to the army.[106]

- Hezekiah Smith, pastor of the First Baptist Church of Haverhill, Massachusetts, was the friend of Generals Washington and Gates as well as many other officers from New England. He served as a chaplain to the Continental Army and occasionally as aide-de-camp to numerous commanders. He boldly declared that the battle of Saratoga was "the grandest conquest ever gained since the creation of the world."[107]

- John Cleaveland of Ipwich, Massachusetts recruited his whole congregation into the Continental Army and then joined himself.[108]

- Thomas Allen of Pittsfield, Massachusetts led the "Berkshire Militia" as chaplain and commander and fought valiantly at the Battle of Bennington, Vermont on August 16, 1777.[109] (Allen's bio is found in chapter 8)

- Samuel Spring of Massachusetts served in the Continental Army as chaplain and participated in the siege of Boston. In September of 1775, he accompanied General Benedict

Arnold (before he had turned traitor) and his troops on the long and perilous invasion of Quebec.[110]

- Peter Muhlenberg of Woodstock, Virginia, received a commission from General George Washington and recruited men from his own church and surrounding area to form the 8th Virginia Calvary. He led them throughout the war fighting in such battles as Charleston, Brandywine, Germantown, Monmouth Courthouse, Stony Point, Morristown, and Yorktown.[111] (Muhlenberg's bio is found in chapter 2)

- John Rosbrugh of the "Forks of the Delaware" in Pittsfield, New Jersey rallied to the aid of Washington's troops as they were retreating across New York. Upon hearing of the retreat, he addressed his congregation and "besought them as patriots and as Christians" to hurry to the aid of Washington and his beleaguered troops. He enlisted as a private and he and his parishioners marched off to war together.[112] (Rosbrugh's bio is found in chapter 1)

- Timothy Dwight of New Haven, Connecticut was an outspoken patriot and served as chaplain under General Putnam in Parson's brigade. Dwight participated in the construction of the defenses at West Point.[113]

- Naphthali Dagget of New Haven, Connecticut and president of Yale, when the British invaded New Haven and approached Yale's campus, rode his horse with a volunteer company of 100 to the top of a hill from which he fired directly at the British Redcoats but then surrendered. While in their captive, he was repeatedly gashed by British bayonets.[114] (Dagget's bio is found in chapter 9)

- James Caldwell of Elizabethtown, New Jersey organized and led a sophisticated group of spies who kept Gen. Washington and his army informed of the enemy's movements. He served as chaplain to the troops and as Assistant Commissary General. He fought alongside his troops and finally gave his life for the cause of liberty.[115] (Caldwell's bio is found in chapter 7)

- Benjamin Trumbull of North Haven, Connecticut served as chaplain and at the Battle of White Plains, was with the division positioned on Chatterton's Hill. Enraged at seeing the retreat of the militia, Trumbull found a musket "and stepping into the ranks fought like a common soldier." Undaunted by the cannon balls exploding all around him he kept up a steady fire with "imperturbable coolness."[116]

- Samuel Kirkland of New York who was a missionary to the Indian tribes of western New York. When the war began, he served as army chaplain and ambassador to the tribes endeavoring to keep them from siding with the British. The service he provided in keeping the frontier of New York solidly in the hands of the Continental Army aided greatly in winning American independence.[117]

- James Hall of Bethany, North Carolina, when hearing of the atrocities perpetrated by the British troops as Cornwallis marched through South Carolina, called his congregation together and urged them to take up arms. The men immediately organized themselves into a cavalry unit and unanimously elected Pastor Hall as their captain."[118]

- John Gano, a Baptist from Virginia, was ministering in New York when the war began. He enthusiastically joined the army as a chaplain and crossed the icy Delaware River with Washington on Christmas night 1776 and was present at the American victory at the Battle of Trenton the next day.[119]

- Daniel McCalla of Charleston, Pennsylvania offered his services to the Continental Congress at the outbreak of the war. He was immediately appointed chaplain of the troops led by Brigadier General William Thompson. At the Battle of Three Rivers in Quebec, along with Gen. Thompson, McCalla and some two hundred other American soldiers were captured as prisoners of war and placed on a prison ship.[120]

- John Witherspoon was president of the College of New Jersey (now Princeton) where he educated many of the Founders such as James Madison. He became deeply involved in the struggle for American independence and was an outspoken patriot. He was elected as a New Jersey delegate to the Continental Congress. When many of the delegates became hesitant to push forward the Declaration of Independence, Witherspoon helped urge them on and was instrumental in getting the document signed. Witherspoon was the only active minister to sign the Declaration.[121] (Witherspoon's bio is found in chapter 11)

- John Steele of Cumberland, Pennsylvania often preached with his flintlock musket beside his pulpit. He was instrumental in raising roughly 3,000 troops in 1774 and served as captain though because of his age, he spent little time in the field.[122]

- Isaac Lewis of Stratford, Connecticut served in the American Army as chaplain and led the men of his church to resist the British as they landed at Norwalk, Connecticut.[123]

- James Latta of Lancaster, County, Pennsylvania served as chaplain and when a good number of the men of his church were drafted, he enlisted in the army and served as a common soldier to encourage them.[124]

- William Graham of Paxton, Pennsylvania (near Harrisburg), when he realized that the young men of his congregation were hesitant to respond to the Governor's call, joined the army himself and by his example, inspired the others to step forward and enlist.[125]

- John Murray of Boothbay, Maine successfully recruited men into the Continental Army. In addition, he served as chaplain and as a currier for the army, carrying messages from one commander to the other. He was so hated by the British that they offered a reward of five hundred pounds for his arrest.[126]

- Joseph Willard, pastor of the First Church in Beverly, Massachusetts, became the president of Harvard in 1781. Willard did "much to kindle and keep alive the general flame of patriotism" in Massachusetts and due "in no small part to his exertions and influence," the community of Beverly sent two companies of soldiers to fight for liberty with Willard in the lead.[127]

- John Craighead of Rocky Spring Church, near Chambersburg, Pennsylvania so stirred the men of his congregation that they organized themselves into a company and went through the entire war with pastor Craighead as their chaplain and captain.[128]

- John Blair Smith, president of Hampden-Sidney College in Virginia, served as captain of a company that rallied to support the retreating Americans after the battle of Cowpens.[129]

- Moses Allen of Midway, Georgia served as the chaplain of the Georgia Brigade. Eventually, Rev. Allen was captured along with other American soldiers and although many officers were pardoned and released, pastor Allen was imprisoned on a prison ship where he eventually died trying to escape. [130] (More about Allen later in this chapter)

- Israel Evans of Pennsylvania became chaplain to the New Hampshire brigade as soon as the war began. He served with distinction during many battles and was considered an ardent patriot in and out of the pulpit. Legend has it that at the Battle of Yorktown, he was standing beside Gen. Washington when a cannonball landed at their feet and sprayed dirt on his hat. Unperturbed, Evans took off his hat and showed it to Washington. The General is said to have responded, "Mr. Evans, you had better take that home and show it to your wife and children."[131] Finally, once the surrender of Cornwallis was complete, Rev. Evans delivered a sermon to the troops standing there in the bloody battlefield with the wreckage of war all around him, lifting his praise to heaven for the great victory and the end of the war.[132]

This is but a sampling of the patriot preachers who did not hesitate to rally to their country's defense when tyranny threatened to strip them of their God-given, unalienable rights.

THE PREACHERS WERE BETTER RECRUITERS THAN THE RECRUITERS

Joseph Fish of Duxbury, Massachusetts was seventy-six years old when the war began. When General Washington issued an urgent call for volunteers, Reverend Fish was called upon to encourage the men of his community to enlist. With the "fire still in his bones" and his patriotism still running high, the Reverend Fish declared,

"Were it not that my nerves are unstrung and my libs enfeebled with age, on such a call as you have, I think I should willingly quit the desk [pulpit], put off my priestly garments, buckle on the harness, and, with trumpet in hand, hasten to battle!"[133]

It was preachers like this who so inspired the Americans to fight. But not only did the preachers make good soldiers, they made great recruiters as well. In fact, out of all they did to promote the American cause, this may well have been one of their most valuable contributions.

For example, the Provincial Congress of Massachusetts authorized pastors Phillips Payson of Chelsea, Massachusetts and Peter Thacher of Maiden, Massachusetts to receive what were called "beating orders" which empowered them to raise two companies of soldiers for the defense of the Massachusetts coastal area.[134] William Emerson, the pastor in Concord, Massachusetts, who was present at the Battle of Concord, was responsible for encouraging many of the Concord men to enlist as minutemen in January 1775 and used his powers of persuasion to recruit many others in the following years.[135]

In the History of Brunswick, we encounter the Rev. Samuel Eaton who had built a reputation as a passionate preacher and supporter of the independence movement. Pastor Eaton was so supportive to "the cause" that on April 29, 1775, he was asked to address a meeting in his hometown of Harpswell, Maine about the impending conflict with England. This meeting was called to address the battles of Lexington and Concord that had occurred just ten days earlier. This is the record of the proceedings:

> "After the business of this meeting was concluded, Reverend Samuel Eaton, of Harpswell, who was present at the meeting, was invited to address the people. He did so and made a stirring and eloquent appeal to their patriotism. He so aroused the spirit and temper of the people, that, carried away by excitement, several of them, under the lead of the chairman of the meeting, Brigadier Thompson, seized Mr. Vincent Woodside, one of the

most prominent and outspoken opposers, who held a commission under the king, and attempted to force him to renounce British rule."[136]

Rev. Eaton's oratory skills were such, that combined with fervent and passionate devotion to the cause of independence, he was able to ignite the crowd to actively engage in the cause for independence and liberty and, which it is safe to assume, also began to identify Tories in their midst.

In addition to recruiting soldiers, the pastors were also invaluable in helping to keep up the spirits of the soldiers and the people, especially during the darker days of the war when the suffering and discouragement were at their worst. Their commitment to country and liberty and the sacrifice necessary to preserve the two was demonstrated time and time again as they challenged and sometimes pled with the colonists to persevere until the war was won. Thomas Allen of Pittsfield, Massachusetts served his country in this manner by convincing General Benjamin Lincoln's discontented and discouraged brigade, which was about to walk away from the conflict, to remain and continue to fight for liberty.[137]

THEY DIDN'T WANT A WAR

"War was not our object or wish: on the contrary, we deprecated it as a dreadful calamity, and continued to hope, even against hope, that the gentler methods of petitioning and remonstrating might obtain a redress of grievances. The war, on our part, was not a war of ambition, but a justifiable self-defense against the claims of an arbitrary power, which was attempting to wrest from us the privileges we had all along enjoyed, and to subject us to a state of abject servitude. In this light it was viewed by the nations of Europe, and even by some of the most illustrious characters in both houses of the

British parliament, who, in their public speeches, have justified our resistance, and acquitted us from the guilt of the blood that has been spilt.

It was after we had been treated with repeated insults and injuries—after our dutiful petitions had been rejected with contempt—after the British administration had held up the high claim of authority to make laws, binding us in all cases whatsoever; the plain language of which was, we have authority and power to do with you as we please; and if you will not quietly submit, and deliver up your earnings to support us in our luxury and extravagance, and be hewers of wood and drawers of water for us, we will lay waste your country with fire and sword, and destroy you from under heaven—it was after the sword had been drawn, and blood shed on the plains of Lexington, and on the fatal Bunker-hill, so that no alternative remained, but either absolute submission or open resistance—it was, I say, after all this, that the representatives of the people in Congress chose the latter, declared for independence, and relying on the justice of their cause, and the aid of the Almighty, resolved to support it by force of arms. (Jeremiah 18:7-10)"[138]

These were the thoughts of Pastor Samuel McClintock, a man who lost three of his four sons for the cause of liberty. McClintock was the pastor of the Congregational Church in Greenland, New Hampshire and made the above remarks on June 3, 1784 in his sermon in Portsmouth, New Hampshire to that state's legislature, not long after the New Hampshire state constitution was adopted.

Samuel Sherwood was a pastor who could see the gathering storm of war on America's horizon. On August 31, 1774, while delivering his sermon in New Haven, Connecticut, he, hoping war could be averted, made this appeal for the people to pray that war would never come:

"Let us be deeply affected with the present critical and alarming situation of our public affairs; and unite in fervent prayers to that God who is higher than the kings of the earth, that he would graciously interpose for our relief; that he would avert the impending storms of vengeance, and favor us with peace and tranquility, and the full enjoyment of all our valuable liberties and privileges; that our rulers may feed us according to the integrity of their hearts, and guide us by the skillfulness of their hands."[139]

It must be understood that these patriot preachers were not bloodthirsty warmongers spoiling for a fight – they, instead, were men who were just as committed to the teachings of Christ and the eternal salvation of individuals as any other generation of preachers/pastors. They, along with the many of the other Founders, believed they had exhausted every option to prevent the effusion of blood. Eventually though, the obstinacy of the British Crown and the increasing brutality of the British Regulars stationed in the colonies became too much for the colonists to bear and made it impossible for them to hold out hope for a peaceful solution. With the added tension caused by some of the Sons of Liberty who seemed committed to "agitating" as much as they were to "demonstrating," the powder keg was bound to blow.

It must also be noted that in the years preceding the conflict, many of the pastors who later marched off to war had originally been against breaking away from Great Britain, having been voices of moderation and conciliation. They had preached that the only righteous war was one that was defensive in nature and that they should never start a war but only engage in armed conflict if it was thrust upon them and thus could not be avoided. Consequently, when the British fired on the Lexington Minutemen, for many of these men, conscientious objection was out and the fight was on.

One pastor who, early on, had been against fighting the British was Congregationalist pastor Samuel Phillips Payson of Chelsea,

Massachusetts. But as soon as the British attacked the colonists at Lexington and Concord, Payson experienced an immediate and permanent change of heart. The following is an account of his reaction to the attack upon the Lexington minutemen as he fought the British in their retreat down Battle Road to Boston:

> "There, too, was the amiable and learned Payson, of Chelsea. He was so adverse to bloodshed and all the horrors of war that he had felt it his duty to preach patience and even submission. His bolder and more resolute brethren near him took such umbrage at this that they refused to let him preach in their pulpits. They wanted no conciliatory doctrines taught to their people. The brutal outrage at Lexington transformed this peaceful scholar and meek divine into the fiery, intrepid soldier, and seizing a musket he put himself at the head of a party, and led them forward to the attack. The gentle voice that had so long spoken only words of peace suddenly rung like that of a prophet of old. A body of British soldiers advancing along the road [from Concord back to Boston], he poured into them such a destructive volley that the whole were slain or taken prisoners. He was a man of peace and conciliation, but the first citizen's blood that crimsoned the green sward made a clean sweep of all his arguments and objections, and he entered with his whole soul into the struggle."[140]

Compelled to fight! That's how the colonists and preachers, in particular, felt. In their estimation, they had no choice but to fight. The feelings of the Americans were clearly communicated in Moses Mather's message, "America's Appeal To The Impartial World." Originally published anonymously in 1775, the message was known to be the work of Moses Mather, graduate of Yale and pastor for sixty-four years in Darien, Connecticut. In it, Mather said,

"At a time when we are called upon to surrender our liberties, our religion, and country; or defend them at the point of the sword, against those, that were our friends, our brethren, and allies (whose swords, and ours, till lately were never drawn but for mutual defense; and in joint battalions, cemented in love, affinity, and valor, have wrought wonders, vanquished armies, and triumphed over the power of mighty potentates), nothing will inspire our councils with unanimity, our resolves with firmness, and render the exertions, the noble struggles of a brave, free and injured people, bold, rapid and irresistible, like a right understanding of the necessity and rectitude of the defense, we are compelled to make, in this unnatural contention."[141]

PASTOR AND PARISHIONER MARCHED TOGETHER

Perhaps the only way to visualize the tandem of pastor and parishioner marching off to war together to fight for American independence is to transport ourselves back in time through the eyes of one who was there and see it as he saw it when the waves of war were breaking all around him. In James Dabney McCabe's 1876 work, we find the following example.

In Stockbridge, Massachusetts, there lived a deacon by the name Mr. Cleveland who, with a fellow member of his church, had been selected to sound the alarm in the event of a British attack. Deacon Cleveland's seventeen-year-old son recalled how the little village of Stockbridge came to life when they received the news that the British had fired upon the minutemen of Lexington and Concord. This is how he recalled that April morning in 1775:

"One quiet Sabbath morning, when all was still, as it ever was in that peaceful valley on that holy day, he was suddenly startled by the report of a musket. On going out to ascertain what it meant, he saw his father in the back yard with the discharged piece in his hand. Before he had time to express his wonder, another report broke the stillness of the Sabbath morning, and as the smoke curled up in the damp atmosphere, he saw in the neighboring yard one of the chief pillars of the church, standing with his musket in his hand. He paused astounded, not knowing what awful phenomenon this strange event portended. He said that he thought the judgment day had come. But in a few moments he noticed men hurrying along the hitherto deserted street, with weapons in their hands. One by one they entered his father's gate, and gathered on the low stoop. The flashing eye and flushed cheek told that something eventful had transpired – and there had.

When the report of those two muskets echoed along the sweet valley of the Housatonic and up the adjacent slopes, the sturdy farmers knew what it meant. The father, just preparing for the duties of the sanctuary, heard it, and, flinging aside his Sabbath garments, hastily resumed his work-day dress, and taking down his musket strained his wife and children in one long farewell embrace to his bosom, then turned from the home he might never see again. The young man bucked on his knapsack, and amid sobs and tears shut the little farm gate behind him, the fire in his eye drying up the tears as fast as they welled to the surface. Although the heart heaved with emotion, the step was firm and the brow knit and resolute.

In a short time the little porch was crowded with men. A moment after, Dr. West, the pastor, was seen slowly descending the hill toward the same place of rendezvous. It was a cold, drizzly morning, and as, with his umbrella over his head, and the Bible under his arm, he entered the dooryard, his benevolent face revealed the emotion that was struggling within. He, too, knew the meaning of these shots; they were the signals agreed upon to inform the minutemen of Stockbridge that their brethren in the East had closed with the foe in battle. He ascended the steps, and, opening the Bible, read a few appropriate passages, and then sent up a fervent prayer to Heaven. When he ceased, the rattling of arms was heard. A short and solemn blessing closed the impressive scene, and before twelve o'clock twenty men, with knapsacks on their backs and muskets on their shoulders, had started on foot for Boston, nearly two hundred miles distant."[142]

CHAPLAINS WERE NO SISSIES!

"Thou profane, wicked-monster of falsehood and perfidy... your late infamous proclamation is as full of notorious lies, as a toad or rattle-snake of deadly poison – you are an abandoned wretch.... Without speedy repentance, you will have an aggravated damnation in hell...you are not only a robber, a murderer, and usurper, but a wicked Rebel: A rebel against the authority of truth, law, equity, the English constitution of government, these colony states, and humanity itself."[143]

This was the open letter that Ipswich, Massachusetts pastor, John Cleaveland, writing under the pseudonym Johannes of Eremo,[144] wrote to British General Thomas Gage on June 17, 1775 and published for all to see in the *Essex Gazette* on July 13, 1775. If there was one word that described the patriot preachers, it was "gutsy!" Consider the following examples:

- David Ely of Huntington, Connecticut, was such a zealous patriot that he, ignoring the fact that his church was in an area populated by a large number of Tories, preached liberty and independence so ardently that the Tories threatened that "when the rebellion was put down, they would hang him on an oak that stood near his own church."[145]

- Josiah Stearns of Epping, New Hampshire told his sons, "If the cause succeeds, it will be a great blessing to the country; but if it should fail, your old father's head will soon be a button for a halter [hangman's noose]!"[146]

- Nathaniel Bartlett of Redding, Connecticut, like Pastor David Ely, was so outspoken for independence that the local Tories, who were numerous in western Connecticut, threatened to hang him if the opportunity presented itself. Due to threats on his life, he was obligated to make his pastoral visits with a loaded musket in hand along with his Bible. He stored gunpowder in a bin he constructed in the attic of his house for the Redding citizens in the event of a British attack (discovered years later by his son Rev. Jonathan Bartlett).[147]

The patriot preachers took quite seriously the words in the Declaration of Independence:

"And for the support of this declaration, with a firm reliance on the protection of Divine Providence, we mutually pledge to each other our lives, our fortunes and our sacred honor."

They were literally willing to give their all for the cause. They left their families and churches behind, many gave their possessions, some gave their lives, and some sacrificed the lives of their wives and children. For these godly men, no price was too great to pay for the sake of their liberty and country.

Although as pastors, they normally earned small salaries and had little in worldly possessions, many willingly sacrificed part, or all of those salaries for the war effort. Although we will never know for certain everyone who did, we do know the stories of a few. We know that Nathaniel Taylor of New Milford, Connecticut; Josiah Stearns of Epping, New Hampshire; James Pike of Somersworth, New Hampshire; and David Sanford of Medway, Massachusetts did.[148] Thomas Allen, pastor in the small frontier community of Pittsfield, Massachusetts, loaned the government large amounts of money and even sold his watch to raise money for the cause.[149]

On December 11, 1783, George Duffield recalled the sacrificial spirit exhibited by the colonists, in general, and the preachers, in particular:

> "Who does not remember the general language, when the war commenced? Cheerfully to pay one half of our property, to secure our rights."[150]

Moses Mather summed up the willingness of the Black Regiment to make whatever sacrifice was needed in his 1775 sermon:

> "Let none be disheartened from a prospect of the expense; though it should be to the half, or even the whole of our estates. Compared with the prize at stake, our liberty, the liberty of our country, of mankind, and of millions yet unborn, it would be lighter than the dust on the balance: For if we submit, adieu forever; adieu to property, for liberty will be lost, our only capacity of acquiring and holding property."[151]

In addition to being willing to voluntarily surrender their worldly possessions in the fight for liberty, many of the pastors had their possessions forcibly taken from them and destroyed by the British. Consider:

- David Caldwell, though from Pennsylvania, pastored a church in North Carolina. It was recorded by Caldwell's biographer that "News of Caldwell's activities provoked the British general to offer a two-hundred-pound reward for his capture. Caldwell was forced to hide out in the swamps before and during the Battle of Guilford Courthouse, March 15, 1781." [152]

- Hezekiah Ripley, the pastor of Greens Farms Congregational Church in Greens Farms, Connecticut, as a Chaplain in the Continental Army, was described as an ardent supporter of the cause of independence. But at the same time, he was also known as "benevolent, forgiving & full of charity for the faults of others." In addition, he was described as "...an ardent supporter of the cause of the Revolution & in consequence his home at Freen Farms with its furniture, and part of his library were burned by the British in 1779." [153]

Of course, we cannot forget preachers like Samuel McClintock of Greenland, New Hampshire whose family sacrificed three of their four sons for liberty. [154] The sacrifices of Samuel McClintock and countless others, known and unknown, provide moving illustrations of the price the preachers of the Black Regiment were willing to pay to establish a republic. This stands as stark evidence of the depth of their conviction.

ARMY CHAPLAINS – AN INDISPENSABLE ASSET TO THE ARMY

The office of military chaplain has changed significantly since the Black Regiment first took its stand against the British Regulars at Lexington/Concord in 1775. In 1864, during the War Between the States, Joel Headley noted the significant changes that had taken place in the role of chaplain in the eighty-nine years since the Revolution:

"It is difficult in these days, when chaplains in the army are looked upon simply as a necessary part of its methodical organization, a set of half officers, half civilians who are not allowed to fight, and often cannot preach, to get a proper conception of those times when their appeals thrilled the ranks, and made each hand clutch its weapon with a firmer grasp, and when their prayers filled each heart with a lofty enthusiasm. Then the people composed the army; and when the man of God addressed the crowding battalions, he addressed the young men and old men of his flock, who looked up to him with love and reverence, and believed him almost as they did the Bible. Could the history of each volunteer band, as it left its native valley, the enthusiasm kindled by the pastor's address, the courage imparted by his solemn parting blessing, and assurance that God smiled on them, be given, we should have a revolutionary page that would thrill the heart."[155]

The importance of providing clergymen to minister to the troops was understood from the beginning of the war. The commanders of the Continental Army knew the value of the comfort and encouragement the chaplains provided to battle weary troops – especially in the darkest hours. Because of their stature, they played a significant role in many encounters. Their spiritual ministry, sometimes combined with their leadership of their churchmen on the battlefield, made the office of chaplain a vital position in the command structure of the Continental Army.

George Washington, while serving as a young colonel in the French and Indian War, had learned early in his military career how critical the ministry of the chaplain could be to the success of an army. As supreme commander of the Continental Army, he respected and admired the bravery, courage, and toughness of the patriot preachers and was convinced they would play a significant role in helping to secure victory for the colonies. Because of their moral influence and ability to inspire the soldiers, Washington employed them extensively in his army for the entirety of the war.

Even so, in the early days of the conflict, there were too few paid chaplains officially serving in the army to effectively meet the spiritual needs of the soldiers. Gen. Washington put forth a major effort to convince the Continental Congress to make provisions for the inclusion of paid chaplains in his army. In December of 1775, he wrote to Congress:

"I have long had it in my mind to mention it to Congress, that frequent applications have been made to me respecting the chaplains' pay, which is too small to encourage men of abilities. Some of them who have left their flocks are obliged to pay the parson acting for them more than they receive. I need not point out the great utility of gentlemen, whose lives and conversation are unexceptionable, being employed in that service in this army. There are two ways of making it worthy the attention of such. One is an advancement of their pay; the other, that one chaplain be appointed to two regiments. This last, I think, can be done without inconvenience. I beg leave to recommend this matter to Congress, whose sentiments hereon I shall impatiently expect."[156]

In the summer of 1776, with the need for chaplains still urgent, Gen. Washington reiterated his previous request to Congress. In Washington's request, he made accommodations to Congress by reducing the number of Chaplains requested but also requested that the Chaplains be paid a livable wage.[157] The Continental Congress finally heard Washington and granted his request. Eight days after he received Congressional approval, he issued the following general order:

"New York, July 9, 1776: The honorable Continental Congress having been pleased to allow a chaplain to each regiment, with the pay of thirty-three and one-third dollars per month, the colonels or commanding officers of each regiment are directed to procure chaplains —

accordingly persons of good character and exemplary lives — to see that all inferior officers and soldiers pay them a suitable respect, and attend carefully upon religious exercises. The blessing and protection of Heaven are at all times necessary, but especially is it in times of public distress and danger. The General hopes and trusts that every officer and man will endeavor so to live and act as becomes a Christian soldier, defending the dearest rights and liberties of his country."[158]

Consequently, the General required that his soldiers, when possible, regularly attend Sunday worship services each week.[159] During the darkest days of the awful winter at Valley Forge in 1777-78, Washington had ministers such as Peter Muhlenberg, Joab Houghton, and David Avery preach to the discouraged and beleaguered troops to prop up their sagging morale. Undoubtedly, the preaching of the Black Regiment, in addition to the arrival of French General Von Steuben and the ability of the Continental Army to obtain food and other provisions, helped pull the army through that bitter winter and helped save its ranks from being destroyed by low morale and desertion.

"COUSIN AMERICA HAS ELOPED WITH A PRESBYTERIAN PARSON!"

Horace Walpole, the son of England's Prime Minister, Robert Walpole, told the British Parliament that there was no use in fretting over it, "Cousin America has eloped with a Presbyterian parson."[160] In addition to the ministerial gifts of the patriot preachers, they possessed other abilities, such as the ability to agitate the masses that significantly increased their value to the army. Historian James Byrd wrote, "Peter Oliver lamented that 'it was in vain to struggle against ... the Gospel of ... [the] black Regiment.' Clergy fed 'the Frenzy of Anarchy' into such a 'political Enthusiasm, that the Minds of the most pious Men seemed to be wholly absorbed in the Temper of Riot.' Oliver even pointed to one minister who called on the people to 'Fight up to your Knees in Blood.'"[161]

Though as human as anyone else, these preachers, were, for the most part, exemplary men of strength and fortitude and had earned the respect of all around them. It is not difficult to see then, why the men of their congregations and communities were so inspired by their example – so much so, that they were willing to follow them straight into the jaws of war.

In fact, the British believed that the patriot preachers and their reformed Calvinist/Whig-inspired preaching had been so successful, they officially laid the blame for the war on them. King George III called the war a "Presbyterian rebellion."[162] As previously noted, Horace Walpole, the son of the British Prime Minister, also blamed the Presbyterian preachers. A Tory by the name of Galloway who was an ardent supporter of King George wrote, "I fix all the blame of these extraordinary American proceedings upon them (Presbyterians). ... the Presbyterians have been the chief and principal instruments in all these flaming measures; and they always do and ever will act against government, from that restless and turbulent anti-monarchical spirit which has always distinguished them ..."[163] Captain Johann Heinrichs, a member of the Hessian Jager Corps, writing from Philadelphia on January 18, 1778, also penned the blame for the war on the Presbyterians when he wrote, "Call this war, my dearest friend, by whatsoever name you may, only call it not an American Rebellion, it is nothing more nor less than an Irish-Scotch Presbyterian Rebellion."[164]

Historian George Bancroft wrote, "The Revolution of 1776, so far as it was affected by religion, was a Presbyterian measure."[165] Even though the British singled out the Presbyterians for particular blame because of their strong and vocal support for American independence, preachers from practically every denomination, including Lutherans, Baptists, Congregationalists, Methodists, and Episcopalians eventually joined the fight, earning themselves the intense hatred of the British as well.

In 1774, British General Thomas Gage, newly appointed as the military governor of Massachusetts by King George, evidenced the "bad blood" most British harbored toward the Black Regiment when he refused to appoint a day of fasting and prayer as had been the custom of every governor of Massachusetts in years previous. His stated reason for refusing to declare the proclamation was "the request was only to give an opportunity for sedition to flow from the pulpit."[166]

No doubt Gage's angst was due, in part, to the annual election sermon Gad Hitchcock, pastor of Pembroke Church in Boston, had delivered to the Massachusetts legislature on May 25, 1774. Gen. Gage, an unexpected guest at the event, was infuriated when Hitchcock had had the audacity to boldly call for resistance against the British.[167] Many of Gage's supporters had stomped out of the gathering, insulted that a preacher would be so brash and bold in the general's presence.[168]

But Hitchcock was not the only patriot preacher to raise the ire of Gen. Gage. When Samuel Langdon, president of Harvard, preached before the Massachusetts Legislature on May 31, 1775, he also incurred the wrath of Gage. On June 12, just days after Langdon delivered the election sermon, Gen. Gage responded by saying: "To complete the horrid profanation of terms and of ideas, the name of God has been introduced in the pulpits to excite and justify devastation and massacre."[169]

As was mentioned earlier, John Cleaveland's June 17, 1775 letter to General Gage in which he called the General a "profane, wicked-monster of falsehood" who was in danger of having "an aggravated damnation in hell,"[170] did not endear Cleaveland or the other patriot preachers to Gen. Gage either.

In that same month, a British sympathizer in New York wrote to a friend in London criticizing the Black Regiment for their, as he called it …

"most wicked, malicious and inflammatory harangues
.... spiriting their godly hearers to the most violent
opposition to Government; persuading them that the
intention of the Government was to rule them with a
rod of iron, and to make them all slaves; and assuring
them that if they would rise as one man to oppose
these arbitrary schemes, God would assist them ...
that now was the time to strike, whilst Government at
home was afraid of them; together with a long string of
such seditious stuff, well calculated to impose on the
poor devils their hearers, and make them run into every
degree of extravagance and folly, which, if I foresee
aright, they will have leisure enough to be sorry for."[171]

Jonathan Sewall, John Adams' classmate at Harvard, was
among those extremely critical of the Black Regiment. Sewall, a
Tory to the core, believed the preachers were fabricating fanciful
stories when they preached about British tyranny. He claimed,

"The simple, unmeaning mechanic, peasant, and
laborer, who had really no Interest in the Matters of
the Controversy, hoodwinked, inflamed and goaded by
their *spiritual drivers*, fancied they saw civil and religious
tyranny advancing with hasty strides; and thus the
Flames soon spread thro these provinces, and by the help
of Kindred Spirits on the other side of the Atlantic it at
length spread thru the continent."[172]

Probably no greater example of the intense hatred the British
had for the preachers can be found than in the story of Pastor
Ebenezer Prime of Huntington, New York. Born on July 21, 1700
in Milford, Connecticut, Prime was seventy-six years old when
the Declaration of Independence was signed. He graduated Yale
in 1718 and at the age of nineteen started his long tenure as a
preacher of the gospel, a ministry that would span six decades.

He spent his entire ministry preaching in Huntington, New York, situated on Long Island.

When the war began in Lexington/Concord in 1775, Prime was already enjoying the last years of his life and was preparing to close his earthly chapter to begin his heavenly one. But the war invigorated the old patriot preacher and, feeling it his service to God, he began to preach once more the Scriptural virtues of liberty, encouraging his congregation to fight for those liberties and against British tyranny. One biographer wrote of him: "To one who had no future in this world, nothing but a solemn sense of duty to his God and his country could have aroused him to enlist in a struggle, the end of which he never expected to see."[173]

When the American forces suffered their humiliating and disastrous defeat at the Battle of Long Island, New York on August 27, 1776, Rev. Prime and his son were forced to flee for safety to a remote part of the area. Well aware of his firm stand for American independence, the British possessed a peculiar hatred for Prime calling him "the Old Rebel." Consequently, Prime was forced to live out the rest of his elderly days in seclusion and hiding.

Alfred V. Sforza in his article, "Old Burying Ground (17th Century) & Fort Golgotha (1782)," provides information on what happened to Pastor Prime and the indignities he and his neighbors suffered as a result of the British occupation of their town (The town endured six and one-half years of occupation by British troops from Sept. 1, 1776 – Mar. 1783). As the British occupied Huntington, Prime's congregation, because they shared his patriotism and disdain for the British, were forced to abandon their homes and flee for their lives along with their pastor. The British destroyed their property and converted Prime's church into a military depot and stables; submitting it to every desecration they could imagine. They also occupied his house and destroyed his personal library by tearing up his books and burning them.[174]

Saddened, but not subdued, Prime continued to minister to his refugee congregation and resorted to preaching in private homes or anywhere else his congregation could gather. He died in the early fall of 1779 without ever seeing the victory of the cause he had so strongly supported. His body was buried in the graveyard next to the then dilapidated and desecrated church from which he had been driven three years before.

In November of 1782, the British commander, Colonel Benjamin Thompson (later known as Count Rumford), who was in charge of the British forces in the area, ordered Prime's church to be dismantled and the wood used to build Fort Golgotha (a fitting name under the circumstances) on the very site of the church and graveyard where Prime was buried. The insult was further compounded when Col. Thompson forced the citizens of Huntington to provide the labor needed for construction of the fort – even forcing them to destroy the graveyard with their own shovels and axes. Imagine the indignity of the townsfolk being forced to destroy their own church and then use the timbers to construct a British fort on top of their ancestral cemetery. In addition, the local militia, which had been forced into service in the British military, was given the order to oversee the whole horrendous spectacle.

As the graveyard was leveled to make way for Fort Golgotha, over one hundred tombstones were removed and used to build ovens, fireplaces, and flooring for the fort. The citizens noted that the bread baked in these ovens often came out with the inverted tombstone inscriptions stamped on the crust. To add insult to injury, Col. Thompson had his tent situated in such a way that the opening was at the head of Rev. Prime's grave. The Colonel claimed that in doing so, "he might tread on the old rebel every time he went in or out."[175]

After occupying the fort for only a few months, the British were forced to evacuate Huntington in March 1783. As one final insult to the citizens of Huntington and the memory of Rev. Prime, Col. Thompson had his troops burn all of the available wood in the area so that the citizens would have a more difficult time heating their dwellings and cooking their meals. Once the Redcoats were gone, it took the citizens of Huntington only a few months to tear down the hated Fort Golgotha. In 1784 they were able to rebuild their beloved Old First Church where it remains to this day.

As a fitting epitaph to Ebenezer Prime and a scathing condemnation of Col. Thompson's dastardly attempt to desecrate Prime's memory and legacy by walking on his grave every time he entered or exited his tent, Joel Headley wrote:

> "But the venerable patriot was beyond the reach of his insults and his rage, safe with the God whom he had served, and to whose protection he had in life committed without wavering his suffering country."[176]

What was true for Pastor Prime eventually became true for all of the Black Regiment preachers. Although the British worked to humiliate, insult, and exterminate them, in the end, their efforts proved unsuccessful. And of course, history records that their courageous stand led to victory and independence from the clutches of a system of government they had grown to despise.

One thing is for certain, the preachers of the Black Regiment could not be accused of being timid or bashful about their opinions. Certainly, no one had to wonder what they believed.

CRUEL AND INHUMANE TREATMENT

As we have seen, the deep seeded hatred the British harbored for the Black Regiment was based in their belief that these preachers were primary contributors to the colonists' "rebelling" against England. Thus, with their anger fueled by this belief, the British leveled exceptional cruelty on the preachers when they were captured. Joel Headley wrote:

> "A chaplain [in the 19th century], when taken prisoner, is usually treated with great courtesy and consideration, but there was a class of clergymen and chaplains in the

Revolution, whom the British, when they once laid hands on them, treated with the most barbarous severity. Dreading them for the influence they wielded, and hating them for the obstinacy, courage and enthusiasm they infused into the rebels, they violated all the usages of war among civilized nations, in order to inflict punishment upon them."[177]

Because the Black Regiment preachers were considered such trophies of war, they became high priority targets for the British. Consequently, the Redcoats sought to kill them and their families whenever they had the opportunity. For example, Presbyterian pastor James Caldwell, the pastor of the First Presbyterian Church in Elizabethtown, New Jersey, was a particularly bold and outspoken Black Regiment preacher. He had rallied the colonists to fight by preaching things like, "There are times when it is as righteous to fight as well as to pray."[178] The British so hated Caldwell that they eventually killed his wife, and not long afterwards, an assassin who many believed was hired by the British killed Pastor Caldwell himself. (Caldwell's bio is found in chapter 7)

If a preacher was unfortunate enough to be captured in battle, the British sometimes executed them on the spot. John Rosbrugh serves as a good example. Captured on the evening of the Second Battle of Trenton, he was brutally murdered by the Hessians under the command of a British officer – even though he had surrendered. (Rosbrugh's story is found in chapter 1).

Those captured preachers who were not executed were often imprisoned on prison ships. There they experienced such horrendous conditions that some considered it a fate worse than death. Crowded inside these ships, the prisoners almost suffocated breathing the foul air. The filth, unfit food, and close quarters often caused sickness and diseases to spread throughout the population. It is said that the bodies of prisoners who died were often not even given a descent burial, but were instead, left on the shores to decompose. It takes little effort to imagination this terrible scene.

Rev. Moses Allen, brother of Pastor Thomas Allen, was captured in December of 1778 during the Battle of Savannah, Georgia and was incarcerated in such a prison ship. After enduring the horrors and suffering of that ship for weeks, Allen jumped overboard in the hope that he could swim to safety and freedom. Unfortunately, in his weakened condition, he was simply unable to swim to the shore and drowned. It is said that when his body was thrown onto the muddy shore, some of his fellow prisoners who were also members of his church, requested they be allowed to give their pastor a descent burial. Tragically, their request was denied and the corpse of the thirty-year-old patriot preacher was allowed to disgracefully decay in the mud on the shore.

Knowing they could face a similar fate, all of the patriot preachers understood the great risk they were taking by being so outspoken. But even in the face of such danger, they refused to be silent and hide in the shadows. As was mentioned earlier, Josiah Stearns of Epping, New Hampshire, knowing the terrible fate that certainly awaited him in the event that the Americans lost the fight, told his sons, "If the cause succeeds, it will be a great blessing to the country; but if it should fail, your old father's head will soon be a button for a halter [hangman's noose]!"[179]

The preachers' fears of being hanged as traitors were real and not imagined. The Founders themselves, were also convinced that if the war was lost, they too would meet the same awful fate. For example, in 1811, Dr. Benjamin Rush wrote to John Adams reminiscing back to the time when they both had signed the Declaration of Independence. Rush specifically recalled how most of them had expected to be executed for their actions:

"Do you recollect the pensive and awful silence which pervaded the House when we were called up, one after another, to the table of the President of Congress to subscribe what was believed by many at that time to be our own death warrants?"[180]

Rush went on to recall the story of the conversation he overheard between Elbridge Gerry and Col. Benjamin Harrison during that signing event. Attempting to lighten the solemn atmosphere prevailing in the hall, Col. Harrison, himself a Virginia delegate, commented to Massachusetts delegate Gerry:

"'I shall have a great advantage over you, Mr. Gerry, when we are all hung for what we are now doing. From the size and weight of my body I shall die in a few minutes, but from the lightness of your body you will dance in the air and hour or two before you are dead.'"[181]

Rush then recalled that Harrison's comments "procured a transient smile, but it was soon succeeded by the solemnity with which the whole business was conducted.'"[182][183]

Benjamin Franklin also recognized the gravity of what declaring independence from England meant, especially if the colonies were not victorious. Although considered a joke today, Franklin certainly was not kidding when he commented to his fellow *conspirators*, "We must hang together, gentlemen, or else we shall most assuredly hang separately."[184]

Although we often shroud the events of 1776 in patriotic glory and portray the Founders and patriot preachers as "bigger than life" heroes, the truth is, most of them did not see it that way. Unlike we who have the luxury of hindsight, these men and women had no way of knowing whether their efforts would succeed or fail. They certainly entertained no false illusions about the consequences they would face if the war went badly for them.

Chapter 4

"THE SHOT HEARD 'ROUND THE WORLD" CAME FROM THE PULPIT

66 "The pulpits have thundered!"[185] – John Adams's exclamation on hearing that the patriot preachers were speaking out for liberty and independence.

"Oh what a glorious morning this is."[186] – Samuel Adams's reported exclamation on the morning of April 19, 1775, upon hearing of the stand of Pastor Jonas Clark and his Minutemen against the British Redcoats at Lexington.

"It must never be forgotten that religion gave birth to Anglo-America society. In the United States, religion is therefore mingled with all the habits of the nation and all the feelings of patriotism, whence it derives a peculiar force."[187] Alexis de Tocqueville

"The American Revolution occurred in a religious atmosphere. It is indeed high time that we repossess the important historical truth that religion was a fundamental cause of the American Revolution."188 Carl Bridenbaugh, historian

"The colonial clergy created the religious climate that made it possible for the American Revolution to take place. ... This righteous rebellion began in the churches before spilling out into the streets of Boston and the rural regions of the colonies. In 1776 mixing politics and religion was as common as drinking smuggled tea."189 James L. Adams, author and journalist

In the preface to his work, *The Chaplains And Clergy Of The American Revolution,* Joel T. Headley wrote:

"He who forgets or underestimates the moral forces that uphold or bear on a great struggle, lacks the chief qualities of a historian. It is unquestionably true that, if the clergy of New England had from the outset taken the decided and determined stand against the cause of the colonies, which they did for it, the result would have been totally different. ... Those who were chaplains during the French and Indian war became at its close pastors of churches, and although most of those who were alive at the breaking out of the Revolution were too old to become chaplains once more, they still held to their former belief in the right of resistance, and taught it in their congregations. ... They were humble pastors, from whose flocks were drawn the numberless little companies of minutemen ... In every quiet little valley and sequestered nook in New England, the pastor had taught the doctrines of freedom, and preached the duty of resistance to oppression."190

How fitting that "the shot heard around the world," that initiated America's War for Independence was fired in Jonas Clark's churchyard in Lexington, Massachusetts. In many ways, the sound of that flintlock as it "cracked" the cool morning air on April 19, 1775 was actually not the first shot of the Revolution. The patriot preachers had been firing volleys from their pulpits at what they considered British tyranny and injustice for decades.

PASTORS WERE HIGHLY ESTEEMED IN EIGHTEENTH CENTURY AMERICA

The fact that the preachers were so outspoken against the British was significant because ministers held great sway and influence over the lives of the colonists. A pastor was generally held in the highest esteem and was considered among the most important people in town. Of course they were not perfect, but typically, of all the people, they were usually the best educated, especially in the case of the Presbyterians (many of them were graduates of schools like Harvard, Yale, and Princeton), and thus, the most informed about current news. The preachers were not only beloved, but because of their knowledge and ministry, they were greatly respected as well. Journalist/historian Joel Headley observed, "The clergy wielded twofold power – as individuals and as representatives of a profession which in New England dominated the State."[191]

The fact that his pulpit provided a regular forum from which he could pontificate from God's Word concerning the central issues of life made the pastor the central figure of the community. While generally men of godliness, honor, and trustworthiness, the pastors of the eighteenth century had earned for themselves the right to be heard and their influence was considerable. Consider this description of Jonathan French, pastor of South Church in Andover, Massachusetts, written by the Honorable Josiah Quincy, himself a lawyer, patriot, and principal spokesman for the Boston Sons of Liberty:

> "The whole space before the meeting-house was filled with a waiting, respectful, and expecting multitude. At the moment of service, the pastor issued from his mansion, with Bible and manuscript sermon under his

arm, with his wife leaning on one arm ... Then followed every other member of the family, according to age and rank, making often, with family visitants, somewhat of a formidable procession. As soon as it appeared, the congregation, as if moved by one spirit, began to move towards the door of the church; and, before the procession reached it, all were in their places. As soon as the pastor entered the church the whole congregation rose, and stood until the pastor was in the pulpit and his family were seated, — until which was done, the whole assembly continued standing. At the close of the service, the congregation stood until he and his family had left the church, before any one moved towards the door. Forenoon and afternoon the same course of proceeding was had, expressive of the reverential relation in which the people acknowledged that they stood towards their clergymen." But this was not " obedience;" for there was no " authority," and no wish for it. The idea was foreign to New England; for resistance to it was the proximate cause of her colonization. It was a nobler, voluntary offering of respect, ..."[192]

In 1763 when Pastor Ebenezer Baldwin's sister, Bethiah, was preparing to visit, he wrote the following to prepare her, "You must expect if you come to Danbury to be a good deal noticed and perhaps gazed at, for to be the Minister's sister you know in a Country Town is a considerable thing."[193]

Not only did their congregations and fellow citizens honor and respect these men of God, but the leaders of government did as well. Consider the 1774 letter written from the First Provincial Congress of Massachusetts to the ministers of Massachusetts:

"Reverend Sirs: When we contemplate the friendship and assistance our ancestors, the first settlers of this province (while overwhelmed with distress), received from the pious pastors of the churches of Christ, who, to enjoy the rights of conscience, fled with them into this land, then a savage wilderness, we find ourselves filled with the most grateful sensations. And we cannot but acknowledge the goodness of Heaven in constantly supplying us with preachers of the gospel, whose concern has been the temporal and spiritual happiness of this people.

In a day like this, when all the friends of civil and religious liberty are exerting themselves to deliver this country from its present calamities, we cannot but place great hopes in an order of men who have ever distinguished themselves in their country's cause; and do, therefore, recommend to the ministers of the gospel in the several towns and other places in the colony, that they assist us in avoiding that dreadful slavery with which we are now threatened, by advising the people of their several congregations, as they wish their prosperity, to abide by, and strictly adhere to, the resolutions of the Continental Congress," at Philadelphia, in October, 1774, as the most peaceable and probable method of preventing confusion and bloodshed, and of restoring that harmony between Great Britain and these colonies, on which we wish might be established not only the rights and liberties of America, but the opulence and lasting happiness of the whole British empire. Resolved, that the foregoing address be presented to all the ministers of the gospel in the province."[194]

With their knowledge and opinions so highly valued and embraced, it is no wonder then, how these men, once they engaged in the discussion about British tyranny, became the strongest voice for liberty and independence in the colonies. Having earned the trust of the people, the pastors leveraged this influence to liberty's advantage. Historian Alice Baldwin wrote, "They stood before the people as interpreters of God's will. Their political speeches were sermons, their political slogans were often Bible texts. What they taught of government had about it the authority of the divine."[195] Colonial, lawyer, and British Loyalist Daniel Leonard articulated this same concept when he wrote, "What effect must it have had upon the audience to hear the same sentiments and principles, which they had before read in a newspaper, delivered on Sundays from the sacred desk, with a religious awe, and the most solemn appeals to heaven from lips, which they had been taught from their cradle to believe could utter nothing but eternal truths."[196]

And what's more, when these preachers spoke out, they were not bashful about it. For example, consider how Jonathan Mayhew preached in the 1750s that Americans had no choice but to resist British tyranny. (John Adams listed Jonathan Mayhew among the five "first and foremost" patriots who produced the great political awakening that made the Revolution possible.[197] Robert Treat Paine called Mayhew "The Father of Civil and Religious Liberty in Massachusetts and America."[198]) In his January 30, 1750 sermon, "A Discourse Concerning Unlimited Submission And Non-Resistance To The Higher Powers," preached in the West Meeting House in Boston, Mayhew emphatically declared:

> "Tyranny brings ignorance and brutality along with it. It degrades men from their just rank into the class of brutes; it damps their spirits; it suppresses arts; it extinguishes every spark of noble ardor and generosity in the breasts of those who are enslaved by it; it makes naturally strong and great minds feeble and little, and triumphs over the ruins of virtue and humanity. This is true of tyranny in every shape: there can be nothing great and good where its influence reaches. For which reason it becomes every friend to truth and human kind, every lover of God and the Christian religion, to bear a part in opposing this hateful monster."[199]

On April 3, 1755, while preaching at Wilmington, Massachusetts to a company of American soldiers under the command of Captain Phinehas Osgood, Isaac Morrill, pastor of the Second Church of Christ in Wilmington, said, "And are we willing to give up our civil Rights and Privileges, and become subjected to Tyranny and arbitrary Government? And are we willing to give up our Religion? Oh for God's sake, let us think of our Danger, and labor to prevent our Ruin...Your All lays at Stake."[200] John Rodgers, pastor of the First Presbyterian Church in New York City, warned the government of Great Britain, "We have so long tasted Sweets of civil and religious Liberty, that we cannot be easily prevailed upon to submit to a Yoke of Bondage, which neither we nor our Fathers were able to bear."[201]

Even though these patriot preachers had been speaking out against British rule and what they saw as tyranny for years, they came to understand that "firing shots" from their pulpits was not enough; so when the time came, some of them actually loaded their flintlocks and fired them as well. These preachers did not just talk about fighting for liberty, they went and actually fought for it on the battlefields. An example of the typical role the patriot preachers and their churches played can be seen in the following account by Richard Frothingham:

> "In Danvers, Massachusetts the deacon of the parish was elected captain of the minutemen and the minister his lieutenant. The company, after its field exercise, would sometimes repair to the meetinghouse to hear a patriotic sermon, or partake of an entertainment at the townhouse, where the zealous sons of liberty would exhort them to fight bravely for God and their country. At Lunenburg, the minute company, after going through several military maneuvers, marched to a public house, where the officers had provided an elegant entertainment for the company, a number of the respectable inhabitants of the town, and patriotic ministers of the towns adjacent. They then marched in military procession to the meetinghouse,

where the Rev. Mr. Adams delivered an excellent sermon, suitable to the occasion, from Psalm 27:3."[202]

When Peter Muhlenberg laid aside his clerical robe in Woodstock, Virginia for a Continental Army uniform, he was not alone. He was only one of hundreds of patriot preachers and spiritual leaders who had grown up hearing about the Christian's responsibility to *establish* and *defend* liberty. Historian Carl Bridenbaugh observed that the roots of these religious principles clearly extended "well beyond 1700 into the previous century"[203] and were taught by pastors from America's earliest days. Historian Alice Baldwin pointed out that the New England preachers had taught the principles of life, liberty, and property long before they were enshrined in the Declaration of Independence in 1776:

> "No one can fully understand the American Revolution and the American constitutional system without a realization of the long history and religious associations which lie back of these words; without realizing that for a hundred years before the Revolution men were taught that these rights were protected by divine, inviolable law."[204]

Using the Scriptures and Whig political philosophy, these patriot preachers believed and preached that all civil laws were preempted by, and founded in, God's law. Considering the Bible supreme in all matters, including government, and gleaning from the writings of William Blackstone, Baron Charles Montesquieu, John Locke, the patriot preachers believed that God's law created a universal law they called *natural law*. With the addition of Christ's *law of liberty* taught in the New Testament, the patriot preachers believed this "sphere of divine law" should heavily influence the thoughts and actions of all colonists – especially those who served in government, and thus, felt the freedom to critique the actions of government leaders.

At the heart of their understanding of law and justice was the concept that any law or constitution that violated God's *natural law* was no law at all. Therefore, the patriot preachers, many in government, and ultimately, the majority of the people in 18th century America concluded any laws that contradicted the basic rights given to man by God were null and void and thus, were unworthy of submission. Additionally, of particular importance was their belief that governments had to obey the law as well as its subjects. Alice Baldwin wrote,

"No single idea was more fully stressed, no principle more often repeated, through the first sixty years of the eighteenth century, than that governments must obey law and that he who resisted one in authority who was violating that law was not himself a rebel but a protector of law."[205]

The profundity of this point must not be overlooked. The concept that law bound *even the King* was revolutionary thought for that time, but it became a deeply rooted principle that buttressed the call for American independence.

Sadly, today this fundamental underpinning of the War for Independence is given little coverage by most media and academics. As Duke University historian Alice Baldwin pointed out, "The significance of the belief in the binding character of law upon God and man seems to have escaped many who write of the Revolutionary philosophy. It is fundamental to any understanding of American constitutional thought."[206]

So, combining this belief with Great Britain's abuse of power and their continued violation of the colonists' basic understanding of law, the patriot preachers were highly motivated to make impassioned pleas to their congregations to resist the tyranny that threatened their very liberties; especially religious liberty which they believed was under considerable threat. As far as they were concerned, liberty had to be preserved at all costs.

Consider, Ezra Stiles' 1760 sermon, "A Discourse on the Christian Union," first preached on April 23, 1760 to a small gathering of the Reverend Convention of the Congregational Clergy of the Colony of Rhode Island in Bristol, Massachusetts and later to a larger audience in Boston in 1761. In it, he pointed out the importance of Christians being unified in the effort to defend the "jewel of liberty":

> "The right of conscience and private judgment is unalienable; and it is truly the interest of all mankind to unite themselves Into one body, for the liberty, free exercise, and unmolested enjoyment of this right, especially in religion....God be thanked we are not embarrassed with subscriptions and oaths to uninspired rules for defining truth, in this land of liberty, where the SCRIPTURES are professedly our only RULE....And being possessed of the precious jewel of religious liberty, a jewel of inestimable worth, let us prize it highly, and esteem it too dear to be parted with on any terms; ... Our cause is one, ... Let us be cemented together by forbearance, fellowship, union....Let the grand errand into America never be forgotten."[207]

WATCHMEN ON THE WALL

The patriot preachers believed that they were God's watchmen over liberty. Seeing themselves then, as guardians, they took this responsibility quite seriously, taking to heart such biblical passages as:

> "... When I bring the sword upon a land, if the people of the land take a man of their coasts, and set him for their watchman: [3]If when he seeth the sword come upon the land, he blow the trumpet, and warn the people; [4]Then whosoever heareth the sound of the trumpet, and taketh not warning; if the sword come, and take him away, his blood shall be upon his own head. [5]He heard the sound of the trumpet, and took not warning; his blood shall be

upon him. But he that taketh warning shall deliver his soul. ⁶But if the watchman see the sword come, and blow not the trumpet, and the people be not warned; if the sword come, and take any person from among them, he is taken away in his iniquity; but his blood will I require at the watchman's hand." Ezekiel 33:2-6

Drawing from Old Testament passages, including the one just quoted, many of the patriot preachers believed that the American church was a *descendent* or even *replacement* of the nation of Israel and that its role in America was quite similar to Israel's role in Old Testament times. Although many of us do not embrace this "replacement" belief, it is easy to understand why these preachers came to this position. By the time of the American War for Independence, the nation of Israel and the Jewish people had been practically "lost" to history for some 1700 years. Not having the luxury of seeing the Jews regathered into the Holy Land and witnessing Israel become an officially recognized nation in 1948 as we in the 20th and 21st centuries have, it is easy to understand how many Christians and preachers in the 18th century came to believe that maybe the church in America had become the *extension* or *replacement* of Israel.

Therefore, the patriot preachers believed that just as God had set His watchmen on the walls of Israel centuries before, God had also commissioned them as "watchmen" over the spiritual and civil liberties of Americans. As Alice Baldwin observed,

"To many of the clergy the spirit of the day seemed disorderly and lawless and they feared for the welfare of the government. They believed it their peculiar business to be 'watchmen on the tower,' to scent out and warn against danger and to set men right as to the principles upon which they were to act and the views they were to hold."[208]

For example, in 1774, John Allen, the pastor of the Second Baptist Church in Boston, published an oration, *The Watchman's Alarm*, extolling the virtues of liberty and decrying the curse of tyranny that darkened the world at that time. Just a few months before, on December 3, 1773, he had preached a sermon in which he compared the dark days of Old Testament Israel with the darkness of tyranny that was then cloaking America:

> "Observe, that it was a dark time with the nation [Israel], a dark time with the church of the living God, and a very distressing time respecting the people, when Micah appeared contemporary with Isaiah, as a prophet of the Lord, and a son of liberty, therefore he tells the oppressors of the people, 'the day of the watchmen, and thy visitation cometh.' And is not this the case? Is not the day of the watchmen of America come, who watch for the rights of the people, as the sentinels of the land, to defend them from every invasion of power and destruction? Now their visitation in Providence is come – try the watchmen whether they will stand for God, and the people, or not."[209]

Thankfully for America, the preachers of the Black Regiment proved to be far more faithful watchmen than did those who watched over Israel in the days of Micah and Isaiah. On December 11, 1783, with the darkness of British tyranny now banished from America, Philadelphia Pastor George Duffield commended the patriot preachers for having faithfully fulfilled their duty as "watchmen on the wall": "Nor were those of the sacred order [preachers] wanting to their country, when her civil and religious liberties were all at stake. But, as became faithful watchmen, they blew the trumpet on the walls of our Zion, and sounded an alarm for defense."[210]

CIVIL AND RELIGIOUS LIBERTY ARE INSEPARABLE

The patriot preachers and many political leaders of that day were convinced that civil and religious liberty were inseparable. In his preface to the printed edition of his 1750 sermon, "Unlimited Submission and Non-resistance To the Higher Powers," Jonathan Mayhew wrote, "There is a natural and just union of religious and civil counsels, ... Having earlier still learned from the Holy Scriptures that wise, brave and virtuous men were always friends to liberty."[211]

Those who believed this were convinced that these liberties were so woven together and mutually dependent that to destroy one, was, by definition, to destroy the other. For example, Presbyterian preacher and president of Princeton, John Witherspoon, declared, "There is not a single instance in history in which civil liberty was lost, and religious liberty preserved entire. If therefore we yield up our temporal property, we at the same time deliver the conscience into bondage."[212]

In addition to this, many, including a number of the Founders, believed that only in those nations where Christianity was the dominant faith could the citizens enjoy true liberty. For example, George Washington said,

> "Of all the dispositions and habits which lead to political prosperity, religion and morality are indispensable supports. In vain would that man claim the tribute of patriotism who should labor to subvert these great pillars of human happiness, these firmest props of the duties of man and citizens. ... And let us with caution indulge the supposition that morality can be maintained without religion."[213]

John Adams said,

> "[I]t is religion and morality alone which can establish the principles upon which freedom can securely stand. The

only foundation of a free constitution is pure virtue. ... [W]e have no government armed with power capable of contending with human passions unbridled by morality and religion. ... Our constitution was made only for a moral and religious people. It is wholly inadequate to the government of any other."[214]

Benjamin Franklin said, "[O]nly a virtuous people are capable of freedom. As nations become corrupt and vicious, they have more need of masters."[215] Preaching the opening sermon of the Georgia Provincial Congress in 1775, John Joachim Zubly argued this point when he said, "Survey the globe, and you will find that liberty has taken its seat only in Christendom, and that the highest degree of freedom is pleaded for and enjoyed by such as make profession of the gospel."[216]

When stripped down to its bare bones, the central concept for which the patriot preachers and their congregations were fighting was the freedom to preach, teach, and practice the gospel – the only message, they believed, that could undergird liberty. Believing that British tyranny posed the greatest threat to that gospel, Pastor Samuel Sherwood offered the following counsel to the "Freemen of the Colony of Connecticut" on August 31, 1774:

> "Once more We are awfully threatened with being deprived of the liberty of our consciences, the liberty of professing the important truths of the gospel; and attending those sacred ordinances which God has instituted with a view to advance the glory of the Redeemer, and promote the salvation of his people."[217]

To them, civil liberty's greatest blessing was the latitude it provided for religious liberty. Conversely, they believed tyranny's greatest curse was that it threatened the free practice and preaching of the gospel. For example, on the evening of October 5, 1777, Abraham Keteltas, pastor of the First Presbyterian

Church in Newburyport, Massachusetts, went as far as to say that governmental tyranny was the work of Satan:

"Liberty is the grand fountain, under God, of every temporal blessing, and what is infinitely more important, it is favorable to the propagation of unadulterated Christianity. Liberty is the parent of truth, justice, virtue, patriotism, benevolence, and every generous and noble purpose of the soul. ... How inestimable a blessing then must liberty be, and how inconceivably great its loss! ... But if liberty is thus friendly to the happiness of mankind ... certainly tyranny & oppression are the cause of the devil, the cause which God's soul hates. The Holy Scriptures abound with instances and prophecies of his judgments against tyrants and oppressors;"[218]

As previously stated, the patriot preachers believed civil and religious liberty were inseparable and that the loss of one would inevitably result in the loss of the other. This is evident in the statement written by the ministers of Connecticut encouraging their Christian brethren in Boston to fight on: "The taking away of civil liberty will involve the ruin of religious liberty also. ... Bear your heavy load with Christian fortitude and resolution."[219]

On July 4, 1798, during the eighteenth anniversary of the signing of the Declaration of Independence, Rev. Timothy Dwight, president of Yale, preached the sermon, "The Duty of Americans At the Present Crisis." In it, he emphasized that civil and religious liberty were "conjoined" and were worth fighting for:

"Religion and Liberty are the two great objects of defensive war. Conjoined, they unite all the feelings, and call forth all the energies, of man. Religion and liberty are the meat and the drink of the body politic. Withdraw one of them, and it languishes, consumes, and dies. If indifference to either at any time becomes the prevailing character of a people, one half of their motives to vigorous defense is lost, and the hopes of their enemies are proportionally increased. Here, eminently, they are inseparable. Without religion we may possibly retain the freedom of savages, bears, and wolves; but not the freedom of New England."[220]

So, as the patriot preachers saw war with Great Britain becoming more and more unavoidable, they had already settled in their minds – if fighting commenced, it was their duty to be a part of it.

Chapter 5

THEY COULD NOT AFFORD TO SIT
THIS ONE OUT

Author and Journalist James Adams observed:
"Colonists felt justified in fighting: In the 1770's, in the minds of the majority the issue was a simple one: Colonists' rights were being eroded by the continual encroachment of an unrepresentative government, located 3,000 miles away, in London. They must nip tyranny in the bud, not permit it to grow to full bloom. ... Christian patriots had the solemn duty to resist. Failure to do so in such a just cause would bring them under God's condemnation."[221]

No doubt, Adams provides a point of view that many in support of the War for Independence felt. In their view, Great Britain had gone too far and for this reason, the patriot preachers and their congregations were willing to fight. To them, an honorable death on the battlefield was deemed preferable to a life of servitude under continued British rule/tyranny. On October 25, 1780, Samuel Cooper, pastor of the Brattle Street Church, Boston, Massachusetts, preached, "A Sermon On The Day Of The Commencement Of The Constitution," before Governor John Hancock and the Massachusetts Legislature in which he said:

"Peace, peace, we ardently wish; but not upon terms dishonorable to ourselves, or dangerous to our liberties;

and our enemies seem not yet prepared to allow it upon any other. At present the voice of providence, the call of our still invaded country, and the cry of every thing dear to us, all unite to rouse us to prosecute the war with redoubled vigor; upon the success of which all our free constitutions, all our hopes depend."[222]

Declaring that dying free was better than living under tyranny, Zabdiel Adams, pastor in Lunenburg, Massachusetts, encouraged his fellow Americans to keep up the fight in his 1782 Massachusetts election sermon:

"Expense is not to be regarded in a contest of such magnitude. What can possibly be a compensation for our liberties? It is better to be free among the dead, than slaves among the living. The ghosts of our friends, slain in war; the spirits of our illustrious ancestors, long since gone to rest, who transmitted our fair inheritance to us; a regard to children still unborn, all call upon us to make greater exertions; and will rise up in judgment against us, if, through cowardice, we desert the noble cause, in which, for many years past, we have been engaged."[223]

Patriot Pastor Moses Mather likewise believed Americans, after having tried all peaceful means, had finally been forced into a corner. In his 1775 sermon, "America's Appeal To The Impartial World," Mather said:

"Since then we are compelled to take up the sword, in the necessary defense of our country, our liberties and properties, ourselves and posterity: Let us gird on the harness, having our bosoms mailed, with firm defiance of every danger; and with fixed determined purpose, to part with our liberty only with our lives, engage in the conflict; and nobly play the man for our country, the cities and churches ... and demonstrate to the world, that the free irrepressible spirit, that inspired the breasts and animated the conduct of our brave forefathers; is not degenerated in us, their offspring. With fair pretenses, they invite us to submit our necks to their yoke; but with unheard of cruelties and oppressions, they determine us, to prefer death to submission."[224]

In his May 29, 1776 Massachusetts election sermon, Samuel West went even further than Mather and said that Americans had a "duty" to oppose British tyranny:

"... it will appear that we are in the way of our duty in opposing the tyranny of Great Britain; for, if unlimited submission is not due to any human power, if we have an undoubted right to oppose and resist a set of tyrants that are subverting our just rights and privileges, there cannot remain a doubt in any man, that will calmly attend to reason, whether we have a right to resist and oppose the arbitrary measures of the King and Parliament; for it is plain to demonstration, nay, it is in a manner self-evident, that they have been and are endeavoring to deprive us not only of the privileges of Englishmen, and our charter rights, but they have endeavored to deprive us of what is much more sacred, viz., the privileges of men and Christians; *i.e.,* they are robbing us of the inalienable rights that the God of nature has given us as men and rational beings, and has confirmed to us in his written word as Christians ... We have made our appeal to Heaven, and we cannot doubt but that the Judge of all the earth will do right."[225]

THEY WERE NOT NAÏVE ABOUT THE PROBABLE COST OF INDEPENDENCE

The patriot preachers were well aware that standing against Great Britain might very well cost them their lives, but as they saw it, liberty was worth the sacrifice. So, with a bit of flare and over exuberance at times, in their sermons, writings, and public conversations, they framed the actions of the British as the egregious acts they sometimes were.

It is at this juncture that we, as students of history, must exercise caution and restraint when retelling the stories of the patriot preachers. Their stories speak for themselves and to fall prey to exaggerations and embellishments is simply unnecessary. There are many fanciful accounts of the British brutally tormenting innocent members of the community, and while there is no doubt that isolated atrocities likely occurred during the lead up to actual military hostilities, examples of *extreme* British brutality do not seem to have been common place. Yet, for a number of reasons, some feel the urge to unnecessarily make the story more dramatic than it actually was. For example, the dramatic scene in Mel Gibson's movie, "The Patriot,"[226] where the church is burned while the townsfolk are locked inside, certainly stirs our emotions to a fevered pitch. The problem is there appears to be no account of an actual event of this type ever occurring during the war. (Although Nazi SS troops did do something similar to citizens in a church in Oradour, France on June 10, 1944 – the event some believe may have inspired "The Patriot" scene.)

It is certainly true that the British were well known for their general brutality to the colonists and they seemed particularly committed to desecrating and burning the churches of the patriot preachers. For example, consider the brutal treatment of Pastor Ebenezer Prime and his congregation at the hands of the British (chapter 3), or the burning of the Red House Presbyterian Church in Semora, North Carolina by the British,[227] or the burning of the parsonage and church of James Caldwell in Elizabethtown, New Jersey on the night of January 25, 1780,[228] or how, in the Old South Meeting House, a Congregationalist Church in Boston, the British "ripped out the pews, installed a bar in the first balcony and used Old South, as a riding school for the British Cavalry"[229] – and these are only a few of the many examples that could be mentioned. No doubt, the patriot preachers knew well when they first determined to stand up and speak out against what they saw as British tyranny that they would most probably receive such treatment, but this did not deter them. They refused to remain silent, and in the face of these atrocities, publicly rebuked the British in their sermons and other declarations. Consider:

- The 1777 sermon by Abraham Ketelas: "Behold those houses of God, ... behold those sacred, magnificent, and costly structures, destroyed by fire, and leveled with the ground, or converted into magazines for warlike stores, receptacles for rapine and plunder, riding schools, for the exercise of horsemanship, theatres, for profane and wanton plays, or prisons, for starving, groaning, expiring captives."[230]

- The 1777 sermon by Samuel Webster: "Accordingly they have vented a peculiar spite against the houses of God, defaced and defied thy holy and beautiful sanctuaries where our fathers worshiped thee, turning them into houses of merchandise and receptacles of beasts, and some of them they have torn in pieces and burned with fire."[231]

- The 1780 sermon by John Rogers: "They have, in the course of this war, utterly destroyed more than fifty places of public worship in these states. Most of these they burnt; others they leveled with the ground, and in some places left not a vestige of their former situation; while they have wantonly defaced, or rather destroyed others, by converting them into barracks, jails, hospitals, riding-schools, etc. Boston, Newport, Philadelphia, and Charlestown, all furnished melancholy instances of this prostitution and abuse of the houses of God. And of the nineteen places of public worship in New York, when the war began, there were but nine fit for use when the British troops left it."[232]

Again, even though the British were often brutal when it came to destroying the churches of those fighting for independence, as was stated above, there is no historical evidence that their actions stooped to the level of those depicted in "The Patriot." Yet this scene is so powerful, it becomes riveted into the minds of all who see it and leads the audience to naturally conclude that the British were so evil that they were practically demonic. This, of course, demonstrates the importance of sticking to the facts and allowing those facts to lead where they may.

Pastor Moses Mather knew well the dangers of standing up to the Crown. In 1775, Mather warned of the sufferings the coming struggle for independence would bring. Though older when the war broke out, he was an ardent supporter of the cause and his devotion eventually led to his being arrested and jailed on two separate occasions. In a very real sense, the words he spoke in a 1775 sermon foreshadowed the future sacrifice he would make for the cause:

> "Let none be dismayed at the strength and power of our oppressors; nor at the horrors of war into which we are compelled, for the necessary defense of our rights. Can we expect the laurels, without entering the list? To be crowned without being tried? ... Such is the state of the world, that the way to freedom and glory is a way of danger and conflict. The road to Canaan was through the desert and the deep; and the grave is the subterranean path to celestial bliss."[233]

Pastor Mather truly did walk through his own "desert and the deep" in his fight for liberty. Hated by the local Tories for his strong preaching, he was imprisoned twice because of his stand against the British. In 1779 he was seized at his home and placed in a New York jail for five weeks. Then in 1781, the

British interrupted one of his church services and detained him and some fifty of his members for a number of months.[234] Even though he knew that incurring the wrath of the British could cost him dearly, he refused to remain silent.

As was discussed in greater detail in chapter 3, the British were especially brutal to the patriot preachers if they captured them. Patriot pastor Abraham Ketelas gave an ample description of the disdain the British had for the pastors active in the cause for independence when he wrote, "Behold your ministers mocked, insulted, buffeted, marked out for destruction, for their attachment to religion and liberty, and their zeal against illegal and oppressive measures."[235]

Keteltas, began as a Presbyterian but later began preaching in Dutch and French Reformed churches and served in the Provincial Congress of New York. In his sermon, "God Arising And Pleading His People's Cause," preached in the Presbyterian Church in Newburyport, Massachusetts on October 5, 1777, he articulated, in colorful terms, what he felt about the cause and the cost:

> "Ye cruel and bloody authors of this unjust, unnatural war! What desolation, what misery have ye not brought on this once happy land? How many old men's sighs, and widows' moans! How many orphans water standing eyes; men for their sons, wives for their husbands fate, and children for their parents timeless death, shall rue the hour that ever ye were born, how many tents of affliction? How many weeping Rachels have ye made? How many disconsolate mothers, bewailing the death of their children, and refusing to be comforted, because they are not? ... let the smoking ruins of well finished and valuable houses, by their speechless, but flaming oratory, melt you into tears, over your country's ruin, and enkindle your indignation against her barbarous, unrelenting foes. ... Behold numbers of the most pious

and respectable characters and families, compelled to fly from their habitations and churches, and seek for refuge in the uninvaded parts of the land. ... See our unnatural foes, exulting over the ruins they have made ... Are these things right? ... Can God give a privilege to any man, or number of men, to violate his own sacred and immutable laws? Reason, conscience, humanity, recoil at the horrid thought!"[236]

Though more dramatic than most, Keteltas reveals the passion at the heart of many of the patriot preachers. Among many threats such as the fear of losing the liberty to preach as they saw fit and the very real possibility that the Church of England could be forced on them,[237] many of the preachers felt compelled to confront what they saw as evil. In doing so, they also knew the price could be high and that some most likely would pay the ultimate price by offering up their own lives. But convinced that they were fighting for their very survival and the preservation of the principles they held most sacred, they considered no price too high.

To illustrate just how material that danger was, consider the threat letter that ended up on the desk of John Hancock, president of the Provincial Congress of Massachusetts. The letter, written by the Rev. Samuel Peters, a Tory from Hebron, Connecticut, included the following section celebrating the soon expected arrival of the British Regulars:

"I am in high spirits, six regiments are coming over from England, and sundry men-of-war. So soon as they come, hanging work will go on. Destruction will attend first the seaport towns."[238]

"Hanging work will go on," no insignificant threat – and had the Americans lost the war, the British might very well have made good on that threat. Thus, the colonists were convinced that if they did not fight, the only other alternative left was to submit to British tyranny.

For the patriot preachers and their compatriots, theirs was no mere experiment in self-government – they were committed to winning their independence and securing their unalienable rights, including self-governance. In this regard, they were not speaking in pithy clichés and political rhetoric, but as the historical record verifies, they were willing to back up their words with political and military actions; and to that end, the patriot preachers played their part.

PROPAGANDA PLAYED A PIVOTAL
ROLE – EVEN IN SERMONS

It is important to understand that central to the success of the American Revolution (or any revolution for that matter) was the ability to persuade large numbers of people to support the cause, and in this regard, propaganda was a critical tool. Political pamphlets, broadsides, and even election sermons,[239] played a major role in persuading the colonists to separate from Great Britain. But, it is important to remember that propaganda, by definition, often involves the embellishment of the facts and is often a huge dose of passion and exuberance "seasoned" with the truth. It is easy to imagine how the people were more quickly stirred to action when incited by cries like, "the redcoats are burning churches" than they were by "the King is violating our unalienable rights." To be fair, we must admit that the sermons presented throughout this book served a dual purpose. First, they were sound, biblical sermons preached, typically from a reformed theological persuasion, using the Bible to teach the principles of right government and the proper use of authority. But these sermons were also extremely useful as propaganda to provide a reasonable, Scriptural basis for defying the King and his unreasonable, unlawful rule of the colonies.

Honestly, it is very difficult for we 21st century Americans who have enjoyed liberty from birth, to understand what it was like to have the British forcing upon the colonists what they viewed as unreasonable policies; policies that ran against the very grain of individual liberty – a liberty free from the monarchical rule of the King. This was no small issue. If we are to understand what motivated those who fought for independence in 18th century America, then we must attempt to walk in their shoes and try our best to feel what they felt.

Of the many things that motivated the colonists to take their stand against the British, the one issue that seems to have been foremost in their minds was the continued insistence of King George and the Parliament to flex their muscles by operating outside what the colonists understood to be legal. After repeated, but unsuccessful appeals for relief, many had concluded that nothing short of complete independence would solve the problem. In the minds of these colonists, King George had become a tyrant and British rule had become tyranny.

So, convinced that every freedom loving American, especially Christians, had an obligation and a sacred duty to serve and defend their country, the patriot preachers challenged the colonists to stand up and do their duty. This can clearly be seen in John Hurt's 1777 message to the troops in New Jersey entitled, "The Love Of Our Country":

"The liberty we contend for is not the license of a few to tyrannize over multitudes, but an equal freedom to all, ... These are circumstances which give a sanction to patriotism, and not only justify, but demand our most active resolutions to promote the welfare of our country by all those methods which become a civilized and numerous people, born with an instinctive love of liberty. If we bear a true and cordial affection for our country, we shall be warm and active in her cause; a calm concern is inconsistent with true patriotism, which gives ardor to the coldest breast and makes even cowards brave. ... so much the greater ought to be our resolution to maintain it, and the more scandalous is our folly if we lose it."

Hurt went on to emphasize that, in his opinion, it was a great sin for citizens who enjoyed the benefits of a lawful society to then be unwilling to defend their country:

"God has assigned each of us our station, and a part which we are obliged to discharge in carrying on the great work of social happiness. If, then, I neglect the part appointed me, I am highly unjust; because I take a share of the benefits of society, and yet leave the burden to be borne by others. A greater injustice than this can scarcely be conceived. He who injures particulars is indeed an offender, but he who withholds from the public the service and affection to which it is entitled, is a criminal of a far higher degree, as he thereby robs a whole body of people, and deprives the community of her just demand. ... if, in short, any be wanting in pursuing the benevolent principle, by directing his talents to their proper ends, he deserves to be treated as a common spoiler, ... We see, then, how closely the kind Creator has connected our interest with our duty, and made it each man's happiness to contribute to the welfare of his country.[240]

As we will see in chapter 14, the patriot preachers were no mob of rebels and anarchists who had traded their call to preach for the power of military conquest. They were, instead, respected ministers who believed in something so strongly that they were willing to fight and, in some cases, die for it. As tensions continued to grow and armed conflict began, the patriot preachers became part of a larger community of people from Connecticut to Georgia struggling to be free and who ended up playing a key part in the War for Independence – whether from behind the pulpit or on the actual battlefield.

HOW SUCCESSFUL WERE THEIR SERMONS?

But how successful were the efforts of the patriot preachers? It certainly appears that by using highly effective tools including pulpit messages, election sermons, and recollections of the war, the preachers came across loud and clear. Their efforts, combined with those of the other supporters of independence and liberty, caused men to take to the field in numbers sufficient enough that the British were never really able to occupy much more than the seaport cities.

How many Americans actually joined the cause for independence? We may never know for certain. Because of a letter written by John Adams, it has been believed for years that approximately one third of Americans supported the cause, approximately one third remained loyal to the British Crown, and approximately one third labored to remain neutral. In recent years, modern historians have challenged those numbers and have suggested that the actual number who supported the war was much higher. Professor William F. Marina, Professor Emeritus of History at Florida Atlantic University, explains:

> "Recent historians of the Loyalists, such as William Nelson, have estimated them [Americans who supported the war] at no more than a sixth of the population. If that estimate is correct, the only alternative to a massive American majority is a very large neutral group. But if that were so, how can the collapse of the legitimacy of British institutions even before the outbreak of fighting, which will always tend to polarize the neutrals, be explained? Further, the patriots managed not only to subdue the internal Loyalist opposition, which had the support of the British army, Hessian mercenaries, and Indian allies, but also to mount an assault on Canada."[241]

So if the number of Americans who engaged in the struggle for independence was as high as some modern historians believe, the patriot preachers may have been more successful than even they knew. Of course, we will probably never know for certain, at least quantitatively, the full impact they had on the cause. But what we do know is that in countless communities and towns, both large and small, the preachers did their part to ensure that those around them were made aware of the level of the crisis.

In any event, many historians continue to suggest that had those who occupied the pulpits during the time leading up to and during the actual war not supported and promoted the effort for independence, it might not have succeeded. As Professor Marina states, even though there were likely large majorities in favor of independence, those majorities needed to be stirred to passion as Pastor Cummings had suggested in 1781. Who but the patriot preachers could have pulled this off? At the very least, it certainly appears that their labors were not in vain. In 1860, historian John Wingate Thornton wrote:

"Thus it is manifest, in the spirit of our history, in our annals, and by the general voice of the fathers of the republic, that, in a very great degree, To the Pulpit, the Puritan Pulpit, we owe the moral force which won our independence. ... They prepared for the struggle, and went into battle, not as soldiers of fortune, but ... with the Word of God in their hearts, and trusting in Him. ... England sent her armies to compel submission, and the colonists appealed to heaven."[242]

In March 1898, while speaking in a chapel service at Emory College in Oxford, Georgia, Methodist Bishop Charles B. Galloway emphasized the "iron" of the men who founded America:

"Mighty men they were, of iron nerve and strong hand and unbalanced cheek and heart of flame. God needed not reeds shaken by the wind, not men clothed in soft raiment; but heroes of hardihood and lofty courage to be the voice of a new kingdom crying in this Western wilderness. And such were the sons of the mighty who responded to the divine call. Bishop Hurst says: 'With some exceptions they were the wheat of the Old World. Unlike many of our recent immigrants, they came to make here their permanent homes. They cut the last ties that bound them to the elder civilization, and entered heart and soul, for life of death, into the struggle of this new and rising land. Besides, they were religious men, swayed by religious principles, who feared God, and Him only. They were men of intelligence, far-sighted, who had been trained in the rough discipline of an age that tried men's souls, and they were thus able to lay broad and deep the foundations of a republic whose cornerstones are freedom and law.'"[243]

As we will see in the following chapters, many of them were not content with only leading out in a "political" sense, but, when the time came, they led out in a "physical" sense as well and marched off to war with their congregants, friends, and neighbors. The following chapters highlight the individual stories of a few of these great patriot preachers – stories whose telling is long overdue.

Chapter 6

JONAS CLARK: "THE MINUTEMAN PASTOR" (1730 – 1805)

"... no better spot [Lexington, Massachusetts] on the continent could have been found for the British first to try the terror of their arms, and make the experiment to subjugate the Colonists by force. His [Jonas Clark's] congregation was ripe for revolution, ready to fight and to die rather than yield to arbitrary force."[244]

Journalist/historian Joel Headley

NO BETTER PLACE THAN LEXINGTON

For the sake of American independence, the British could have chosen no better place to begin hostilities than in the sleepy little town of Lexington, Massachusetts. It was there that one of the most ardent patriot preachers plied his trade – Pastor Jonas Clark. In many ways, this man, along with Peter Muhlenberg, embodies the prototypical patriot preacher. Of course, it is important to distinguish the patriot preachers from the larger body of clergy in the 18th century. Not all preachers supported the cause of liberty and independence and either remained neutral or loyal to the Crown. But Jonas Clark was anything but loyal to the Crown or neutral; yet at the time, he probably had no idea of the significant role he was destined to play in the massive drama that was about to play out around him.

For quite some time, as war with Great Britain seemed imminent, like so many other "Minutemen" groups throughout New England, Pastor Clark and the men of his church and community had been regularly mustering together to drill in military exercises to prepare themselves for the coming fight. This fact, as it turned out, would have a huge impact on what happened in Lexington that spring day in 1775. But just as important, perhaps even more, were Clark's persuasive writing and speaking activities. Quite possibly, his greatest fight against the British was carried out using the weapons of his mind, pen, and oratory skill rather than his musket. Using Clark's 1773 writings protesting the British tea tax, Theodore Gilman, Governor of the New York Society, testified to how well Clark had trained his people for the coming conflict:

> "These papers so full of learning and patriotism were an education to the men of Lexington. The citizens of no other town were so well instructed in their rights and duties for God and Country. They were like trained gladiators and when the hour of trial came, they knew their duty and did it. It was Jonas Clark who had trained and instructed them."[245]

Without a doubt, there was probably no other pastor in New England who had better prepared himself and his congregation for the coming struggle than Clark. Events would unfold on April 19, 1775 that would transform all of that training and preparation from an academic exercise into a significant role that many, to this day, consider providential.

Born in 1730, Jonas Clark received his formal education at Harvard, graduating when he was twenty-two. Immediately upon leaving Harvard, he began preparing himself for the ministry and was ordained in 1755 when the first church in Lexington called him to be their third pastor – a post he would hold for fifty years until his death in 1805.

Serving as the successor to the church's second pastor, John Hancock, the grandfather of the famous Founder, John Hancock, president of the Continental Congress, was no small task but Clark was certainly up to the challenge. Hired for the yearly salary of eighty pounds and twenty cords of wood, once he was settled in Lexington, Clark gave himself fully to the Gospel ministry, faithfully ministering to the needs of his Lexington congregation.

Powerful in the pulpit and persuasive in everyday life, Clark boldly proclaimed the truths of God's Word every Sunday. It was said of his preaching:

"His voice was so powerful and agreeable, and when excited by his subject, which was often the case, it extended far beyond the bounds of the meeting-house, and could be heard distinctly by those who were anywhere in the immediate neighborhood."[246]

Along these same lines, historian Alice Baldwin wrote,

"For years before the Stamp Act, he [Jonas Clark] is said to have preached Sunday after Sunday and explained in many a town meeting the doctrines of natural and constitutional rights and the rights of resistance."[247]

A man of deep commitment and firmly held beliefs, Jonas Clark was not one to sit by, waiting for something to happen. Aggressively proactive, his temperament seems to have perfectly suited him for his part in America's struggle for independence.

An ardent patriot, Clark was not one to shy away from controversial subjects and he did not hesitate to preach the principles of religious and civil liberty from his Lexington pulpit. As the relationship between Great Britain and the colonies deteriorated, Clark expounded even more frequently upon the principles of godly government and the Christian's responsibility to resist tyranny. He declared to his people, "[We must be prepared to] Sacrifice our Estates and everything dear in Life,

Yea & life itself, in support of the common cause."[248] William Ware, a preacher in Cambridge, Massachusetts, said of Clark,

"It would not be beyond the truth to assert that there was no person at that time in that vicinity – not only no clergyman, but no other person of whatever calling or profession, who took a firmer stand for the liberties of the country, or was more ready to perform the duties or endure the sacrifices of a patriot than the minister of Lexington. He was considered, moreover, not only as a person of great ardor of temperament as a politician – the first to move himself and set others in motion on great emergencies – but also as a person of great abilities, whose judgment was one more than others to be respected and relied upon. No one than he better understood the state of the question as between the Colonies and England; nor were there any who, earlier than he, or with more talent at the town meetings, and at other places and times, argued the great topics on which differences had arisen, and then, through the representatives of the town, presented the arguments and conclusions at which they had arrived, in papers which he had prepared, to the General Court, at their various session."[249]

The consummate statesman, Pastor Clark was quite influential in writing the official documents of Lexington and greatly contributed to, if not writing completely, Lexington's instructions to their representatives to the Provincial Congress and Council of Massachusetts. This was not uncommon in those days since the local pastor was often the most educated person in the community and was regularly called upon by his neighbors to perform this type of service. In his instructions to William Reed in 1765 and Jonas Stone in 1773, we not only see Clark's writing skills in action, but we also see his firm grasp of the crisis the colonies faced:

"... that the world may see and future generations know that the present (generation) both know and value the rights they enjoyed and did not tamely resign them for chains and slavery. ... as far as consistent with allegiance and duty to our rightful sovereign, such measures should be promoted as would preserve the invaluable rights and liberties we at present possess."[250]... that thus, whether successful or not, succeeding generations might know that we understood our rights and liberties and were neither afraid or ashamed to assert and maintain them, and that we ourselves may have at least the consolation in our chains, that it was not through our neglect that this people were enslaved."[251]

Charles Hudson, expert on the history of Lexington, said this about the persuasive power of Clark's pen:

"Few towns are able to furnish from their records, papers as numerous, elaborate and able as Lexington ... [as] the able state papers which emanated from her village clergyman, Rev. Jonas Clark. ... So fully and clearly are the grievances under which our fathers labored and the causes which gave rise to the American Revolution set forth (in Mr. Clark's writings) that if all other records were destroyed and all recollections blotted from the memory, the faithful historian could from the instructions given to the representatives of Lexington and other papers found on our records emanating from the pen of Mr. Clark, trace the developments of oppression from year to year, and state the true causes of that struggle."[252]

Clark made an indelible mark on the citizens of Lexington specifically, and on the citizens of Massachusetts generally. Interestingly, Jonas Clark's wife, the former Lucy Bowes, was the granddaughter of the Rev. John Hancock who had pastored the Lexington church from 1698-1752. This, of course, made her a cousin to the noted patriot, Governor John Hancock, also a grandson of the senior Reverend Hancock. As pastor, the senior Rev. Hancock had once lived in the same house in which Jonas and Lucy Clark lived. Consequently, Gov. John Hancock often visited the Clarks at the parsonage in Lexington and so, during those visits it is reasonable to assume Jonas and John spent many hours discussing the principles of liberty, self-government, and the worsening crisis between the Colonies and Great Britain. Sensing that conflict with Great Britain was imminent, Pastor Clark, like many pastors in New England, began to organize the men of his church and town into a small militia. These groups all over New England formed themselves into groups of "minutemen" – all committing to be prepared in a moment's notice, musket in hand, to fight the British in the event they showed a force of arms.

For weeks on Sunday afternoons after church, Pastor Clark and a deacon named John Parker, a veteran of the French and Indian War and known to all in the area as "Captain Parker," had gathered on the yard of Clark's church to train these minutemen how to fight as soldiers. It must be remembered that the majority of these New England Minutemen were not professional soldiers, but instead, were farmers, merchants, mechanics, blacksmiths, etc. who had no official military training and thus were no match for the well-trained British regulars.

APRIL 19, 1775

On the night of April 18, 1775, the Clarks just happened to be entertaining two special guests in their home who had stopped by while on business for the Continental Congress. The two guests were John Hancock and Samuel Adams. That same night, British Lieutenant Colonel Francis Smith had received orders to march to Concord, Massachusetts and confiscate the munitions that had been hidden there by the colonists. The fact that Hancock and Adams were known to be staying in Lexington, no doubt created an interesting prospect to the British, for if captured, these two American patriots would have been valuable trophies of war. Writing a year after the battle, Jonas Clark commented,

"As both these gentlemen [Samuel Adams and John Hancock] had been frequently and even publicly, threatened, by the enemies of this people, both in England and America, with the vengeance of the British administration: – And as Mr. Hancock in particular had been, more than once, personally insulted, by some officers of the troops in Boston; it was not without some just grounds supposed, that under cover of the darkness, sudden arrest, if not assassination might be attempted, by these instruments of tyranny! To prevent anything of this kind, ten or twelve men were immediately collected, in arms, to guard my house, through the night."[253]

As Col. Smith's British Regulars set out on their march, long before they reached Lexington, they realized their movements had been discovered. The ringing church bells and booming signal guns of the extensive and effective spy system the New England colonists had devised provided sufficient proof to the British that the patriots were aware of their presence and were making preparations to receive them. Bells that normally summoned faithful believers to worship now rallied determined patriots to the defense of liberty.

About this same time, Joseph Warren, president of the Massachusetts Provincial Congress, dispatched Paul Revere and William Dawes to warn the citizens of Lexington and Concord that the British were headed their way. On their famous midnight ride through the Massachusetts countryside, Revere and Dawes warned, "The regulars are coming, the regulars are out!" Recalling the events of that night, Pastor Clark wrote,

"On the evening of the eighteenth of April, 1775, we received two messages; the first verbal, the other by express, in writing, from the committee of safety, who were then sitting in the westerly part of Cambridge, directed to the Honorable John Hancock, Esq. ... informing, 'that eight or nine officers of the king's troops were seen, just before night, passing the road towards Lexington, in a musing, contemplative posture; and it was suspected they were out upon some evil design.'"[254]

Around midnight, Revere and Dawes reached Lexington and the house of Pastor Jonas Clark. Riding up into Pastor Clark's yard, Revere shouted, asking to speak with Adams and Hancock:

"As he loudly demanded to see Adams and Hancock, one of the guards stationed there hushed him, saying that the family had gone to bed and his noise would disturb them. 'Noise?' he is reported to have exclaimed. 'You'll have noise enough before long! The Regulars are coming out!' Hancock opened the front shutters and called down, 'Come in, Revere, we are not afraid of you.'"[255]

An impromptu meeting was convened inside the parsonage and as Adams, Hancock, Clark, Parker, and Revere discussed what their course of action should be, Pastor Clark was asked if the Minutemen would fight. Clark is reputed to have responded, "I trained them for this very hour; they would fight, and, if need be, die, too, under the shadow of the house of God."[256]

(Jonas Clark's purported response to Adams and Hancock can only be sourced to two sources: Journalist/historian Joel Headley's 1860 and CE Hamlin's 1899 accounts. But, given Clark's patriotic passion and his documented involvement in the circumstances surrounding the events at Lexington on April 18-19, 1775, it is highly likely that a conversation similar to this did indeed take place where it is quite probable that he said something like this.)

Once it was agreed upon that a show of force by the men of Lexington was necessary and the meeting concluded, Revere and Dawes set out for Concord to warn the citizens there. Clark historian, Theodore Gilman, wrote,

"Lexington was a subordinate point on the route of the British troops. There was no call to make a stand at Lexington. There on the green, the British soldiers met the devoted band of Lexington men. At Thermopylae a few Greeks stood their ground against the advancing hosts of the Persians, and a reverent world was paid homage to their fortitude ever since. There was no reference to Thermopylae in the writings of Mr. Clark, but the spirit he invoked was the same as ruled the hearts of those heroic Greeks. These 'embattled farmers' were trained by Mr. Clark 'to maintain and defend their rights, privileges and immunities at the utmost peril of their lives and fortunes.'"[257]

By the time the meeting transpired in Clark's house, Lieutenant Col. Francis Smith and his British Regulars were now already well on their way to Lexington. The opening salvo that would light the powder keg was not far away. Pastor Clark described what happened next:

"Between the hours of twelve and one, on the morning of the nineteenth of April, we received intelligence by express, from the Honorable Joseph Warren, Esq.; at Boston, 'that a large body of the king's troops (supposed to be a brigade of about 12 or 1500) [actually closer to 700-800] were embarked in boats from Boston ... Upon this intelligence, as also upon information of the conduct of the officers as above mentioned, the militia of this town were alarmed, and ordered to meet on the usual place of parade; not with any design of commencing hostilities upon the king's troops, but to consult what might be done for our own and the people's safety: And also to be ready for whatever service providence might call us out to, upon this alarming occasion, in case overt acts of violence, or open hostilities should be committed by this mercenary band of armed and blood-thirsty oppressors. ... The militia met according to order; and waited the return of the messengers, that they might order their measures as occasion should require. Between 3 and 4 o'clock, one of the expresses returned, informing, that there was no appearance of the troops, on the roads, either from Cambridge or Charlestown; and that it was supposed that the movements in the army the evening before, were only a feint to alarm the people. Upon this, therefore, the militia company were dismissed for the present, but with orders to be within call of the drum ... we had no notice of their [British] approach, 'till the brigade was actually in the town, and upon a quick march within about a mile and a quarter of the meeting house and place of parade. ... However, the commanding officer [Captain John Parker] thought best to call the company together,–not with any design of opposing so superior a force, much less of commencing hostilities; but only with a view to determine what to do, when and where to meet, and to dismiss and disperse. ... Accordingly, about half an hour after four o'clock, alarm guns were fired, and the drums beat to arms; and the militia were collecting together."[258]

Just before daybreak, Capt. John Parker positioned the some seventy-seven minutemen on the green in front of their church in a two-lined formation for battle. (Although there were more than seventy-seven minutemen in Lexington, this was all who could manage to reassemble before Major John Pitcairn's Redcoats were upon them.) The minutemen who stood on the yard of the Lexington meetinghouse ranged in age from young William Diamond, a sixteen-year-old drummer, to a number of men who were actually too old for such action. (Fifty-five of the seventy-seven were over the age of thirty.) Outnumbered almost ten to one, the minutemen were hopelessly outmanned and outgunned.

Convinced that God would only honor a defensive war, Black Regiment preachers like Jonas Clark had preached the importance of not initiating a fight – only to respond in self-defense if the British started one. Therefore, Captain Parker made certain that his men understood that they were not to be the first to open fire. In fact, the plan appears to have been only to offer a strong protest against the audacious, militaristic actions of the British – not to bring about an actual clash of arms and bloodshed. Their stand was may have been intended to "display" their muskets, not to "discharge" them, unless they were forced to do so in self-defense. Accordingly, Capt. Parker gave the order to his men: "Stand your ground, don't fire unless fired upon. But if they mean to have a war, let it begin here."[259] Then Pastor Clark recalled,

"In the meantime, the troops having thus stolen a march upon us ... when within about half a quarter of a mile of the meeting house, they halted, and the command was given to prime and load ... Immediately upon their appearing so suddenly, and so nigh, Capt. Parker, who commanded the militia company, ordered the men to disperse, and take care of themselves and not to fire. – Upon this, our men dispersed;–but many of them, not so speedily as they might have done, not having the most distant idea of such brutal barbarity and more than savage cruelty, from the troops of a British king, as they immediately experienced! – For, no sooner did they come in sight of our company, but one of them, supposed to be an officer of rank, was heard to say to the troops, 'Damn them; we will have them!' – Upon which the troops shouted aloud, huzza'd, and rushed furiously towards our men. – About the same time, three officers (supposed to be Col. Smith, Major Pitcairn and another officer) advanced, on horse back, to the front of the body, and coming within 5 or 6 rods of the militia, one of them cried out, 'ye villians, ye Rebels, disperse; Damn you, disperse!' – or words to this effect. One of them (whether the same, or not, is not easily determined) said, 'Lay down your arms; Damn you, why don't you lay down your arms!'"[260]

After a short time of staring down the Regulars, Capt. Parker, believing the Minutemen had made their point, ordered the Minutemen to disperse. It was at this moment that someone discharged what many witnesses claimed sounded like a pistol. (Clark claimed it was one of the British officers) Pastor Clark then described the sound of the first shot that rang out:

> "The second of these officers, about this time, fired a pistol towards the militia, as they were dispersing. – The foremost, who was within a few yards of our men, brandishing his sword, and then pointing towards them, with a loud voice said to the troops, 'Fire! – By God, fire!' – Which was instantly followed by a very heavy and close fire upon our party, dispersing, so long as any of them were within reach. – Eight were left dead upon the ground! Ten were wounded. – The rest of the company, through divine goodness, were (to a miracle) preserved unhurt in this murderous action! … In short, so far from firing first upon the king's troops; upon the most careful inquiry, it appears, that but very few of our people fired at all; and even they did not fire till after being fired upon by the troops, they were wounded themselves, or saw others killed, or wounded by them, and looked upon it next to impossible for them to escape.'"[261]

America's War for Independence had begun. Historian R. Don Higginbotham wrote, "Lexington was hardly a battle, and yet a war had begun. The United States was born in an act of violence lasting but fifteen to twenty minutes."[262]

When the smoke had cleared and the British had marched on, Pastor Clark stood surveying the green in front of his church stained red with patriot blood glistening in the April sun. On the ground lay Jonas Parker, "the strongest wrestler in Lexington,"[263] who had first been hit in the leg by a British musket ball and was then bayoneted in the stomach by a Redcoat. There lay John Brown having taken a ball to the head. Asahel Porter lay on the ground shot in the back as he walked away from the Redcoats. Robert Monroe's body lay dead, shot dead right where he had stood when the minutemen first formed for battle. There also lay Samuel Hadley and Isaac Muzzey. Jonathan Harrington lay dead on his doorstep; though fatally wounded, he had been able to crawl back to his own house before he died. And finally, there lay Caleb Harrington, Jonathan's brother, dead on the doorstep of the church, killed while going for more gunpowder.[264] Pastor Clark's men truly had died "under the shadow of the house of God" – a fitting place for the initial offerings sacrificed on the altar of American liberty.

Then there were the wounded. Ten Massachusetts men in all – including Prince Estabrook, a black slave. It is believed that Estabrook got off two shots before being wounded, with the second hitting no less than Major Pitcairn himself, the British commander.

Appropriately, on April 19, 1776, just one year after the battle, Jonas Clark preached the first anniversary sermon. Entitled, "The Fate of Blood-thirsty Oppressors, and God's tender Care of His distressed People," Clark, in addition to rehearsing the events of the battle, declared that by shedding the innocent blood of the Lexington citizens, the British had proved themselves unlawful oppressors that he had always believed and preached that they were. The following excerpt provides a flavor of this famous and impassioned address:

"At length on the night of the eighteenth of April, 1775, the alarm is given of the hostile designs of the troops.

The militia of this town are called together, to consult and prepare for whatever might be necessary, or in their power, for their own, and common safety; though without the least design of commencing hostilities, upon these avowed enemies and oppressors of their country. In the mean time, under cover of the darkness, a brigade of those instruments of violence and tyranny, make their approach, and with a quick and silent march, on the morning of the nineteenth, they enter this town. And this is the place where the fatal scene begins! They approach with the morning's light; and more like murderers and cut-throats, than the troops of a Christian king, without provocation, without warning, when no war was proclaimed, they draw the sword of violence, upon the inhabitants of this town, and with a cruelty and barbarity, which would have made the most hardened savage blush, they shed INNOCENT BLOOD! But, O my God! How shall I speak! Or how describe the distress, the horror of that awful morn, that gloomy day! Yonder field can witness the innocent blood of our brethren slain! And from thence does their blood cry unto God for vengeance from the ground! There the tender father bled, and there the beloved son! There the hoary head, and there the blooming youth! And there the man in his full strength, with the man of years! They bleed, they die, not by the sword of an open enemy (with whom war is proclaimed) in the field of battle; but by the hand of those that delight in spoil, and lurk privily that they may shed innocent blood! But they bleed, they die, not in there own cause only; but in the cause of this whole people: In the cause of God, their country and posterity. And they have not bled, they shall not bleed in vain. Surely there is One that avengeth, and that will plead the cause of the injured and oppressed; and in His own way and time, will both cleanse and avenge their innocent blood. And the names of Munroe, Parker, and others, that fell victims to the rage of bloodthirsty oppressors, on that gloomy morning, shall be had in grateful remembrance, by the people of this land, and transmitted to posterity, with honor and respect, throughout all generations."[265]

After his initiation at the Battle of Lexington, Jonas Clark did not fade into the background, but instead, stayed in the forefront of the struggle, intensifying his efforts to ensure that America won the war and secured its liberty. One of the key services he provided was that of statesman. By assisting in writing the laws and the new constitution of Massachusetts, Clark helped to ensure that these laws reflected the very principles that were being defended on the battlefield.

Once the new Massachusetts Constitution was adopted and the Massachusetts state elections were held, Pastor Clark was chosen to preach the election sermon on May 31, 1781. With the room occupied with such notables as Gov. John Hancock, Lt. Gov. Thomas Gushing, and the members of the Senate and House of Representatives, Clark reminded the crowd that the war, not yet won, required their continued support, diligence, and courage:

> "O my fathers and brethren, all, all is yet at stake All may yet be lost, if we rise not as one man to the noble cause. How inglorious must it be to fail at the last. Where then the pleasing scenes of liberty and independence, where the glorious foundations of safety and freedom which our civil constitution has laid? They vanish — they are gone — they are lost forever. Is this possible? Can it be? Forbid it righteous Heaven, forbid it O my country."[266]

Clark continued to faithfully preach to his congregation in Lexington until a few months before his earthly journey came to an end in 1805. The fact that his sermons remained popular among the people for years and continued to be published right up until his death attests to the effectiveness of his life and ministry. Anne Fisher, historian of the First Parish Church in Lexington, wrote this about Clark's fifty years of ministry:

> "Although Reverend Clarke will long be remembered for his role as friend and counselor to John Hancock, grandson of Pastor Hancock, Samuel Adams and other Massachusetts patriots, he by no means ignored his duties in the parish. During his ministry 365 gave a profession of faith, 10 were admitted to the church by letter from other churches, 69 owned the covenant and 1069 were baptized. ... After more than 50 years of ministry, Mr. Clarke died in 1805 at the end of an era."[267]

In the sermon he preached on the first anniversary of the Battle of Lexington, Jonas Clark had predicted the impact the battle would have on liberty, both in America and Great Britain. Even he could not have realized the full extent to which he was correct when he said:

> "But it is not by us alone, that this day is to be noticed. This ever-memorable day is full of importance to all around, to this whole land and nation; and big with the fate of Great Britain and America. From this remarkable day will an important era begin for both America and Britain. And from the nineteenth of April, 1775, we may venture to predict, will be dated, in future history, THE LIBERTY or SLAVERY of the AMERICAN WORLD, according as a sovereign reign God shall see fit to smile or frown upon the interesting cause, in which we are engaged."[268]

Chapter 7

JAMES CALDWELL:
"THE REBEL HIGH PRIEST"
(1734 – 1781)

"There are times when it is righteous to fight as well as to pray."[269]

Pastor James Caldwell

A famous ditty of the day went like this: "Who's that riding in on horseback? Parson Caldwell, boys; Hooray! Redcoats call him 'Fighting Chaplain,' how they hate him! Well they may!" Often wearing two pistols into the pulpit when he preached, James Caldwell was one of the fieriest of the Presbyterian preachers to fight for American independence. He was born on April 14, 1734, the youngest of seven children born to John and Margaret Caldwell. The Caldwell's were Scots-Irish settlers of French Huguenot descent who came to America, first landing in New Castle, Delaware on December 10, 1727. Having descended from Huguenot blood whose ancestors had been driven from their homeland in France to Scotland and Ireland, the Caldwell line inherited the "spirit" of the Scotch Covenanters and possessed a deep hatred for tyranny and the tyrants who perpetrated it. As devout Presbyterians, they were in search of a home where they could worship God in peace, as they understood God's word.

Settling for a short time in Lancaster County, Pennsylvania, the Caldwell's eventually migrated to what was then the edge of the frontier in Charlotte County, Virginia. But since the Church of England held great sway in that area, John and Margaret found that the religious liberty they so longed for was not yet theirs. John, along with other Presbyterians, sent a delegation to Virginia's governor requesting his permission to found a Presbyterian settlement in a place called Cub Creek. The governor granted his permission and the church was organized in 1738 under a tree and later met in a log building they constructed.

Consequently, James grew up in the frontier of Virginia where he learned the values of hard work, commitment, and faith. Early on, it became evident that he was destined for the ministry and after attending school, he enrolled in the College of New Jersey (later named Princeton University) where he studied subjects like Greek, Hebrew, logic, and rhetoric. After graduating in 1759, James studied for the ministry under the personal tutelage of Dr. Samuel Davies, president of the College of New Jersey. On March 11, 1760, he applied for a minister's license, and after successfully completing the requirements, was ordained in 1761 by the presbytery of New Brunswick, New Jersey. Full of passion and ready to preach, young Caldwell immediately began the search for a pastoral position. He submitted his name to the First Presbyterian Church of Elizabethtown, New Jersey, one of the oldest churches in the area. Having been without a pastor for some eighteen months, the congregation was anxious to find a new leader. Consequently, Caldwell was given an opportunity to preach a trial sermon for the church, and one who heard that first sermon, and many more thereafter, recalled many years later, "His superior capacity for extemporaneous speaking, his animated, impressive and captivating eloquence in the pulpit, and his fervent piety, rendered him uncommonly interesting to every audience, and excited for him, high esteem, both at home and abroad...."[270]

Recognizing his gifts as a preacher and leader, the Elizabethtown congregation immediately elected Caldwell as their pastor. The young pastor wasted no time and went right to work soon earning the respect and love of his new congregation. Approximately one year later on March 14, 1763, James Caldwell married Miss Hannah Ogden, of Newark, a descendant of one of the Pilgrims who came to America on the Mayflower.

Although the congregation at Elizabethtown was comprised mostly of laborers, shopkeepers, and farmers, there were a striking number of political figures and military leaders who would play a significant role in the founding of America, such as:

- Jonathan Dayton – who would serve as an officer in the Continental Army and as a representative for New Jersey to the Constitutional Convention.

- Francis Barber – who would serve as a colonel in the Continental Army and who was a personal friend of George Washington.

- Oliver Spencer – who would serve as a major in the Continental Army.

- Elias Boudinot – the future President of the Continental Congress, Congressman from New Jersey, and one of the men who would help found the American Bible Society.

- William Livingston – future Governor of New Jersey and signer of the U.S. Constitution.

- Abraham Clark – future delegate to the Continental Congress, signer of the Declaration of Independence, and New Jersey U.S. Congressman.[271]

Ministering to people of such character and patriotism helped to bring out similar qualities in Caldwell and placed him in a very influential position as the conflict with England grew more and more imminent.

Pastor Caldwell had an incredibly fruitful ministry in Elizabethtown as historian William Sprague attested:

> "By God's grace, Caldwell's energy and forceful preaching contributed to the growth of the congregation. They soon

added a sixteen-foot extension to the rear of the church. By 1776, there were 345 "pew renters." His days were filled with the standard pastoral duties: visiting the sick, conducting weddings and funerals, attending to building matters, and helping to plant new churches. He preached two sermons every Sunday, pouring out his heart and soul: 'As a preacher, he was unconsciously eloquent and pathetic; rarely preaching without weeping himself, and at times he would melt his whole audience into tears.'"[272]

Even though his church responsibilities at Elizabethtown kept him quite busy, Caldwell found time for other ministry opportunities as well. He retained close ties to Princeton, his alma mater, and assisted the institution by serving as a trustee. In addition, he traveled throughout Virginia with the school's president, John Witherspoon, raising financial assistance for the college. Caldwell was also active in other humanitarian/ Christian efforts such as: helping promote missionary work in Africa and among the Indians in North America, helping to found a society that assisted widows and children of deceased Presbyterian ministers, and serving on a committee to examine the Presbyterian Church's position on slavery.[273]

As tensions between the colonies and Great Britain increased, Caldwell was in the middle of the debate. As the rhetoric for American independence increased, Caldwell's personal rhetoric increased apace. In 1770, he was asked to serve on a committee for the purpose of documenting England's tyrannous acts against religious freedom in America. Once the committee's work was completed, they listed the following abuses:

"1) Permits were required in order to build a church and to preach the Gospel; 2) the doors of churches were to remain open (presumably so that spies could listen in); 3) a ban on preaching in private homes; 4) imprisonment of dissenting ministers; and, 5) members of dissenting congregations were taxed to support the established church. ... Between 1774-1785, the Presbytery sent six requests to the Virginia Legislature pleading for religious liberty."[274]

An ardent patriot through and through, and completely unashamed of publicly proclaiming his displeasure with the British, Caldwell earned the adoration of most colonists and the contempt of the British. At the May 1775 Presbyterian Synod, while serving with fellow patriot preacher, John Witherspoon, Caldwell worked hard to build support for the cause of American independence among his fellow Presbyterians.

Sunday after Sunday, Pastor Caldwell stood in his pulpit churning out sermons calling upon Christians to rise up and throw off British rule. He was famous for regularly making incendiary comments like, "There are times when it is righteous to fight as well as to pray."[275] Convinced that war with Great Britain was unavoidable, he offered his services to resistance organizations such as Essex County's Committee and Council of Safety. No doubt it was the charged rhetoric from the pulpit in support of independence from men like Pastor James Caldwell that caused the British to hate the Presbyterians so much and that led them to eventually blame the war on them.

When words turned into war at Lexington and Concord, the call to arms shot out across the colonies. Immediately, New Jersey offered up its first brigade commanded by Colonel Jonathan Dayton, a member of Caldwell's church. Without hesitation in June 1776, Caldwell joined his friend's command and was quickly elected as the chaplain of the regiment commanded by Col. Ebenezer Elmer. Pastor Caldwell was not the only member of his church in Elizabethtown to join the cause, eighty-three men on the membership rolls of the church also appeared on the muster rolls of the Continental Army – thirty-one as officers and fifty-two as enlisted men.[276]

Just days after joining the army, Caldwell and his regiment were encamped at Johnstown, New York when they heard the news that the Continental Congress had signed a "Declaration of Independence." Upon hearing this, the troops were ecstatic with joy and a great celebration ensued. Col. Elmer recorded the festive spirit that filled the camp that day:

> "At 12 o'clock the assembly was beat, that the men might parade in order to receive a treat, and drink the States' health. When, having made a barrel of grog, the Declaration was read, and the following toast was given by Parson Caldwell: 'Harmony, honor and all prosperity to the free and independent United States of America — wise legislators — brave and victorious armies both by sea and land to the United States of America.' When three hearty cheers were given and the grog flew round amain."[277]

As their chaplain, Pastor Caldwell accompanied his regiment wherever it went and had almost endless opportunities to provide much needed ministry to the soldiers. Tireless in his duties, Caldwell did not restrict his services to the army, but also ministered to the surrounding townspeople when he could. He was often invited to preach in the churches near the army encampments, to baptize their new converts, and even to preach the funerals of their fallen in battle. This new "itinerate ministry" not only kept Caldwell incredibly busy, but also served to spread his reputation far and wide as Journalist/Historian Joel Headley attested:

> "The timid were to be encouraged, the hesitating brought over to the side of liberty, and the Tories met and baffled at every point. Hence, he would be on the Sabbath with his parish, the next day in the army, and then traversing the county to collect important information, or set on foot measures to advance the common cause. … The darker the prospects became, the higher rose his resolution, and the more complicated and disheartening the condition of the army grew, the more persevering were his efforts, and the more tireless his unsleeping activity. He seemed

ubiquitous, for scarcely would he be reported in one place when his presence was announced in another, and nothing seemed to escape his keen, penetrating scrutiny. His spies were everywhere, and the enemy could not make a movement that eluded his watchful eye. The aid he furnished at this time to the American army in keeping it advised of every step taken by the invading force was of incalculable service."[278]

Nearly a century after James Caldwell served as the pastor of First Presbyterian Church, Elizabethtown, Nicholas Murray served as its pastor. Well-acquainted with the history of Caldwell, Murray wrote:

"He was a man of such unwearied activity, that no amount of bodily or mental labor could fatigue him. Feelings of the most glowing piety and of the most fervent patriotism occupied his bosom at the same time, without the one interfering with the other. He was one day preaching to the battalion, the next providing the ways and means for their support, the next marching with them to battle; if defeated, assisting to conduct their retreat; if victorious, offering their united thanksgivings to God; and the next, offering the consolations of the gospel to some dying parishioner, or pouring the oil of consolation into the wounds of the afflicted."[279]

In the fall of 1776, having been away from home for weeks traveling with the army, Caldwell returned home to Elizabethtown on leave to see his family and catch up on his pastoral duties. His stay was cut short by Gen. Washington's demoralizing defeat at Long Island, New York and his subsequent retreat across New Jersey with Cornwallis hot on his heels. With the American defeat and the British on the prowl, fear seized the hearts of the citizens of Elizabethtown and the town was evacuated with the people fleeing to the countryside for safety.

Although consumed with making certain his family was safely out of harm's way, Caldwell did not shrink from his duties to his suffering country. He was known to have developed a very useful network of spies who, sometimes at great personal risk, provided valuable intelligence directly to General Washington. An indication of how much Washington valued the work of Caldwell's group is evident in the following excerpt from a letter he wrote to Caldwell:

> "...and I shall expect whenever it comes to you, you will not lose a moment in forwarding it to me, by a trusty hand, on whose activity and care you can depend; and when there is any thing particularly interesting you will send duplicates for fear of accidents. As the obtaining good and certain intelligence is a matter of great importance to us, I must entreat you to continue your other exertions for procuring such as may be depended on..."[280,281]

When it appeared that the British had departed, the citizens of Elizabethtown returned home to find their town in ruins, their houses burglarized, and their orchards destroyed. The British soldiers had rifled through every structure taking anything they wanted – often destroying what they left behind. Caldwell found his church vandalized, his personal library ransacked, and many of his papers stolen or destroyed. The pastor and his congregation immediately went to work cleaning up the mess and repairing the damage. On the following Sunday morning they were back in their church worshipping their Lord and praying for judgment to fall on their enemies.

Like others in the Black Regiment, Caldwell's enthusiastic patriotism did not go unnoticed by the British. As one writer put it, his "zeal and activity did not fail to render him obnoxious to the enemy, and no effort was spared to do him injury. A price was set upon his head."[282] Living with this looming threat hanging over him, Caldwell began to fear for his own life and the lives of his wife and children. Even so, his commitment to the cause did not waver, though in the end, it would cost he and his wife their lives.

With threats on his life, a bounty on his head, branded with titles such as "Rebel Priest" and "High Priest of the Rebellion" by the British and Tories alike, those of lesser resolve would have shrunk back from the conflict – but not James Caldwell. Instead, Pastor Caldwell began going about armed in order to defend himself and his family. As strange as it may seem today, it was not uncommon for him to climb into his pulpit on Sundays wearing two pistols while men from his congregation hid in the church belfry keeping a keen eye on lookout for a British raiding party.[283] Once in his pulpit, Caldwell would place the pistols on his pulpit, open his Bible, and deliver his sermon. When the sermon was finished, he would put the pistols back in his belt, walk to the back of his church, and greet his congregation. In his memoir of James Caldwell, Pastor Nicholas Murray commented on this rather strange scene:

> "To us, in these days, all this looks very strange in a minister of the gospel of peace; but there is an old proverb which well says that 'circumstances alter cases.' He would not be a tory — he could not be a neutral, his temperament forbid it — and the principles which led him to defend his country also taught him to defend himself. The foolish principles of 'non resistance' were yet unborn."[284]

As 1777 arrived, because of the reputation he had earned as an ardent patriot, Caldwell was presented with a new opportunity to aid his fledgling country: serving as Assistant Commissary General for the Continental Army. Essentially, Caldwell's new job was to find, secure, and distribute all of the supplies necessary for the army. With things in such short supply throughout the colonies, this was a challenging new addition to his role as chaplain. Finances were so tight that on one occasion he actually borrowed money in his own name to pay the debts owed to the suppliers by the army. Caldwell himself wrote, "Solemn promises were made to me upon entering the New Department of a supply of money. I have been obliged to pay considerable sums of money to those from whom I borrowed interest, because I could not obtain the Certificates at the time promised. And must I yet wait longer? I hope not."[285]

Early in the war, many of the men, privates and commanders alike, endured the added hardship of serving without many of the accouterments necessary – especially shoes. It is said that during the march to the Delaware River in the bitter cold and snow of December 25, 1776 in preparation for the Battle of Trenton the next day, approximately one third of Washington's soldiers were without shoes.[286] One of Gen. Washington's aids, Colonel John Fitzgerald, noted in his personal journal on the evening of Dec. 25, 1776, "It is fearfully cold and raw and as snowstorm is coming. The wind northeast beats into the faces of the men. It will be a terrible night for those who have no shoes. Some of them have tied only rags about their feet: others are barefoot, but I have not heard a man complain."[287] Some historians have written that the soldiers recalled seeing many of the men leaving bloody footprints in the snow as they marched.

The following appeal written to Commissary General Caldwell by General William Maxwell requesting a new pair of boots illustrates just how desperate the need was: "Dear Sir: My old boots will neither keep out wind or water; if you can help me with a pair I would come down some day to have my measure taken. I have never had a pair of Boots or Shoes from the Publik yet, but it seems now that those who serve the Publick have no other place to go for these necessarys, or at least are not able to go any other place. I am, Dear Sir, Your Most Obedient Humble Servant, [General] Wm. Maxwell."[288]

In the face of such challenges, Chaplain Caldwell did the best he could to meet the soldiers' needs. Even though the situation was daunting and discouraging, Caldwell regularly wrote of his trust in God. How he maintained his strong spirit of patriotism is evidenced by his correspondence:

"...the enemy may from the situation of Head Quarters, effectually ruin this fine Country before Winter – Cut off the source of many supplies to the Army and reduce to absolute poverty several thousand families most faithful in the good cause – But Jehovah reigns, and I am sure all will be well. We do not despond – We are determined to yield our Country but by inches, and sell them dear."[289]

In addition to its inability to properly outfit the soldiers, the Continental Congress was often unable to pay them as well. As can be imagined, this greatly demoralized the troops, often pushing them to the brink of desertion. But as their chaplain, Caldwell was able to stir the soldiers' patriotism through his preaching and personal conversation and succeeded in persuading many to fight on and endure their trials and hardships for the sake of the cause.

Even amidst the dark days there was opportunity for humor. Consider the story told by Nicholas Murray about the day Abraham Clark, a member of Caldwell's church and future U.S. congressman, came to visit the pastor in his army office in Chatham, New Jersey:

"Over the door of the office of Caldwell in Chatham, were the letters D.Q.M.G., being the initials of Deputy Quarter Master General. Perceiving Mr. Clark approaching the door he went to meet him, and found him intently gazing upon the above letters. 'What' said he, 'are you looking at so earnestly?' 'I am looking' replied Clark, 'at those letters, and I am striving to comprehend what they mean.' 'Well, what do you think they mean,' asked Caldwell. 'I cannot conceive,' replied his friend, 'unless they mean 'Devilish Queer Minister of the Gospel.'"[290]

As was stated earlier, as the British moved ever closer to Elizabethtown, the Caldwells and other citizens of Elizabethtown moved back and forth between Elizabethtown and the small village of Connecticut Farms nearby for safety as the tide of war ebbed and flowed in the various battles and occupations around the area. With his parsonage and church unoccupied much of the time, they were converted for use as a hospital for sick and wounded American soldiers who were often forced to sleep on the floor and eat their meals on the church pews. Consequently, the church itself was often hardly fit for Sunday services. Nevertheless, Caldwell and his congregation worshipped in the building anyway as the congregation was often forced to stand for the entire service since there were no seats available.[291] Unfortunately, when the British finally occupied Elizabethtown, to show their intense hatred for Caldwell and his people, they and local Tories burned the parsonage and church on the night of January 25, 1780.[292]

Emboldened by the fall of Charleston, South Carolina to General Cornwallis in May 1780, British Loyalists called for an increased British presence in New Jersey and New York. The British high command agreed, and in June, General Clinton moved out with his troops and Lieutenant General Baron Wilhelm von Knyphausen, a Hessian general, marched towards Elizabethtown with some five thousand soldiers.

Concerned once again for his family's safety, Pastor Caldwell relocated them to Connecticut Farms, a place thought safe from the British. The night before Gen. Knyphausen's army reached Elizabethtown, Caldwell spent one more night at home with his family. But in the early hours of the morning, he was awakened by the news that the enemy was approaching:

> "Mounting his horse with haste he started for headquarters with the information. He had proceeded but a short distance, however, when he began to have serious fears for his wife and family that he had left

behind. The former, when she bade him good-bye, told him that she had no apprehensions for her own safety, for the enemy, she said, would not harm her and her little children [the six older children having been sent away to safety]. He had often left them in a similar way before and always found them safe on his return, but now he was oppressed with unusual anxiety, and after striving in vain to shake it off turned his horse and galloped back. As he rode up to the door his wife came out to inquire what he wanted. He told her that he wished her and the children to accompany him to camp, for he felt very uneasy about leaving them behind. But she knowing they would encumber his movements, smiled at his fears, saying there was no danger at all, and declined entirely to leave the house. In the mean time she went in and brought from the breakfast table a warm cup of coffee. While he sat on his horse drinking it the enemy came in sight. Handing back the cup, and flinging her a hasty farewell, and commending her to the care and mercy of the God in whom they both trusted, he struck his spurs into his horse and dashed away."[293]

The Battle of Connecticut Farms was the last real battle of proportions in the North. General Knyphausen believed that Washington's discouraged army stationed at Morristown, New Jersey could be easily crushed, thus allowing the British to take the offensive in the North. Unfortunately for the Caldwell's, Hannah and the rest of the family were right in the middle of the eye of the storm that was gathering over the little village of Connecticut Farms – a storm that would ultimately take Hannah Caldwell's life. The actual story of how Hannah Caldwell was killed is disputed. Various accounts tell of how she was apparently shot by a British soldier. The following account records how many believe it happened:

"Mrs. Caldwell herself felt no alarm. She had hid several articles of value in a bucket and let it down into the well; and had filled her pockets with silver and jewelry. She saw that the house was put in order, and then dressed herself with care, that should the enemy enter her dwelling, she might, to use her own expression, "receive them as a lady." She then took the infant in her arms, retired to her chamber, the window of which commanded a view of the road, towards which the end of the house stood, and seated herself upon the bed. The alarm was given that the soldiers were at hand. But she felt confidence that no one could have the heart to do injury to the helpless inmates of her house. Again and again she said "They will respect a mother." She had just nursed the infant and given it to the nurse, who was in the room. The girl, Abigail, was standing by the window. A soldier left the road, and crossing a space of ground diagonally to reach the house, came to the window of the room, put his gun close to it, and fired. Two balls entered the breast of Mrs. Caldwell; she fell back on the bed, and in a moment expired. He wore a red coat, and is generally supposed to have been a British soldier. Some have attributed the act to a refugee. The little girl received in her face some of the glass when the two balls entered, both of which took such deadly effect.

After the murder, Mrs. Caldwell's dress was cut open, and her pockets were rifled by the soldiers. Her remains were conveyed to a house on the other side of the road; the dwelling was then fired and reduced to ashes with all the furniture. The ruthless soldiers went on in their work of destruction, pillaging and setting fire to the houses, piling beds and clothing in the street and destroying them, till the village was laid waste."[294]

(This account taken from AmericanRevolution,org describing the events of that day are a worthy read and describe, in some detail, how Mrs. Caldwell was most probably killed. The debate over how she died will probably never be completely resolved, but this account most likely describes what happened.)

While Hannah Caldwell was dying from her wound in the little village of Connecticut Farms, James Caldwell was but a short distance away with the army at a place called Short Hills. Standing beside General Lafayette, he looked through an eyeglass toward Connecticut Farms and seeing the smoke of the burning buildings rising high into the sky, exclaimed, "Thank God, the fire is not in the direction of my house."[295] Unfortunately, he was gravely mistaken.

Later that evening in camp, Caldwell overheard a few soldiers whispering something about Mrs. Caldwell. Immediately, he knew that something terrible had happened and, pressing the soldiers, learned that his wife had been killed. The next morning, under a flag of truce, the pastor rode to Connecticut Farms. Finding the town a "heap of smoking ruins," he made it to the building where the body of his wife lay. There, James Caldwell gathered his children around the lifeless body of their wife and mother and grieved the loss together.[296] Speaking of this tragedy years later, the Hon. Samuel L. Southard said of Hannah Caldwell, "her children were baptized to piety and patriotism in a mother's blood."[297]

As the British continued their march toward Springfield, New Jersey, burning and pillaging as they went, James Caldwell was busy burying his wife. Eulogizing her, he said,

> "Mrs. Caldwell was of so sweet a temper, and so prudent, benevolent and soft in her manners, that I verily believe she had not upon earth one personal enemy; and whatever rancor the enemy felt against myself for my public conduct and political character, I have no reason to believe there was any person among them under the

influence of any personal difference, or private revenge. I cannot therefore esteem it the private action of an individual. No officer interfered to preserve the corpse from being stripped or burnt, nor to relieve the babes left thus desolate among them. Many officers, indeed, showed their abhorrence of the murder, and their tenderness for the babes; why did they not set a sentinel over the corpse, till the neighboring women could have been called? They knew she was a lady of amiable character and reputable family; yet she was left half the day stripped in part, and tumbled about by the rude soldiery; and at last was removed from the house before it was burnt, by the aid of those who were not of the army. From this I conclude the army knew the will of their superiors; and that those who had benevolence dared not show it to this devoted lady."[298]

Hannah Caldwell's remains were laid to rest in the cemetery next to their church in Elizabethtown. There the church erected a stone above her grave with the following inscription:

"Hannah Caldwell was killed at Connecticut Farms by a shot from a British Soldier. Cruelly sacrificed by the enemies of her husband and her country … Here lies the remains of a Woman who exhibited to the World a bright Constellation of the female virtues. On that memorable Day, never to be forgotten when a British Foe invaded this fair Village and fired even the temple of the Deity. This peaceful daughter of Heaven retired to her hallowed apartment imploring Heaven for ye pardon of her Enemies. In that Sacred Moment She was by the bloody Hand of a British Ruffian dispatched like her Divine Redeemer through a Path of Blood to her long wished for native Skies."

Significantly, since 1857, the official seal of Union County, New Jersey has been a depiction of the moment when the Redcoat is shooting Hannah Caldwell through the window of her home. With his wife buried and his children safely in the care of friends, James Caldwell rode to Springfield to rejoin the army as they prepared to engage the British there. On June 23, 1780, as Gen. Knyphausen's troops neared Springfield, they were met by American troops under the command of Colonel Israel Angell waiting in an apple grove just across the Rahway River. Outnumbered almost five to one, the Americans stood their ground as the British let loose a furious volley of hundreds of muskets and six cannons, whose iron and lead hail blew away huge chunks of wood from the apple trees – killing many Americans in the process. In the midst of this melee, Chaplain Caldwell moved up and down the lines reassuring the men. At one point in the fight, he overheard some of the soldiers crying, "Wadding! Give us wadding." The Americans had a severe problem: they were quickly running out of precious wadding, thus rendering their flintlocks all but useless.

According to numerous accounts, Caldwell responded by mounting his horse and galloping to the First Presbyterian Church of Springfield. Running inside, he gathered up as many Isaac Watts hymnals as he could carry and quickly returned to the battlefield. Throwing the hymnbooks to the soldiers, Caldwell yelled out for them to tear out the pages and use them for wadding. As the men stuffed Isaac Watts' hymns down the barrels of their muskets, Caldwell could be heard shouting over the din of battle, "Giv'em Watts boys! Put Watts into 'em!"[299] Journalist/Historian Joel Headley wrote, "With a laugh and a cheer they pulled out the leaves, and ramming home the charges did give the British Watts with a will."[300] Caldwell's actions at the Battle of Springfield made such an impression that Washington Irving made them famous by telling the story in his popular biography of George Washington in the 1850s.

Even though the Americans were greatly outnumbered at Springfield, they were not outfought. Successfully holding their ground for some twenty-five minutes, they eventually turned the British Regulars back – and the "Rebel High Priest" from Elizabethtown, New Jersey had once again successfully stood his ground.

With the subsequent retreat of Knyphausen from Springfield and the destruction of the bridge at Elizabethport, fighting in New Jersey quieted down and a relative peace prevailed throughout the region. This cessation of hostilities in and around Elizabethtown allowed Pastor Caldwell to refocus his efforts on ministering to his congregation through the remaining months of 1780 and into 1781. But as God would have it, the end was near for the "Rebel High Priest."

During the British occupation of New York City, a family by the name of Murray had shown great kindness to New Jersey citizens held prisoner there. Since some of these prisoners were from Elizabethtown, Miss Beulah Murray traveled to Elizabethtown to visit the families of these prisoners. On November 24, 1781, with the intention of escorting her into town, James Caldwell drove his carriage to the wharf to meet Miss Murray as she arrived at Elizabeth Point under a flag of truce. In 1858, William Buell Sprague recounted the story of Pastor Caldwell's untimely death:

> "A sentry was kept up, at that time, at the Port. Tying his horse outside the sentinel, Mr. Caldwell proceeded to the wharf, and taking with him Miss Murray, placed her in his carriage, and then returned to the boat for a small bundle that belonged to her. Thus he passed three times the man who was keeping guard. With a small package in his hand he was returning a second time to his carriage, when the sentinel ordered him to stop, thinking probably that there was something contraband in the bundle. He replied that the bundle belonged to

the young lady in his carriage. The sentinel said that it must be examined. Mr. Caldwell turned quickly about to carry it back to the boat, that it might be opened there, when the fatal ball struck him. The Captain of the guard hearing the report of a gun, looked round and saw Mr. Caldwell staggering before him. He ran and caught him in his arms, and laid him on the ground, and without speaking a word, he almost instantly expired, — the ball having passed through his heart."[301]

James Caldwell's body was placed in Robert Twigley's wagon on a bed of straw and taken to the house of Mrs. Noel, a friend of the Caldwell family. "The Rebel High Priest" was buried on November 28, 1781 beside his beloved wife Hannah. Rev. Nicholas Murray wrote the following about the funeral:

"The funeral was one of the most solemn this town has ever witnessed. The concourse assembled on the occasion was immense. The Rev. Dr. McWhorter, of Newark, preached the funeral sermon from Ecclesiastes 8:8, and after the service was ended, the corpse was placed on a large stone before the door of the house of Mrs. Noel, where all could take a view of the remains of their beloved pastor. When this affecting ceremony was over, and before the coffin was closed, Dr. Boudinot came forward, leading nine orphan children, and placing them around their father's bier, made an address of surpassing pathos to the multitude in their behalf. It was an hour of deep and powerful emotion, and the procession slowly moved to the grave, weeping as they went. And as they lifted their streaming eyes to Heaven, they besought the blessing of God upon the orphan group, and upon their own efforts to resist and vanquish their oppressors."[302]

Mrs. Noel, the longtime and faithful friend of the family, took the children into her home and was successful in organizing an effort to raise funds for their rearing and education. The likes of General Marquis de Lafayette and Elias Boudinot rallied to the Caldwell children's support – even Gen. George Washington donated one hundred dollars.[303] All of the children grew up to live productive and meaningful lives and many of them advanced to significant positions in the church and government.

As to the man who shot Caldwell, his name was James Morgan, a disgruntled member of the New Jersey militia. Morgan was known by townspeople as a ruthless man with a serious drinking problem. By some accounts it is said that when one of his children had fallen into a well and drowned, the enraged Morgan had taken the dead child's body by its arms and had beaten the bereaved mother with it. Only because neighbors heard her cries and came to her rescue did Mrs. Morgan escape possible death at the hand of her enraged husband.[304]

Immediately after shooting Caldwell, Morgan was taken into custody by the authorities and later tried for murder. His exact motivation for killing the pastor was never determined but it was rumored that he was bribed by the British to do so. Whatever his motive, Morgan was easily convicted of murder and was sentenced to hang on January 28, 1782. Nicholas Murray recorded the events of that cold January day:

> "The day appointed for his execution arrived. His grave was made in the northwestern corner of the churchyard in Westfield, away from all other graves; some even objecting to have his remains placed within the enclosure. He asked the privilege of seeing his grave and was taken to it by the Sheriff. He was then conducted to the Church, where, in accordance with an old English custom, which had not then fallen into disuse, a sermon was preached by the Rev. Mr. Elmer of New Providence, from the text, 'O do not this abominable thing which I hate.' The prisoner was seated in a chair in the aisle before the pulpit; but seemed in no way impressed either with the discourse

or with the awfulness of his situation. He was conducted from the Church to the place of execution, (a hill north of the Church of Westfield, called Morgan's hill to this day,) by Noah Marsh, High Sheriff of the County of Essex, assisted by Isaac Clark and James McMannis, constables, and escorted by a company of Light Horse commanded by Captain Samuel Meeker of Springfield, and a company of Infantry commanded by Captain John Scudder of Westfield."[305]

Earlier, in a January 16, 1782 letter written from Philadelphia by Congressman Abraham Clark to Captain Benjamin Winans of Elizabethtown, Congressman Clark expressed the feelings of admiration many held for James Caldwell:

"I suppose by this time that the murderer of Mr. Caldwell has been tried and received his doom: but that will not restore our loss, which will be long felt in Elizabethtown. I hope you will not be in a hurry to get another, for few can be found fit to succeed him that is gone. I have one or two in my mind that might answer, but I think that they could not be got till the end of the war, as they are chaplains of the army."[306]

The magazine, *Leben, A Journal of Reformation Life*, noted,

"James Caldwell lived a full life. One marvels at the breadth of his service to his country and his Savior. It is easy to imagine that he might have gone on to serve his country in the new Republic as one of the Founding Fathers."[307]

The monument erected over James Caldwell's grave bears the inscription:

"This Monument is erected to the memory of the Rev. James Caldwell, the pious and fervent Christian, the zealous and faithful Minister, the eloquent Preacher, and a prominent leader among the worthies who secured the independence of his country. ... Be of good courage, and let us behave ourselves valiantly for our people, and for the cities of our God, and let the Lord do that which is good in his sight. The glory of Children are their Fathers. The memory of the just is blessed."

In 1848, Rev. Nicholas Murray gave this fitting tribute to James Caldwell:

"He was a man of unwearied activity, and of wonderful powers of both bodily and mental endurance. Feelings of the most glowing piety and the most fervent patriotism occupied his bosom at the same time, without at all interfering with each other. He was one day preaching to the battalion – the next, providing the ways and means for their support – the next, marching with them to battle; if defeated, assisting to conduct their retreat – if victorious, offering their united thanksgivings to God – and the next, carrying the consolations of the Gospel to some afflicted or dying parishioner. Down to the present hour, the aged ones speak of him with tearful emotion. Never was a pastor more affectionately remembered by a people.....May the church never want such ministers, nor the state such patriots as was Caldwell. May the names of the ministers of the gospel who aided in securing for our country the freedom which it enjoys ever live in the memory of a grateful people and country. His name will be cherished in the Church and in the State so long as virtue is esteemed or patriotism honored."[308]

Chapter 8

THOMAS ALLEN: "THE FIGHTING PARSON" (1743 – 1810)

"Valiant soldiers! I exhort and conjure you to play the man. … let no suffering appear too severe for you to encounter for your bleeding country. God's grace assisting me, I am determined to fight and die by your side rather than flee before our enemies or resign myself to them. Rather than quit this ground with infamy and disgrace, I should prefer leaving this body of mine a corpse on the spot. … may the God of heaven take us all under His protection and cover our heads in the day of battle and grant unto us His salvation."[309]

Pastor Thomas Allen's pre-battle speech to his men

Thomas Allen was born in Northampton, Massachusetts to Joseph and Elizabeth Allen on January 17, 1743. Thomas was born into a family with a rich Christian heritage. His grandfather was a deacon in the church pastored by the First Great Awakening preacher, Jonathan Edwards, and apparently a portion of his grandfather's heritage was passed down to Thomas.

Allen's parents made certain that he received an education that would adequately prepare him for the work of the ministry. He enthusiastically took to his studies and graduated Harvard in 1762 at the young age of nineteen.

Not long afterwards, on December 9, 1763, Thomas was invited to preach as a candidate for the pastoral position of the

Pittsfield Congregational Church situated in the frontier of western Massachusetts. The congregation liked what they heard and called him to be the first pastor in Pittsfield. Hired for the salary of sixty pounds and forty cords of wood per year, he was ordained on April 18, 1764 and officially began his pastoral duties in Pittsfield on March 5, 1764 where he continued to minister for the next forty-six years. Pastor Allen immediately jumped into his work, the fruits of which soon began to bear testimony to his unique giftedness as thirty-one new members were added to the church in his first year – quite a number considering the sparse population of western Massachusetts in the 1760s.

In 1768, Thomas married Elizabeth Lee, of Salisbury, Connecticut, daughter of Rev. Jonathan Lee. A descendant of William Bradford, the noteworthy Pilgrim and second governor of Plymouth Plantation, Elizabeth, like Thomas, descended from an illustrious spiritual lineage. The two became effective ministers to their flock in Pittsfield and came to raise a large family of twelve children, one of which, William, became a minister himself. Writing about his father, William recalled,

> "My father was of middle height, and slender, vigorous, and active; of venerable gray hairs in his age; of a mild, pleasant, affectionate countenance; hospitable to all visitors, and always the glad welcomer of his friends. As he was very honest and frank, and had a keen sense of right and wrong, and as he lived when high questions were debated, it is not strange that those whom he felt called upon to oppose should have sometimes charged him with indiscreet zeal; but he cherished no malice, and his heart was always kind and tender. Simple and courteous in his manners, sincere in his communications, and just in his dealings, he set his parishioners an example of Christian morals. The atonement of the Divine Redeemer, the evangelical doctrines of grace, and their application to the practical duties of life in the various relations of society,

were the favorite subjects of his public sermons and private conversations. He explained them without the formality of logic, but with a happy perspicuity of style, and recommended and enforced them with apostolic zeal. As he wrote out most of his sermons in Weston's shorthand, he usually, in his preaching, read them from his notes; but he threw into them, with but little action, great fervor of spirit. Sometimes, in his extemporary addresses at the Communion-table, his trembling voice and kindling eye and animated countenance were quite irresistible."[310]

Along with his fervent religious beliefs, Pastor Allen possessed a patriotic passion and embraced Whig political sentiments.[311] Driven by this political conviction, in the years leading up to the war with Great Britain, Allen was one of the most outspoken proponents in Massachusetts for a constitutional government that would ensure that neither the King nor Parliament could undermine the people's liberties. As the head of "The Berkshire Constitutionalists," Pastor Allen spoke all over the region promoting the need for a written constitution for Massachusetts at gatherings of every sort from town meetings to regional conventions. It was said of him that he was "restless in his endeavors" and his efforts eventually began to pay dividends. *The History of Pittsfield (Berkshire County), Massachusetts* records this of Allen's influence:

"A large majority of the people acceded to his doctrines. The towns and county conventions adopted resolutions, addresses, and memorials in accordance with them, and often drafted by him; while most of the committees of inspection were remodeled in order to secure vigor in prosecuting the measures adopted by his advice. ... It is a conspicuous proof of the power of Mr. Allen's earnestness, eloquence, and personal consideration, that a single address by him was sometimes sufficient to revolutionize the entire sentiment of a town against the wishes of its own most prominent citizens, and that his teachings impressed upon the people of Berkshire political characteristics which remain strongly marked to this day; for it was in this fiery campaign, rather than in his subsequent political career, that he had the opportunity to inculcate those enduring principles whose deep root among these hills, and wide-spread influence wherever the sons of Berkshire have found a home, are ascribed to him by those most familiar with the intellectual history of the county. In argument, he was logical, and not unskilled in the subtler arts of oratory. In appeal, he was vehement and earnest; impassioned often to a degree that carried him to extremes in his expressions concerning opponents, and to something like exaggeration in his denunciation of measures. Righteous indignation was not greatly tempered by any thing in the composition of his mind."[312]

Allen's passionate patriotism and oratory had a moving effect upon an audience – a fact that infuriated the Tories. Those who heard him preach said that his messages "together with his private exhortations, had the desired effect, and the people were influenced to the degree the preacher designed."[313] *The History of Pittsfield* noted that the secret to Allen's persuasiveness was that his political passion was fuelled by his spiritual passion: "His political [life] was an outgrowth of his spiritual life. ... In the private exercises of devotion he was constant; and, however he may have at times thrown off the etiquette of his sacred profession, there is abundant evidence that its essential spirit was preserved and its essential duties were performed in the most trying moments of military and political excitement."[314]

Possessing strong anti-British sentiments, Allen was the first in Pittsfield to declare himself a "nonconformist" to King George. Along with most enlightenment thinkers of the day, he believed the British Crown had no "divine right" to govern and resistance to King George's unjust actions, rather than being treasonous, was the responsibility of every freedom-loving American. It was said that Allen had,

> "An innate hatred of oppression and injustice, a zealous devotion to any cause to which his sense of right attached him, a personal character which carried weight with the people, and a happy faculty for enforcing his opinions both with the tongue and the pen, completed the qualities which eminently fitted him to be a leader in times of revolution. Placable to his own enemies, he was an excellent hater of the foes of his country, chief among which he classed the Tories and George the Third."[315]

It is not surprising, then, that Pastor Allen succeeded in earning the intense hatred of the Tories. Journalist/historian J. T. Headley wrote that Allen was "closely watched, and his name sent down to Gen. Gage as the most dangerous character to the king's cause in the western part of the Colony."[316] The fact that he was a preacher provided no special protection from the British. He knew that if ever caught, the consequences could be grave. But this very real possibility did not dissuade him in the least. His deep devotion to liberty and intense dislike for those who did not share his sentiments drove him to do all within his power to see that the enemies of liberty were confronted and stopped. He assisted in confiscating the property of Tories who owed the Continental government and helped see to it that the proceeds were deposited in the treasury. In his defense of liberty, Pastor Allen was ruthless. One wrote that Allen "marked the conspirators, put some of them in chains, and drove others over the border in affright. Though by profession a man of peace, in this great struggle he was a man of blood."[317]

This, of course, earned him a great number of enemies. Three of the leading Tories in the Pittsfield area, Col. William Williams, Woodbridge Little, and Major Israel Stoddard, enraged by his preaching and political activities, formally charged him with "treason, rebellion and sedition."[318] Unfortunately for the Tories, the charges were thrown out of court and Pastor Allen was a free man. Allen put this freedom to work by intensifying his crusade to rid Massachusetts of British domination.

Allen's dislike for British rule and King George was so strong that his feelings had not abated long after the war was over. This is evidenced in his experience while visiting London in 1799; sixteen years after America had won its independence. After seeing King George in a procession heading to Parliament, Allen wrote,

> "This is he who desolated my country; who ravaged the American coasts; annihilated our trade; burned our towns; plundered our cities; sent forth his Indian allies to scalp our wives and children; starved our youth in his prison-ships; and caused the expenditure of millions of money, and a hundred thousand precious lives. Instead of being the father of his people, he has been their destroyer. May God forgive him so great a guilt!"[319]

As the contention between the colonies and Great Britain intensified, so did Allen's sermons and political activities. A member of the seven-man Committee of Safety and Correspondence for Pittsfield, Pastor Allen actively helped prepare his congregation and neighbors for the war he knew was coming. Aware that if Canada fell into the hands of the British, America's hopes for independence could well be dashed, Allen contributed insight and intelligence for a military expedition to secure the forts at Ticonderoga and Crown Point. Once launched, Allen, knowing that the secrecy of the expedition was of upmost importance to its success, wrote to General Seth Pomeroy on May 4, 1775:

> "Sir – I have the pleasure to acquaint you that a number of gentlemen from Connecticut went from this place last Thursday morning ... on an expedition

against Ticonderoga and Crown Point, expecting to be reinforced by men from the grants above here, a post having previously taken his departure to inform Col. Ethan Allen of the design, and desiring him to hold his Green Mountain Boys in actual readiness. The expedition has been carried on with the utmost secrecy, as they are in hopes of taking the forts by surprise. ... We earnestly pray for success in this important expedition, as the taking of those places would afford us a key to all Canada. There is, if the accounts are to be depended upon, not more than twenty soldiers at each fort. There are a large number of cannon, and I hear four as excellent brass cannon as we could wish. Should success attend the expedition, we expect a strong reinforcement will be sent from the western part of Connecticut, to keep those forts, and to repair and fortify them well. ... Our Tories are the worst in the Province – all the effect the late and present operations have laid upon them is, they are mute and pensive, and secretly wish for more prosperous days to toryism. As to your important operations, sir, you have the fervent prayers of all good men that success may attend them. I hope God will inspire you with wisdom from above in all your deliberations, and your soldiers with courage and fortitude, and that Boston will speedily be delivered into your hands – the General thereof, and all the king's troops – that that den of thieves, that nest of robbers, that asylum for traitors and murderers, may be broken up, and never another red coat from England set foot on these shores.

I have been concerned, lest General Gage should spread the small pox in your army. May heaven protect your army from his wicked wiles. May you be shielded, sir, in the day of battle, and obtain a complete victory over those enemies of God and mankind."[320]

Allen's letter to Gen. Pomeroy on a previous occasion provides clear evidence of his unique involvement in the early days of the war. As the correspondence indicates, his duties were numerous – from requisitioning supplies and reconnoitering the enemy to ensuring that the intelligence made it to the appropriate commanders:

"Sir – I shall esteem it a great happiness if I can communicate any intelligence to you that shall be of any service to my country. In my last I wrote to you of the northern expedition. Before this week ends we are in raised hopes here of hearing that Ticonderoga and Crown Point are in other hands. Whether the expedition fails or succeeds, I will send you the most early intelligence, as I look on it as an affair of great importance. ... Our militia this way, sir, are vigorously preparing for actual readiness. Adjacent towns and this town are buying arms and ammunition. As yet, there are plenty of arms to be sold at Albany; but we hear, that, by order of the Major. Etc., no powder is to be sold there for the present. The spirit of liberty runs high there, as you have doubtless heard by their post to our headquarters. I have exerted myself to disseminate the same spirit in King's district, which has of late taken surprising effect. The poor Tories at Kinderhook are mortified and grieved, are wheeling about, and begin to take the quick step. New York Government begins to be alive in the glorious cause, and to act with great vigor. ... I fervently pray, sir, that our Council of War may be inspired with wisdom from above, to direct the warlike enterprise with prudence, discretion, and vigor. O, may your councils of deliberation be under the guidance and blessing of heaven."[321]

Allen's letter to Gen. Pomeroy also reveals his insight into military strategy and his awareness of the future needs of the army. For example, once he learned of the munitions and cannons available at Fort Ticonderoga and Crown Point, he instinctively understood that they would most likely be extremely handy in the defense of Boston. Allen wrote to Pomeroy,

> "... an intelligent person, who left Ticonderoga Saturday before last, informs me that ... there are cannon enough at Crown Point ... That he saw the old Sow (a large cannon taken at the siege of Louisburg), from Cape Breton, and a number of good brass cannon, at Ticonderoga. Should the expedition succeed, and should the Council of War send up their order for the people this way, to transport by land twenty or thirty of the best of the cannon to headquarters, I doubt not but the people in this country would do it with expedition. We could easily collect a thousand yoke of cattle for the business."[322]

As it turns out, Allen's instincts were correct. Later that summer, Gen. Washington laid siege to Boston but was greatly hindered in his efforts in driving out the British because he had no artillery with which to do the job. General Washington thus dispatched General Henry Knox in the cold of early December to begin the herculean effort of traveling to Fort Ticonderoga and transporting the artillery and ammunition back to Boston. Eventually, this formidable trek across New York and Massachusetts would come to be known as the "Noble Train of Artillery."[323] As the caravan proceeded across New York and eventually, through the Berkshires, a good number of locals volunteered to help the procession, confirming what Rev. Allen had written to General Pomeroy: "Should this expedition succeed, and should the Council of War send up their orders for the people this way to transport by land twenty or thirty of the best cannon to head quarters, I doubt not but the people in this country would do it with all expedition. We could easily collect a thousand yoke of cattle for the business."[324]

Incredibly, Gen. Knox and his critical cargo made the trek in some fifty-six days, arriving in Cambridge, Massachusetts on

January 24, 1776. By early March, Knox's guns from Ticonderoga were in place and were frowning down from Dorchester Heights on the British in Boston. When the British commander, Gen. William Howe, saw the guns, he was amazed that the Americans had accomplished such a miraculous feat in such a short time and in such inclement weather. Knowing he had no option but to surrender Boston to Washington and his army, Howe agreed to evacuate Boston without burning the town, if Washington agreed not to open fire. On March 17, 1776, some 11,000 British soldiers and loyalists sailed out of Boston harbor in a fleet of 120 ships.

Even though at this point he was clearly aiding the cause, Pastor Allen had not yet completely thrown in his lot with the American army. But August of 1776 would change all of that. When the British routed Gen. Washington and his army at the Battle of Long Island on August 27, 1776, Pastor Allen knew he could remain at home and out of the fray no longer. He immediately joined the army as chaplain of the "Berkshire Militia."[325] As chaplain, Allen prayed with, preached to, and encouraged the soldiers – just as a good man of God would do. But when the time for fighting came, with musket in hand, he was standing right there beside his fellow soldiers in the thickest of the fighting.

In July 1777, when the British General, John Burgoyne, marched against Fort Ticonderoga, Pastor Allen was there with Gen. Arthur St. Clair and his men to help stop his advance. Convinced that the fall of the fort would clear the way for Burgoyne and his Redcoats to invade New York and likely deal a deathblow to the American cause, Allen was prepared to sacrifice himself for the cause. Content not only to pray and fight with his men, he was ready to die with them if necessary and was determined to set an example of courage and patriotism to bolster the sagging spirits of his men.

Even though the Americans were outnumbered almost two to one, Allen was certain that Ticonderoga's fortifications and the resolve of the American soldiers were more than enough to offset the British numbers. However, as Dr. Paul Walker of the Army Corp of Engineers and historian to the Office of the Chief of Engineers points out, there was something that Rev. Allen could not have known – Ticonderoga was vulnerable to British forces from Sugar Loaf Hill. Until Col. Trumbull pointed this out in his engineering analysis, Ticonderoga was thought to be too far away from the hill to be in any danger, thus explaining Allen's confidence of success.

Unaware of the real need to retreat and of the fact that Gen. St. Clair was, at that very moment, conducting a council of war discussing plans for evacuating the fort, Pastor Allen, showing his courage and patriotism, stood on a cannon platform and delivered this rousing speech to the troops under his pastoral care – soldiers who would soon learn that they, unfortunately, were going to have to abandon Ft. Ticonderoga:

> "Valliant soldiers, yonder are the enemies of your country, who have come to lay waste and destroy, and spread havoc and devastation through this pleasant land. They are mercenaries, hired to do the work of death, and have no motives to animate them in their undertaking. You have every consideration to induce you to play the man, and act the part of valiant soldiers. Your country looks up to you for its defense; you are contending for your wives, ... you are contending for your children, ... for your houses and lands, for your flocks and herds, for your freedom, for future generations, for every thing that is great and noble, ... You must, you will, abide the day of trial. You cannot give back whilst animated by these considerations.

Suffer me, therefore, on this occasion, to recommend to you, without delay to break off your sins by righteousness, and your iniquities by turning to the Lord. ... I must recommend to you the strictest attention to your duty, ... Valliant soldiers, should our enemies attack us, I exhort and conjure you to play the man. Let no dangers appear too great, let no suffering appear too severe, for you to encounter for your bleeding country. Of God's grace assisting me, I am determined to fight and die by your side, rather than flee before our enemies, or resign myself up to them. ... Rather than quit this ground with infamy and disgrace, I should prefer leaving this body of mine a corpse on this spot. ... And may the God of Heaven take us all under his protection, and cover our heads in the day of battle, and grant unto us his salvation."[326]

To the great disappointment of Pastor Allen and his men, the Americans were never given a chance at Burgoyne's forces. While firing hardly a shot, the American forces surrendered the fortifications that had been so hard won months before by the gallant fighting of Ethan Allen and his Green Mountain Boys. Still unaware that the surrender was most likely the correct move on Gen. St. Claire's part, Allen and his men marched away humiliated. As the Americans retreated to Saratoga, New York, apparently still unaware of the true reason Fort Ticonderoga had been surrendered, a disillusioned and downcast Thomas Allen refused to accompany them, returning home to Pittsfield instead. Summing up Allen's resolve, one historian wrote, "He [Allen] felt that had he commanded at Ticonderoga, its ramparts, though carried at last by the overwhelming foe, would first have been baptized in blood."[327]

Pastor Allen had been home in Pittsfield only a few days when he received correspondence from Gen. John Stark requesting the assistance of the Berkshire Militia in resisting the advance of Lieutenant Colonel Friedrich Baum and his Hessians against the town of Bennington, Vermont. Even though Stark had washed his hands of the Continental Congress, swearing not to serve under a Congress which did not recognize his value to the war effort having promoted less able men than himself to higher commands, Allen knew him to be a fierce fighter.

Once Stark's request for troops reached Pittsfield, the citizens rallied at the town meeting house. Although still smarting from the retreat at Ticonderoga, the fires of Allen's patriotism were rekindled by this new call to arms. Holding his musket, Allen stood before his neighbors and delivered a rousing speech encouraging his fellow patriots to join him in hurrying to Gen. Stark's aid. With many of Pittsfield's men already in the field serving with the Continental Army, those still at home responded to the urgent call. *The History of Pittsfield* records the effect Allen's speech had on his neighbors: "Twenty-two men enrolled themselves in all, under the command of Lieut. William Ford, an officer who saw much service in those days. With him served the veteran Col. Easton, Rev. Mr. Allen, Capts. Charles Goodrich, James Noble, and William Francis, Lieuts. Joseph Allen (second in command), Josiah Wright, and Rufus Allen. ... Mr. Allen set out in the old sulky ... going to war in his chariot, like the heroes of classic and scriptural story."[328]

Having been called out to fight on numerous occasions only to be refused the opportunity to face their enemy on the field of battle, Allen and the members of the Berkshire Militia were determined to engage the enemy this time – even if they had to do it by themselves. Only their confidence in Gen. Stark's reputation as a fighting man could have inspired the Pittsfield patriots to march the some thirty miles to Bennington in a drenching rain. But march they did, reaching Stark and his men on the night of August 16. Even though Pastor Allen's confidence in Stark was solid, after arriving in the army's camp, he made his way to the general's headquarters to discover for himself if the Berkshire Militia would finally get the opportunity to actually engage the

British regulars in battle. Historian Edward Everett wrote about the meeting between Allen and Stark:

"Among the re-enforcements from Berkshire county came a clergyman [Rev. Mr. Allen] with a portion of his flock, resolved to make bare the arm of flesh against the enemies of his country. Before daylight on the morning of the 16th, he addressed the commander as follows: 'We, the people of Berkshire, have been frequently called upon to fight, but have never been led against the enemy. We have now resolved, if you will not let us fight, never to turn out again. Gen. Stark asked him 'If he wished to march then, when it was dark and rainy.' 'No,' was the answer, 'not just this minute.' 'Then,' continued Stark, 'if the Lord should once more give us sunshine, and I do not give you fighting enough, I will never ask you to come again.'"[329]

"I PUT OUT THAT FLASH!"

The next day, Stark led his army, including the Berkshire Militia, on to the field to meet Baum's Hessians. As the American units were being deployed on the field, a member of the Berkshire Militia said to Allen:

"'We will do our own fighting today.' 'Yes,' said he [Pastor Allen], 'we shall have a good time at the enemy, but we are not quite ready yet, we must first join in prayer;' and there, under the August sky, he lifted up his earnest prayer, that God would give them the victory. ... [He] prayed to the God of armies that He would 'teach their hands to war, and their fingers to fight.' The prayer was offered with that fervent earnestness for which its author was remarkable; and it inspirited the men like the harangue of a trusted commander. There were many who attributed the glorious success of the following day to the efficiency of the Berkshire parson's morning prayer. … He had no intention, however, of doing the praying, and letting his congregation do all of the fighting. He meant to fight himself, and if the example of their pastor could make them brave, he resolved there should be no cowards among the Berkshire men that day."[330]

Once Pastor Allen and the Berkshire Militia were positioned within easy sight of the Hessians, the "fighting parson" walked out in front of the American lines and stood on the stump of a fallen tree to address the enemy. Calling out to the Hessians and local Tories, many of whom were known personally by Allen, the pastor offered them the opportunity to surrender. His offer was received with the exclamation, "There's Parson Allen: let's pop him!"[331] Then a volley of Hessian musket fire was sent his way. As the lead flew around him, riddling the tree upon which he stood, one of the balls shot through his hat. Undaunted, Allen stepped down from the stump and returned to his men. His conscience clear, having given them the chance to surrender, Pastor Allen requested a musket and began to fire. Standing by his brother, Lieut. Joseph Allen, and knowing that he was a better shot than Joseph, Allen turned to his brother and said, "'Joe, you load, and I'll fire,' and so they fought side by side God's own battle on that warm August day."[332] In fact, it is believed that Allen's flintlock was the first American gun to fire that day – well before the order to fire was given![333] In his own account of the battle, Allen recalled,

> "The action was extremely hot for between one and two hours. … The blaze of the guns of the contending parties reached each other. The fire was so extremely hot,–and our men easily surmounting their breastworks, amid peals of thunder and flashes of lightning from their guns, without regarding the roar of their field pieces,–that the enemy at once deserted their cover, and ran; and in about five minutes their whole camp was in the utmost

confusion and disorder. All their battalions were broken in pieces, and fled most precipitately; at which instant our whole army pressed after with redoubled ardor, pursued them for a mile, made considerable slaughter among them, and made many prisoners. ... This action which redounds so much to the glory of the great Lord of the heavens and God of armies, affords the Americans a lasting monument of the divine power and goodness, and a most powerful argument of love to and trust in God. ... May all be concerned to give God the glory, whilst we commend the good conduct of the officers and soldiers in general on so important an occasion!"[334]

After the hard fought victory, Pastor Allen did as he always did – focused his energy on ministering to the wounded and dying. He spent the night of the 16th and all the next day serving the suffering. On the following day, Saturday, August 18, though no doubt bone weary, Allen saddled up his horse and rode some thirty miles to Pittsfield, arriving that night to preach the next day in his own pulpit. A few days later, one of the members of Allen's congregation asked if it was true that he had fought at Bennington like a common soldier. The following conversation ensued:

"'Yes,' he said, 'I did, it was a very hot, close battle, and it became every patriot to do his duty.' 'Well, but,' said the parishioner, 'Mr. Allen, did you kill anybody?' "No,' he replied. 'I don't know that I killed anybody; but I happened to notice a frequent flash from behind a certain bush, and every time I saw that flash one of our men fell. I took aim at the bush, and fired. I don't know that I killed anybody, but I put out that flash.'"[335]

Thomas Allen was not the only patriot in the Allen family; as was mention above, his brother Joseph was a lieutenant in the Continental Army, and another brother, Moses, was a chaplain in a Georgia unit. Equally courageous as Thomas, Moses also exposed himself to harm's way in battle and was eventually captured by the British at the Battle of Savannah, Georgia on December 29, 1778 and placed on a prison ship, where he eventually died trying to escape. (More about Moses Allen's attempted escape in chapter 3)

With Moses gone, Thomas could not bear the thought of his brother's widow and child living alone so far away. So he determined to go to Georgia and bring them back to Pittsfield to live with him. In typical Allen style, Thomas undertook the perilous journey on horseback, riding hundreds of miles through enemy territory, no doubt often being forced to ride extra distances in order to avoid towns and areas occupied by the British. Eventually reaching Georgia, he decided against transporting his sister-in-law and young nephew back through the enemy occupied territory he had just travelled and instead, chose to travel back to Pittsfield by boat. Even though this was almost as dangerous as the land route, they finally made it safely to Pittsfield and at long last, Pastor Allen was able to shelter his sister-in-law and young nephew in the safety of his own home.

When the war finally ended, Pittsfield celebrated with parades and numerous gatherings. Pastor Allen preached a message of thanksgiving to God for the American victory and the birth of their new government. With God's blessing, he predicted a glorious future for his beloved country. In the years following, he remained active in the political arena and became a statesman for his new republic.

In 1786, believing Shays' Rebellion posed a threat to the fledgling Union, Allen once again rose up to defend his country. He spoke out against the insurgents and used his sizeable influence to raise resistance to stop what he believed to be an attack on liberty. In doing so, he incurred the intense hatred of his enemies who threatened to take him prisoner and haul him to New York. Again, in typical Thomas Allen fashion, he kept loaded guns in his bedroom and dared his enemies to come and get him. As it turned out, Allen's critics left the old veteran alone and never made good on their threats. Unfortunately, the enemies Allen earned during this time remained embittered to him for the rest of his life.[336]

With a life as full and eventful as his had been, one would think that Thomas Allen would have been ready to settle into an easy retirement and coast on in to heaven. But he had one more great adventure left in him. In 1799, his oldest daughter, who had married a merchant from Boston, was visiting London when she unexpectedly died, leaving behind an infant child. With her husband in the West Indies on business, the child was orphaned in Great Britain with no one to care for him. Unable to bear the thought of his grandchild in the care of strangers, Allen decided to sail to England and bring him back to Pittsfield. Bidding farewell to his congregation, he boarded passage on the *Argo*.

Out in the Atlantic, *Argo's* crew noticed that they were being followed by a ship that appeared to belong to the French, who were now America's enemies. Fearful that the French were planning to attack, the *Argo's* captain called together the passengers to determine whether they should make a run for it, surrender, or turn and fight. After a short discussion, all on board decided that fighting would be far better than the prospect of being thrown into a French prison. The fighting spirit of '76 rose up once again within the old patriot preacher, and Allen requested permission to speak to the men and pray with them for the strength to fight courageously. With the battlefield voice of old, Pastor Allen's words inspired *Argo's* crew and passengers with the same fire that had so empowered the Continental soldiers twenty years before.

As the unknown ship neared, to the great relief of everyone on the *Argo*, it turned out to be British – not French (Ironically, now the British were America's allies). Overjoyed, Allen again called all of the passengers together and this time prayed a prayer of thanksgiving to God for His divine protection.

Once in England, Allen made the acquaintances of numerous Christian leaders, including John Newton, the ex-slave trader, famous preacher and hymn writer. In the short time he was there, Allen and Newton developed a strong relationship that kindled a new appreciation for world missions in Allen, a passion that would mark his last few years in the ministry. After securing his grandchild, Pastor Allen made the arduous journey back across the Atlantic, finally arriving in Pittsfield six months after he had originally departed.[337]

Pastor Thomas Allen faithfully ministered to the congregation in Pittsfield for forty-six years. With death approaching, his mind clear and his faith unshaken, he whispered, "Come, Lord Jesus, come quickly!" Just before he died, one of his children warned that if he did not eat something soon, he would not live much longer. Allen responded, "Live! I am going to live forever."[338] On February 11, 1810, the "Fighting Parson" passed from this life to eternal life. It was said of Thomas Allen, that he was,

> "Noble by nature, an earnest Christian, a faithful minister of the Gospel, a brave patriot – his name should be inscribed high on the monument that commemorates his country's independence."[339]

Chapter 9

NAPHTALI DAGGETT:
"GUN-PACKING PROFESSOR"
(1727 – 1780)

British officer: "'If I let you go this time, you rascal, will you ever fire again on the troops of His Majesty?' Naphtali Daggett: 'Nothing more likely.'"[340]

Daggett's response to a British officer during the Battle of Yale

Naphtali Daggett was born in Attleborough, Massachusetts on September 8, 1727 to Ebenezer and Mary Daggett. When just a young man, Daggett was befriended by Rev. Solomon Reed, who determined to see to it that Naphtali received a formal education. Rev. Reed made arrangements for Naphtali to be educated by Rev. James Cogswell of Plainfield, Connecticut who ran a school for boys. After studying under Dr. Cogswell, Naphtali moved to Abington, Massachusetts where he continued his studies under Reverend Reed.

In 1744, Reverend Reed helped Naphtali enroll in Yale where he earned a reputation as a noted scholar and theologian. Rev. Ezra Stiles, president of Yale, said of Daggett, "he was a good classical scholar, well versed in moral philosophy and a learned Divine."[341] Daggett graduated from Yale in 1748 and was ordained by the Presbytery of Suffolk County, Long Island, New York on August 10, 1749. On September 18, 1751, he became the pastor of the Presbyterian Church in Smithtown, New York situated on the north shore of Long Island where he served until

1756 when he was selected as Yale's Professor of Divinity. Pastor Daggett officially began his duties at Yale on March 4, 1756 and continued to serve there until his death in 1780.

When Dr. Thomas Clap, the first President of Yale, resigned his position in September 1766, Daggett was chosen to serve as the interim president. Though he believed himself to be a gifted pastor, theologian, and scholar, he was hesitant to assume the role because he felt he was not an able administrator. When Yale's trustees agreed to assume the school's administrative and fund raising duties, Daggett reluctantly agreed to take the position and became the second president of Yale – a position he held until 1777.

Elizur Goodrich, Congressman and Professor of Law at Yale, described Daggett as, "of about the middle height, strong framed, inclining to be corpulent, slow in his gait, and somewhat clumsy in his movements."[342] According to Yale historian, Brooks Kelley, Daggett had "hot blood coursing through his veins which made him a fiery patriot."[343] This "hot blood" caused him to become an outspoken critic of the British and their many abuses of the colonists' rights.

When the Stamp Act was imposed on the colonies in 1765, King George appointed Jared Ingersoll, a British loyalist, as Stamp Master of Connecticut. Because of American animosity toward the Act, Ingersoll became one of the most hated men in Connecticut. Daggett was the first to publicly attack Ingersoll in print in an article published in the *Connecticut Gazette* on August 9, 1765 in which he called Ingersoll a traitor.[344] As public outcry reached a fevered pitch, a mob of infuriated New Haven citizens threatened to hang Ingersoll. Soon thereafter, he was forced to resign his post.

When the shots rang out at Lexington and Concord, the campus of Yale was thrown into a patriotic fervor and quickly raised a company of student-soldiers. When Gen. George Washington travelled to Cambridge to take command of the

American Army, he visited the Yale campus to the shouts and cheers of a large crowd of students and townspeople. With great fanfare, Yale's company of student-soldiers marched and performed military maneuvers for the General.[345] Noah Webster, a Yale student at that time, wrote about the experience, "In the morning they were invited to see a military company of students at Yale College perform their manual exercises. They were surprised at the precision of the students who then escorted them to the Neck Bridge. It fell to my humble lot to lead this company with music."[346]

As Daggett had predicted, he did indeed make a much better professor than college president. With the war intensifying, he determined that his time as Yale president was nearing an end and tendered his resignation, effective immediately after the commencement ceremony of 1777. He continued to serve as professor of divinity but surrendered the leadership of the college to Reverend Ezra Stiles, a more able administrator.

In 1779, rumors began to circulate that British Major General William Tryon and his troops were planning to invade Connecticut. And as one might imagine, the effect of this news created quite a stir among the citizens of New Haven as one writer recorded: "The place was immediately thrown into great alarm, and a meeting was called to deliberate on what was to be done. Counsels were various as to the best course to pursue, but Dr. Daggett declared that whatever else was determined upon, one thing was clear, the citizens must fight."[347]

The rumors turned out to be true and on the evening of July 5, 1779, Gen. Tryon and some twenty-five hundred British regulars from New York landed on the Connecticut shore about five miles south of the center of town. Once news reached the campus, the company of student-soldiers numbering roughly one hundred, organized their company and prepared to make a brief stand in the hope of providing a little extra time for the citizens of New Haven and Yale to evacuate the area. In 1849, Rev. Elizur

Goodrich, a Yale student at the time of the battle, recounted the amazing clash of arms that happened that July 4:

"In common with others of the students, I was one of the number; and I well remember the surprise we felt the next morning, July 5th, as we were marching over West Bridge towards the enemy, to see Dr. Daggett riding furiously by us on his old black mare, with his long fowling-piece in his hand ready for action. We knew the old gentleman had studied the matter thoroughly, and satisfied his own mind as to the right and propriety of fighting it out; but we were not quite prepared to see him come forth in so gallant a style to carry his principles into practice. Giving him a hearty cheer as he passed, we turned down towards West Haven at the foot of the Milford Hills, while he ascended a little to the West, and took his station in a copse of wood where he seemed to be reconnoitering the enemy, like one who was determined to 'bide his time.'

As we passed on towards the South, we met an advanced guard of the British; and taking our stand at a line of fence, we fired upon them several times, and then chased them the length of three or four fields, as they retreated; until we suddenly found ourselves involved with the main body, and in danger of being surrounded. It was now our turn to run, and we did for our lives. Passing by Dr. Daggett in his station on the hill, we retreated rapidly across West Bridge, which was instantly taken down by persons who stood ready for the purpose, to prevent the enemy from entering the town by that road.

In the mean time, Dr. Daggett, as we heard the story afterwards, stood his ground manfully, while the British columns advanced along the foot of the hill – determined to have the battle himself as we had left him in the lurch; and using his fowling-piece now and then to excellent effect, as occasion offered, under the cover of the bushes.

But this could not last long. A detachment was sent up the hillside to look into the matter; and the commanding officer coming suddenly, to his great surprise, on a single individual in a black coat blazing away in this style, cried out, 'What are you doing there you old fool, firing on His Majesty's troops?' 'Exercising the rights of war,' says the old gentleman. The very audacity of the reply, and the mixture of drollery it contained, seemed to amuse the officer. 'If I let you go this time, you rascal,' says he, 'will you ever fire again on the troops of His Majesty?' 'Nothing more likely,' said the old gentleman, in his dry way. This was too much for the flesh and blood to bear; and it is a wonder they did not put a bullet through him on the spot."[348]

Rev. Goodrich then went on to elaborate on how the British mistreated Daggett once he was captured:

"However, they dragged him down to the head of the column, and as they were necessitated by the destruction of West Bridge to turn their course two miles farther North to the next bridge above, they placed him at their head and compelled him to lead the way. I had gone into the meadows, in the mean time, on the opposite side of the river, half a mile distant, and kept pace with the march as they advanced towards the North. It was, I think, the hottest day I ever knew. The stoutest men were almost melted with the heat.

In this way they drove the old gentleman before them at midday under the burning sun, round through Westville about five miles into the town, pricking him forward with their bayonets when his strength failed, and when he was ready to sink to the ground from utter exhaustion. Thus they marched him into New Haven, shooting down one and another of the unoffending inhabitants as they passed through the streets, and keeping him in utter uncertainty whether they had not been reserving him for the same fate. When they reached the green, he was recognized by one of the very few Tories in the place, who had come forward to welcome the troops, and at his request was finally dismissed.

His life was, for some time, in danger from extreme exhaustion, and from the wounds he had received. He did, however, so far recover his strength as to preach regularly in the chapel, a part of the next year; but his death was no doubt hastened by his sufferings on that occasion." [349]

In 1855 at the age of ninety-one, Rev. Payson Williston, a 1783 graduate of Yale, recalled the battle of seventy-six years before:

"You are of course aware of the patriotic spirit which he evinced at the time of the attack of the British on New Haven, and of the rude treatment he received from them, disabling him somewhat afterwards. It was my lot to mingle in that scene as a member of the Artillery company who opposed the British who landed on the West side of New Haven harbor; and I distinctly remember the President's coming up and addressing to us patriotic and earnest words, bidding us go on and fight; and he rushed along himself, and very soon after came near paying for his patriotism with his life."[350]

Ironically, a 1757 Yale graduate, Edmund Fanning, was the son-in-law of British Gen. Tryon and many credited Fanning's influence and the daring stand of the student militia for the fact that the British did not destroy New Haven and the Yale campus. With the exception of some plundering by the Redcoats, the campus and town sustained little damage. One of the reasons pillaging was kept to a minimum was that the British spent a good deal of their time in New Haven sleeping off the huge quantity of rum they had stolen and consumed. On July 6, just two days after the battle, the British moved on, and New Haven and Yale were saved.

As Rev. Goodrich recalled, Daggett wavered between life and death for days from the heat exhaustion and bayonet wounds he sustained during his clash with the enemy, but unfortunately, his strength was so diminished by the ordeal that some sixteen months later on November 25, 1780, Naphtali Daggett traded this earthly struggle for his heavenly reward. It was said, "He was borne to the grave, one more added to the list of noble souls who felt that the offer of their lives to their country was a small sacrifice."[351]

Chapter 10

GEORGE DUFFIELD: "PASTOR OF 'THE CHURCH OF THE PATRIOTS.'"
(1732 – 1790)

"Nor were those of the sacred order wanting to their country, when her civil and religious liberties were all at stake. But, as became faithful watchmen, they blew the trumpet on the walls of our Zion, and sounded an alarm for defense."[352]

George Duffield commending the
Black Robed Regiment in 1783

George Duffield was a man well prepared for the struggle in which he would play a significant role. In the early 1760s, the qualities that equipped him for liberty's fight which would take place a little over a decade later became evident while he ministered to a number of churches situated in the raw and rugged frontier of central Pennsylvania.

During that time, the Indians in that part of Pennsylvania were often hostile to the colonists thus, the members of Duffield's church often attended church while heavily armed. When the Indians engaged in acts of violence, the colonists would launch expeditions into the wilderness to punish the offenders with Pastor Duffield often accompanying them. This rough and ready attitude helped to endear him to the people of that area and consequently, his reputation as a preacher who was not afraid to stand and fight began to grow.

It is said that in those days, the situation was so dangerous that in the little community of Monaghan, Pennsylvania the colonists had to build fortifications around their church building. During the Sunday services, members of the congregation manned these defenses to guard against surprise attacks from Indian tribes in the area. It was in this wild and untamed wilderness that Duffield's ministry "metal" was tempered. It is no wonder that when the fight with Great Britain came, he was ready.[353]

George Duffield was born on October 7, 1732 in Lancaster County, Pennsylvania to George and Susanna who were both of French Huguenot descent, having immigrated to America from Ireland around 1720 and settling in Pequea, Pennsylvania. George and Susanna made certain that young George received a solid education eventually leading to his graduation from Princeton in 1752. Four years later in 1756, he was licensed to preach and soon afterwards married Elizabeth Blair on March 1, 1756. Unfortunately Elizabeth died the very next year. Two years later, George married Margaret Armstrong, the sister of Gen. John Armstrong. Duffield's ministry continued to grow and in 1761 he was ordained as pastor of the church in Carlisle, Pennsylvania. Preachers were in short supply in that sparsely populated region of Pennsylvania, so, in addition to his ministerial duties at Carlisle, Pastor Duffield also ministered to two other congregations in Big Spring (later renamed Newville), and Monaghan (later renamed Dillsburg).

In 1772, after eleven years of faithful ministry to the pioneer settlers of the Pennsylvania frontier, Pastor Duffield was called to the Old Pine Street Presbyterian Church (later renamed the Third Presbyterian Church) in Philadelphia where he continued to pastor until his death in 1790. It was during his ministry there that he became a staunch advocate for American independence and lobbied continuously for it. The news of his strong stand against what he believed to be British tyranny began to spread across the region and Duffield became quite popular, with large crowds flocking to hear him wherever he spoke. Like the other preachers in the Black Regiment, he was loved by the patriots and hated by the Tories/British. It was said of Duffield that he:

> "...provided leadership during the Revolution during the stamp Act and against the king's unconstitutional taxation; Duffield proclaimed "to arms, to arms" and argued for liberty. In such strains of impassioned eloquence did he sustain his high argument for liberty, and pour his own brave, glowing soul into his excited listeners, till they were ready, when he ceased, to shout, 'To arms! To arms!'"[354]

Shortly after Pastor Duffield and his family settled into their new home and ministry in Philadelphia, an event occurred that perfectly illustrated the level of hated some harbored toward him. Having received an invitation to speak at the famous First Presbyterian Church of Philadelphia, he gladly accepted. But when the designated Sunday evening came, Duffield arrived at the church only to discover that a number of the church's leaders, who disliked his robust patriotism, had locked the building so that he and the large crowd that had gathered were unable to enter. Undaunted, Duffield and his audience began searching for another way into the building and, finding a window they could pry open, lifted the preacher up and through it. Once inside the church, they unbolted the doors and the enthusiastic crowd filed inside to hear him preach.[355]

In the legendary story as recorded in the History of the First Presbyterian Church,[356] as Duffield was beginning his sermon, word was working its way to Jimmy Bryant, a British magistrate in Philadelphia. Once Bryant learned that the patriot preacher was promoting his propaganda to a large crowd of rebels at First Presbyterian, he rushed to the church to stop the service. Hurrying into the building, he pushed his way through the crowd, down the aisle, and interrupted Duffield by declaring the gathering an illegal assembly. As Duffield paused at the interruption, Bryant began reading the Riot Act aloud. Robert Knox, a large man who was a member of the church and an officer in the American militia, rose and ordered Bryant to stop. Declaring that he would not, Bryant proceeded to read the Act. With a louder and more commanding tone, Knox again demanded that Bryant cease. Bryant, disregarding this warning as well, continued to read.

At this point, Knox began making his way toward the magistrate. Working his way through the crowd, Knox eventually reached Bryant and seizing him, dragged him down the aisle and thrust him through the doors of the church and outside. Surprised, infuriated, and greatly humiliated at his rough expulsion from the meeting, Bryant, wise enough to know his limits, wisely walked away. Duffield, seemingly unshaken by the whole escapade, once order had been restored, resumed his sermon to the great delight of the crowd.

The following day, Pastor Duffield was summoned to appear before the King-appointed mayor to answer to the charge of aiding and abetting a riot. When the mayor demanded that Duffield supply bail for his release until trial, the pastor respectfully refused, declaring his innocence and asserting his rights as a minister of Jesus Christ. Duffield insisted that, rather than inciting a riot, he had been carrying out his legal responsibilities as a duly ordained minister of the Gospel and that the only one guilty of inciting a riot was Mr. Bryant, the King's magistrate.

Personally sympathetic to the pastor, the mayor explained that if he released him without charging him and demanding bail, it would be he who would find himself in prison instead of the pastor. Wanting desperately to avoid escalating the problem, the mayor offered to allow Duffield's many friends in the courtroom to help with his bail. Respectfully, Duffield declined the offer. Flustered and growing increasingly concerned for his own welfare, the magistrate went as far as to offer himself as bail for Duffield. Once again the pastor declined stating that as a minister of Christ, he had broken no laws and that the only lawbreaker was Mr. Bryant who interrupted a lawful Christian assembly.

The mayor was in a dilemma. Confident that if he locked up the pastor, not only would he have to deal with the opposition of the local citizens, but additionally, he would have to contend with the "Paxton Boys," a volunteer militia some one hundred miles away in the Pennsylvania frontier, who had already resolved to march to Philadelphia and free Duffield by force of arms if necessary. With no apparent options that would not precipitate a full-scale riot, the mayor decided to postpone his decision for a few days and allowed Duffield to go free. In the end, with local sentiment decidedly in Duffield's favor and with the threat of insurrection spreading, the mayor determined to allow the incident to simply blow over and never required Duffield to appear before his court again.[357]

Rather than dampening his resolve, the incident invigorated Duffield and he returned to his own pulpit more vocal than ever. As his reputation as a patriot grew, so did his influence. Drawn to his strong message of truth and liberty, the members of the Continental Congress, when in Philadelphia, often attended his church. Patriots like John Adams, who called Duffield a man of genius and eloquence, were often seen seated in the pews of the patriot preacher's church. Soon, the Old Pine Street Presbyterian Church became known as "The Church of the Patriots."[358]

The profound influence Duffield had on the Founders is seen in John Adams's response to a sermon Duffield preached on May 17, 1776 in which he compared King George to the Egyptian pharaoh who refused to free the Israelites. Writing home to Abigail about how the sermon had impacted his own thinking, Adams commented,

> "Is it not a saying of Moses, 'Who am I that I should go in and out before this great people?' When I consider the great events which are passed, and those greater which are rapidly advancing, and that I may have been

instrumental in touching some springs, and turning some small wheels, which have had and will have such effects, I feel an awe upon my mind, which is not easily described. Great Britain has at last driven America to the last step, complete separation from her; a total, absolute independence."[359]

Duffield was so beloved and respected by the delegates of the first Continental Congress that when its first chaplain switched his allegiance to the British, they named Duffield as one of their new chaplains.[360] In addition, just two days after the Declaration of Independence was signed, Pastor Duffield was appointed by Governor Morton to be the Chaplain to the Pennsylvania militia.[361] Choosing to leave his pulpit for the service of liberty and his fellow citizens, Duffield was absent from his church for the majority of the war. It was noted by historians that numerous men from Duffield's church followed his patriotic example: "Duffield left the church for the duration of the War. Sixty men from his congregation followed him into the army, many serving with distinction. John Steele was field officer the day Cornwallis surrendered at Yorktown. William Linnard launched cannon fire on the Hessians at the Battle of Germantown. George Latimer was so effective in fighting the British that a reward was offered for his capture — dead or alive."[362]

Duffield's ministry while serving as a Chaplain was both fruitful and daring as he fearlessly and consistently placed himself in harm's way. For example, as Journalist/historian Joel Headley writes, in 1776, with the British occupying Staten Island and the American army encamped across the river in New Jersey, Duffield assembled the soldiers in an orchard for Sunday worship. Climbing into the fork of a tree, he began the service by leading the men in a familiar hymn. As the soldiers lifted their voices toward heaven, the Redcoats on Staten Island heard their singing, trained their cannons on the orchard, and opened up a withering fire in hope of silencing their worship. As the iron hail came crashing through the trees, the Americans were momentarily hushed by the shock. Unwilling to give the British the satisfaction they sought, Duffield climbed down out of the tree and as the cannon shot whizzed through the air around him, led the soldiers to a safer place behind a small hill where they resumed their church service.[363] But George Duffield's commitment to the cause did not go unnoticed by the British; it came at a high cost as they placed a bounty of fifty pounds on his head.[364] Like most of the other patriot preachers, he knew that if the British ever captured him, they would make good on their threat. An event that occurred in the early days of 1777 drove home to Duffield how very real this looming threat was.

On January 2, 1777, just seven days after Washington and his army routed the Hessians at the Battle of Trenton, New Jersey, the British mounted a counter offensive triggering a second clash at Trenton. During the battle, the British murdered Duffield's friend, Pastor John Rosbrugh, from Pittsfield, New Jersey. Even though he had surrendered, Rosbrugh was mercilessly bayoneted to death while begging for his life. His mutilated body was left lying in a pool of blood (more about Rosbrugh in chapter 1). Hearing of his friend's death, Duffield, with the aid of a member of Rosbrugh's church, saw to it that their fallen compatriot received a decent Christian burial.[365]

J.T. Headley wrote that the Rosbrugh incident was a solemn reminder to Duffield that the British believed "every such rebel parson was more dangerous to the cause of the King than a whole regiment of militia."[366] Duffield and the rest of the Black Regiment were painfully and fully aware that this war was much more than a mere demonstration of religious fervor; to them, it was a real life-and-death struggle against the forces of tyranny and evil. Soon after his friend's murder, Duffield had an additional experience that emphasized the extreme danger he was in when he barely escaped being captured by the British.

As Gen. Washington and his army continued their retreat across New Jersey to slow the British, they destroyed the bridges over the rivers and streams once the army was safe on the other side. Exhausted from days of moving from place to place and from endless hours of ministering to the troops, Duffield was welcomed into the home of a local patriot to catch some much-needed rest. While he was sound asleep, the American army passed without his notice and were preparing to destroy the only remaining bridge over which he could cross to safety. Oblivious to the danger, Pastor Duffield was nearly trapped on the wrong side of the river practically guaranteeing his capture and perhaps even the same fate as that of his friend John Rosbrugh. Suddenly, there came a persistent rapping at the door and the excited warning of a local Quaker who respected Duffield and knew what the Redcoats would do if they captured him. Awakened and alarmed by the news, Duffield quickly collected himself, thanked his Quaker friend and his host, mounted his horse, and raced across the bridge just as the American soldiers were preparing to destroy it.[367]

Duffield's valiant stand for liberty came with more than a personal cost; it cost his Philadelphia church dearly as well. For earning the title, "The Church of the Patriots," Gen. Howe's Redcoats took sweet revenge on the church once they occupied Philadelphia in 1777. To dishonor and desecrate the church, they first exposed it to the insults and injuries of serving as a hospital for British soldiers during which time these foes of liberty burned the pews and pulpit to keep the place warm. Once gutted by this indecency, its floor was covered with dirt and the British used it as their stables where they frequently enjoyed equestrian sporting activities in the main auditorium. But the worst insult was the burial by the Redcoats of some one hundred Hessian mercenaries in the church cemetery.[368]

For all of the hardships George Duffield and his church were forced to endure for liberty, he remained a man of strong faith and faithfulness, learning to fully depend on his Lord for his strength and supply. For example, on one of the rare times when he was at home on leave from his duties as chaplain, he was informed by his son on a Saturday evening that the family was completely destitute of food and had nothing left to eat. Duffield, confident of God's care, comforted his son with the assuring words, "My son, the Lord will provide." The next day at church, a member of his congregation handed him a sealed letter, and as was his habit, Duffield refused to open it until the Sabbath had passed. The next morning when he opened the envelope, inside he found more than enough money to care for his family's needs for quite some time.[369]

By his patriotism, service on the battlefield, and his kindness to the soldiers, Duffield endeared himself both to the army and to his country. Faithful in all things, he refused to abandon his duties as chaplain even during the brutal winter of 1777-78 as the army suffered at Valley Forge. During that terrible time of cold and privation when the troops had little to wear and even less to eat, it was Duffield and the other patriot preachers in the camp who moved about encouraging the soldiers with words of hope from God's Word. But the soldiers were not the only ones who benefited from the ministry of chaplain Duffield; he and his fellow Black Regiment preachers provided much needed ministry to a number of the officers, no doubt including General Washington. It is impossible to know the true impact the patriot preachers' ministry provided to liberty's cause during those dark months at Valley Forge.

After suffering seven years of the hardships and privations of the war, once it was over, Pastor Duffield returned to his ministry at the Old Pine Street Church in Philadelphia where he spent the rest of his life rebuilding what the British and the war had destroyed. In post war Pennsylvania, he became an extremely active leader among the Presbyterians and served as the first official clerk of their general assembly. In 1785, he received an honorary

Doctor of Divinity degree from Yale. George Duffield continued to faithfully minister to his congregation in Philadelphia until his death at the age of fifty-eight. On February 2, 1790, the day Duffield died, one more member of the Black Robed Regiment made his way into the presence of God and the greatest liberty of all.

Chapter 11

JOHN WITHERSPOON:
"THE PATRIOTS' PASTOR"
(1723 – 1794)

"For my own part of property I have some, of reputation more. That reputation is staked, that property is pledged on the issue of this contest; and although these gray hairs must descend into the sepulcher, I would infinitely rather they should descend thither by the hand of the executioner than desert at this crisis the sacred cause of my country."[370]

John Witherspoon urging the signing of the Declaration of Independence

"There is not a single instance in history in which civil liberty was lost, and religious liberty preserved entire. If therefore we yield up our temporal property, we at the same time deliver the conscience into bondage."[371]

John Witherspoon, "Dominion of Providence Over the Passions of Men," 1776

Not every member of the Black Regiment served in the army or fought on the field of battle – some fought battles in the halls of government. So it was with the Presbyterian preacher named John Witherspoon, the only vocational minister to sign the Declaration of Independence.

John Witherspoon was born on February 5, 1723 in Gifford, Scotland to James and Anne Witherspoon. James was the pastor of the parish of Yester, a few miles from Edinburgh, Scotland and was descended from the great preacher and reformer John Knox who was described as the, "prime instrument of spreading and establishing the reformed religion in Scotland,"[372] and, as Charles Augustus Goodrich in 1829 suggests, Mary, Queen of Scots, was "more afraid of his prayers, than of an army of ten thousand men."[373] So John Witherspoon came from a long and distinguished bloodline of men and women of strong Christian character.

Young John was sent to the public school at Haddington, Scotland where he quickly earned a reputation for his intelligence, love of learning, and quick wit. At the age of fourteen, he began attending the University of Edinburgh where he graduated seven years later. He was licensed to preach in 1743 and, although he was offered a position to serve as his father's associate in Yester, John chose instead to take a pastorate in the parish of Beith in west Scotland and was ordained in 1745 when he began his ministry there.

Just as Witherspoon was settling into his ministry in Beith, the Jacobite uprising of 1745 came to Scotland. Charles Edward Stuart was at war with England in an attempt to recapture the English throne for the House of Stuart. When the Scots landed in Scotland, Witherspoon, young and adventurous, showed early on the "Black Regiment" spirit that would characterize his ministry later. Some have written that Witherspoon helped raise a militia company and marched to Glasgow to fight against the "Bonnie Prince Charles." (There is some disagreement among commentators and academics about this story. Some contend Witherspoon raised a militia and fought while others argue that he was only an observer and unintentionally got caught up in the fight.)

What is certain is that on January 17, 1746, at the Battle of Falkirk, Witherspoon and other friends were taken prisoner and imprisoned in the Castle Donne. They were held there until Charles was defeated at the Battle of Culloden on April 16, 1746.[374]

Once free, Witherspoon immediately returned to his parish in Beith. In 1747, he was invited to become the pastor of a much larger congregation in Paisley, Scotland. An eager Witherspoon accepted the call and during his years there, he met and married his wife, Elizabeth, and together they had ten children of whom only five survived to adulthood. The years in Paisley were a time of fruitful ministry for the Witherspoon's but they were also a time of testing as the Presbyterian Church in Scotland dealt with the liberal teachings that were beginning to creep in. A natural leader, Witherspoon assumed the leadership of a group of conservative preachers who fought to maintain the denomination's doctrinal purity. His fiery sermons attacking the moral decay in the church and the Scottish society made him a popular voice in Scotland. Dr. John Rogers wrote this about Witherspoon's preaching:

> "… always interesting and instructive in the pulpit, he was assiduous in the discharge of every parochial duty when out of it. And his preaching generally turned on those great, distinguishing, and practical truths of the gospel, which, in every Christian country, most affect and attach the hearts of the great body of the people."[375]

Founding Father and signer of the Declaration of Independence, Dr. Benjamin Rush, said that Witherspoon's way in the pulpit was "'solemn and graceful,' his voice melodious, and his sermons 'loaded with good sense and adorned' with 'elegance and beauty' of expression."[376] But what impressed Rush most about Witherspoon's preaching was the fact that he did not use notes when he spoke – an uncommon practice in a time when preachers, according to Rush, had the "too common practice of reading sermons."[377] Others noted that Witherspoon also did not use gestures or flowery language when he preached. Princeton historians write, "The story is told of a visitor who, observing that Witherspoon's enthusiasm for gardening was confined to growing vegetables, remarked, 'Doctor, I see no flowers in your garden,' to which came the reply, 'No, nor in my discourses either.'"[378]

In 1766, seeking a scholar to serve as their president, the College of New Jersey (later Princeton) found John Witherspoon a qualified candidate and issued an invitation for him to come to America and become the school president. However, because of friendships she had made in Paisley and her fear of sailing across the Atlantic Ocean, Mrs. Witherspoon refused to leave Scotland for America. Empowered by the trustees of Princeton, Richard Stockton and Dr. Benjamin Rush continued to urge the Witherspoon's to come to America. Stockton told Witherspoon that "he could be of untold service to religion and learning in America"[379] if he accepted the presidential post at Princeton. Rush encouraged, "Your talents have been in some measure buried but at Princeton they will be called into action, and the evening of your life will be much more effulgent than your brightest meridian days have been."[380] Finally, in 1768, after two years of continued appeals, Elizabeth Witherspoon agreed to move.

The Witherspoon's and their five children arrived in Philadelphia in August 1768 accompanied by a gift of some three hundred books for the college library. Exuberant tutors and students greeted them and a great celebration was held that night on the Princeton campus. Later that month, on August 17, John Witherspoon was inaugurated as the sixth president of Princeton.

Once his family was settled into their new home and he had settled into his new responsibilities at Princeton, President Witherspoon found that the college was not as healthy as he had hoped. Funding was low and enrollment was down. So, the president took to the road, accompanied by fellow Presbyterian Black Robe preacher James Caldwell, traveling from Massachusetts to Virginia, preaching from town to town in the hope of raising support for the school. After visiting Williamsburg, Virginia, the *Virginia Gazette* reported that Witherspoon "preached to a crowded audience in the Capital yard (there being no house in town capable of holding such a large crowd) and gave universal satisfaction."[381] But the real payoff came when the crowd contributed some fifty-six pounds to Princeton.

Not only did Witherspoon's preaching/fundraising tour secure much needed resources for the school, it also exposed his Scottish brogue preaching to his new American audience. While in Virginia, he encouraged the Madison's of Montpelier, Virginia to enroll their son, James, into Princeton – which they did in 1771, thus placing the young James Madison under his tutelage.

It did not take Witherspoon long to prove himself a capable and outstanding college president. His impact on Princeton was powerful and positive. In addition to helping to restore the financial stability of the school, he also strengthened its academic program by adding courses like Hebrew, French, government/politics, and international law to the curriculum. Dr. John Rogers noted Witherspoon's contributions, "But the principal advantages it derived, were from his literature; his superintendancy; his example as a happy model of good writing; and from the tone and taste which he gave to the literary pursuits of the college."[382] Princeton's own historians note:

"He [Witherspoon] had a quality contemporaries were inclined to describe as 'presence.' One of his students, a later president of the College, recalled that Witherspoon had more presence than any other man he had known, except for General Washington. ... He brought to Princeton a fresh emphasis upon the need of the church for a well-educated clergy, a purpose to which the college had been dedicated at the time of its founding, but by men who at the height of a stirring religious revival may well have given first place to the church's need for a 'converted' ministry."[383]

But one of Witherspoon's most impactful and enduring contributions was his influence on the young men who were preparing themselves for service in the ministry and government. While preaching Witherspoon's funeral, Dr. John Rogers wrote,

"He was, in many respects one of the best models on which a young preacher could form himself. It was a singular felicity to the whole college, but especially to those who had the profession of the ministry in contemplation, to have such an example constantly in view. Religion, by the manner in which it was treated by him, always commanded the respect of those who heard him, even when it was not able to engage their hearts. An admirable textuary; a profound theologian, perspicuous and simple in his manner; an universal scholar, acquainted with human nature; a grave, dignified, solemn speaker; he brought all the advantages derived from these sources, to the illustration and enforcement of divine truth."[384]

Remarks from those at Princeton University point out that its founders intended for the school to prepare young men to engage in both religion and politics and that President Witherspoon, touting his Whig political philosophy, played a major role in helping the institution to realize that goal: "The founders had hoped too that the College might produce men who would be 'ornaments of the State as well as the Church,' and Witherspoon realized this hope in full measure. ... He did not hesitate to teach both politics and religion."[385]

Historian, John Fea of Messiah College, observes that Witherspoon, believing humans, due to their fallen nature, are "prone to self-interest and passion-driven jealousies that must be controlled by a strong centralized government,"[386] quite naturally, instilled this same conviction into his students such as James

Madison. Madison went on to argue these very principles later in *Federalist 10*. Madison, of course, also played a major role in winning America's independence and was one of the principle authors of the U.S. Constitution.

Clearly, Witherspoon was successful in producing men who would eventually have a profound impact on their culture and their churches. As Princeton boasts,

> "His students included, in addition to a president and vice-president of the United States, nine cabinet officers, twenty-one senators, thirty-nine congressmen, three justices of the Supreme Court, and twelve state governors. Five of the nine Princeton graduates among the fifty-five members of the Constitutional Convention of 1787 were students of Witherspoon."[387]

Even though Witherspoon had his differences with British rule in the colonies, in the early days of the debate over American independence, he steered clear of the controversy, refusing to call the King a tyrant, claiming that it was a false accusation and undignified to speak of governmental authority in such a fashion. But by 1770, with the political atmosphere heating up and Princeton students beginning to publicly demonstrate against British injustice, it became impossible for him to remain silent. Eventually, the old "rebel spirit" that had driven him to participate in the conflicts in Scotland in the 1740s rose up within Witherspoon anew and pushed him into the struggle. He began preaching sermons and giving speeches in favor of American independence, even using a Princeton commencement speech as an opportunity to promote the American cause.

In 1774, as John Adams was returning to the Continental Congress in Philadelphia, he took time to visit Princeton. Following that visit, he wrote in his diary, "Doctor Witherspoon enters with great spirit into the American cause. He seems as hearty as a Friend as any of the Natives – an animated son of liberty."[388]

But even though Witherspoon was fully engaged in the political scene, his passion for the Gospel and the cause of Christ remained undiminished. It is significant to note that when John Adams called Witherspoon an "animated son of liberty," he also wrote, "but first, he was a son of the Cross."[389] (This should give pause to those who claim that preachers who engage in politics are doing so at the expense of preaching the Gospel.)

Having proven himself to the people of New Jersey as a true American patriot, John Witherspoon was elected to the New Jersey Provincial Congress where he served for two years. At the same time, he was also chosen to serve on that colony's Committees of Correspondence and Safety. By 1776, he had become so respected that the Continental Congress asked him to deliver a special sermon to the legislators on May 17, 1776, a day the Congress had designated as a day of national prayer and fasting. Witherspoon's sermon, "The Dominion of Providence Over the Passions of Man," a scathing criticism of British rule in America, was an instant success and quickly became a classic. (Today the sermon is considered one of the most important sermons preached in American colonial history.) In response, the British immediately labeled him a rebel and traitor.

In June 1776, fed up with the rule of British magistrates in America, Witherspoon led out in the effort to remove from power Gov. William Franklin, the royal governor of New Jersey, who had repeatedly opposed the will of the people. In the proceedings against the governor, Witherspoon served as a type of prosecuting attorney.

Just one day after deposing the governor, Witherspoon was chosen by the citizens of New Jersey to represent them in the Continental Congress. Taking his seat just days before the Declaration of Independence was signed, he became an outspoken member of the Congress; having arrived in time to support Richard Henry Lee's resolution for independence that had been presented earlier on June 7. As deliberation wound down to the actual vote, some delegates remained hesitant to declare independence – and with good reason. Among other concerns, they knew that by doing so, they would be considered traitors by the British and would most probably be executed if captured. In stark contrast, it appears that there was no such hesitation in John Witherspoon. According to a number of accounts, he stood and gave this moving speech:

> "There is a tide in the affairs of men, a nick of time. Mr. President [John Hancock], that noble instrument [the Declaration of Independence] upon your table, which insures immortality to its author, should be subscribed this morning by every person of this house. He that will not respond to its accents and strain every nerve to carry into effect its provisions is unworthy the name of freeman. For my own part of property I have some, of reputation more. That reputation is staked, that property is pledged on the issue of this contest; and although these gray hairs must descend into the sepulcher, I would infinitely rather they should descend thither by the hand of the executioner than desert at this crisis the sacred cause of my country."[390]

In his book, *The Story of Princeton*, Edwin M. Norris writes, "During the debate, when timid members hesitated and the fate of the Declaration hung in the balance, it was the unwavering resolution of such staunch patriots as Doctor Witherspoon that carried the day. His speech on that memorial occasion has often been quoted."[391] Norris draws from the account of Dr. John M. Krebs who was there when Witherspoon gave his rousing speech and witnessed the scene in the Continental Congress. Krebs recounted this of Witherspoon's effect on the Congress:

> "Every eye went to him with the quickness of thought, and remained with the fixedness of the polar star. He cast on the assembly a look of inexpressible interest and

unconquerable determination, while on his visage the hue of age was lost in the flush of burning patriotism that fired his cheek."[392]

After Witherspoon was seated, another delegate rose to declare, "We are not yet ripe for a revolution." To which Dr. Witherspoon responded, "In my judgment, Sir, we are not only ripe but rotting."[393]

It is important to understand that these were not just hollow words spoken in a moment of patriotic passion; they came from the deeply held convictions of one who was willing to sacrifice all to defend them. But John was not the only Witherspoon in the family who held strong personal beliefs about liberty and independence – two of his sons joined the Continental Army. Sadly, the Witherspoon's would come to experience first hand the ultimate cost of liberty when one of those sons, James, a 1770 graduate of Princeton, was killed on October 4, 1777 at the Battle of Germantown.

Because of his political engagement, John Witherspoon placed Princeton in the forefront of the debate over religious liberty in America; so much so, that it eventually came to be known as the "seedbed" of the revolution.[394] As was mentioned earlier, because of the leading role Presbyterians like Witherspoon played in the fight for independence, King George called the conflict a "Presbyterian rebellion."[395] When Horace Walpole, son of British Prime Minister Robert Walpole, told Parliament that "Cousin America had eloped with a Presbyterian parson,"[396] perhaps it is fair to presume that the "Presbyterian parson" to whom Walpole was referring may very well have been none other than John Witherspoon.

Consequently, when the British invaded New Jersey and occupied Princeton in November 1776, they apparently vented their hatred for Witherspoon and the Presbyterians by desecrating Nassau Hall, burning the library, and destroying other parts of the school. Interestingly, Witherspoon and the school were avenged just one month later when Washington and his army defeated the Redcoats at the Battle of Princeton on January 3, 1777.

In addition to being a man of resolve and action, John Witherspoon was also a man of wit and humor as well. For example, throughout his life, he battled with insomnia, often causing him to become extremely drowsy after eating. As can be imagined, this posed a great challenge for him in the long, almost endless debates that often took place in the Continental Congress. It was his sense of humor that aided him in dealing with this often-embarrassing disorder. On one occasion, he actually made a motion on the floor of the New Jersey Congress that daily sessions should end before dinner. His motion having lost, tongue in cheek, he warned his fellow members: "... there are two kinds of speaking that are very interesting...perfect sense and perfect nonsense. When there is speaking in either of these ways I shall engage to be all attention. But when there is speaking, as there often is, halfway between sense and nonsense, you must bear with me if I fall asleep."[397]

A man of significant insight, Witherspoon's intuition often served him and his country well. For example, when Thomas Paine, whose popularity was soaring because of the success of his work, "The American Crisis," was nominated as a candidate for Secretary of the Committee on Foreign Affairs in 1777, according to John Adams, Witherspoon objected to the appointment, claiming that Paine was not a safe man for the job.[398] Because of Paine's popularity, Witherspoon's criticism created quite the stir. But his vindication soon came when his suspicions proved to be correct when Paine began embracing extremely unorthodox religious/political views, thus disqualifying himself.

As both a minister and an elected official, John Witherspoon forthrightly defended the right of preachers/pastors to serve in government. In 1777, when learning that the Georgia legislature had made it illegal for preachers to run for political office, an enraged Witherspoon wrote this stinging rebuke:

"In your paper of Saturday last, you have given us the new Constitution of Georgia, in which I find the following resolution, 'No clergyman of any denomination shall be a member of the General Assembly.' I would be very well satisfied that some of the gentlemen who have made that an essential article of this constitution, or who have inserted and approve it in other constitutions, would be pleased to explain a little the principles, as well as to ascertain the meaning of it.

Perhaps we understand pretty generally, what is meant by a clergyman, viz. a person regularly called and set apart to the ministry of the gospel, and authorized to preach and administer the sacraments of the Christian religion. Now suffer me to ask this question: Before any man among us was ordained a minister, was he not a citizen of the United States, and if being in Georgia, a citizen of the state of Georgia? Had he not then a right to be elected a member of the assembly, if qualified in point of property? How then has he lost, or why is he deprived of this right? Is it by offence or disqualification? Is it a sin against the public to become a minister? Does it merit that the person, who is guilty of it should be immediately deprived of one of his most important rights as a citizen? Is not this inflicting a penalty which always supposes an offence? Is a minister then disqualified for the office of a senator or representative? Does this calling and profession render him stupid or ignorant? I am inclined to form a very high opinion of the natural understanding of the freemen and freeholders of the state of Georgia, as well as of their improvement and culture by education, and yet I am not able to conceive, but that some of those equally qualified, may enter into the clerical order: and then it must not be unfitness, but some other reason that produces the exclusion. Perhaps it may be thought that they are excluded from civil authority, that they may be more fully and constantly employed in their spiritual functions. If this had been the ground of it, how much more properly would it have appeared, as an order of an ecclesiastical body with respect to their own members. In that case I should not only have forgiven but approved and justified it; but in the way in which it now stands, it is evidently a punishment by loss of privilege, inflicted on those, who go into the office of the ministry; for which, perhaps, the gentlemen of Georgia may have good reasons, though I have not been able to discover them.

But besides the uncertainty of the principle on which this resolution is founded, there seems to me much uncertainty as to the meaning of it. How are we to determine who is or is not a clergyman? Is he only a clergyman who has received ordination from those who have derived the right by an uninterrupted succession from the apostles? Or is he also a clergyman, who is set apart by the imposition of hands of a body of other clergymen, by joint authority? Or is he also a clergyman who is set a part by the church members of his own society, without any imposition of hands at all? Or is he also a clergyman who has exhorted in a Methodist society, or spoken in a Quaker meeting, or any other religious assembly met for public worship? There are still greater difficulties behind: Is the clerical character indelible? There are some who have been ordained who occasionally perform some clerical functions, but have no pastoral charge at all. There are some who finding public speaking injurious to health, or from other reasons easily conceived, have resigned their pastoral charge, and wholly discontinued all acts and exercises of that kind; and there are some, particularly in New England, who having exercised the clerical office some time, and finding it less suitable to their talents than they apprehended, have voluntarily relinquished it, and taken to some other profession, as law, physic, or merchandise—Do these all continue clergymen, or do they cease to be clergymen, and by that cessation return to, or recover the honorable privileges of laymen?

I cannot help thinking that these difficulties are very considerable, and may occasion much litigation, if the article of the constitution stands in the loose, ambiguous form in which it now appears; and therefore I would recommend the following alterations, which I think will make every thing definite and unexceptionable.

'No clergyman, of any denomination, shall be capable of being elected a member of the Senate or House of Representatives, because {here insert the grounds of offensive disqualification, which I have not been able to discover} Provided always, and it is the true intent and meaning of this part of the constitution, that if at any time he shall be completely deprived of the clerical character by those by whom he was invested with it, as by deposition for cursing and swearing, drunkenness or uncleanness, he shall then be fully restored to all the privileges of a free citizen; his offence shall no more be remembered against him; but he may be chosen either to the Senate or House of Representatives, and shall be treated with all the respect due to his brethren, the other members of Assembly.'"[399]

Having received such sharp criticism from one as well known and esteemed as Dr. John Witherspoon, the Georgia legislature soon repealed the law and, thanks to Witherspoon, preachers in Georgia were free once again to exercise "one of their most important rights as a citizen."

Witherspoon's service to the Continental Congress was tireless and prolific, spanning from June 1776 to November

1782. Among his many acts of service, he served as Chaplain to the Congress, appointed to that position by John Hancock, he served on some one hundred committees, was outspoken on the floor in most debates, helped draft and sign the Articles of Confederation, assisted in organizing the interim government for the colonies during the war, and was active in American foreign policy – serving on the equivalent of today's Committee on Foreign Affairs. In 1829, historian Charles Goodrich wrote of Witherspoon's service,

"For the space of seven years, Dr. Witherspoon continued to represent the people of New Jersey in the general congress. He was seldom absent from his seat, and never allowed personal considerations to prevent his attention to official duties. Few men acted with more energy and promptitude; few appeared to be enriched with greater political wisdom; few enjoyed a greater share of public confidence; few accomplished more for the country, than he did, in the sphere in which he was called to act. In the most gloomy and formidable aspect of public affairs, he was always firm, discovering the greatest reach and presence of mind, in the most embarrassing situations."[400]

But among his great accomplishments while a member of the Continental Congress, none eclipsed his being the only vocational minister to sign the Declaration of Independence, second only to his assisting in the drafting of, and signing the Articles of Confederation.

In 1779, Witherspoon voluntarily resigned from the Continental Congress to return to private life. Shortly thereafter, he also resigned his post at Princeton to Dr. Samuel Smith, his son-in-law, and moved to Tusculum, his country home. But the citizens of New Jersey were not quite ready to say goodbye to John Witherspoon and in 1781, elected him one more time to the Congress, where he served for one more year, resigning in 1782.

Witherspoon spent the last years of his life helping to rebuild Princeton from the damages it incurred from the ravages of the war. During those years, he served two more terms in the New Jersey Legislature (1783-89), helped ratify the U.S. Constitution in 1787, in 1789 chaired a committee in the New Jersey legislature to abolish slavery,[401] and led out in the reorganization of the Presbyterian Church in America. Sadly, in 1789, his beloved Elizabeth died and two years later, having recently turned seventy, John Witherspoon married Ann Dill, the twenty-three year old widow of Dr. Armstrong Dill. Though the significant age difference no doubt raised the eyebrows of some and caused a good deal of talk, their marriage was strong enough to allow Witherspoon to father two more children. Historian Charles Goodrich described Witherspoon's last years:

> "Bodily infirmities began at length to come upon him. For more than two years before his death, he was afflicted with the loss of sight, which contributed to hasten the progress of his other disorders. These he bore with a patience, and even with a cheerfulness, rarely to be met with in the most eminent for wisdom and piety. Nor would his active mind, and his desire of usefulness to the end, permit him, even in this situation, to desist from the exercise of his ministry, and his duties in the college, as far as his strength and health would admit. He was frequently led into the pulpit, both at home and abroad, during, his blindness; and always acquitted himself with his usual accuracy, and frequently with more than his usual solemnity and animation."[402]

In the end, John Witherspoon did his part in helping the colonies win their independence from Great Britain and to establish a republican form of government in North America that would emphasize the individual liberties of the people and the principle of the "consent of the governed." Historian, Raymond

Frey of Centenary College in Hackettstown, NJ, summed up Witherspoon's contributions in this way:

"Although we can only guess about his influence in forging the U.S. Constitution and the Bill of Rights, his many essays and sermons, published widely in both American and European newspapers, reveal a man who was deeply committed to the idea of religious liberty. As the only member of the clergy in Congress at that critical time of our nation's beginning, John Witherspoon's strong and outspoken conviction to liberty of conscience, shared by many of the founders, became a cornerstone of individual rights. It is therefore no accident that the very first amendment to the Constitution to be ratified, and its very first sentences – guarantee and preserve freedom of worship in America."[403]

On November 15, 1794, the great patriot preacher departed this world for his heavenly home. His epitaph reads:

"Beneath this marble lies interred the mortal remains of John Witherspoon D.D. LL.D. a venerable and beloved President of the College of New Jersey. He was born in the parish of Yester, in Scotland, on the 5th of February, 1722, O.S. And was liberally educated in the University of Edinburgh; invested with holy orders in the year 1743, he faithfully performed the duties of his pastoral charge, during five and twenty years, first at Beith, and then at Paisley. Elected president of Nassau Hall, he assumed the duties of that office on the 13th of August, 1768, with the elevated expectations of the public. Excelling in every mental gift, he was a man of pre-eminent piety and virtue and deeply versed in the various branches of literature and the liberal arts. A grave and solemn preacher, his sermons abounded in the most excellent doctrines and precepts, and in lucid expositions of the Holy Scriptures. Affable, pleasant, and courteous in familiar conversation, he was eminently distinguished in concerns and deliberations of the church, and endowed with the greatest prudence in the management and instruction of youth. He exalted the reputation of the college amongst foreigners, and greatly promoted the advancement of its literary character and taste. He was, for a long time, conspicuous among the most brilliant luminaries of learning and of the Church. At length, universally venerated, beloved, and lamented, he departed this life on the fifteenth of November, 1794, aged 73 years."[404]

Section II:

How they thought

As I mentioned at the beginning of this book, the patriot preachers found ways to merge their theological conclusions into a cohesive set of principles using Whig political philosophy and the after-effects of the Enlightenment period. These principles served as a means of justification as they prepared their congregations and communities for the coming conflict they sensed was just around the corner. Drawing from these principles, they stood before their congregations Sunday after Sunday and thundered against what they perceived to be British tyranny. On top of that, many published their sermons providing an even wider distribution for their arguments. Suffice it to say that these pastors were highly effective in persuading large numbers of Christians to resist the British. In fact, this ability to articulate their ideas, seasoned with a sense of "divine permission/commission," in support of independence was likely their greatest contribution to the independence effort.

In this section, we will transition our discussion from "how these preachers fought" to "how they thought." It must be understood that these were thinking men to say the least – they were serious students of the Scriptures, of history, and of political philosophy and their sermons certainly reflected this. To be sure, our culture is very different from theirs, but even so, there may be lessons we can learn from these patriot preachers that will help us to more effectively engage our culture here in the 21st century.

It must also be emphasized that these preachers were far from being a bunch of rabble-rousers intent on starting a war – only a psychotic would wish for war (much more about this in Chapter

14). At times, they spoke prophetically and on other occasions they spoke politically, but they all longed for peace. Yet, as they built their case against what they considered the tyrannical and unlawful actions of their King and Parliament, they reached a point where they understood that independence and possible war were inevitable and became convinced that they must make whatever sacrifice was necessary to defend their liberties – especially their religious liberty. So in the end, regardless of how we might critique or disagree with their theology and politics, their motives, sincerity, and influence seem undeniable.

Like the Black Regiment who put their theological conclusions into action, we must do the same. Although our views may differ from theirs in some ways, our goal should be essentially the same – to provide maximum individual liberty so that the Gospel can be freely preached and God's kingdom can be advanced. If we boil the arguments and actions of the patriot preachers down to their core, I'm convinced that's what they were trying to do.

The take away lesson from these preachers is simple: "Truth and liberty are two of the most valuable gifts God has given us and if our theology does not spur us to action to defend them, then what good is it?" The effect of the patriot preachers' beliefs was profound as they lived them out in their communities, preached them from their pulpits, and in many cases, took them all of the way to the battlefield. Do we hold our beliefs as deeply as they held theirs, and are we as driven to action and sacrifice as were they?

Chapter 12

"A 'RIGHTEOUS' WAR"

"Those fathers accomplished the Revolution on a strict question of principle."[405]

Daniel Webster

Admittedly, the image of a pastor standing in front of his congregation holding his Bible high, encouraging his people to march off to war (at times led by him), seems strange to us today. But these were men of principle, men who would rather die than to compromise those principles.

The above quote from Daniel Webster is from a speech delivered to the U.S. Senate on May 7, 1834 where he was pointing out that the War for Independence was indeed driven by principle. And what was that principle? Webster went on to elaborate:

> "The Parliament of Great Britain asserted a right to tax the colonies in all cases whatsoever; and it was precisely on this question that they made the Revolution turn. The amount of taxation was trifling, but the claim itself was inconsistent with liberty; and that was, in their eyes, enough. ... They poured out their treasures and their blood like water, in a contest in opposition to an assertion, which those less sagacious, and not so well schooled in

the principles of civil liberty, would have regarded as barren phraseology, or mere parade of words."[406]

Webster's words accurately describe the concepts many in the Black Regiment came to believe and preach from their pulpits.

For example, in 1775, Pastor Jacob Duche emphasized that Americans were going to war armed with more than muskets and black powder – they were going armed with principles: "Possessed, therefore, of these principles – principles upon which the present constitution of Britain was happily settled ... I trust it will be no difficult matter to satisfy your consciences with respect to the righteousness of the cause in which you are now engaged."[407] That same year, Pastor Moses Mather articulated what was at the very core of the debate, "Thus, the question is reduced to a single point, either the parliament hath no such power over the persons and properties of the Americans as is claimed, or the Americans are all slaves. ... For, deprive us of this barrier of our liberties and properties, our own consent; and there remains no security against tyranny and absolute despotism on one hand and total abject, miserable slavery on the other." [408] Along those same lines, Pastor Samuel Langdon declared to his audience that the British were attempting to, "compel us to submit to the arbitrary acts of legislators who are not our representatives, and who will not themselves bear the least part of the burdens which, without mercy, they are laying upon us."[409] Historian John Wingate Thornton framed the debate like this:

"The question was, really, 'Does the British Parliament, three thousand miles off, in which we have neither voice nor vote, own us, three million people, souls and bodies?' The people considered the matter, and gradually got ready to fight about it, seeing no more 'divine right' of parliaments than of kings"[410]

As the uneasy relationship between the colonies and England continued to deteriorate, the Black Regiment began to make an argument that marked a critical turning point in the liberty debate. They began to insist that their struggle was not only a political war, but was much more than that – it was a *righteous* war. Trusting their pastors, many members of their congregations also began to see the war as authorized by God. Therefore, "armed" with their arguments, the patriot preachers became convinced that their cause was a righteous one. For example, on May 31, 1775, Samuel Langdon, an ordained Congregational pastor, preached that the Most High would vindicate the colonists:

> "If God be for us, who can be against us? The enemy has reproached us for calling on his name, and professing our trust in him. They have made a mock of our solemn fasts, and every appearance of serious Christianity in the land. On this account, by way of contempt, they call us *saints;* and, that they themselves may keep at the greatest distance from this character, their months are full of horrid blasphemies, cursing and bitterness, and vent all the rage of malice, and barbarity. And may we not be confident that the Most High, who regards these things, will vindicate his own honor, and plead our righteous cause against such enemies to his government, as well as our liberties."[411]

Langdon's words not only expressed his own feelings, but also echoed the beliefs of many of the other patriot preachers as well. For them, the war was "God's War" and there was little doubt in their minds that they were doing God's service as they marched headlong into it. On October 5, 1777, Abraham Keteltas, who embraced reformed theology and believed in a "providential history of America"* – one in which America was a "chosen" nation of God, argued that the War was God's war. Using a bit of hyperbole, Keteltas declared:

"Our cause therefore, my dear brethren, is not only good, but it has been prudently conducted: Be therefore of good courage; it is a glorious cause: It is the cause of truth, against error and falsehood; ... the cause of the oppressed against the oppressor; ... of liberty, against arbitrary power; of benevolence, against barbarity, and of virtue against vice. It is the cause of justice and integrity, against bribery, venality, and corruption. ... It is the cause, for which heroes have fought, patriots bled, prophets, apostles, martyrs, confessors, and righteous men have died: Nay, it is a cause, for which the Son of God came down from his celestial throne, and expired on a cross— it is a cause, for the sake of which, your pious ancestors forsook all the delights and enjoyments of England."[412]

William Gordon echoed the same message in his July 4, 1777 election sermon to the General Court of Massachusetts as he said, "A variety of particulars conspire to evidence, that it becomes us to say of this great event that it was from the Lord. ... I have not a doubt but that we are fully authorized, by reason and religion, for thus separating; and am persuaded that we are justified by the disinterested and impartial world."[413]

---

* God's providential hand in history is subjectively assumed by evangelicals but can rarely be objectively proven. Generally speaking, providential history, as the patriot pastors understood it, was an assumption that God supernaturally ordained the creation of America. This, of course, cannot be objectively proven scripturally, but is more a "felt" assumption based on circumstantial evidence and the very loose "connecting the dots" philosophy, than it is an objective fact. Though I certainly see God's hand in our history and certainly believe Christians played a significant role in our founding, I personally do not embrace the "subjective" approach to interpreting history.

The patriot preachers' resolve was not only heard and felt in their sermons, but in their prayers as well. For example, in the spring of 1777, with the Continental Army having suffered crushing defeats at the Battle of Long Island, New York, the subsequent fall of New York City, and the fall of Fort Washington, all precipitating the retreat of General Washington and his army from the region, Samuel Webster, pastor in Salisbury, Massachusetts, ended his May 28, 1777 election sermon to the Massachusetts House of Representatives with this prayer:

> "Awake, Lord, for our help, and come and save us. Awake, Lord, as in ancient times. … Lord, raise a dreadful tempest and affright them, and let thy tremendous storms make them quake with fear, and pursue them with thine arrow, till they are brought to see that God is with us of a truth, and fighteth for us, and so return to their own lands, covered with shame and confusion, and humble themselves before thee, and seek to appease thine anger by a bitter repentance for their murderous designs."[414]

Many other patriot preachers prayed similar prayers seeking God's intervention in their cause of liberty. Four years after Pastor Samuel Webster prayed God's "tempest" upon the British, Pastor Judah Champion was said to have prayed:

> "Oh, Lord! We view with terror and dismay the approach of the enemies of Thy holy religion. Wilt thou send storm and tempest to toss them upon the sea, and to overwhelm them in the mighty deep, or scatter them to the uttermost parts of the earth. … We beseech Thee, moreover, that Thou do gird up the loins of these Thy servants, who are going forth to fight Thy battles. Make them strong men, … Hold before them the shield, … Give them swift feet, … and swords, terrible as that of Thy destroying angel,"[415]

Reminiscent of numerous Old Testament characters, these preachers were weaving passionate biblical/political ideas into their prayers calling upon the Lord for deliverance from what they believed was British tyranny. Developing a near Exodus narrative to describe the events of the 1770's became an essential part of the role the patriot preachers played. As Professor James P. Boyd puts it, "no biblical narrative surpassed the Exodus in identifying the major themes, plots, characters, and subplots of the Revolution. Revolutionaries could not get enough of the Exodus story. They saw in the Exodus the providential hand of God, which would orchestrate the Revolution."[416]

Some may legitimately ask, "How could men of God, standing every Lord's Day in the pulpits across the colonies, who held the Word of God and its principles in such high esteem, so willingly support, encourage, and even participate in a war?" Although there is no simple answer to this question, their belief that every effort to avoid war had failed and their understanding of what Scripture taught about an "offensive" and a "defensive" war, certainly were contributing forces.

THEY WERE CONVINCED DIPLOMACY HAD FAILED AND THEIR LIBERTY WAS HANGING IN THE BALANCE

It must be remembered that when they declared their independence from Great Britain, the colonists believed they had exhausted all possible options for some type of compromise with Great Britain and therefore had no other choice – other than to surrender their God-given rights. In the Declaration itself, they attempted to delineate the lengths to which they had gone to avoid separation and possible armed conflict with their "mother country":

> "In every stage of these Oppressions We have Petitioned for Redress in the most humble terms: Our repeated

Petitions have been answered only by repeated injury. A Prince whose character is thus marked by every act which may define a Tyrant, is unfit to be the ruler of a free people. ... Nor have we been wanting in attentions to our British brethren. We have warned them from time to time of attempts by their legislature to extend an unwarrantable jurisdiction over us. We have reminded them of the circumstances of our emigration and settlement here. We have appealed to their native justice and magnanimity, and we have conjured them by the ties of our common kindred to disavow these usurpations, which, would inevitably interrupt our connections and correspondence. They too have been deaf to the voice of justice and of consanguinity. We must, therefore, acquiesce in the necessity, which denounces our Separation, and hold them, as we hold the rest of mankind, Enemies in War, in Peace Friends."[417]

Then, making their appeal to "the Supreme Judge of the world for the rectitude of our intentions," and with "a firm reliance on the protection of divine Providence," they declared their independence and prepared for war.

The patriot preachers stressed to their audiences that separation and possible war were the furthest from their intentions. For example:

- On the first anniversary of the Battle of Lexington, Pastor Jonas Clark reminded his audience: "... the connection of America with Britain ... might have been preserved inviolate to the end of time. And it may be added, that there is no just ground to suppose, that it would have ever entered the heart of Americans, to have desired a dissolution of so happy a connection with the Mother-Country, or to have sought independence of Britain, had they not been urged, and even forced upon such an expedient, by measures of oppression and violence, and the shedding of innocent blood."[418]

- Samuel Langdon preached in his May 31, 1775 Massachusetts election sermon at Watertown, Massachusetts: "We have used our utmost endeavors, by repeated humble petitions and remonstrances, ... to prevent such measures ... But our King, as if impelled by some strange fatality, is resolved to reason with us only by the roar of his cannon and the pointed arguments of muskets and bayonets."[419]

- Abraham Keteltas echoed this same point in his 1777 sermon: "... all our assemblies on the continent, and the Congress at two several times, have endeavored, by the most humble and earnest petitions to the throne, to prevent the fatal war, which now rages and desolates our land. ... and it was not until every pacific measure failed, and our petitions were scornfully treated, and rejected, and a powerful fleet and army had actually invaded us and shed our blood; that we took up arms, in behalf of our lives and liberties."[420]

- In his July 4, 1777 sermon preached before the General Court of Massachusetts, William Gordon declared: "This continent complained of real grievances, and humbly petitioned. ... Instead of being heard and relieved, the yoke was increased by fresh acts of cruelty, and new burdens laid upon the continent. Our first grievances were spoken of as if not real; and as though we complained without cause, ... we were at once plunged into a defensive war, ... Still we were desirous, if possible, of an accommodation. We therefore petitioned again, without rising in our requests, only enlarging them to take in new grievances. Instead of having them redressed, we were deemed and were to be treated as rebels."[421]

- On April 19, 1781, Henry Cumings reminded the citizens of Lexington, Massachusetts: "Had our petitions and prayers been properly regarded, and moderate pacific measures pursued, we should have entertained no thoughts of a revolt; for even after hostilities had commenced, we were ardently desirous of continuing united with our mother country, if such an union could have been preserved, without making a sacrifice of our liberties."[422]

The Black Regiment argued that, even with all of the intense effort the colonists had put forth to salvage the peace and avoid bloodshed, King George and his parliament still refused to relent from their heavy-handed and hard-nosed dealings; and rather than relenting, the British had stubbornly intensified their stranglehold. Because of this, the patriot preachers were certain that, under the circumstances, there was no way that the colonies could settle for peace under the terms the British were offering. Moses Mather emphatically made this point in 1775:

"To be reconciled to Great-Britain upon unjust terms, is to be reconciled to injustice, ruin and slavery; until they shall have condemned the measures that have been pursued against America, recalled their fleets and armies, … and given up the claim of power in parliament, to dominion over us, they cannot expect that we will treat with them, about future connections."[423]

Convinced the British were forcing the conflict, the Black Regiment went on to place the blame squarely on them. On December 18, 1765, long before the war, Stephen Johnson of Lyme, Connecticut, sometimes referred to as the "forgotten patriot" of Lyme, clearly pointed to the British as the aggressors even then when he said, "May we not ask who is the aggressor, he that invades the right of a free people, or they who defend only what is their own?"[424] Pastor John Cleaveland of Ipswich, Massachusetts, writing about the obstinacy of the British, said, "[S] he is become cruel as the Ostrich, more cruel than Sea-Monsters towards their young ones! Her Measures tend not only to dissolve our political Union to her as a Branch of the British Empire, but to destroy our Affection to her as the Mother State."[425] In 1777, Abraham Keteltas cried out, "Ye cruel and bloody authors of this unjust, unnatural war! What desolation, what misery have ye not brought on this once happy land?"[426] The Presbyterian preacher and delegate to the Continental Congress, John Witherspoon, asked, "Is it not manifest with what absurdity and impropriety they have conducted their own designs? ... they have by wanton and unnecessary cruelty forced us into union."[427] On the sixth anniversary of the Battle of Lexington, Henry Cumings declared, "The pride, avarice and ambition of Great Britain, gave rise to the present hostile contests. From this source originated those oppressive acts, which first alarmed the freemen of America; and provoked them, after petitioning in vain for redress, to form plans of opposition and resistance." [428]

Clearly, those who embraced the War for Independence felt forced into the conflict and compelled to fight. Even before hostilities had erupted, in 1775 Moses Mather made this point quite clear:

> "Since then we are compelled to take up the sword, in the necessary defense of our country, our liberties and properties, ourselves and posterity: ... With fair pretenses, they invite us to submit our necks to their yoke; but with unheard of cruelties and oppressions, they determine us, to prefer death to submission. [429]

Then, months after the war had ended, on December 11, 1784 while looking back at the causes of the late war, Pastor George Duffield summed up the choice he believed those who supported the war had faced at the outset of the conflict:

> "Hard alternative! to resign liberty, or wage this hazardous war. And yet none other remained. ... But *Liberty* was the

prize. She chose "Freedom or Death" as her motto; and nobly resolved on war with all its horrors; that at least, her last expiring groan might breathe forth freedom."[430]

Essentially, the patriot preachers were convinced that King George had violated the original charters and compacts that Great Britain had made with the colonies. This belief is clearly reflected in Samuel Langdon's 1775 Massachusetts election sermon when he said, "The most formal and solemn grants of kings to our ancestors are deemed by our oppressors as of little value, and they have mutilated the charter of this colony in the most essential parts, upon false representations, and new invented maxims of policy, without the least regard to any legal process."[431]

Believing this, the patriot preachers took the next step and declared that since the King had violated the compacts and charters, the colonists were relieved of their allegiance to them. Moses Mather made this point when he proclaimed:

"The king by withdrawing his protection and levying war upon us, has discharged us of our allegiance, and of all obligations to obedience: ... He having violated the compact on his part, we of course are released from ours; and on the same principles, if we owed any obedience to parliament (which we did not) we are wholly discharged of it. We are compelled to provide, not only for our own subsistence, but for defense against a powerful enemy: Our affections are weaned from Great Britain, ... the king, contrary to his design, hath discharged us of our allegiance and forced us from our dependence, and we are become necessarily independent, in order to preservation and subsistence, and this without our act or choice. And is it a crime to be, what we can't help but be? It is not from a rebellious spirit in the Americans, but unavoidable necessity, that we are become so?"[432]

Given this, the Black Regiment was not bashful to call the actions of the British exactly what they believed they were – tyranny. This is what Pastor William Gordon called it when he said in 1777: "We are not fighting against the name of a king, but the tyranny; and if we sailor that tyranny under another name, we only change our master without getting rid of our slavery. ... Now is the golden opportunity for banishing tyranny as well as royalty out of the American states, and sending them back to Europe, from whence they were imported."[433]

With the deeply felt conviction that the British intended to run roughshod over their "unalienable, God-given rights," the patriot preachers began calling their congregations to the defense of their fundamental liberties. This is exactly what Samuel Sherwood told his New Haven, Connecticut audience on August 31, 1774 when he said, "We are further threatened with being deprived of all our civil privileges, and brought under a most cruel, arbitrary and tyrannical kind of government."[434] Philadelphia pastor, George Duffield, went even further by asserting that it seemed clear to him that the British aimed to "subjugate" the Americans under an absolute tyranny:

> "The British monarch had formed a design to reduce these states, then British colonies, into absolute vassalage. A venal Parliament had approved the unrighteous purpose, and passed a decree to bind us in all cases, both civil and religious, to the obedience of such laws as they might deem meet to enact. ... But whatever might have been the motive, America was marked out for servile submission or severe subjugation, and the power of Britain employed to accomplish the end."[435]

Pastor Samuel Langdon warned, "America is threatened with cruel oppression, and the arm of power is stretched out against New England ... to compel us to submit to the arbitrary acts of legislators who are not our representatives, and who will not themselves bear the least part of the burdens which, without mercy, they are laying upon us." [436] Moses Mather was able to boil down the question into a "simple point" when he succinctly argued:

"Thus, the question is reduced to a single point, either the parliament hath no such power over the persons and properties of the Americans as is claimed, or the Americans are all slaves. ... he that hath authority to restrain and control my conduct in any instance, without my consent, hath in all. And he that hath right to take one penny of my property, without my consent, hath right to take all." [437]

So, convinced that tyranny was the enemy and liberty the goal, the preachers told their people that it was their *duty* to defend their rights. This is what Samuel West told the Massachusetts legislature in 1776 when he said, "We ought ever to persevere with firmness and fortitude in maintaining and contending for all that liberty that the Deity has granted us. It is our duty to be ever watchful over our just rights, and not suffer them to be wrested out of our hands by any of the artifices of tyrannical oppressors." [438] Three years later, Pastor Samuel Stillman reminded the Massachusetts Supreme Court that liberty, not political power, was the prize for which they were fighting when he preached, "We are engaged in a most important contest; not for power, but freedom. We mean not to change our masters, but to secure to ourselves, and to generations yet unborn, the perpetual enjoyment of civil and religious liberty, in their fullest extent." [439]

The Black Robes were so intent on defending their liberties that they were willing to forego any offer of peace that would in any way diminish them. In 1780, Samuel Cooper declared that peace at the price of liberty was not a peace worth having:

"Peace, peace, we ardently wish; but not upon terms dishonorable to ourselves, or dangerous to our liberties; and our enemies seem not yet prepared to allow it upon any other. At present the voice of providence, the call of our still invaded country, and the cry of every thing dear to us, all unite to rouse us to prosecute the war with redoubled vigor; upon the success of which all our free constitutions, all our hopes depend."[440]

Knowing that if the colonists were going to retain their rights and liberty that war was practically inevitable, Moses Mather was completely transparent with his Hartford, Connecticut audience about the approaching hardships of war. Even so, he encouraged them with the admonition, "Let none be dismayed at the strength and power of our oppressors; nor at the horrors of war into which we are compelled, for the necessary defense of our rights. Can we expect the laurels, without entering the list? To be crowned without being tried? ... Such is the state of the world, that the way to freedom and glory is a way of danger and conflict."[441]

THE "RIGHT KIND" OF WAR

Although the patriot preachers disdained the thought of war and its resulting suffering and death, they believed that some wars were *just* and could even be seen as *righteous*. This belief is evidenced in the words of Henry Cumings as he reasoned on April 19, 1781 that God sometimes gives His people "a spirit of opposition" and "stirs them up to make a resolute resistance" against evil:

> "[A]nother way wherein God restrains the wrath of man, is, by rousing those who suffer, ... to stand in their own defense; and inspiring them with courage and resolution, to oppose and resist, to the utmost, all the mischievous efforts of ... those proud aspiring mortals, who would, if possible, rob them of their natural rights, and plunge them into a state of servility. ... When God purposes to restrain the wrath of his people's enemies, he usually rouses a spirit of opposition, stirs them up to make a

resolute resistance, and animates and excites them to the most vigorous efforts for the maintenance of their rights."[442]

But, the patriot preachers emphasized that in order for a war to be righteous, it had to be defensive in nature. In other words, a righteous war had to be fought in the defense of truth and to protect the innocent – not in quest or aggression. For example, consider the "Artillery Sermon" delivered in Boston on June 1, 1767 by Daniel Shute to the troops of the Continental Army on the anniversary of the election of their officers. Long before the war was actually upon them, Pastor Shute was laying the philosophical groundwork, as he saw it, for a defensive, righteous war:

> "DEFENSIVE war is then right according to the constitution of God, and supported by the written declarations of his will; and in particular, is consistent with the rules of the gospel; for all the dissuasives therein, from anger, wrath and revenge, and all the persuasives to meekness, forgiveness and charity, are reconcileable to the principles of natural religion, which allow and require the defence of our being, with all the privileges of being, in every capacity, private or public."[443]

In 1775, Moses Mather expressed the same sentiments:

> "Hence, it is evident, that man hath the clearest right, by the most indefensible title, to personal security, liberty, and private property. And whatever is a man's own, he hath, most clearly, a right to enjoy and defend; to repel force by force; to recover what is injuriously pillaged or plundered from him, and to make reasonable reprisals for the unjust vexation. And, upon this principle, an offensive war may sometimes be justifiable, viz. when it is necessary for preservation and defense."[444]

The message that God would only honor a defensive war had made its mark. Proof of this can be seen in the resolution passed by the Provincial Congress of Massachusetts on March 30, 1775 that urged the Massachusetts "Army of Observation" to prepare themselves to fight only a *defensive* war:

> "That whenever the Army under command of General Gage, or any part thereof to the Number of Five Hundred, shall march out of the Town of Boston, with Artillery and Baggage, it ought to be deemed a design to carry into execution by Force the late acts of Parliament, the attempting which, by the Resolve of the late Honorable Continental Congress, ought to be opposed; and therefore the Military Force of the Province ought to be assembled, and an Army of Observation immediately formed, to act *solely on the defensive* so long as it can be justified on the Principles of Reason and Self Preservation and no longer."[445]

Understanding this causes the command that Captain John Parker gave to the Lexington Minutemen on April 19, 1775 to make perfect sense. When he said, "Stand your ground, don't fire unless fired upon. But if they mean to have a war, let it begin here," Parker was no doubt voicing a principle he had been hearing from his pastor, Jonas Clark, for years.

JUSTIFIED BY BRITISH BRUTALITY

As the patriot preachers continued to focus on the "unjust vexation and plundering" of the British, they contributed to a growing sense among the colonists that their cause truly did meet God's self-defense standard for war and that the British had to be stopped or perhaps the plundering and the carnage might come to their doorsteps as well. This concern was, in fact, valid. Consider the behavior of the British during a little known battle called the Battle of Menotomy (now called Arlington,

Massachusetts) that was fought on April 19, 1775 as a part of the Lexington/Concord battles.

As the British were pulling back into the security of Boston, they were forced to fight a running battle against the Militia who gathered from all around the surrounding area determined to give the Redcoats a difficult march down what is today called "Battle Road." As the Brits moved down the road, they used small flanking forces to keep the main column safe from attack by the militia. During the course of the march, one of these flanking companies came into Menotomy and while both sides fought viciously, the British are remembered that day for being particularly ruthless. Their actions were so vicious in fact, that a British Lieutenant named Barker wrote of the plundering by the Redcoats that day, "[they] hardly thought of anything else; what was worse, they were encouraged by some officers."[446]

One particular part of the fight that illustrates Barkers angst involves the fight in the Russell House. As the militia took cover in this house, British regulars stormed it and the bloody scene inside is hard to describe. As historian Thomas Fleming recounts, "Eleven militiamen, including seven from Danvers, died during hand-to-hand fighting in the Russell house. The struggle raged from cellar to attic, the odds heavily in favor of the British trained in use of the bayonet. Foster claimed that three or four of his men surrendered only to be 'butchered with savage barbarity.'"[447] Fleming goes on to describe other infamous actions of the Brits that day:

> "When the British burst into the home of Deacon Joseph Adams, they found Mrs. Adams in bed, holding her newborn and flanked by her daughters, aged 20 and 14. Nine-year-old Joel Adams peered from under the bed. 'Why don't you come out here?' asked one of the soldiers. 'You'll kill me,' the boy replied. 'No, we won't,' the soldier said. The boy came out and watched the soldiers prowl through the house, stealing silver and jewelry. They then

ordered the family out of the house, broke up some chairs in the parlor and set them ablaze."[448]

While not every battle went this way, enough of them did to begin to create a picture in the minds of the colonists of a ruthless and vicious British soldiery – an image that was used by many to exhort the colonists to fight; and fight they did.

Even in the light of the willingness of some British soldiers to carry out atrocities such as these, the patriot preachers, in most cases, continued to insist that Americans should only fight in a defensive posture and never initiate bloodshed. This, they believed, was in keeping with the Scriptures and the principles of the "Just War Theory."[449] But even though most patriot preachers did not believe God honored *starting* a fight, they definitely believed He approved of *finishing* one if it was thrust upon them. For example (and without debating their hermeneutic), consider the following two sermon excerpts; one preached by Ezra Stiles and one by Henry Cumings. Ezra Stiles, Congregational minister and president of Yale, preached an election sermon to the General Assembly of Connecticut in Hartford, Connecticut on May 8, 1783 in which he argued; "War, in some instances, especially defensive, has been authorized by Heaven." Cummings while pastoring a Congregational church in Billerica, Massachusetts, placed his arguments squarely in line with enlightenment philosophy of the time by stating, "They who would be glad to 'live peaceably with all men,' are often unhappily forced into contention, and obliged to take arms, and engage in hazardous contests, in order to defend their lives and liberties, against the evil designs of unreasonable men,"[450]

Fifteen years after the war had ended, the patriot preachers were still reminding the people of the primary reason to fight a defensive war – to secure men's God-given liberties, of which religion liberty was viewed as most important. On July 4, 1798, on the twenty-second anniversary of the signing of the Declaration of Independence, Timothy Dwight, Congregational pastor in

Connecticut and president of Yale, argued in his sermon that religion (Christianity) and liberty were not only worth fighting for, but were properly fought for:

"Religion and Liberty are the two great objects of defensive war. ... Withdraw one of them, and it languishes, consumes, and dies. If indifference to either at any time becomes the prevailing character of a people, one half of their motives to vigorous defense is lost, and the hopes of their enemies are proportionally increased. Here, eminently, they are inseparable. Without religion we may possibly retain the freedom of savages, bears, and wolves; but not the freedom of New England. If our religion were gone, our state of society would perish with it; and nothing would be left, which would be worth defending. Our children of course, if not ourselves, would be prepared, as the ox for the slaughter, to become the victims of conquest, tyranny, and atheism. ... Where religion prevails ... a nation cannot be made slaves, nor villains, nor atheists, nor beasts. [451]

So, believing the war was just and, in their view, actually the work of God, many of these preachers unashamedly endorsed the conflict. Consider the following two examples:

- William Smith, pastor of Christ Church in Philadelphia, preached on June 23, 1775, "But let not this discourage you, yea, rather let it animate you with a holy fervor, a divine enthusiasm, ever persuading yourselves that the cause of virtue and freedom is the cause of God upon earth;"[452]

- John Rogers, New York City pastor, peached on December 11, 1780, "They [British] hereby taught us ... the necessity of maintaining our independence, or perishing in the struggle. ... It is much to be lamented, that the troops of a nation [England] that have been considered as one of the bulwarks of the reformation, should act as if they had waged war with the God whom Christians adore. They have, in the course of this war, utterly destroyed more than fifty places of public worship in these states. Most of these they burnt; others they leveled with the ground, and in some places left not a vestige of their former situation; while they have wantonly defaced, or rather destroyed others, by converting them into barracks, jails, hospitals, riding-schools, etc. ... of the nineteen places of public worship in New York, when the war began, there were but nine fit for use when the British troops left it."[453]

The Black Regiment made no bones about it – the war was a righteous cause and the colonists, especially the Christians, had no choice but to fight against what they believed was British tyranny. As we have seen, this was no new message; many of the patriot preachers had been making a case against British rule for years, long before military hostilities began in 1775. In fact, ten years before the war had become a foregone conclusion, Jonathan Mayhew had defended the right of Americans to defy the British government by resisting the Stamp Act. In his sermon, "The Snare Broken," preached in Boston on May 23, 1766, Mayhew contended that the colonists possessed natural rights as men and, therefore, also retained the right to petition the Parliament with their grievances. In this famous sermon which was as much a political argument as it was anything else, Pastor Mayhew used a number of "taken for granted" sections to make the point that the King and Parliament had underestimated the colonists' right to claim the fundamental "rights of men." Deeply tilling the ground of freedom nearly a full decade before the Declaration of Independence was written, Mayhew argued:

> "It shall, therefore, be taken for granted, that the colonies had great reason to petition and remonstrate against a late act of Parliament, as being an infraction of these rights, and tending directly to reduce us to a state of

slavery. ... The colonists are men, and need not be afraid to assert the natural rights of men; they are British subjects, and may justly claim the common rights, and all the privileges of such, with plainness and freedom. ... Let none suspect that, because I thus urge the duty of cultivating a close harmony with our mother country, ... I mean to dissuade people from having a just concern for their own rights, or legal, constitutional privileges. ... Power aims at extending itself, and operating according to mere will, wherever it meets with no balance, check, control or opposition of any kind. For which reason it will always be necessary, as was said before, for those who would preserve and perpetuate their liberties, to guard them with a wakeful attention; and ... to oppose the first encroachments on them. ... After a while it will be too late."[454]

Because of the high regard with which the colonists held Mayhew and other like-minded preachers, they no doubt believed the Black Regiment's sermons granted a kind of "pastoral approval" for resistance to King George and the Parliament. With the Crown's continued diminishing of the rights and liberties of the colonists and the increased cruelty of the British soldiers upon the American citizenry, the people were primed for action. The Black Regiment's unapologetic call for the armed defense of life, liberty, and property provided the very justification many colonists were waiting for. It could be said that *the British provided the powder, the preachers loaded the gun, and the colonists pulled the trigger.*

No message could be more illustrative of this fact than the one from the pastor who was at the very epicenter of the opening salvo of the conflict, the fiery patriot himself – Jonas Clark. As was shown in his short biography in Chapter 6, for some two decades before the redcoats fired those first shots in his churchyard in

Lexington, Clark had been pounding out the message of truth and liberty from his pulpit.

"The Fate Of Bloodthirsty Oppressors, And God's Care Of His Distressed People" was the sermon Jonas Clark preached on April 19, 1776 during the first commemoration of the Battle of Lexington. In a well-reasoned, generally political sermon, seasoned with biblical and historical precedents that supported his contention, Clark defended the colonists' right to fire back once the British had struck the first blows – thus establishing the war as "defensive" and satisfying *Jus Ad Bellum* principles of "Just War Theory."[455] Upon reflection, Pastor Clark argued that it would be God who would avenge the events that took place not only on the Lexington Green the previous year, but also of the War in general:

> "At length on the night of the eighteenth of April 1775, the alarm is given of the hostile designs of the troops. The militia of this town are called together, to consult and prepare for whatever might be necessary, or in their power, for their own, and common safety; though without the least design of commencing hostilities, upon these avowed enemies and oppressors of their country. In the mean time, under cover of the darkness, a brigade of those instruments of violence and tyranny, make their approach, and with a quick and silent march, on the morning of the nineteenth, they enter this town. ... They approach with the morning's light; ... without provocation, without warning, when no war was proclaimed, they draw the sword of violence, upon the inhabitants of this town, and with a cruelty and barbarity, which would have made the most hardened savage blush, they shed INNOCENT BLOOD! ... Yonder field can witness the innocent blood of our brethren slain! ... Surely there is One that avengeth, and that will plead the cause of the injured

and oppressed; and in His own way and time, will both cleanse and avenge their innocent blood. ... First, God's word and promise, in which He assures His people, that notwithstanding the violence of their enemy against them, and the distress and sorrow their oppressors may have caused them, by shedding innocent blood among them; yet they shall never avail to overthrow, or destroy them; but they shall assuredly be redeemed and delivered out of their hands, and restored and established, as His Church and people, in a flourishing state."[456]

Put yourself in the shoes of the average member of a congregation where one of these patriot preachers preached. Imagine how moving it must have been to hear impassioned words like those of Jonas Clark as they were preached Sunday after Sunday reflecting the heart and soul of their pastor, the central figure of their community. In this particular case, to hear the patriot who had helped lead those courageous minutemen of Lexington on the first day of the War must have been incredibly inspiring to that audience. With men like Clark preaching and leading as they did, the colonists came to see themselves as fighting a *holy war* for their religious and civil liberty. Author James Adams observed:

> "As most of the militiamen were members of his own church, Clarke had seen to it that Sunday after Sunday they were exposed to the kind of patriotic preaching guaranteed to produce 'Christian soldiers.' ... The appeal to Scripture to fortify a political position was common among Puritan preachers. When the showdown came with the British, the colonists had been properly conditioned to take up arms and resist, and few people fight as fiercely as those who believe they are engaged in a holy war. The majority of Americans perceived their Revolution as a righteous rebellion."[457]

But not only did the messages of these patriot preachers resonate with their congregations and communities, they also caused grave concerns among the British and their sympathizing Tories. Thus, realizing the significant force the patriot preachers were to the war effort, Tory pamphleteer Daniel Leonard, writing under the pseudonym of the "Massachusettensis," said:

> "When the clergy engage in political warfare, religion becomes a most powerful engine, either to support or to overthrow the state. What effect it must have had upon the audience, to hear the same sentiments and principles, which they had read before in a newspaper, delivered on Sundays from the sacred desk with religious awe, and the most solemn appeals to Heaven, from lips, which they had been taught from their cradles, to believe could utter nothing but eternal truths."[458]

BELIEVING THE WAR A "HOLY CAUSE," THEY PREACHED CURSES ON THOSE WHO WOULD NOT FIGHT!

It becomes fairly obvious that the members of the Black Regiment were absolutely convinced in their own minds that the war was a *righteous* cause and that all liberty-loving colonists should join the fight. So, adamant in this belief, some declared the actions of the British as a sin to Almighty God. For example, in 1776, Samuel West told the Massachusetts Legislature, "But because we were not willing to submit to such an unrighteous and cruel decree, ... instead of hearing our complaints, and granting our requests, they have gone on to add iniquity to transgression, by making several cruel and unrighteous acts." [459]

Consistent in their thinking, some of the patriot preachers reasoned that if what the British were doing to the colonists was a sin, then it was certainly a comparable sin for any colonist, especially those who called themselves Christians, to refuse to

stand up and fight against those sinful deeds. This is what Samuel
Sherwood claimed in his sermon in New Haven, Connecticut
on August 31, 1774. Sherwood criticized the pastors who
would, as he said, "for one sweet delicious morsel to themselves"
sell out their country by not participating in defending liberty.
Samuel West added to this argument by condemning those
who thought they were doing God's work by standing idly by
while British atrocities were being committed all around them
by declaring:

> "There are some who pretend that it is against their
> consciences to take up arms in defense of their country;
> but can any rational being suppose that the Deity can
> require us to contradict the law of nature which he has
> written in our hearts, a part of which I am sure is the
> principle of self-defense, which strongly prompts us all
> to oppose any power that would take away our lives, or
> the lives of our friends? ... Thus some have thought they
> did God service when they unmercifully butchered and
> destroyed the lives of the servants of God; while others,
> upon the contrary extreme, believe that they please God
> while they sit still and quietly behold their friends and
> brethren killed by their unmerciful enemies, without
> endeavoring to defend or rescue them. The one is a sin of
> omission, and the other is a sin of commission, and it may
> perhaps be difficult to say, under certain circumstances,
> which is the most criminal in the sight of Heaven. Of this
> I am sure, that they are, both of them, great violations of
> the law of God. ... Nor can I wholly excuse from blame
> those timid persons who, through their own cowardice,
> have been induced to favor our enemies, and have refused
> to act in defense of their country; ... to indulge cowardice
> in such a cause argues a want of faith in God; [460]

While taking a bit of hermeneutical latitude in his April
20, 1778 sermon, Jacob Cushing added himself to the list of

preachers condemning those who would not draw their swords for the cause of freedom:

> "If this war be just and necessary on our part, as past all doubt it is, then we are engaged in the work of the Lord, which obliges us (under God mighty in battle) to use our 'swords as instruments of righteousness, and calls us to the shocking, but necessary, important duty of shedding human blood;' not only in defense of our property, life and religion, but in obedience to him who hath said, 'Cursed be he that keepeth back his sword from blood.' ... The honor and glory of God, and the salvation of your country under God, call aloud upon all. Duty, interest, liberty, religion and life, every thing worth enjoyment, demand speedy and the utmost exertions."[461]

IF THERE WAS GOING TO BE A FIGHT, THEY WANTED A CLEAN ONE

Having concluded that all efforts to avoid war had failed, having established, from their perspective, that there was such a thing as a righteous war, having listed the abuses and atrocities of the British and shown them to be the aggressor, having shown that it was, as they understood it, biblical and legal to overthrow a tyrannical government, and having declared that it was time to fight for liberty, the Black Regiment insisted that, if Americans had no alternative but to fight a war to free themselves from British oppression, they must execute that war in keeping with "Just War Principles." In carrying out "the cause of God" as they saw it, the patriot preachers demanded a clean fight and urged their fellow colonists to conduct the war honorably as Christian soldiers. This call for honorable behavior on the battlefield is evident in the 1777 sermon of John Hurt as he preached to the Continental troops in New Jersey:

"National affection, therefore, if it be derived from a true principle, must necessarily inspire a moral conduct, must incline us to quit every baneful vice, to contract the circle even of what we call innocent amusements, and, instead of looking out for daily parties of pleasure, it will prompt us rather to make a constant festival of human kindness, the most delicious of all entertainments to a generous mind. If we behave thus, then we are patriots indeed. It is thus we are to arm ourselves against our unprincipled enemies; who, though they should not dread our strength, will certainly stand in awe of our virtue. Whilst we act in this manner, our professions will not only meet with full applause from men, but also with the approbation of God,"[462]

Likewise, Jacob Cushing challenged the Americans to reflect an "honorable and shining character" and fight as "good soldiers of Jesus Christ" in his sermon delivered in Boston on April 20, 1778:

"Above all, let me recommend and urge it upon you, to strive for a more honorable and shining character; I mean, that of true Christians, good soldiers of Jesus Christ; and to fight manfully under his banner, as the high priest of your profession, and great captain of your salvation. Then whatever service he shall call you to, or sufferings allot you; wherever he shall lead, you will cheerfully follow, be ready to face the enemy and every danger, and meet death with calmness and intrepidity, whenever arrested, and be conquerors through him."[463]

In Springfield, Massachusetts on Dec 14, 1787, well after the war was over, Pastor Joseph Lathrop articulated the sentiment of the patriot preachers when he said, ""We lately thought it worth defending by our arms: it is still worth securing by our virtue."[464]

While not perfect, even in the fog of war, when passions can lead to acts barbarism, the patriot preachers and many of the regular soldiers as well, sought to perform on the battlefield with as much moral and spiritual honor as possible. As one author put it:

> "It has been asserted, indeed, that there scarcely ever was a body of men collected for war so humane and moral, and who returned to their farms so little corrupted, as those who composed the American army; and the religious liberty which the new republic established, was so complete, that the dearest rights and interests of men were eminently promoted by the revolution."[465]

Likewise, John Witherspoon declared that it was piety and inward principle that made good, patriotic soldiers: "[I]n times of difficulty and trial, it is in the man of piety and inward principle, that we may expect to find the uncorrupted patriot, the useful citizen, and the invincible soldier."[466]

Certainly, the patriot preachers were under no false illusions. They were painfully aware that the patriotic feelings that were necessary to carry out a war of this magnitude could ignite passions in men in the heat of battle that could make them capable of committing excesses that were all but criminal. On April 19, 1781, Rev. Henry Cummings addressed these "patriotic passions" declaring that even though he was no "advocate for outrages," neither reason nor religion required "the total suppression of the passions" and that it was "both rational, and a duty, to stir them up" when the crisis demanded. Cummings forthrightly pointed out that the "enkindled wrath" of battle was capable of:

> "... transporting the passions, in some instances, among individuals, into criminal excesses. But even these excesses of the passions, have, by Providence, been made to conspire with better principles, and more laudable

springs of action, to strengthen the opposition to British tyranny, and check the career of British rage and cruelty.

Far be it from me to justify any excesses of wrath and anger. I am no advocate for outrages, even on the most provoking occasions. But I cannot but observe, that, as on the one hand, it will not be denied, that the human passions have, in some instances, among particular persons broken forth into a criminal excess of riot; so, on the other, it cannot but be acknowledged, that there have been many instances of a very culpable indifference and tameness of temper, which, without any emotion, could behold the impending ruin of the country, or have quietly submitted to concessions fatal to liberty.

We are not to suppose, that either reason or religion requires the total suppression of the passions. It is both rational, and a duty, to stir them up into exercise, when suitable objects are presented to view. None of our original passions are in themselves vicious. They become vicious only by their exorbitancy. It is the excess of them that is criminal. While they are tempered with prudence and discretion, and kept within due bounds, they may be indulged to advantage upon many occasions. … patriotism without feeling or sensibility, is a mere name."[467]

Some wonder how "men of the cloth" could believe and preach such things. Even though historians and others will interpret for themselves the validity of claims like Cummings' and the other patriot preachers, it must be remembered that they decried the tyranny of Great Britain and most believed that America had been raised up and sustained by God's Providence" – even on the battlefield. This theological bias towards seeing Providence at work in the struggle for independence naturally tilted their view of the excesses that happen in a life or death struggle when passions are raised.

Sadly, in the fog and passion of war, the preachers' admonitions to fight morally were not always adhered to by all American soldiers. But the Black Regiment preachers had done their duty and cannot be blamed for the evil actions of the few who disregarded their call for virtuous behavior. Thankfully, in most cases, the citizens took to heart the pastoral admonitions for honorable behavior. The following incident illustrates just how respectful of authority the Americans remained as they protested the British government.

In September of 1774, some fifteen hundred citizens from Barnstable, Plymouth, and Bristol counties in Massachusetts gathered outside the Superior Court in Barnstable County to peacefully protest the court and judge who had been installed by the British and who, though unaccountable to the colonists, was paid by the taxes they were forced to pay. On that day, the colonists adopted this "code of regulations" for resisting British tyranny which read in part:

> "Whereas a strict adherence to virtue and religion is not only well-pleasing in the sight of Almighty God, and highly commendable before men, but hath a natural tendency to good order, and to lead mankind in the paths of light and truth: Therefore, Resolved, That we will ... not offer violence to any persons, or use any threatening words, otherwise than such as shall be approved of and accounted necessary by our community for the accomplishing the errand we go upon; and that we will carefully observe an orderly, circumspect, and civil behavior, as well towards strangers and all others as towards those of our own fellowship. ... so that our righteousness may plead our cause, and bear a public testimony that we are neither friends to mobs, or riots, or any other wickedness or abomination." [468]

"That we are neither friends to mobs, or riots, or any other wickedness or abomination" – this was the attitude of the vast majority who stood against what they saw as British tyranny. This, of course, serves to refute the accusation by some that the Americans who supported independence were just a mob of lawless rebels or anarchists (more on this subject in Chapter 14). In fact, according to the patriot preachers, the Americans were not in rebellion at all but were, instead, lawfully defending their rights by participating in a righteous conflict. This is what Samuel Langdon, president of Harvard and pastor of the North Church in Portsmouth, New Hampshire, had to say on May 31, 1775:

> "Our late happy government is changed into the terrors of military execution. Our firm opposition to the establishment of an arbitrary system is called *rebellion*, and we are to expect no mercy but by yielding property and life at discretion. This we are resolved at all events not to do; and therefore, we have taken arms in our own defense, and all the colonies are united in the great cause of liberty."[469]

This is no doubt the spirit with which Pastor Samuel Cooper said on October 25, 1780:

> "It is doubtless the ardent desire of everyone now present, to see a speedy and happy end to the war. ... The appeal has been made to heaven, and heaven has hitherto supported us, and restrained the wrath of our enemies. Trusting in God therefore, we should take courage still to *stand fast in the liberties, wherewith he has made us free,*"[470]

The patriot preachers believed the war was a righteous struggle and they did their level best to support and execute it as such – to them, liberty was worth the cost.

Chapter 13

THEY BOLDLY PREACHED RELIGION
AND POLITICS FROM THEIR PULPITS

Historian James L. Adams wrote,
"Freedom was not born a bastard. It was birthed in blood during the American Revolution, when church and state were still married. Separation would come later. The Founding Fathers called only for separation – not divorce. Only in the later half of this century has the United States Supreme Court held that church and state should be legally divorced. As a result of having its religious roots cut out from under it, freedom currently suffers from an identity crisis."[471]

As Adams points out, America was born in a time before church and state were separated/divorced. The patriot preachers of the 17th and 18th centuries saw civil and religious liberty as virtually inseparable and believed that to lose one necessarily meant to lose the other. To suggest the possibility of their separation would have been foreign to them. In 1860, historian John Wingate Thornton wrote, "They invoked God in their civil assemblies, called upon their chosen teachers of religion for counsel from the Bible, and recognized its precepts as the law of their public conduct. The Fathers did not divorce politics and religion, but they denounced the separation as ungodly."[472]

Suffice it to say, their understanding of combining religion with politics/government was very different from today's understanding, and like a pendulum, the idea of integrating religion into politics has swung almost completely in the other direction. Today, it is considered out of place to mention God, let alone Jesus, in most public assemblies. As a result, for the majority of Americans including Christians, it is difficult to envision the world in which these United States were birthed. To the modern mind heavily influenced by "separation of church and state" mentality, it seems inconceivable that there could have ever been a time in America when Christian principles were embraced in politics/government and where preachers routinely preached about "politics" from their pulpits.

That said, it is important to note that even though it seems evident that the Founders intended to create a religious-friendly government that was neither hostile to religion nor supportive of any one particular expression, what is crystal clear is that they had no intention of creating a theocracy. In a way, that was the very thing from which they were fighting to free themselves, i.e., the King's Church of England. Nevertheless, in the 21st century, it is hard for many to fathom just how large a role the church played in the government of the colonies from the earliest days. For example, of the original thirteen colonies, all founded by different Christian denominations, nine had a state church.[473] As historian James Adams contends: "Seventeenth century Puritan New England saw the state as the church's enforcer. The church set the standards, and the state policed them."[474]

Even though religion's role in the individual state governments lessened to a degree in the decades after the war, the founder/framer generation did not believe that a lessened role should mean an insignificant one. They believed the "link" between civil and religious liberties was indivisible. To quote James Adams again:

"After the Revolution, the church-state roles gradually reversed, but the original relationship was not put asunder. The state now looked to the church to nurture the kind of Christians who would make good citizens. Mere morality would never produce "political prosperity." Religion was the taproot of the tree of liberty, … In the minds of this eighteenth-century people, religious and civil freedom were intertwined. Losing one meant losing the other. A rent in the political fabric, even a small rip, could eventually lead to the unraveling of all those religious and political rights their Puritan forefathers had won on the battlefields, under Cromwell. Their ancestors had left their comfortable homeland for the hallowed 'errand into the wilderness' in order to freely exercise those rights."[475]

The patriot preachers had been preaching this for years. For instance, Episcopalian, William Smith, pastor of Christ Church in Philadelphia, Pennsylvania wrote on June 23, 1775, "Religion and liberty must flourish or fall together in America. We pray that both may be perpetual."[476] John Witherspoon offered this prayer during the sermon he preached on May 17, 1776, just one month before he was elected to the Continental Congress: "God grant that in America true religion and civil liberty may be inseparable, and that the unjust attempts to destroy the one, may in the issue tend to the support and establishment of both."[477] When Samuel Langdon preached the annual election sermon to the General Court of New Hampshire on June 5, 1788, he warned, "And if our religion is given up, all the liberty we boast of will soon be gone."[478]

Obviously, many of the clergymen of the 18th century believed in a strong link between religion and liberty and therefore felt an obligation under God and to their congregations to address the subject of politics/government from their pulpits. This belief was so intense, that the patriot preachers were willing to risk all to defend it.

Yet, some argued then, as they do now, that politics and religion must be kept separate. Just seventeen years after the War for Independence was over, New York pastor, John M. Mason, preached a sermon in which he expressed his astonishment that there were actually people who believed it was wrong to mix politics and religion:

> "Yet religion has nothing to do with politics! Where did you learn this maxim? The bible is full of directions for your behavior as citizens. It is plain, pointed, awful in its injunctions on rulers and ruled as such: yet religion has nothing to do with politics. You are commanded 'in all your ways to acknowledge him, In every thing, by prayer and supplication, with thanksgiving, to let your requests be made known unto God, And whatsoever ye do, in word or deed, to do all in the name of the Lord Jesus." Yet religion has nothing to do with politics! Most astonishing! And is there any part of your conduct in which you are, or wish to be, without law to God, and not under the law of Christ? Can you persuade yourselves that political men and measures are to undergo no review in the judgment to come? That all the passion and violence, the fraud and falsehood, and corruption which pervade the systems of party, and burst out like a flood at the public elections, are to be blotted from the catalogue of unchristian deeds, because they are politics? Or that a minister of the gospel may see his people, in their political career, bid defiance to their God in breaking through every moral restraint, and keep a guiltless silence because religion has nothing to do with politics? I forbear to press the argument farther; observing only, that many of our difficulties and sins may be traced to this pernicious notion. Yes, if our religion had had more to do with our politics; if, in the pride of our citizenship,

we had not forgotten our Christianity: ... it would have been infinitely better for us at this day. ...

That religion has, in fact, nothing to do with the politics of many who profess it, is a melancholy truth. But that it has, of right, no concern with political transactions, is quite a new discovery. If such opinions, however, prevail, there is no longer any mystery in the character of those whose conduct, in political matters, violates every precept, and slanders every principle, of the religion of Christ. But what is politics? Is it not the science and the exercise of civil rights and civil duties? And what is religion? Is it not an obligation to the service of God, founded on his authority, and extending to all our relations personal and social?"[479]

John Mitchell Mason came by his convictions honestly. He was only six years old when the Declaration of Independence was signed, and by the time the war had ended, he had entered his teen years having grown up in the midst of America's great struggle for independence. He was intimately acquainted with the price of the struggle and when he preached about the Founders and their intentions, he knew well of that which he spoke. John Mitchell Mason was imminently familiar with the ministry of the Black Robed Regiment because his father, Dr. John Mason, was among its ranks. The senior Mason was a pastor in New York City when the war broke out and as such, was an outspoken critic of the British. Pastor Mason was a chaplain in the New York militia and later enlisted as a chaplain in the Continental Army. With young John Mitchell coming of age under his father's courageous example, a deep and abiding love of liberty was impressed upon him. John Mitchell went on to become a Presbyterian minister and spent his life ministering in New York. Like his father, he believed preachers should be engaged in the political as well as the spiritual life of the country. Even though he was not "technically" a member of the original Black Robed Regiment, John Mitchell was certainly a bona fide member of the second generation of the "Regiment" and was an early spiritual/political influencer of America.

The Black Regiment not only believed in mixing politics and religion; they believed that it was wrong not to do so. In their day, unlike today, the people believed that delivering sermons containing strong political content was a regular part of the preaching responsibilities of their pastors. In the preface to his 1860 book, *The Pulpit of the American Revolution*, John Wingate Thornton wrote:

> "The Fathers did not divorce politics and religion, but they denounced the separation as ungodly. Indeed, the clergy were generally consulted by the civil authorities; and not infrequently the suggestions from the pulpit, on election days and other special occasions, were enacted into laws. The state was developed out of the church. The annual election sermon bears witness that our Fathers ever began their civil year and its responsibilities with an appeal to heaven, and recognized Christian morality as the only basis of good laws."[480]

The accuracy of Thornton's claim is confirmed by the request the Massachusetts Provincial Congress made to the clergy of New England on November 23, 1775. The Massachusetts legislators encouraged their preachers to follow the suggestion of the Continental Congress and "make the question of the rights of the colonies and the oppressive conduct of the mother country a topic of the pulpit on weekdays."[481]

The Black Regiment not only enthusiastically complied with the Continental Congress' request on weekdays, but they obliged themselves to do so on Sundays as well. Historian Alice Baldwin categorized these messages as "politico-religious sermons" and noted that the Continental Congress recognized just how valuable they were in motivating the colonists to engage in the fight for liberty and independence.[482] Believing that the church and the state were essentially "attached at the hip," the Continental Congress and the provincial congresses of the individual colonies encouraged the setting aside of special days throughout the year for the colonists to fast, pray, and give thanks to God for His blessings and to request His aid.

Emphasizing the inseparability of church and state, Urian Oakes, pastor in Cambridge, Massachusetts and president of Harvard, wrote:

"According to the design of our founders and the frame of things laid by them, the interest of righteousness in the commonwealth and holiness in the Churches are inseparable ... To divide what God hath conjoined ... is folly in its exaltation. I look upon this as a little model of the glorious kingdom of Christ on earth. Christ reigns among us in the commonwealth as well as in the church and hath his glorious interest involved and wrapped up in the good of both societies respectfully."[483]

In the introduction to his three-part discourse, "Unlimited Submission And Non-Resistance To The Higher Powers," Jonathan Mayhew wrote,

"It is hoped that but few will think the subject of it [politics] an improper one to be discoursed on in the pulpit, under a notion that this is preaching politics, instead of Christ. However, to remove all prejudices of this sort, I beg it may be remembered that 'all Scripture is profitable for doctrine, for reproof, for correction, for instruction in righteousness.' Why, then, should not those parts of Scripture which relate to civil government be examined and explained from the desk [pulpit], as well as others? Obedience to the civil magistrate is a Christian duty; and if so, why should not the nature, grounds, and extent of it be considered in a Christian assembly? Besides, if it be said that it is out of character for a Christian minister to meddle with such a subject [politics], this censure will at last fall upon the holy apostles. They write upon it in their epistles to Christian churches; and surely it cannot be deemed either criminal or impertinent to attempt an explanation of their doctrine."[484]

Then as Mayhew began the main body of his sermon, he said:

"It is evident that the affairs of civil government may properly fall under a moral and religious consideration, at least so far forth as it relates to the general nature and end of magistracy, and to the grounds and extent of that submission which persons of a private character ought to yield to those who are vested with authority. ... It is the duty of Christian magistrates to inform themselves what it is which their religion teaches concerning the nature and design of their office. And it is equally the duty of all Christian people to inform themselves what it is which their religion teaches concerning that subjection which they owe to the higher powers."[485]

Even though it is undeniable that the patriot preachers saw no problem with mixing politics and religion as they preached the gospel, they certainly understood that the salvation of men and women's souls was of utmost importance. Consider the words of William Gordon in his message on December 15, 1774:

"The pulpit is devoted, in general, to more important purposes than the fate of kingdoms, or the civil rights of human nature, being intended to recover men from the slavery of sin and Satan, to point out their escape from future misery through faith in a crucified Jesus, and to assist them in their preparations for an eternal blessedness. But still there are special times and seasons when it may treat of politics."[486]

But in addition, for that generation of preachers, preaching the Gospel meant more than just telling someone how to find Christ and receive eternal life. They believed it also meant taking the Scriptures and instructing their congregations about growing in grace and moving forward in their salvation. They found this admonition in passages such as Hebrews 6:1:

"Therefore leaving the principles of the doctrine of Christ, let us go on unto perfection; not laying again the foundation of repentance from dead works, and of faith toward God."

To them, salvation not only produced a saved soul, it produced a saved lifestyle as well. They believed this saved lifestyle included good marriages, good parenting, good character, good work habits as well as full engagement in the civil, as well as the spiritual life of the society. But they also believed that a society where individuals had the religious liberty to worship and serve God as they understood Scripture was the best environment for this to take place. Thus, they saw a very clear link between external liberty (civil liberty) and internal liberty (religious liberty) and believed that these two kinds of liberty were mutually dependent on one another. For example, in his 1773 Massachusetts election sermon, patriot preacher Charles Turner of Duxbury, Massachusetts articulated his "blended" view of civil and religious liberty when he said:

"[W]hen the civil rights of a country receive a shock, it may justly render the ministers of God deeply thoughtful for the safety of sacred privileges – for religious liberty is so blended with civil, that if one falls it is not to be expected that the other will continue."[487]

William Smith, the Episcopalian pastor of Christ Church in Philadelphia, Pennsylvania, vocalized this same view in his 1775 sermon, "The Crisis of American Affairs":

"[W]e know that our civil and religious rights are linked together in one indissoluble bond, we neither have, nor seek to have, any interest separate from that of our country; nor can we advise a desertion of its cause. Religion and liberty must flourish or fall together in America. We pray that both may be perpetual."[488]

This bond was considered so indissoluble that historian Carl Bridenbaugh wrote that, in America, "Religion and politics could never again be distinguished one from another after the uproar created in the colonies by the Stamp Act."[489] On May 17, 1776, John Witherspoon, who just weeks after would help "push" the delegates of the Continental Congress to sign the Declaration, delivered a sermon at Princeton in which he contended that civil and religious liberty were inseparable and that an attack upon one was necessarily an attack upon the other:

"... our civil and religious liberties, and consequently in a great measure the temporal and eternal happiness of us and our posterity, depended on the issue [independence]. ... There is not a single instance in history in which civil liberty was lost, and religious liberty preserved entire. If therefore we yield up our temporal property, we at the same time deliver the conscience into bondage. ... God grant that in America true religion and civil liberty may be inseparable, and that the unjust attempts to destroy the one, may in the issue tend to the support and establishment of both."[490]

Even British preachers like Anglican Bishop, Thomas Newton, D.D., Bishop of Bristol, England, understood the strong link between civil and religious liberty. In 1754 he said:

"... the Scriptures, though often perverted to the purposes of tyranny, are yet, in their own nature, calculated to promote the civil as well as the religious liberties of mankind. True religion and virtue, and liberty, are more nearly related and more intimately connected with each other than people commonly consider."[491]

So, motivated by their belief that God's word spoke to every area of life, the Black Regiment considered it their duty to instruct their people about the nature and proper function of government, as they understood it. As far as they were concerned, no area was "off limits" to the pulpit. Therefore, they did not hesitate to give their opinions about who they thought deserved to be elected and those who did not. For example, consider again Samuel West's 1776 Massachusetts election sermon. In this excerpt, West spoke directly to his fellow preachers, challenging them to preach about government:

> "My reverend fathers and brethren in the ministry will remember that, according to our text, it is part of the work and business of a gospel minister to teach his hearers the duty they owe to magistrates. Let us, then, endeavor to explain the nature of their duty faithfully, and show them the difference between liberty and licentiousness; and, while we are animating them to oppose tyranny and arbitrary power, let us inculcate upon them the duty of yielding due obedience to lawful authority. In order to the right and faithful discharge of this part of our ministry, it is necessary that we should thoroughly study the law of nature, the rights of mankind, and the reciprocal duties of governors and governed. By this means we shall be able to guard them against the extremes of slavish submission to tyrants on one hand, and of sedition and licentiousness on the other."[492]

Jonathan Edwards, Jr., pastor of the White Haven Church in New Haven, Connecticut and son of the famous Great Awakening preacher, Jonathan Edwards, preached the following to his fellow preachers in his 1794 Connecticut election sermon:

"We who are employed in the work of the ministry are deeply interested in this subject [government]. We are interested in the prosperity of the state, and are peculiarly interested in this means of prosperity on which I have been insisting. It is our business to study and teach Christianity, and thus to promote the political good of the state, as well as the spiritual good of the souls of our hearers. This is a noble employment, to fidelity and zeal in which, not only the motives of religion call us, but even those of patriotism. Therefore if we have any love to religion and the souls of men; nay if we have any public spirit and love to our country, let us diligently study the evidences, the nature, the doctrines and duties of Christianity, and inculcate them with all plainness, assiduity and perseverance, giving line upon line and precept upon precept."[493]

On May 8, 1800, John Smalley, student of Rev. Ezra Stiles and pastor in Farmington (New Britain), Connecticut, preached that year's Connecticut election sermon entitled, "On The Evils Of A Weak Government." Though non-committal early on concerning the colonies' declaring independence from Great Britain, Smalley eventually became an outspoken proponent of the struggle and encouraged his fellow preachers and believers to stand against British tyranny. In this sermon, he encouraged preachers to "declare all the counsel of God," and rebuked those who were fearful to do so:

"The ministers of the gospel, are thought to have no concern with the temporal happiness of mankind: doubtless, the good way for them, whether the old way or not, is to confine themselves very much to their spiritual vocation. Doubtless their principal business is, to save the souls of those who hear them. But in order to [do] this … Ministers must not 'shun to declare all the counsel of God,' both to rulers and subjects, if they would be 'pure from the blood of all men.' In a word, they must do what in them lies to make all their hearers good Christians; for without this they can never get them to heaven; and they need do no more, to make them peaceable and orderly members of society on earth."[494]

"ELECTION" AND OTHER "POLITICAL" SERMONS

The patriot preachers seized every opportunity to speak out publically and to advocate for a distinctly republican form of government. Though the definition of republicanism changes somewhat in specifics from writer to writer, generally, most scholars agree that republicanism emphasizes individual sovereignty and civic virtue supported by the general concept of the "rule of law." As many of the colonists' saw it, under a republican form of government, individual rights would not be subject to the whims of a sometimes-fickle king, but would instead be constrained by the limits of the law – codified in written constitutions.

The patriot preachers were driven to proclaim these concepts every time they had a chance. In addition to preaching them from their pulpits on Sundays, they also pontificated on them during the numerous special occasions that occurred throughout the year.

For example, one of these was the Thursday or Fifth Day Lecture which occurred each year in Boston. The Lecture was established in 1633 by the Massachusetts preacher John Cotton as a special occasion for guest preachers to expound on the biblical principles of government. This annual event was considered so vital and was so popular that it continued to be observed until the middle of the nineteenth century.[495] Additionally, special days of thanksgiving, fasting, and prayer were regularly called by governors of the individual colonies as well as by the Continental Congress, providing yet another opportunity for the patriot preachers to preach politics. While this practice may seem odd to us today, it was commonplace in the 17th and 18th centuries. Hardly a holiday passed without the Black Regiment taking the opportunity to educate the people.

These preachers were also regularly invited to speak to military units in sermons appropriately called "Artillery Sermons." These times afforded them a prime opportunity to provide their biblical perspective on the principles of liberty, government, and the responsibility to defend the rights of men against tyranny. Gatherings commemorating historic moments like the Boston Massacre, the battles of Lexington and Concord, the Fourth of July, the end of the war, the deaths of George Washington and other significant Founders, etc. were all employed for this purpose.

But of all the opportunities available for preaching "political theology," none was more important to the patriot preachers than the annual Election Sermon. These sermons were delivered to the lawmakers of the colonies/states after the annual elections were completed as they were preparing to begin their new legislative year. The entire governing body of the colony/state, including the governor, lieutenant governor, and the elected members of the legislature would be invited, along with local citizens, to listen to a leading local preacher whose task was to remind the legislators of what God required of government and that they would someday give an account to Him for the way they governed in the coming legislative year. In addition to sometimes being published in the newspapers, these important sermons were commonly immortalized by being published by the legislature and then distributed throughout the area in pamphlet form.

The tradition of the election sermon can be traced all of the way back to the 1630s with the Connecticut election sermon of Rev. Thomas Hooker and the Massachusetts election sermon of Rev. Nathaniel Ward in 1641.[496] The delivery of the election sermon continued as a major part of the beginning of the legislative year in the colonies/states for decades. For example, Massachusetts observed the election sermon for some 250 years and Connecticut did so for approximately 150 years. As time passed, more and more of the colonies/states began the practice with such states as Vermont in 1778 and New Hampshire in 1784.[497] In 1860, historian John Thornton said this about the election sermon:

> "The annual 'Election Sermon,' a perpetual memorial, continued down through the generations from century to century, still bears witness that our fathers ever began their civil year and its responsibilities with an appeal to Heaven, and recognized Christian morality as the only basis of good laws."[498]

RELIGION IS CRITICAL TO LIBERTY AND GOOD GOVERNMENT

The Founders believed religion, Protestant Christianity specifically, was essential to ensuring the liberty and success of a free society. Strongly convinced of this, the patriot preachers taught that government and religion were friends. As far as they were concerned, whatever promoted God's kingdom also promoted individual liberty. John Witherspoon emphasized this in his sermon on May 17, 1776:

> "That he is the best friend to American liberty, who is most sincere and active in promoting true and undefiled religion, and who sets himself with the greatest firmness to bear down profanity and immorality of every kind. Whoever is an avowed enemy to God, I scruple not to call him an enemy to his country."[499]

According to Witherspoon, if men would govern themselves and "bear down profanity and immorality of every kind," they would help to create a more virtuous society and thus create an environment where liberty could flourish. To him and many leaders of that era, religion was indispensable to that end.

Just ten days after Witherspoon preached the above message, Phillips Payson, pastor in Chelsea, Massachusetts, addressed this same subject in his Massachusetts election sermon:

"I must not forget to mention religion, both in rulers and people, as of the highest importance to the public. ... The importance of religion to civil society and government is great indeed, as it keeps alive the best sense of moral obligation, a matter of such extensive utility, especially in respect to an oath, which is one of the principal instruments of government. The fear and reverence of God, and the terrors of eternity, are the most powerful restraints upon the minds of men; and hence it is of special importance in a free government, ... For this, and other reasons, the thoughtful and wise among us trust that our civil fathers, from a regard to gospel worship and the constitution of these churches, will carefully preserve them, and at all times guard against every innovation that might tend to overset the public worship of God, ... Let the restraints of religion once be broken down ... and we might well defy all human wisdom and power to support and preserve order and government in the state."[500]

Two days later, Samuel West preached the same theme to the Massachusetts lawmakers:

"And as nothing tends like religion and the fear of God to make men good members of the commonwealth, it is the duty of magistrates to become the patrons and promoters of religion and piety, and to make suitable laws for the maintaining public worship, and decently supporting the teachers of religion. Such laws, I apprehend, are absolutely necessary for the well being of civil society. Such laws may be made, consistent with all that liberty of conscience which every good member of society ought to be possessed of;"[501]

As the war raged on, the patriot preachers continued to stress this same message. This is what Simeon Howard, pastor of the West Church in Boston, preached in that year's election sermon on May 31, 1780:

"… it is of great importance to their happiness that religion and virtue generally prevail among a people; and in order to this, government should use its influence to promote them. Rulers should encourage them, not only by their example, but by their authority; and the people should invest them with power to do this, so far as is consistent with the sacred and inalienable rights of conscience, … Without such care in government, there is danger that the people will forget the God that is above, and abandon themselves to vice; or, to say the least, impiety and vice are much less likely to become general where such care is taken than where it is not. Taking this care of religion is so plain and important a duty, that the government which should wholly neglect it would not only act a very unwise and imprudent part with respect to themselves, but be guilty of base ingratitude and a daring affront to Heaven."[502]

In 1783 as the war was coming to a close, Ezra Stiles, the president of Yale, emphasized to the Connecticut General Assembly that holiness, not just secular happiness, was the "true" end of all government:

"Give us, gentlemen, the decided assurance that you are friends of the churches, and that you are the friends of the pastors, who have certainly in this trying warfare approved themselves the friends of liberty and government. … the morals of Christianity are excellent. It enjoins obedience to magistracy, justice, harmony, and benevolence among fellow citizens; and, what is more, it points out immortality to man. … That our system of dominion and civil polity would be imperfect without the true religion; or that from the diffusion of virtue among the people of any community would arise their greatest secular happiness: which will terminate in this conclusion, that holiness ought to be the end of all civil government. ... We err much if we think the only or chief end of civil government is secular happiness."[503]

When the war was over and people of the states were creating the United States, the patriot preachers continued to emphasize the importance of religion. They reminded the people that, just as they had needed the Lord's assistance to win the war, they would equally need His intervention to establish good government and a moral society. For example, on June 3, 1784, on the occasion of the completion of the New Hampshire state constitution, Samuel McClintock preached the following to that state's lawmakers:

"As religion has a manifest tendency to promote the temporal as well as eternal interests of mankind, it is the duty of rulers to give all that countenance and support to religion that is consistent with liberty of conscience. ... The religion of Christ, where it has its proper influence on the hearts and lives of men, will not fail to make the best rulers and the best subjects."[504]

On May 12, 1785, Samuel Wales, Congregational pastor in Connecticut and professor of divinity at Yale, declared to the General Assembly of Connecticut that, "The practice of religion must therefore be considered as absolutely essential to the best state of public prosperity,"[505]

The patriot preachers also feared the calamities that would come upon their society if the people ever strayed from the essentials of Christianity. Joseph Lathrop, pastor of the Congregational Church in West Springfield, Massachusetts, warned:

"Political liberty depends on national virtue. Prevailing vice sooner or later introduces national slavery. Under almost any form of government a virtuous people will be free and happy. But a people sunk in corruption must be wretched. Their government, however liberal in its principles, will be severe in its administration, because they can subsist under no other."[506]

Samuel Langdon, president of Harvard and pastor of the Congregational Church in Hampton Falls, New Hampshire, warned in his 1788 election sermon:

"If you neglect or renounce that religion taught and commanded in the Holy Scriptures, think no more of freedom, peace, and happiness; the judgments of heaven will pursue you. Religion is not a vain thing for you because it is your life: ... And if our religion is given up, all the liberty we boast of will soon be gone;"[507]

George Washington declared February 19, 1795 as a day of thanksgiving and prayer for the entire country. On that day, Bishop James Madison, Episcopal Bishop and president of the College of William and Mary, preached the following:

"[V]irtue is the vital principle of a republic, ... remember, that in the same proportion as irreligion advances, virtue retires; ... Nothing, then, can be a greater stimulus to a virtuous government, to adopt the most energetic measures, that religion and every species of virtue may be encouraged:"[508]

ESTABLISHING OR ENCOURAGING RELIGION?

Believing as they did that civil and religious liberties were strongly linked together, the patriot preachers believed that government should do more than simply "tolerate" religion – some believed government had an *obligation* to encourage it and even participate in it. Though by today's standards, they would probably be accused of trying to create a theocracy, in their day, they were able to walk a fine line between *supporting* and *requiring* religion in civic life. For example, consider the preaching of Samuel Stillman, pastor of the First Baptist Church of Boston and delegate to the 1787 Constitutional Convention. In his May 29, 1779 sermon preached before the Supreme Court of Massachusetts, he juxtaposed the government's legal responsibility to *encourage* religion against its illegal attempt to *establish* religion. In doing so, he illustrated the delicate and tenuous balance of keeping the two "kingdoms" from overstepping their bounds and emphasized that government's only real function in religion was to be a *loose* support. In this necessary read, Stillman declared:

> "It may be said, that religion is of importance to the good of civil society; therefore the magistrate ought to encourage it under this idea. ... As a *magistrate,* he should be as a nursing father to the church of Christ, by protecting all the peaceable members of it from injury on account of religion; and by securing to them the uninterrupted enjoyment of equal religious liberty. The authority by which he acts he derives alike from *all the people;* consequently he should exercise that authority *equally* for the benefit of *all,* without any respect to their different religious principles. They have an undoubted right to demand it. ... On the other hand, if the magistrate destroys the equality of the subjects of the state on account of religion, he violates a fundamental principle of a free government, establishes separate interests in it, and lays a foundation for disaffection to rulers and endless quarrels among the people.
>
> Happy are the inhabitants of that commonwealth ... in which all *are protected* but none *established.* Permit me, on this occasion, to introduce the words of the Rev.

Dr. Chauncey, whose age and experience add weight to his sentiments. 'We are in principle against all civil establishments in religion. We desire not, and suppose we have no right to desire, the interposition of the state to establish our sentiments in religion, or the manner in which we would express them. It does not, indeed, appear to us, that God has entrusted the state with a right to make religious establishments.' ... To which I take the liberty to add the following passage of a very ingenious author: 'The moment any religion becomes national, or established, its purity must certainly be lost, because it is impossible to keep it unconnected with men's interests; and if connected, it must inevitably be perverted by them.'

Upon the whole, I think it is a plain as well as a very important truth, that the *Church of Christ* and a *commonwealth are essentially different.* The one is a *religious* society, of which Christ is the sole head, and which he gathers out of the world, in common, by the dispensation of his gospel, governs by his laws in all matters of religion, a complete code of which we have in the sacred Scriptures; and preserves it by his power.

The other is a *civil* society—originating with the people, and designed to promote their *temporal interests*—which is governed by men, whose authority is derived from their fellow-citizens, and confined to the affairs of this world.

In this view of the matter, the line appears to me to be fairly drawn between *the things that belong to Caesar* and *the things* that belong to God."[509]

By insisting that religion be *encouraged* while not being *established*, they assigned to their government a challenging task. Legislators of that day generally embraced these ideas and, rather than shying away from religion, generally saw the support of religion as a part of their duty to the community. It is at this point where many today make a huge error – they confuse *encouraging* religion with *establishing* it.

Although encouragement and establishment may seem similar, in truth, they are actually worlds apart. Understanding this, the patriot preachers and the Founders wanted to restrict government from *imposing* religion while not *impeding* it. They certainly did not want the same situation in America that existed in Great Britain with the Church of England. There, the king was not only the head of the government, but was also the head of the church and could use his authority to force the citizens to embrace his religious beliefs. This was the very situation the patriot preachers fought a war to prevent!

To guard against repeating this fatal error, the Framers of the Constitution placed a limit on the federal government with the First Amendment to the Constitution by restricting *Congress* from establishing a state religion/church and from prohibiting the free exercise of religion. (Interestingly, this restriction only applied to the federal congress – not the state governments. This remained the case until federal courts created the "Incorporation Doctrine" out of thin air. Now the restrictions previously placed exclusively on Congress are being forced upon the state governments – a "doctrine" many of the Framers, no doubt, would reject.)

Unlike today, people of that time understood the phrase "establishment of religion" to be a clear reference to the government-established Church of England. They understood that men's freedom to publicly practice their religion was an unalienable right given them by God – a right that government had no power to restrict or to seize. They did not believe government *allowed* them to practice their religious beliefs publicly; they believed they received that right from God. But equally important, they did not see public expression of religion to be an *establishment* of religion as many do today. The Founders would be astonished and completely bewildered when today's federal courts interpret "establishment of religion" to mean:

- Reading the Bible aloud at school

- Praying at a school function

- Displaying the Ten Commandments on public property

- Erecting a nativity scene on public property

- Singing Christmas carols at school

As we have seen, the thirteen colonies were heavily Christian and almost exclusively Protestant. They could not have imagined the impact the coming European and eventual worldwide immigration would have on the philosophical/religious makeup of the United States. They would not have believed that the general population could experience such moral decline as it has over the decades; resulting in the pluralistic society we have today. Consider the fact that in 1775, of the roughly 2.5 million people in America, it is estimated that there were likely only 2,000 Jewish (less than 1%) in the population.[510] In addition, it is widely held that Catholics in the 1790 census numbered no more than 30,000.[511] The majority of the remaining population considered themselves as Protestant Christians. In our day, it is practically impossible to conceive of just how thoroughly "Christian" the colonies were. This, of course, had a huge impact on how the colonists viewed religion and government.

So even though they did not want a federally *established* religion, they also believed the "new" federal government had no authority to limit the unalienable religious rights of its citizens to worship God publicly. They believed the citizens of the individual states could make their own laws concerning religious expression.

Obviously, this is very different from our understanding today. Outlawing Bible reading, prayer, Christmas carols, nativity scenes, and Ten Commandments displays in public buildings would be anathema to most 18th century Americans. Though arguments against the above activities may have some merit, I am convinced that most reasonable people, given the proper information and time to think it through, would agree that a nativity scene on the courthouse lawn does not equal "establishing" a state church/ religion that citizens are forced to endorse or join. Instead, most reasonable people understand that when these activities are *allowed* on public property, government is simply recognizing the right of the citizens to freely express the generally held religious/ philosophical ideas that reflect the beliefs of the majority of those in that community. Conversely, in a community where a secular majority exists that might disallow the erection of a nativity scene on their local courthouse lawn, I would personally respect that decision as well. Although I might not agree with the decision, I would not force my views on the majority – although I might move to another community.

The Founders' intent was clear – religion needed to be protected from the federal government, the federal government did not need to be protected from religion. They endeavored to foster a healthy intercourse *between* government and religion where religion would be encouraged while not established.

WHAT THEY ACTUALLY PREACHED IN
THOSE ELECTION SERMONS

So what subjects did the patriot preachers address when they preached those election sermons? Although space will not permit a thorough answer to this question (see author's handbook: *Election Sermons of the Black Robed Regiment*), a quick listing of some of the topics they covered gives one a pretty good idea. Consider these points often superbly made in these sermons:

- Human government was instituted by God.
- Man's sinful nature makes government necessary.
- Government is subordinate to the laws of God.

- Principles of good government are found in Scripture.
- The purpose of government is the public good.
- The power of government lies with the people.
- Government must act according to the law.
- What despotic government is and how it must be resisted.
- The defense of liberty is God's will.

Just imagine the impact it would have on our government today if those who govern were exposed to biblically sound sermons about the purpose and accountability of government. Believing that government was as much an institution of God as the family and the church, the Black Regiment did not hesitate to preach on the biblical definition and grounds of good government. How we could use this type of preaching today.

Chapter 14

THEY WERE NOT REBELS & ANARCHISTS

"A continued submission to violence is no tenet of our church."[512]

This is how patriot Pastor William Smith, Episcopalian pastor in Philadelphia, PA, emphatically stated the position of many colonists on June 23, 1775. Having warned King George that he must govern lawfully if he intended to retain the cooperation of the colonies, they felt they had no other option but to resist the King's clear intention to not only ignore the colonists' pleas, but to double down on his oppressive rule as well.

Having been taught by their pastors to honor and submit to those who ruled over them, the colonists were hesitant to enter into conflict. They simply would not take up arms hastily, but labored over the issue for more than ten years – all the while doing everything within their power to avoid bloodshed. But, they had also been taught that a tyrannical government either had to be *righted* or *replaced*. Elizur Goodrich, pastor of the Congregational Church in Durham, Connecticut, a graduate of Yale and a close friend of Rev. Ezra Stiles, president of Yale, articulated this very message before the Connecticut General Assembly:

"Honor and respect are due to rulers: ... When a constitutional government is converted into tyranny, and the laws, rights and properties of a free people are openly invaded, there ought not to be the least doubt but that a remedy ... is provided in the laws of God and reason, for their preservation; nor ought resistance in such case to be called rebellion."[513]

These are hardly the words of a wild-eyed rebel bent on anarchy. Rather, they are the well-reasoned arguments of a law-abiding individual – arguments derived from the intertwining of Whig political philosophy and republicanism. The clear intention of the Americans was to execute an honorable and lawful separation from Great Britain. John Adams, who was greatly influenced by the sermons of the Black Robed Regiment and regularly attended the Boston church of Black Regiment preacher Samuel Cooper, made this clear on February 20, 1775 when he defended the Americans' right to resist the British through "lawful opposition":

> "We are not exciting rebellion. Opposition, nay, open, avowed resistance by arms against usurpation and lawless violence, is not rebellion by the law of God or the land. Resistance to lawful authority makes rebellion."[514]

Benjamin Franklin, also greatly influenced by Pastor Cooper by his regular correspondence with him, shared these same sentiments. While being questioned by the British House of Commons in 1766, Franklin was asked what the Americans' temper towards Great Britain was before 1763. Franklin responded, "The best in the world. They submitted willingly to the government of the crown, and paid, in all their courts, obedience to acts of Parliament. ... They had not only a respect, but an affection for Great Britain,"[515] He was then asked about their present temper to which he answered, "O, very much altered."[516] Just ten short years later, he and fifty-five other patriots skillfully articulated in their "Declaration of Independence" the great effort they had put forth to "fix" things with Great Britain and King George:

"In every stage of these Oppressions We have Petitioned for Redress in the most humble terms: ... We have appealed to their native justice and magnanimity, and we have conjured them by the ties of our common kindred to disavow these usurpations, ... They too have been deaf to the voice of justice and of consanguinity."[517]

With all of their efforts having failed, there was nothing left for the Founders to do but separate – that is, if they wanted to be free. They, of course, understood that this would most probably mean war, but even so, they vowed to hold the British as "enemies in war and in peace friends."

NO ANARCHY HERE

Writing in the midst of the war, Francis Hopkinson, signer of the Declaration of Independence, gave a simple, but effective definition of the meaning of a "true" rebellion:

"But it has often been said, that America is in a state of rebellion. Tell me, therefore, what is Rebellion? It is when a great number of people, headed by one or more factious leaders, aim at deposing their lawful prince without any just cause of complaint in order to place another on his throne. Is this the case of the Americans? Far otherwise. They have repeatedly declared, with the most solemn protestations, that they were ready to support, with their lives and fortunes, the present king of Great Britain, ... and only requested, in return the enjoyment of those rights, which the British constitution confirms to all his subjects; and without which, the boasted freedom of that constitution is but a solemn mockery and an empty name."[518]

In 1821, obviously long after the war, John Quincy Adams debunked the theory that the Founders were anarchists:

"[T]here was <u>no</u> anarchy.... [T]he people of the North American union and of its constituent states were associated bodies of civilized men and Christians in a state of nature but not of anarchy. They were bound by the laws of God (which they all) and by the laws of the Gospel (which they nearly all) acknowledged as the rules of their conduct."[519]

Far from being rebels and anarchists, the founding generation was executing a *lawful separation* from a tyrannical government. They did not board ships and sail to England to usurp the throne, they *legally* sought the freedom to live and govern the way they thought best – while allowing the British to do the same. Deeply intellectual/spiritual individuals and having thought it through completely, the Founders/Framers were well aware of the gravity of their actions and fully anticipated and embraced the potentially disastrous consequences of separating from England. As was mentioned earlier, Benjamin Franklin had warned his fellow delegates that they could all very well be hanged for treason for their actions.

Franklin's statement reflects the intense solemnity with which these men took their stand for liberty. Historian John Thornton said of the Founders/Framers, "His Majesty called them 'rebels,' and they soon declared and proved themselves to be neither subjects nor rebels, but a free people."[520]

On July 5, 1802, while speaking at the twenty-sixth anniversary of the signing of the Declaration of Independence, William Emerson, pastor of the First Church in Boston, told his Boston audience:

"Here, then, you find the principles, which produced the event, we this day commemorate. They were the principles of common law and of eternal justice. They were the principles of men, who sought not to subvert the government, under which they lived, but to save it from degeneracy; not to create new rights, but to preserve inviolate such, as they had ever possessed, … Such was the American Revolution. It arose not on a sudden, but from the successless petitions and remonstrance of ten long years. It was a revolution, not of choice, but of necessity."[521]

As we have seen, the colonists had shown an amazing amount of restraint and willingness to go the second mile in attempting to work out a compromise with Great Britain – all in the face of repeated insults and abuses. So to accuse them of reckless rebellion stretches credulity beyond the breaking point. This fact was articulately expressed in a November 9, 1772 article in the *Boston Gazette* written by "Mr. Humanity," whom most believed to be a preacher:

> "[It is] my firm opinion that the Americans would be justified in the sight of Heaven and before all nations of mankind, in forming an independent government of their own, and cutting off every son of Adam that dared to oppose them by force – Great Britain has robbed them, sent her armies to enslave them, and totally cancelled all obligations to continue their connection with her another day …"[522]

No doubt, the patriot pastor in Weston, Connecticut, Samuel Sherwood, spoke for most in the Black Regiment when he said:

> "I am a firm friend to good order and regularity; … That authority and government be supported and maintained so as to promote the good of society, the end for which it was instituted; perfectly consistent with which, a people may keep a watchful eye over their liberties, and cautiously guard against oppression and tyranny, which I detest and abhor, and solemnly abjure."[523]

Samuel Langdon, patriot preacher and president of Harvard, expressed the same sentiments as those of Sherwood when he preached in his 1775 election sermon:

"On your wisdom, religion, and public spirit, honored gentlemen, we depend, to determine what may be done as to the important matter of reviving the form of government, and settling all the necessary affairs relating to it in the present critical state of things, that we may again have law and justice, and avoid the danger of anarchy and confusion."[524]

Responding to the accusation that Americans were nothing more than rebels, Pastor John Cleaveland wrote articles that were published in the April 18, 25, 1775 issues of the Massachusetts *Essex Gazette*. The articles said in part:

"To the Inhabitants of New England, Greeting. Men, Brethren and Fathers: Is the time come, the fatal era commenced, for you to be deemed rebels, by the Parliament of Great Britain? Rebels! Wherein? Why, for asserting that the rights of men, the rights of Englishmen belong to us. ... We are, my brethren, in a good cause; and if God be for us, we need not fear what man can do."[525]

In that same year, Moses Mather made an almost identical statement in a sermon when he said, "And are the Americans chargeable with treason and rebellion, for yielding to the irresistible impulses of self-preservation and acting under and in pursuance of the royal license and authority of their king?"[526] Further contrasting the difference between a people in rebellion and a people fighting for their God-given rights, pastor Samuel West said:

"They [British] can have no right any longer to style us rebels; for rebellion implies a particular faction risen up in opposition to lawful authority, ... But when war is declared against a whole community without distinction, and the property of each party is declared to be seizable, this, if anything can be, is treating us as an independent state."[527]

THE QUESTION THEY HAD TO ANSWER: "WHEN IT IS RIGHT TO OVERTHROW A GOVERNMENT?"

Long before the war began, Pastor Jonathan Mayhew understood that the God-given, unalienable rights of Americans were in jeopardy. He knew that the taxes levied without the colonists' consent and intolerable acts like the Stamp Act were only symptoms of a greater, deeper problem – an overbearing government. Mayhew would argue that it was a tyrannical government that had crossed the Atlantic and was bent on enlarging its power at the expense of the colonists' rights. For example, when Great Britain repealed the Stamp Act on March 18, 1766, they had done so mostly because of the lost income from diminished trade caused by colonial boycotts of British goods and the threat of increased violence – not because they believed it was the right thing to do. Mayhew's suspicions were confirmed when Parliament, while in the process of repealing the Stamp Act, passed the Declaratory Act. This act declared that Parliament had the same authority in the American colonies as it did in England and could pass any laws it chose – laws as equally binding on the colonists as they were on those living in England. Actions like these made the Americans realize that the time for reasonable discourse was running out. So, on May 23, 1766, just weeks after the repeal of the Stamp Act, Mayhew made it clear that the real point of contention between the Americans and the British was the abuse of the colonists' natural rights by the British:

> "The colonists are men, and need not be afraid to assert the natural rights of men; they are British subjects, and may justly claim the common rights, and all the privileges of such, with plainness and freedom. ... It shall be taken for granted that this natural right is declared, affirmed, and secured to us, as we are British subjects, by Magna

Carta; all acts contrary to Which are said to be *ipso facto,* null and void:"[528]

Convinced that the British government's acts against the colonies were "illegitimate," the patriot preachers taught and preached that it was the duty of Christians to rise up and replace such a government. In 1918, Alice Baldwin explained just how these preachers defined "proper" law and the type of government that deserved the submission of the people:

> "Probably the most fundamental principle of the American constitutional system is the principle that no one is bound to obey an unconstitutional act. ... No single idea was more fully stressed, no principle more often repeated, through the first sixty years of the eighteenth century, than that governments must obey law and that he who resisted one in authority who was violating that law was not himself a rebel but a protector of law."[529]

In general, the argument being advanced by the patriot preachers was this: God first gave rights to the people and the people, by consent, could enter into a covenant and form a government to protect and administer those rights. In this covenant, the same laws that bound the people also bound the government. But they also believed that if government ever violated its covenant with the people, it forfeited its right to govern and therefore invalidated itself. Moses Mather articulated this principle in simple terms in his sermon to his Hartford, Connecticut audience in 1775:

> "The question is not whether the king is to be obeyed or not; for the Americans, have ever recognized his authority as their rightful sovereign, and liege lord; have ever been ready, with their lives and fortunes, to support his crown and government, according to the constitutions of the nation, ... But the question is, whether the parliament of Great Britain hath power over the persons and

properties of the Americans, to bind the one, and dispose of the other at their pleasure? ... to induce and compel a servile submission; is treason against the kingdom, of the deepest dye, and blackest complexion: whereby the constitution, that firm foundation of the nation's peace, and pillar of government that supports the throne, is shaken to its very basis; the kingdom rent, and divided against itself; and those sons of thunder that should be the protectors of its rights, are become its destroyers."[530]

Twenty-seven years later as he looked back to the time of the war, William Emerson made the same argument that Mather had made to justify the war:

"Was it, then, right in the colonies to resist the parliament, and wrong to resist the king? No. For the king had joined the latter to oppress the former, and thus became, instead of the righteous ruler, the tyrant, of this country, to whom allegiance was no longer due. ... Americans called themselves free, because they were governed by laws originating in fixed principles, and not in the caprice of arbitrary will. They held, that the ruler was equally obliged to construct his laws in consonance with the spirit of the constitution, as were the people to obey them when enacted; and that a departure from duty on his part virtually absolved them from allegiance. ... Who is the rebel against law and order, the legislator ordaining, or the citizen resisting, unconstitutional measures?"[531]

So, according to the Black Regiment, was there ever a time when it was acceptable to resist government and not be considered in rebellion? Joseph Lathrop, patriot pastor of the Congregational Church in West Springfield, Massachusetts, provided an emphatic answer to that question:

THEY WERE NOT REBELS & ANARCHISTS

"Perhaps it will be asked, 'Is there no case in which a people may resist government?' Yes, there is one such case; and that is, when rulers usurp a power oppressive to the people, and continue to support it by military force in contempt of every respectful remonstrance. In this case the body of the people have a natural right to unite their strength for the restoration of their own constitutional government."[532]

As far as the Black Regiment was concerned, it was possible for a king to "un-king" himself and for a seated government to "unseat" itself by violating its rightful authority. Jonathan Mayhew had made this point abundantly clear some twenty-six years before the war broke out:

"... the Parliament which first opposed King Charles's measures, and at length took up arms against him, were not guilty of rebellion, ... for he had, in fact, un-kinged himself long before, and had forfeited his title to the allegiance of the people. ... Cromwell and his adherents were not, properly speaking, guilty of rebellion, because he whom they be headed [King Charles] was not, properly speaking, their king, but a lawless tyrant; ... Common tyrants and public oppressors are not entitled to obedience from their subjects by virtue of anything here laid down by the inspired apostle [Apostle Paul]. ... For a nation thus abused to arise unanimously and resist their prince, even to the dethroning him, is not criminal, but a reasonable way of vindicating their liberties and just rights: it is making use of the means, and the only means, which God has put into their power for mutual and self defense. And it would be highly criminal in them not to make use of this means. It would be stupid tameness and unaccountable folly for whole nations to suffer one unreasonable, ambitious, and cruel man to wanton and riot in their misery."[533]

In the event that the government "unseated" itself or the king "un-kinged" himself, the patriot preachers believed that this government should be viewed as tyrannous. Since they believed God hated tyranny, they preached that the people not only had the right, but the responsibility to resist that government at all costs. This is how Samuel Langdon articulated this principle: "If the great servants of the public forget their duty, betray their trust, and sell their country, or make war against the most valuable rights and privileges of the people, reason and justice require that they should be discarded, and others appointed in their room, without any regard to formal resignations of their forfeited power."[534] Therefore, having concluded that King George and the British government had indeed "un-kinged" and "unseated" themselves, the pastors unashamedly declared that it was time to throw off British tyranny and follow the course Jefferson and the others outlined in the Declaration of Independence:

> "… when a long train of abuses and usurpations, pursuing invariably the same object evinces a design to reduce them under absolute despotism, it is their right, it is their duty, to throw off such government, and to provide new guards for their future security."

Four years before the Declaration had specified the citizens' "right and duty" to throw off a tyrannical government, John Allen had preached that message in his sermon in the Second Baptist Church, Boston. The sermon was so powerful and made such an impact on the colonists that it was reprinted seven times, making it the sixth most popular sermon pamphlet published in pre-revolution America. In it, Allen proclaimed:

> "For that king is not worthy to reign, that does not make the rights of his people the rule of his actions: Knowing this, that he receives all his power, and majesty, from them; and how can he think that he has any right to rule over them, unless he rules in their hearts by inviolable

maintaining their rights? For as the ministers of the gospel (when in their proper place) are no otherwise than the people's servants; so the king is no more than the servant of the people: And when at any time, he is unfaithful, as the people's servant, they have a right to say to him, 'give an account of thy stewardship, that thou mayest be no longer steward.' ... That it is no rebellion to oppose any king, ministry, or governor, that destroys by any violence or authority whatever, the rights of the people. Shall a man be deemed a rebel that supports his own rights? It is the first law of nature, and he must be a rebel to God, to the laws of nature, and his own conscience, who will not do it. ... It is no more rebellion, than it is to breathe. ... So that if the king of England is not happy let him thank himself for it: It is not his people's fault—it is his own. For that king is not worthy to reign, that does not make the *rights* of his people the rule of his actions:"[535]

In closing this chapter, I feel it is important to reemphasize that the patriot preachers were not wild rebels and anarchists who wanted war – they were well-reasoned men who wanted peace and a friendly relationship with Great Britain. This sentiment was clearly articulated by William Gordon as he preached a sermon observing the first anniversary of the signing of the Declaration of Independence. In the sermon, he said, "May the spirit of wisdom return speedily to the British councils, that so Britain may soon recover our friendship and secure our connection by commercial treaties, ere it is too late, and her ruin is sealed!"[536]

* For more information on how the Black Regiment justified "righteous resistance" to the British Crown, two sermons are a must read:

- Jonathan Mayhew's three-part discourse, "Discourse Concerning Unlimited Submission And Non-Resistance To The Higher Powers"

- Samuel West's sermon, "Discourse VI, Election Sermon"

These two sermons can be found in the companion booklet to this book entitled, *The Sermons of the Black Robe* and can be purchased from our online bookstore at www.resonance.com.

Chapter 15

"PREACHING POLITICS IN THE 21ST CENTURY"

"It is sometimes said that ministers must not preach politics. ... They would have to toe hop, and skip, and jump through two-thirds of the Bible if they did not, for there is not another book on the face of God's earth that is so full of commerce and business and government, and the relations between the governing and the governed, as this same Bible. ... And yet, in these later days, we have these ineffable men who tell us that we must not preach in the pulpit about public affairs, and who would scourge out of the sanctuary a full half of the Bible. Infidels!"[537]

This is how Henry Beecher Ward, the Presbyterian abolitionist and pastor of the Congregational Church in Brooklyn, New York, responded on March 19, 1863 to those who were insisting that preachers should not address political issues from their pulpits. Sadly, that same debate continues to this very day.

Here in the 21st century, there is a wide range of opinion concerning whether preachers/pastors should engage in politics from their pulpits. On one extreme are pastors who simply will not touch the subject in their pulpits. Stating reasons such as a fear of the IRS revoking the church's "tax-free status," a strict understanding (I believe misguided) of the "separation of church and state," to their firm belief that the pulpit is simply no place for politics (as they define it), these preachers refuse to address the subject. On the other end of the spectrum are pastors who turn to the Old Testament and conflate America with Israel and insist that America must be "taken back" by Christians who can then reestablish the rule of Mosaic Law. In the middle are those such as myself who believe that God established the institution of government, and although the answers to man's deepest problems are not political and cannot be solved by government, still, Scripture has much to say about government and those principles should be preached from the pulpit.

Of course, in large part, this debate turns on how we define "politics." If we define politics as the struggle between political parties to determine which party will be in power and/or the inside jockeying that determines who runs those parties, then I agree, there is no place for that in the pulpit. I certainly would never encourage any preacher to become a political hack for a particular party. But, if we define politics as the struggle to ensure that fair and just government is maintained in order to protect the fundamental, God-given, unalienable rights of Americans, then I believe those principles should be addressed from the pulpit and preachers should unashamedly bring God's Word to bear on the subject.

As far as I can determine, this is how the patriot preachers defined politics and, as we have seen, had no reservations about addressing the subject of government from their pulpits. As historian Frank Moore wrote, "The preachers of the Revolution did not hesitate to attack the great political and social evils of their day."[538] What's more, they believed the spiritual atmosphere of the culture was a direct reflection of the pulpit and church. Some one hundred years after the Black Regiment had passed from the scene, a nineteenth century evangelist by the name of Charles Finney expressed this belief to his fellow preachers:

"Brethren, our preaching will bear its legitimate fruits. If immorality prevails in the land, the fault is ours in a great degree. If there is a decay of conscience, the pulpit is responsible for it. If the public press lacks moral discrimination, the pulpit is responsible for it. If the church is degenerate and worldly, the pulpit is responsible for it. If the world loses its interest in religion, the pulpit is responsible for it. If Satan rules in our halls of legislation, the pulpit is responsible for it. If our politics become so corrupt that the very foundations of our government are ready to fall away, the pulpit is responsible for it.[160] ... Politics are part of a religion in such a country as this and Christians must do their duty to the country as a part of their duty to God. ... Christians seem to act as if they think God does not see what they do in politics. But I tell you He does see it, and He will bless or curse this nation, according to the course Christians take."[539]

As a pastor myself, I understand the struggle preachers face as they grapple with this dilemma. None of us wants to be guilty of "prostituting" our call in order to become nothing more than a political pundit. I know the fear that can envelop a man as he contemplates the repercussions that no doubt will come his way as he prepares to deliver a sermon that addresses political/governmental issues. I can easily understand why many simply decide to avoid this conflict altogether and play it safe. Unfortunately, playing it safe in the pulpit has helped to get us into the deplorable mess we are in today. For example, undercover reporters have just released videos revealing that some Planned Parenthood facilities are selling parts of aborted babies to the highest bidder.[540] Recently, the owners of an Oregon bakery, claiming that it would force them to violate their deeply held Christian beliefs, refused to make a wedding cake for a lesbian couple and were fined $135,000 in damages.[541] In another story, the U.S. Army recently kicked out a decorated Green Beret with an 11-year Special Forces career for shoving an Afghan police commander (whom he had trained) who was accused of raping a boy and beating up his mother when she reported the incident.[542] Finally, America is on the verge of authorizing an agreement with Iran that will enable them to eventually develop a nuclear intercontinental ballistic missile, thus giving nuclear power to and making us the allies of a government that has vowed to wipe the nation of Israel off of the map and has chanted "Death to America" (while the agreement was being drawn up). Need I say more?

I admit that it is difficult to preach about such things, but can we preachers remain silent in the face of these insanities and atrocities – or ones even worse than those mentioned above – it that's possible? If we preachers do not provide the biblical perspective on issues like these to our congregations, then who will? I believe the time for playing it safe in the pulpit has passed.

"JUST AS LONG AS IT DOES NOT HAPPEN IN MY LIFETIME"

So how did our culture go from being primarily a "Christian" culture in the 18th century to being the polarized, pluralistic one it is today where the progressive/liberal forces seem committed to ridding the public sector of any religious expression whatsoever? Maybe something Thomas Paine wrote on December 23, 1776 explains the attitude that has allowed this "spiritual drift" to occur. Even though Paine later embraced aberrant political and spiritual philosophies and thus, discredited himself, the truths he articulated concerning the price of freedom in his *The Crisis* are still viable nonetheless:

> "THESE are the times that try men's souls. The summer soldier and the sunshine patriot will, in this crisis, shrink from the service of their country; but he that stands by it now, deserves the love and thanks of man and woman.

Tyranny, like hell, is not easily conquered; yet we have this consolation with us, that the harder the conflict, the more glorious the triumph. What we obtain too cheap, we esteem too lightly: it is dearness only that gives every thing its value. Heaven knows how to put a proper price upon its goods; and it would be strange indeed if so celestial an article as FREEDOM should not be highly rated. ...

I once felt all that kind of anger, which a man ought to feel, against the mean principles that are held by the Tories: a noted one, who kept a tavern at Amboy, was standing at his door, with as pretty a child in his hand, about eight or nine years old, as I ever saw, and after speaking his mind as freely as he thought was prudent, finished with this unfatherly expression, 'Well! Give me peace in my day.' Not a man lives on the continent but fully believes that a separation must some time or other finally take place, and a generous parent should have said, 'If there must be trouble, let it be in my day, that my child may have peace;' and this single reflection, well applied, is sufficient to awaken every man to duty."[543]

Although Paine's words were penned two hundred and thirty-nine years ago, his words are as relevant today as if they had been written last week. Sadly, we find the same attitude as that of the self-centered tavern keeper dominating many in our culture today. Like him, many, including a good number of evangelical Christians, remain apathetic and unengaged in the face of "national" calamity. Like him, they, too, excuse themselves by saying, "Just give me my 'golden parachute' and then someone else can fix things when I'm dead and gone." They willingly admit that it is sad that we appear to be running our culture into the ditch, but they just hope and pray that the really "bad stuff" does not happen in their lifetime. They seem perfectly content with leaving the dirty job of cleaning up the mess to their children and grandchildren. It has been rightly observed that, "America's founders were willing to sacrifice their own prosperity for their posterity; today's Americans seem willing to sacrifice their posterity for their own prosperity."

This terrible situation is further exacerbated by the lack of political involvement among Christians. For example, although voting is the easiest to fulfill of all our civic duties, of the approximately 60-80 million self-professed evangelicals in these United States, only some fifty percent even bother to vote.[544] Worse still, of the other fifty percent who do not vote, most are not even registered to vote! Just imagine what influence evangelicals would have if the majority voted the biblical values they claim to believe. Sadly, in addition to many Christians "sitting it out" in elections, exit polls in recent presidential elections have indicated that some 20-25 percent of evangelicals who do vote actually cast their votes for candidates who reject the very values evangelicals embrace![545]

Of course, many Christians argue that politics is a dirty business and as Christians, they just can't get involved in such a godless enterprise. Claiming that they are too focused on "spiritual things" to be concerned with secular matters like political activism, these believers apparently think that the political process that determines who writes and enforces the laws and policies of our government is of little spiritual consequence. Separating their world into "the secular" and "the spiritual," they carefully avoid anything they label as "secular" even though the Bible makes no such distinctions. On the contrary, Scripture teaches that, to the Christian, all things, with the exception of clearly delineated sinful things, are spiritual and should be done as "unto the Lord":

> "Unto the pure all things are pure: but unto them that are defiled and unbelieving is nothing pure;" Titus 1:15

> "Servants, be obedient to them that are your masters according to the flesh, ... as unto Christ; ... but as the servants of Christ, ... ⁷With good will doing service, as

to the Lord, and not to men: [8]Knowing that whatsoever good thing any man doeth, the same shall he receive of the Lord, whether he be bond or free." Ephesians 6:5-8

"And whatsoever ye do, do it heartily, as to the Lord, and not unto men; [24]Knowing that of the Lord ye shall receive the reward of the inheritance: for ye serve the Lord Christ." Colossians 3:23-24

Interestingly, these same Christians do not seem to consider things like careers, sports, hobbies, etc. as "secular" and have no qualms about participating in them. Ironically, if these believers were as equally engaged in the culture war as they are in their careers, sports, hobbies, etc., our culture might not be in the terrible fix it is in today.

Having accepted the myth of separation of church and state, these believers, along with many of their pastors, seem convinced that it is sinful and violates some civil or religious law to mix politics and religion. When challenged to provide solid biblical justification for this position, they resort to offering "spiritualized" interpretations of Scripture as they define the Christian mission in a way far different from their patriot preacher ancestors, who as we saw, "did not divorce politics and religion, but denounced the separation as ungodly."[546] Modern Christians should be grateful that the founding generation did not think like they do or America would probably be flying the Union Jack.

THERE IS A REASON WHY POLITICS HAS BECOME SO "DIRTY."

If politics is dirty, then I submit it is because Christians abandoned it. Contrary to popular belief, politics is not inherently "dirty" – especially since God established the institution of human government in the first place. The late preacher, Adrian Rogers, once said, "God created human government. It is, therefore, inconceivable that God would create government and then tell His people to stay out of it any more than He would ordain the family and then tell us not to get involved. ... Our job is not to try and change society through government, but to change people with the Gospel so they can influence the government. Our nation needs more righteous people to get involved in government."[547] Unfortunately, "staying out of it" is exactly what Christians have been doing for decades and the results have been catastrophic.

Although many preachers today may choose to ignore this fact, the principle of government is mentioned throughout Scripture. It shows up as early as Genesis 9 when God established it to protect human life in the days after the flood of Noah. In Genesis 11, we find man's first recorded gross misuse of government as Nimrod attempts to establish a one-world government. In Genesis chapters 37-50, the correct and incorrect use of governmental power is a significant part of Joseph's story. Government and law are major themes in the books of Exodus, Leviticus, Numbers, and Deuteronomy. Most of the heroes of the Old Testament, including Abraham, Joseph, Moses, Joshua, King David, King Solomon, and Daniel, were all involved in government in some way, with some actually serving as government officials. Matthew, Jesus' disciple, was a tax collector and Nicodemus, a convert and significant follower of Jesus, was a member of the Jewish Sanhedrin – the Jewish equivalent to the U.S. Supreme Court. Jesus even endorsed human government by commanding His followers to "render to Caesar the things that are Caesar's." At His mock trial, Jesus reminded Pilate that his power as governor came from God, through the divine institution of government. Jesus faithfully paid His taxes. He endorsed the concepts of private property ownership, free market capitalism, and the individual's responsibility to work for a living – all issues of government and/or economics. Clearly, the Bible is filled with references to government and stories about how believers have been engaged in government from the beginning.

Most Christians agree that God established three institutions to provide for a civil society: the home, the state, and the church, and most readily agree that without protecting and promoting all three of these institutions, lawful human society cannot exist. But ironically, when it comes to preaching about these three institutions today, many preachers steer clear of government claiming it is unbiblical to get "political" in the pulpit – even though government has a direct and significant influence in the lives of their congregants.

POLITICS WAS NOT ALWAYS ABOUT POLITICAL PARTIES

One of the reasons modern preachers give for not preaching about government is that they do not want to be seen as endorsing a particular political party. They claim that if they do, they will not only have violated the "sanctity" of the pulpit, but they will also have alienated a portion of their congregation who supports the opposite party. I must attest to the truth that in today's church, it is very difficult to preach on "so-called" political issues without being accused of promoting a particular political party or attacking another and I completely understand a preacher's/ pastor's trepidation concerning this issue. But, it is essential to understand that political parties did not even exist in the days of the Black Regiment. Their generation would find today's often venomous, partisan bickering back and forth between Democrats and Republicans revolting and unproductive. The only parties in existence then were the ones Thomas Jefferson referred to in his letter to Henry Lee on August 10, 1824:

> "Men by their constitutions are naturally divided into two parties: 1. Those who fear and distrust the people, and wish to draw all powers from them into the hands of the higher classes. 2. Those who identify themselves with the people, have confidence in them, cherish and

consider them as the most honest and safe, although not the most wise depository of the public interests. In every country these two parties exist, and in every one where they are free to think, speak, and write, they will declare themselves. Call them, therefore, Liberals and Serviles, Aristocrats and Democrats, or by whatever name you please, they are the same parties still, and pursue the same object."[548]

To many colonists, preaching politics meant discussing the deeper, biblical principles and concepts that define the basic rights of men, individual liberty, and the primary functions of government. Essentially, they believed politics was the ongoing debate about liberty and tyranny – not whose political party was best. Unfortunately, our modern view of politics is very different. For so many, political debate is less about what is right and wrong and more about the "competition" that determines whose party is in power (even though, in most cases, it doesn't seem to matter since both parties essentially govern the same way once they're in power). Even more disturbing is the fact that many today seem completely incapable of getting beyond party politics and to the real debate about the foundational principles that determine the destiny of our republic.

The Founders had grave concerns about the formation of political parties in American politics and the subsequent division and confusion they would bring. They were convinced that if a "party spirit" were ever allowed to develop in America, the factions it would create and the damage it would do might eventually destroy the republic they had labored so hard and long to establish – a prophetic vision that has, unfortunately, come to pass. On October 2, 1780, in a letter to Jonathan Jackson, John Adams discussed this fear:

> "There is nothing which I dread so much as a division of the republic into two great parties, each arranged under its leader, and concerting measures in opposition to each

other. This, in my humble apprehension, is to be dreaded as the greatest political evil under our Constitution."[549]

In his 1796 farewell address, President George Washington warned of the potential problem parties could cause:

"In contemplating the causes which may disturb our Union, it occurs as matter of serious concern that any ground should have been furnished for characterizing parties by geographical discriminations, Northern and Southern, Atlantic and Western; whence designing men may endeavor to excite a belief that there is a real difference of local interests and views. One of the expedients of party to acquire influence within particular districts is to misrepresent the opinions and aims of other districts. You cannot shield yourselves too much against the jealousies and heart burnings which spring from these misrepresentations; they tend to render alien to each other those who ought to be bound together by fraternal affection. ... They serve to organize faction, to give it an artificial and extraordinary force; to put, in the place of the delegated will of the nation the will of a party, often a small but artful and enterprising minority of the community; ... they are likely, in the course of time and things, to become potent engines, by which cunning, ambitious, and unprincipled men will be enabled to subvert the power of the people and to usurp for themselves the reins of government, destroying afterwards the very engines which have lifted them to unjust dominion."[550]

In *Federalist No. 10*, James Madison called these party factions a "mortal disease":

"AMONG the numerous advantages promised by a well-constructed Union, none deserves to be more accurately developed than its tendency to break and control the violence of faction. ... The instability, injustice, and confusion introduced into the public councils, have, in truth, been the mortal diseases under which popular governments have everywhere perished; ... These must be chiefly, if not wholly, effects of the unsteadiness and injustice with which a factious spirit has tainted our public administrations. ... To secure the public good and private rights against the danger of such a faction, and at the same time to preserve the spirit and the form of popular government, is then the great object to which our inquiries are directed."[551]

Interestingly, forty years earlier on May 27, 1747, Charles Chauncy preached to a Boston audience that when voting, Americans should set aside all "party designs" and "private considerations":

"Let me beseech you, sirs, for the sake of this poor people, and for the sake of your own souls, when you shall stand before the dreadful bar of the eternal judgment, to lay aside all party designs and private considerations, and to deliberate upon this great affair, with a single view to the public good, and under the uniform influence of a steady principle of righteousness;"[552]

Sadly, we did not heed these warnings. Today, we find ourselves living in a culture deeply divided by party partisanship where political power is more important than principle. This situation makes it very difficult for modern preachers who actually do want to address the subject of politics. In the midst of this emotionally charged political party tug-of-war, they must navigate around the confusion and contention created by this "party spirit" that now controls the minds of their audiences. To cut through this mental fog and preach about civic responsibility, while at the same time assuring his people that he is not promoting a particular political party, is a difficult and delicate balancing act indeed –

one requiring great courage and commitment. This is, no doubt, why so many of today's pastors shy away from addressing the subject altogether.

Thankfully, this was not true for the patriot preachers of the 18th century – they enthusiastically fulfilled their duty and many of their messages became the basis for the laws of the land. Historian Alice Baldwin noted this when she wrote,

> "The constitutional convention and the written constitution were the children of the pulpit. To the men of New England who had been nourished from their youth on the election sermons and who had been thoroughly enlightened by their pastors in theoretical and practical politics, it was but natural to turn to the ministers when they needed some one to express their ideas of government."[553]

In the 1800's, historian G. W. Balch affirmed the role the patriot preachers played in educating their people about "politics" when he wrote, "All classes were stirred and none more so than the clergy; and here it may well be remarked that from thenceforward, during the entire Revolutionary period, the latter were leaders and the most potent factors in resistance to British oppression. ... In the absence of a numerous newspaper press, the political education of the people then as now in sparsely settled regions was conducted largely from the pulpit — or the stump."[554]

IN AMERICA, CAESAR IS "WE THE PEOPLE"

Because the "political education of the people" is no longer "conducted by the pulpit" as Balch said it was in the 18th century, the average churchgoer in the 21st century has not been taught how to correctly and consistently apply Scripture to their politics. This is why they do not appear to connect the dots between the spiritual and the political and explains why so many Christians are unengaged at the political level. It also explains how some who do engage, at least at some level, can be pro-life, support biblical marriage, reject the welfare state, etc., and yet support candidates, political parties, and/or causes that take the exact opposite position.

We must recognize that in our republican form of governance, the government derives its authority from the consent of the governed and thus, it is "of, by, and for the people." It stands to reason then, that if "we, the people" do not engage in government, it will cease to function properly, or even at all. In our representative republic, Caesar is *the people*. If we Christians intend to obey Christ's command and "render unto Caesar the things that are Caesar's" we must engage in the political process because *we are Caesar*. In a representative republic like ours, our civic duty is a part of our service to God. This is what Evangelist Charles Finney told his fellow preachers back in the 1800s when he said,

> "Politics are part of a religion in such a country as this and Christians must do their duty to the country as a part of their duty to God. ... Christians seem to act as if they think God does not see what they do in politics. But I tell you He does see it, and He will bless or curse this nation, according to the course Christians take."[555]

If we Christians bow out, the only ones left to govern will be those who do not uphold biblical values. It is helpful to remember that John Adams said, "Our constitution was made only for a moral and religious people. It is wholly inadequate to the government of any other."[556] If Christians abdicate their civic responsibilities to unbelievers, they should not be surprised when those unbelievers undermine and destroy the Christian values that have helped to undergird our republic for over 230 years. It has been correctly said that we Americans generally get the kind of government we deserve. So, if godly people do not participate, they have no right to complain when their government becomes ungodly. It is no more complicated than that.

Luckily, there is a relatively easy solution to this problem. If preachers would clearly articulate from their pulpits what Scripture teaches about these issues and then compare the candidates' or political/cultural causes' positions to Scripture, their congregations would not only become more engaged, but do so with a more biblically informed mindset. As it is, most pastors rarely, if ever, mention political issues or candidates/ cultural causes from their pulpits. Many preachers claim that people are smart enough to "figure it out on their own" without explicit instructions from the pulpit. Of course, this may generally be true, but if this approach works so well, then why don't these preachers use the same approach when it comes to issues such as tithing and church attendance and let their people "figure those out on their own" as well?

In His wisdom, God has chosen the "foolishness of preaching" to proclaim His Word, and congregations, like sheep, depend on their shepherds to lead them. The problem is many modern preachers are neglecting to shepherd their people when it comes to the subject of government and politics. What makes this so dangerous is that, in most cases, the average churchgoer assumes that if a particular subject has spiritual implications and is important, their pastor will address it from the pulpit. So if there is some issue he does not address, many naturally assume that that issue is either not significantly addressed in Scripture, is not spiritually important, or is unspiritual altogether. Consequently, these Christians either ignore the subject or simply allow the winds of public opinion to drive their positions and actions rather than Scripture.

This is indeed regrettable because, for the most part, congregations are eager to know what their pastors believe and have to say about a whole host of issues, including politics. This is not because they are unable to form their own opinions; it is because they respect the opinions and judgment of their spiritual leaders – especially if those spiritual leaders are well informed biblically, historically, and culturally.

So, if congregations truly do want to hear the biblical perspective on political issues but their pastors refuse to address them, to whom can they turn – to the dominant news media or to education and Hollywood elites? The church should be the place to hear the well-reasoned, biblical perspective on political/cultural issues. But if the church does not do its job in this regard (as the 18th century church did), Christians are left with few other places to which they can turn.

Facing a similar dilemma when trying to address the subject of slavery, Abraham Lincoln lamented the fact that people in his day discouraged open and public debate on the issue. In a speech given on March 6, 1860 in New Haven, Connecticut, Lincoln lamented:

> "... we must not call it [slavery] wrong in politics because that is bringing morality into politics, and we must not call it wrong in the pulpit because that is bringing politics into religion; we must not bring it into the Tract Society or the other societies, because those are such unsuitable places, and there is no single place, according to you, where this wrong thing can properly be called wrong!"[557]

In a way, the same thing is happening again. Today, there seems to be no place, certainly not most pulpits, where the Bible can be brought to bear on politics.

Sadly, those who do not embrace a biblical worldview have eagerly filled the vacuum created by the silence/absence of the pulpit/church. So, by disengaging from politics, believers, by default, have surrendered the public debate about political issues and the control of their government to non-Christians. It is not surprising then, to see our government (local/state/federal) leaning more and more to the left and away from biblical values.

Lacking the influence of the "salt of the earth" and "light of the world," the institution of government is becoming more and more hostile to biblical values and those who embrace them.

Some three thousand years ago, Solomon warned about the calamities ungodly leaders bring upon a people:

"When the righteous are in authority, the people rejoice: but when the wicked beareth rule, the people mourn." Proverbs 29:2

A government devoid of biblical values, where Christian soldiers are virtually "missing in action," is exactly the opposite of what the Black Robed Regiment intended. They believed that politically engaged Christians were essential for healthy government. Decades before the Black Regiment came along, William Penn, founder of Pennsylvania, said,

"Governments, like clocks, go from the motion men give them; and as governments are made and moved by men, so by them they are ruined too. Wherefore governments rather depend upon men than men upon governments. Let men be good and the government cannot be bad.... But if men be bad, let the government be never so good ..."[558]

In his 1803 election sermon, Matthias Burnett, Pastor of the First Baptist Church, Norwalk, Connecticut, said:

"Let not your children have reason to curse you for giving up those rights and prostrating those institutions which your fathers delivered to you. ... Think not that your interests will be safe in the hands of the weak and ignorant; or faithfully managed by the impious, the dissolute and the immoral. ... Watch over your liberties and privileges–civil and religious–with a careful eye."[559]

In July 1877, James Garfield, twentieth president of the United States, wrote:

"Now more than ever the people are responsible for the character of their Congress. If that body be ignorant, reckless, and corrupt, it is because the people tolerate ignorance, recklessness, and corruption. If it be intelligent, brave, and pure, it is because the people demand these high qualities to represent them in the national legislature.... [I]f the next centennial does not find us a great nation ... it will be because those who represent the enterprise, the culture, and the morality of the nation do not aid in controlling the political forces."[560]

SINCE I AM A CITIZEN OF HEAVEN, WHY SHOULD I EVEN CARE ABOUT POLITICS?

This is the response that many believers give when challenged to engage in politics. In one sense, they are correct. The Apostle Paul wrote in Philippians 3:20, "For our conversation [citizenship] is in heaven; from whence also we look for the Saviour, the Lord Jesus Christ." There is no doubt about it, the Bible clearly teaches that Christians are citizens of heaven and what a glorious truth that is! Accordingly, Jesus taught that we are to be heavenly-minded in this life and "lay up treasures in heaven rather than on the earth." When compared to our heavenly citizenship, our earthly citizenship, no matter the state or country, pales into oblivion. Our relationship to God through faith in Christ and obedience to His will, admittedly, makes our civic duties seem trivial. If one gets the faith/obedience issue wrong, nothing else matters. Jesus said in Matthew 16:26, "For what is a man profited, if he shall gain the whole world, and lose his own soul? Or what shall a man give in exchange for his soul?"

Even so, this does not relieve us of our duty to fulfill our duties to our government – especially here in America where we, as we noted earlier, live in a representative republic. Daniel

Webster, the famous American statesman said, "Whatever makes men good Christians makes them good citizens."[561]

The Apostle Paul was no stranger to a believer's civic responsibility to government. He instructed the Christians in the city of Rome about their obligations as citizens (and remember, these Christians were living under a ruthless dictator) when he wrote in Romans 13:7, "Render therefore to all their dues: tribute [taxes] to whom tribute is due; custom to whom custom; fear to whom fear; honour to whom honour." Paul actually invoked his rights as a Roman citizen on a number of occasions and even used those rights to further the Gospel (Acts 22:22-29, 25:11, 28:19). To Paul's admonition, the Apostle Peter added in 1 Peter 2:17, "Honour all men. Love the brotherhood. Fear God. Honour the king." If Peter and Paul recognized and respected their duties as earthly citizens, is it proper, then, for modern Christians to ignore theirs? Of course not and I am convinced that Christians instinctively know this. But what they may not recognize is that it is a sin for them not to be engaged.

Since Jesus commanded us to, "render to Caesar the things that are Caesar's," it is clear that He *expects us* to fulfill our duties to our government – unless that service clearly contradicts God's principles. James 4:17 teaches that it is a sin for us not to do what we know we should do. Scripture also teaches that in a right relationship with God, everything has spiritual value. The Apostle Paul wrote in Colossians 3:17,23, "And whatsoever ye do in word or deed, do all in the name of the Lord Jesus, giving thanks to God and the Father by him. ... [23]And whatsoever ye do, do it heartily, as to the Lord, and not unto men." In Titus 2:7, Paul admonished, "In all things showing thyself a pattern of good works." Although this admonition obviously directly refers to living according to the sound doctrines of Scripture, by extension it would include "all things" – including civic engagement.

In addition to our *responsibility* to be good citizens, we are also required to be *good stewards* of the good things God has given us. 1 Corinthians says, "Moreover it is required in stewards, that a man be found faithful." James 1:17 adds, "Every good gift and every perfect gift is from above, and cometh down from the Father of lights." Since most of us would agree that liberty is a good gift, we must, therefore, also agree that it is a blessing from God. The question then arises, how is the 21st century church in America doing in its stewardship of the liberty that has been passed down to us? It appears not too well I fear.

John Jay, the first Chief Justice of the U.S. Supreme Court, noted how we American Christians have been favored with a special blessing of liberty when he said, "The Americans are the first people whom Heaven has favored with an opportunity of deliberating upon and choosing the forms of government under which they should live."[562] Because we have been "favored by heaven" with great liberty, we American Christians have much to account to God for in regard to how we have treasured and used this uncommon blessing. In Luke 12:48, Jesus said, "… For unto whomsoever much is given, of him shall be much required: and to whom men have committed much, of him they will ask the more." In other passages like James 3:1, Scripture confirms the principle that those who have received special grace are held to a higher standard than those who have not. Jesus warned the city of Capernaum that because much had been given to them (the Lord's very presence and miracles), much was required of them:

> "And you, Capernaum, who are exalted to heaven, will be brought down to Hades; for if the mighty works which were done in you had been done in Sodom, it would have remained until this day. [24]But I say to you that it shall be more tolerable for the land of Sodom in the day of judgment than for you." Matthew 11:23-24

No doubt, this is what Ezra Stiles had in mind as he preached to the Connecticut General Assembly in 1783: "… the United States are under peculiar obligations to become a holy people unto the Lord our God, on account of the late eminent deliverance, salvation, peace, and glory with which he hath now crowned our new sovereignty."[563] In his book, *Mere Christianity*, C.S. Lewis said:

> "Every faculty you have, your power of thinking or of moving your limbs from moment to moment, is given you by God. If you devoted every moment of your whole life exclusively to His service, you could not give Him anything that was not in a sense His own already."[564]

Jesus warned in Matthew 25 that each one of us will be required to give an account to God for how we have invested the "talents" that have been entrusted to us. How will it go for us American Christians in the judgment when God evaluates how we have invested or squandered our "talent of liberty" He has so graciously given to each of us?

BUT WHY WEREN'T JESUS AND PAUL INVOLVED IN GOVERNMENT?

How often have you heard someone say, "If Christians should get heavily involved in politics, why did Jesus and Paul not say so?" Actually, in way they did.

Of course, it is true that Jesus did not call upon his disciples to lead an armed revolt against the Romans nor did Paul, the great church planter, rally the early church to overthrow Caesar. So does this mean that believers of all eras should stay out of government? If so, how can we defend our Founders for overthrowing the oppressive British Crown? Were they nothing more than a generation of rebels and anarchists? (see Chapter 14) Therefore, it is important that we briefly discuss here the misconceptions that swirl around the positions that Jesus and Paul took concerning government.

First of all, it must be noted that the primary reason Jesus came to this earth was to fulfill what the Scriptures said about Himself and to die as a ransom for sinners – not to reform the government (John 3:16). His kingdom was not of this world or, as He said, His disciples would have used the sword to establish it (John 18:36). For example, when Peter attempted to stop the Romans from arresting Jesus in the Garden of Gethsemane, the Lord told him to sheath his sword. He then proceeded to remind Peter that by dying He was fulfilling the very purpose for which the Father had sent Him. Jesus went on to assure His disciples that if He wanted to resist, He could have called more than twelve legions of angels (60,000-70,000) to defend Him – an ample force considering that 2 Kings 19:35 tells of a single angel dispatching 185,000 Assyrian soldiers in one night. Jesus' came to redeem the lost, not to reform government.

In no way, though, should this be interpreted to mean that Jesus did not intend for His people to engage in government, defend liberty, or protect the innocent from tyrants. As we have already seen, He said we should "Render to Caesar what is Caesar's." Additionally, in Luke 22:36 (a verse with which many are unfamiliar), Jesus told His servants a time would come when they would need to purchase a sword:

> "Then said he unto them, 'But now, he that hath a purse, let him take it, and likewise his scrip [knapsack, luggage]: and he that hath no sword, let him sell his garment, and buy one.'" Luke 22:36

Unlike before, when He had sent out His disciples without money or other provisions (Luke 9-10), in Luke 22 Jesus told His followers to purchase a sword. Why would He have said this? Certainly, it would have been completely inconsistent with Jesus and His message for Him to be implying that He intended the Gospel to be forced upon people at the point of a sword (as Islam does); therefore, He must have had some other reason(s) for making this statement. To me, there seem to be at least two reasons: first, He could have been warning his followers that since they were living in a wicked world, they would need a sword for self-defense, or second, He could have been referring to the "sword of justice" that must be used to enforce law – as Paul wrote in Romans 13:4:

> "... for he [government] beareth not the sword in vain: for he is the minister of God, a revenger to execute wrath upon him that doeth evil."

It would seem clear, to me at least, that Jesus intended for His followers to be prepared to defend themselves and the innocent from criminals and tyrants. This was the motivation of the patriot preachers and I believe should be our motivation as well.

As with Jesus, many also argue that since Paul did not attempt to reform or replace his government, modern believers should not as well. The response to this argument is similar to the one concerning Jesus, with a slight difference. Paul had also been given a specific mission from God – his was to plant the infant Christian church throughout the western world, not to reform and/or replace the Roman government.

Those who use Paul as an excuse for disengaging from politics seem to forget that he did not live in a representative republic as American Christians do. Paul lived under a dictatorship where the people had been subjugated by the Roman emperor and therefore had little or no opportunity to influence their government. Even so, as was mentioned earlier, Paul used his Roman citizenship when he could (Acts 22:22-29, 25:11) and wrote about government in a number of his letters, particularly in Romans 13. Additionally, he took every opportunity to engage the political leaders of his day with the gospel. Examples can be found in his confrontations with King Agrippa, Governors Felix and Festus, and ultimately, with Caesar himself. Certainly, Paul did not piously isolate himself from government claiming that he was too spiritually minded to get involved – even though his opportunities to be involved in government were very limited.

In his 1794 four-volume work, *The History of the Rise, Progress and Establishment of the United States of America*, patriot preacher William Gordon objected to the notion that Christians were bound by Jesus and Paul to surrender their God-given rights to tyrants without offering any resistance, when he wrote:

> "You have frequently remarked, that though the partisans of arbitrary power will freely censure that preacher who speaks boldly for the liberties of the people, they will admire as an excellent divine, the parson whose discourse is wholly in the opposite strain, and teaches that magistrates have a divine right for doing wrong, and are to be implicitly obeyed; men professing Christianity, as if the religion of the blessed Jesus bound them tamely to part with their natural and social rights, and slavishly to bow their neck to any tyrant; as if Paul was faulty in standing up for his Roman privileges, that he might escape a scourging, or falling a sacrifice to the malice of his countrymen, when he appealed unto Caesar."[565]

It is true that Paul did not focus his efforts on correcting the Roman tyranny under which he lived, he did not run for office, he did not encourage his Christian brothers and sisters to vote, nor did he organize believers to overthrow the Romans. But this is because "righting" the government was not his mission and the tyranny under which he lived made involvement practically impossible. To compare Paul's political world to our American republic is like comparing apples to monkey wrenches. But, I am convinced that if Paul were an America citizen writing Romans 13 today, he would absolutely be admonishing American Christians to engage in the political process and take the "salt and light" into their halls of government.

Interestingly, in attempting to obey Jesus' command to "render to Caesar the things that are Caesar's," Paul and the early church did their best to live and work peaceably with their government. In fact, it was Paul who urged:

> "If it be possible, as much as lieth in you, live peaceably with all men." Romans 12:18

It is important to note that a key part of this admonition is the phrase "if it be possible." Clearly, Paul understood that there are times when it is not possible to live peaceably with all men. Our Founders knew this all too well and believed that they had reached this point with the British.

Even though they were very aware of the Scriptures that clearly teach believers to submit to government and to give honor to the authorities over them, the Black Regiment did not believe this meant believers where commanded to offer unlimited submission – especially to tyrants. From passages such as Romans 13, they taught their congregations that government had the authority to demand their respect and obedience; even to the point of its officers using the sword, if necessary, to ensure civil order and justice. But, the patriot preachers also believed that if the government usurped its authority and practiced tyranny, the people had the *right* and the *responsibility* to *replace* that government. They certainly did not understand Paul to teach that government's power was unlimited. For example, consider how Pastor Samuel West clearly articulated this principle:

> "A slavish submission to tyranny is a proof of a very sordid and base mind. ... all good magistrates, while they faithfully discharge the trust reposed in them, ought to be religiously and conscientiously obeyed. ... The reason why the magistrate is called the minister of God is because he is to protect, encourage, and honor them that do well, and to punish them that do evil; therefore it is our duty to submit to them, not merely for fear of being punished by them, but out of regard to the divine authority, under which they are deputed to execute judgment and to do justice. ... if magistrates have no authority but what they derive from the people; ... if the whole end and design of their institution is to promote the general good, and to secure to men their just rights, it will follow, that when they act contrary to the end and design of their creation

they cease being magistrates, and the people which gave them their authority have the right to take it from them again. ... when a people find themselves cruelly oppressed by the parent state, they have an undoubted right to throw off the yoke, and to assert their liberty, ... for, in this case, by the law of self-preservation, which is the first law of nature, they have not only an undoubted right, but it is their indispensable duty, if they cannot be redressed any other way, to renounce all submission to the government that has oppressed them, and set up an independent state of their own, ... No man, therefore, can be a good member of the community that is not as zealous to oppose tyranny as he is ready to obey magistracy. ...

Further: if magistrates are no farther ministers of God than they promote the good of the community, then obedience to them neither is nor can be unlimited; for it would imply a gross absurdity to assert that, when magistrates are ordained by the people solely for the purpose of being beneficial to the state, they must be obeyed when they are seeking to ruin and destroy it. This would imply that men were bound to act against the great law of self-preservation, and to contribute their assistance to their own ruin and destruction, in order that they may please and gratify the greatest monsters in nature, who are violating the laws of God and destroying the rights of mankind. Unlimited submission and obedience is due to none but God alone. ... Whenever, then, the ruler encourages them that do evil, and is a terror to those that do well, i.e., as soon as he becomes a tyrant, he forfeits his authority to govern, and becomes the minister of Satan, and, as such, ought to be opposed. ... Reason and revelation, we see, do both teach us that our obedience to rulers is not unlimited, but that resistance is not only allowable, but an indispensable duty in the case of intolerable tyranny and oppression."[566]

In short, the patriot preachers believed that it was not wrong for a people to resist tyranny if they could. They certainly did not believe that God would have His people stand idle as tyrants trample truth and justice under foot when we have the power to prevent it. Of course, many throughout history, including most in the early church, had no choice in the matter because they had already been subjugated and had no power or opportunity to resist the powers that abused them.

Obviously, few choose tyranny when they can have liberty, and since we Americans are free and still retain the right and ability to prevent tyranny, I believe we have the responsibility to do so. It is clear that generations of believers who preceded us believed this truth. Had they not, we would most likely not enjoy the liberty we do today.

Chapter 16

THE CHURCH AND THE INTERNAL REVENUE SERVICE

"The preachers of the Revolution did not hesitate to attack the great political and social evils of their day ..."[567] Historian Frank Moore

Although the patriot preachers "did not hesitate," many modern pastors not only hesitate, they refuse to attack the great political and social evils of our day. The obvious question is, "Why?" I have asked myself this question time and time again. No doubt there are many answers. As we will see in the next chapter, the pollster George Barna found some interesting answers when he asked that question.

Of course, some honestly do not believe pastors should get involved in politics. For them, it is a matter of conscience. Others are afraid of the criticism and conflicts that will inevitably come their way if they get political. Afraid that members of their own congregations may rise up against them, these pastors fear for their jobs. But beyond these reasons, I believe there are two other reasons:

1. They believe the modern "myth" of separation of church and state.

2. They fear the loss of their church's non-profit, tax-exempt status.

THE "MYTH" OF SEPARATION

Even though neither the Bible nor the Constitution demands a "strict separation of church and state" (as it is most often understood today), many are convinced they do. Although space will not allow a thorough discussion of this subject here, I believe it is important to offer a brief overview.

As we saw in chapter 13, of the original thirteen colonies, all founded by different Christian denominations, nine had an official state church.[568] It is important to remember what historian John Wingate Thornton wrote: "The Fathers did not divorce politics and religion, but they denounced the separation as ungodly."[569] Today, we are told that it is ungodly to "wed" politics and religion – the exact opposite of the founding generation.

As most are aware, much of the "separation" controversy stems from the famous "separation" phrase in Thomas Jefferson's response letter he wrote to a group of Baptists in Danbury, Connecticut on January 1, 1802. In the letter, Jefferson correctly reminded the Baptists in Danbury, who had been told that Congress was intending to endorse a "national" denomination, that the Constitution erected a "wall of separation" between religion and government, restricting the federal government from establishing an "official" church in America. In context, he was explaining that this "wall" existed mainly to protect religion from the federal government – not the federal government from religion.

The very purpose for the Constitution and the Bill of Rights was to limit government – not the people. The thought that Jefferson believed the country needed protection from religion is ludicrous, is the exact opposite of what he was saying, and is contrary to what the Founders intended. The Constitution and subsequent Bill of Rights established freedom "of" religion, not freedom "from" religion. As James L. Adams correctly observed,

"With those words Jefferson was not formulating a secular principle to banish religion from the public arena. Rather he was trying to keep government from darkening the door of the church. ... We dare not muzzle morality in the marketplace or permit the wall of separation to turn into an Iron Curtain of religious repression."[570]

Unfortunately, our courts have been using this misinterpretation of Jefferson's letter as the basis for bad constitutional law for years. This was the opinion of William Rehnquist, former Supreme Court justice:

"But the greatest injury of the "wall" notion is its mischievous diversion of judges from the actual intentions of the drafters of the Bill of Rights. ... The 'wall of separation between church and State' is a metaphor based on bad history, a metaphor which has proved useless as a guide to judging. It should be frankly and explicitly abandoned."[571]

The colonists clearly believed that the colonies/states had the right to "establish" a state church if its citizens chose to do so, and as noted above, the majority of the colonies did just that. But, they also believed that the federal government had no right to meddle in religion other than to foster an atmosphere friendly to it.

This is the environment the French historian and political scientist Alexis de Tocqueville found when he visited America in the 1830s. For almost two years he toured and studied the American culture. Upon returning to France he compiled his notes into his famous work, *Democracy In America* in which he wrote nothing about any such thing as "separation of church and state." In fact, he found quite the opposite. Intrigued with the particularly strong influence Christianity had in the lives of Americans, De Tocqueville wrote,

"Upon my arrival in the United States, the religious aspect of the country was the first thing that struck my attention; and the longer I stayed there, the more did I perceive the great political consequences resulting from this state of things, ... religion is therefore mingled with all the habits of the nation and all the feelings of patriotism, whence it derives a peculiar force. ... In the United States the sovereign authority is religious, ... there is no country in the world where the Christian religion retains a greater influence over the souls of men than in America; ... The Americans show by their practice that they feel the high necessity of imparting morality to democratic communities by means of religion."[572]

Sadly, this is not true of the American culture today. As historian Carl Bridenbaugh observes, "We live in an increasingly secular society. Religiosity in our day (if not actual church-going) declines apace; whereas our fore fathers of the eighteenth century considered piety, religious observance, even theology, as part of their daily existence."[573] I believe this explains why the "myth of separation" is so broadly accepted today. Regrettably, many Americans, preachers in particular, who know little of the history of the concept of the "separation of church and state," insist on ridding the pulpit of anything that even resembles politics – and tragically, our culture is paying a very high price.

LOSING ITS TAX-EXEMPT STATUS

The other key reason that pastors avoid politics in the pulpit is their and their church's fear of losing its tax-exempt status. It is important to understand that the common fear most pastors and congregations have about the church losing its tax-exempt status over political speech is, at least for now, unwarranted. For the record: during the entire history of the Internal Revenue

Service, *not one church has ever lost its tax-exempt status because of political speech!*

The closest any church has ever come was when the Church at Pierce Creek in Binghamton, New York placed full-page advertisements in the October 30, 1992 issues of *USA Today* and the *Washington Times* encouraging Christians not to vote for Bill Clinton for President. Going even further, Pierce Creek even solicited donations within those ads – a step that even the most politically engaged churches would probably not have taken. But even then, Pierce Creek did not lose its tax-exempt status.

The IRS did successfully prosecute the church but the most they were able to do was to revoke the advance letter of tax-exempt status that the IRS had given to the church when it originally filed as a 501(c)(3) organization. Even though this advance letter was revoked, Pierce Creek never lost its tax-exempt status.

(Note: It is important to know that this advance letter of tax-exempt status is not required for a church to be tax-exempt. In fact, a church does not even have to officially file as 501(c)(3) to be tax-exempt – churches are automatically tax-exempt. Whether a church officially files as a 501(c)(3) organization or not, the IRS treats them as such.)

It is interesting to note that in its ruling against the church, the Federal Court of Appeals for the District of Columbia admitted:

"… because of the unique treatment churches receive under the Internal Revenue Code, the impact of the revocation is likely to be more symbolic than substantial. … All that will have been lost is the advance assurance of deductibility in the event a donor should be audited."[574]

The Court went on to state that it knew of no authority, "to prevent the Church from reapplying for a prospective determination of its tax-exempt status and regaining the advance assurance of deductibility …"[575] After the Federal Court's May 12, 2000 ruling, Matt Staver, attorney with the Liberty Counsel, noted,

"Understand that the only thing the Church lost in this case is its advance tax-exempt letter ruling. Contributions given prior to the revocation of the IRS letter are still deductible and are not taxable to the Church. After the letter ruling was revoked, the Church could continue as a church, continue receiving donations, and donors could continue to claim deductions on their income tax return, provided that the Church did not continue to endorse or oppose candidates. If the Church wants an advance letter ruling at some point in the future, it is free to ask for another one. Obviously in the case of the presidential election, the Church could easily cease endorsing or opposing a candidate since the election had transpired."[576]

So essentially, once the election was over, the church could reapply for its letter from the IRS and retain it until, at some time in the future, it decided to endorse another candidate. In which case the IRS would presumably prosecute to revoke that new letter also. If so, the church could simply reapply for another letter, and another, and another and apparently continue repeating the process indefinitely.

According to numerous tax attorneys, even if a church or its pastor endorses a candidate from the pulpit on a given Sunday, the worst conceivable action the IRS could take would be to consider the donations given *on that day only* as non-deductible. The next day the church would return to its "tax exempt posture" since it conceivably would not be "officially" endorsing a candidate on that day.

Additionally, most church members are shocked to discover that, along with allowing political speech from their pulpits, the church can even participate in official lobbying efforts as long as those efforts do not represent a major part of the church's ministry time. In short, as long as the church does not make lobbying its primary function, they are not in violation of IRS regulations.

The bottom line is this: the IRS has very little power to prosecute and take away a church's tax-exempt status. In very real terms, when it comes to limiting religious speech, the IRS is a "paper tiger" – one that pastors and congregations need not fear (At least for now; but if Christians remain politically disengaged, this could change very soon). Therefore, pastors should feel free to boldly proclaim their biblical convictions from the pulpit – even when it comes to politics.

Many of us believe this is something preachers should do regardless of the actions of the government or the IRS. Just like Peter and John in Acts 4, many believe modern preachers should speak out boldly on every subject, no matter the consequences:

> "And they called them, and commanded them not to speak at all nor teach in the name of Jesus. [19]But Peter and John answered and said unto them, 'Whether it be right in the sight of God to hearken unto you more than unto God, judge ye. [20]For we cannot but speak the things which we have seen and heard.' [21]So when they had further threatened them, they let them go, finding nothing how they might punish them, because of the people: for all men glorified God for that which was done." Acts 4:19-21

Of course, some are quick to point out that in Acts 4, the apostles were in jail for preaching the gospel – not politics. Certainly this is true. But the question can justifiably be asked, "If pastors won't speak out on political and social issues because they're afraid of losing their church's tax-exempt status, would they actually be willing to go to jail for preaching the Gospel?" In addition, it is important to note that certain issues like homosexuality/lesbianism and same sex marriage that were once considered spiritual/biblical issues are now considered "political," so can pastors not preach about them any longer? In fact, many of the subjects the Black Regiment considered proper for the pulpit in their day are today considered "political" and are therefore deemed off limits to the modern pulpit. And since the list of what is *spiritual* and what is *political* now appears to be a moving target, who will decide which issues are political and which are spiritual/biblical and thus proper for the pulpit in the future? There is a very real fear that eventually, everything in Scripture that is offensive to the politically correct crowd will be categorized as political or hate speech and will therefore be designated as hate speech if the pastor addresses them from the pulpit.

As followers and spokesmen for Christ, we cannot allow ourselves to be controlled by the fear of man. Preachers, and all believers for that matter, must stand up and preach what we know is right – regardless of what the government says. Like David in Psalms 56:11, we should say, "In God have I put my trust: I will not be afraid what man can do unto me." We must follow the admonition of Jesus in Matthew 10:28: "And fear not them which kill the body, but are not able to kill the soul: but rather fear him which is able to destroy both soul and body in hell." After all, as Paul declared in Romans 8:31, "What shall we then say to these things? If God be for us, who can be against us?"

We can take heart – the battle is not ours. As David said to Goliath in 1 Samuel 17:47, "And all this assembly shall know that the Lord saveth not with sword and spear: for the battle is the Lord's, and he will give you into our hands."

THE CHURCH'S TAX-EXEMPT STATUS IS NOT A "GIFT" FROM GOVERNMENT

I am often amazed as preachers/Christians speak in hushed tones, whispers, and innuendos about political issues when they are at church, as if it is against the law to speak of such things there. They are obviously fearful that the government may hear and take away their tax-exempt status.

The church's tax-exempt status is not a "gift" bestowed by a benevolent government. From the very beginning of our country, the church has been recognized as a sovereign entity that is exempt from taxation. This principle has been affirmed throughout our history, and as recently as 1971, it was confirmed by the U.S. Supreme Court in *Lemon v. Kurtzman*. Writing for the majority, Chief Justice Warren Burger said,

"In Walz [*Walz v. Tax Commission*, 1970] it was argued that a tax exemption for places of religious worship would prove to be the first step in an inevitable progression leading to the establishment of state churches and state religion. That claim could not stand up against more than 200 years of virtually universal practice imbedded in our colonial experience and continuing into the present."[577]

From the time the early settlers landed on North America's shores until 1789 when the U.S. Constitution was ratified, the driving motivation for Americans was to found a country where people would be free to worship God according to the dictates of their own consciences – not according to the dictates of government. This principle was first expressed in documents like the Mayflower Compact and ultimately codified into law in the First Amendment to the U.S. Constitution. It is, therefore, insane to believe that these early Americans made the great sacrifices they made for liberty and freedom to then create a government with the power to limit their freedom of speech, especially religious, and severely punish those who did not comply with its restrictions. This would make absolutely no sense.

In his farewell address, President George Washington pointed out that "morality and religion" are the "two pillars" upon which our republic rests.[578] This is the very reason why John Adams emphasized that our Constitution would "work" only for a people dominated by the Christian faith and that it was "wholly inadequate for the government of any other."[579] Understanding the central role of the church in America, historian John Wingate Thornton wrote in 1860, "The state was developed out of the church"[580] – not the other way around. Historian Alice Baldwin seconded Thornton's declaration when she wrote in 1918, "The

Constitutional Convention and the written Constitution were the children of the pulpit."[581]

It is because the Founders believed the church to be so essential to the survival of the republic that they insisted on protecting it from governmental intrusion by taxation. So they ensured that the church would always be beyond government's reach by recognizing it as tax-exempt. A casual study of our early history reveals how this principle was applied throughout the colonies/states. For example, Virginia exempted churches from paying property taxes in 1777, New York did so in 1799, and Washington D.C. followed suit in 1802. That same year, the Seventh Congress exempted all churches in America from property taxes.[582]

(Note: Even today, parsonages are still exempt from property taxes in all 50 states. The minister's housing exemption, a principle first recognized in America in 1921, was modified in section 107(2) of the Internal Revenue tax code on August 11, 1953 by Representative Peter Mack allowing ministers of the gospel to designate a portion of compensation as a housing allowance and to exclude that amount from income to the extent that it is actually used to provide a home. In presenting the legislation, Rep. Mack declared, "Certainly, in these times when we are being threatened by a godless and antireligious world movement, we should correct this discrimination against certain ministers of the gospel who are carrying on such a courageous fight against this foe. Certainly this is not too much to do for these people who are caring for our spiritual welfare."[583] In 2000, the parsonage exemption was challenged when the IRS questioned the amount Rick Warren, pastor of Saddleback Church in southern California, claimed for his parsonage allowance on his tax returns. Whether or not every member of the court agreed that the amount Warren claimed was fair, they did uphold, in principle, that parsonages should be considered tax-exempt. Due to concerns generated by this challenge, two years later Congress passed the Clergy Housing

Allowance Clarification Act of 2002 which was signed into law by President George Bush on May 20, 2002. Even though this act capped the parsonage exemption at the amount of a home's fair rental value, including furnishings and appurtenances such as a garage, plus the cost of utilities, it reaffirmed the principle of the church's tax-exempt status.)

The Founders also believed government had no authority or right to tax the church because they considered it a sovereign entity. Understanding that a sovereign entity such as the federal government had no authority to tax another sovereign entity such as an individual state, another country, or the church, the Founders considered the church outside the reach of governmental authority and taxation. The following article, "Churches Are Tax Exempt As A Matter Of Constitutional Right," published on OpposingViews.com, clearly explains the issue of the sovereign status of the church:

"There is a distinction between constitutionally separate 'sovereigns.' For one sovereign entity to tax another leaves the taxed one subservient to that authority. This is true both in the symbolic statement of paying the tax and in the practical effect of supporting the sovereign party. So, in our constitutional structure, states may not tax each other, and they may not tax property of the federal government. The District of Columbia does not tax the property owned by foreign governments, and New York does not tax the property owned by the United Nations.

So, too, churches in America are not subservient to the government. The First Amendment to the Constitution requires that 'Congress shall make no law respecting an establishment of religion or prohibiting the free exercise thereof.' The Constitution prevents the government from wielding its authority to control churches. Churches in this way differ from all other businesses and organizations. They are a unique institution whose existence is not derived from government authority, nor even from governmental acknowledgment. Churches preceded the birth of our nation and will remain long after its death. They transcend geographic and ethnic boundaries.

In the 1970 opinion in *Walz vs. Tax Commission* of the City of New York, the high court stated that a tax exemption for churches 'creates only a minimal and remote involvement between church and state and far less than taxation of churches. [An exemption] restricts the fiscal relationship between church and state, and tends to complement and reinforce the desired separation insulating each from the other.'

In *Walz v. Tax Commission*, the Supreme Court noted that the church's 'uninterrupted freedom from taxation' has 'operated affirmatively to help guarantee the free exercise of all forms of religious belief.' The much misunderstood 'separation between church and state' is in truth designed to restrict the sovereignty of each over the other. That is, it is designed to achieve a position for each that is neither master nor servant of the other. Exemption from income taxation is essential for respect of the church as a separate sovereign entity. Otherwise the government has the power to encumber and even terminate churches if such taxes are not punctually paid or cannot be so paid in full."[584]

Additionally, many of the Founders and those who immediately followed them viewed government's power to tax as a huge threat to liberty – especially religious liberty. In 1819, while arguing the case of *McCulloch v. Maryland*, a case that determined whether or not an individual state could tax the First Bank of the United States, Daniel Webster said, "An unlimited power to tax involves, necessarily, a power to destroy."[585] In the Supreme Court's decision in that case, Chief Justice John Marshall wrote:

"That the power of taxing it [First Bank of the United States] by the States may be exercised so as to destroy it, is too obvious to be denied ... the power to tax involves the power to destroy."[586]

Believing that religion, i.e. the Christian Church, was essential to the survival of our republic, the Founders did not grant the federal government the power to tax the church because they believed that power could be used to threaten the free exercise of religion. Concerning this, Erik Stanley, senior legal counsel for the Alliance Defending Freedom, wrote,

"With all of the discussion swirling about whether church leaders can speak freely about electoral candidates from the pulpit, one question frequently comes to the fore: If a church wants to talk about the positions of electoral candidates, it can just give up the 'gift' of tax-exempt status 'bestowed' by the government. That would be simple enough — if it wasn't so completely wrong.

That's because churches receive a tax exemption as a matter of constitutional right, not legislative grace. The U.S. Supreme Court stated decades ago that the power to tax involves the power to destroy, and no surer way to destroy the free exercise of religion exists than to tax it out of existence.

Therefore, tax-exempt status for churches has existed independent of any special grant of privilege from the IRS. Some assume that any tax exemption is a government subsidy. That would be true if the government owned all property and income, but in America, it doesn't. Americans have always placed a high value on the importance of private property. That's a big difference between the United States and many other nations.

Churches derive their tax exemption from the Constitution, and it is therefore not something the government can withdraw without serious damage to the Constitution, itself. For almost the first 200 years of our country's history, that tax exemption was recognized without any stipulations or conditions. Pastors spoke freely from the pulpit, both endorsing and opposing candidates for office without anyone questioning whether they should be tax exempt."[587]

Therefore, since the Founders believed that attacking the church through taxation was necessarily striking at the very foundation of America, they recognized the church as tax-exempt. They considered taxation of the church a violation of the First Amendment since it could prohibit the free exercise of religion. If America began to tax the church, we would be ignoring the original intent of the Founders and more than 200 years of accepted legal thought and practice.

THE JOHNSON AMENDMENT – THE REASON PASTORS FEAR THE IRS

Even when they are armed with this information, many pastors still remain reluctant to speak about politics from their pulpits. With judicial history on their side and the reality that the IRS is a "paper tiger" when it comes to interfering with religious expression, what could possibly continue to intimidate these men of God? The answer is simple – the Johnson Amendment.

For the first century or so of America's existence, pastors were free to endorse and oppose candidates without fearing resistance from their people or intimidation from their government. In fact, their congregations expected them to address political issues and no one during that time suggested that a church should lose its tax-exempt status because its pastor did so. But all of this changed in 1954.

In 1954, then Texas Senator Lyndon Baines Johnson was running for reelection. Johnson's first victory in 1948 was so razor thin, with a margin of only 87 votes, that Coke Stevenson, his challenger, was able to present credible evidence that Johnson had probably stolen the election through fraud. But with some "creative" judicial wrangling, Johnson had been able to use court injunctions to retain his victory. So six years later, when Johnson was running against Dudley Dougherty, a Texas State Representative, he had good reason to fear defeat. Johnson actually was in jeopardy of losing his bid for reelection due to the efforts of two conservative non-profit organizations: Facts Forum and the Committee for Constitutional Government. These groups were making a convincing claim that Johnson was, at the very least, soft on Communism.

Desperately needing to censor these groups or likely lose the race, Johnson, on July 2, 1954, with the assistance of a complicit U.S. Senate, successfully inserted language into the IRS tax code that silenced these groups and swept him into the senate once more. Known since as the "Johnson Amendment," the new language read:

> "Non-profit entities, including churches, cannot participate in, or intervene in (including the publishing or distributing of statements), any political campaign on behalf of *or in opposition to* (italicized words added in 1984) any candidate for public office"[588]

Even though the amendment flew in the face of the Constitution by violating the section of the First Amendment that reads, "Congress shall make no law respecting an establishment of religion, or prohibiting the free exercise thereof; or abridging the freedom of speech," that did not seem to matter to the senators in 1954. It is difficult to understand how they did not see that this new law was a frontal attack on Americans' fundamental right to free speech, but they pushed it right through Congress anyway. More appalling is the relatively little discussion and debate that occurred on the senate floor concerning this far-reaching change to the tax law. After Senator Johnson had been recognized from the senate floor, the following is the only discussion that took place:

Mr. Johnson of Texas: "Mr. President, I have an amendment at the desk, which I should like to have stated."

The Presiding Officer: "The Secretary will state the amendment."

The Chief Clerk: "On page 117 of the House bill, in section 501(c)(3), it is proposed to strike out 'individuals, and' and insert 'individual,' and strike out 'influence legislation.' And insert 'influence legislation, and which does not participate in, or intervene in (including the publishing or distributing of statements), any political campaign on behalf of any candidate for public office.'"

Mr. Johnson of Texas: "Mr. President, this amendment seeks to extend the provisions of section 501 of the House bill, denying tax-exempt status to not only those people who influence legislation but also to those who intervene in any political campaign on behalf of any candidate for any public office. I have discussed the matter with the chairman of the committee, the minority ranking member of the committee, and several other members of the committee, and I understand that the amendment is acceptable to them. I hope the chairman will take it to conference, and that it will be included in the final bill which Congress passes."[589]

With that brief discussion, the Johnson Amendment became the law of the land and the club with which the IRS has intimidated pastors and churches for some fifty-eight years since. Commenting on the Johnson Amendment, Erik Stanley of Alliance Defending Freedom wrote,

"Scholars attest to the fact that the Johnson Amendment was not intended in any way to restrict the free speech of churches on the subject, but it has been used in that manner ever since. It is patently unconstitutional.

If one doubts the impact of this ill-advised piece of legislation, passed by Congress without debate or analysis, one only need take a peek at the activity of organizations like Americans United for Separation of Church and State to see how they wield it as a weapon to keep churches (at least the ones they disagree with) from having a voice. This 'keep your opinions to yourself or else' threat has got to go."[590]

Ironically, the Johnson Amendment does not even mention pastors; it only restricts churches from participating in political campaigns. So in a technical sense, the pastor's right to freely express himself from the pulpit is unaffected by the amendment. Unfortunately, that is not how the amendment has been understood and, instead, it has been used to muzzle pastors and prevent them from speaking their convictions from their pulpits. Some make the argument that since the pastor is a paid employee of the church, when he speaks from the pulpit he speaks officially for his church. On some occasions this may indeed be true, but normally it is not. Ask any preacher and he will tell you that quite often what he says does not necessarily reflect the opinions of those in his church. In fact, as a pastor I have found that I can pontificate with great emphasis from the pulpit on Sunday only to discover that members of my congregation can go out on Monday and do the exact opposite of what I told them just the day before.

The fact is most pastors do not understand themselves to be articulating the opinions and positions of their churches when they preach. Instead, most believe they are articulating the opinions and positions of God, as they understand them, from His Word. Unlike CEOs, pastors are not called to be corporate spokesmen for their churches – they are called to be spokesmen for God.

If a pastor is sincerely concerned about appearing to speak for his whole congregation when he preaches about some particularly controversial subject, all he need do is simply preface his message with the statement that his comments may not necessarily reflect the opinions or positions of all those in his church. In short, just because the pastor takes a position on a particular subject does not necessarily mean that his church takes the same position. Obviously, those who attend a particular church normally do so because they believe that what is preached from the pulpit is God's truth, they do not come to hear the pastor speak "on behalf" of the church.

Additionally, *what does speaking out on political/legislative issues have to do with the non-profit status of the church anyway?* What do political activism and making a profit have in common? Someone has yet to adequately explain why a church ceases to be a non-profit organization simply because it speaks out on a particular candidate or political issue.

ENTER THE ADF AND THE "PULPIT FREEDOM INITIATIVE"

When people ask, "So what can my church do?" Or, when preachers ask, "So what can I do?" I respond by encouraging them to join other groups who are fighting the good fight in some arena. Although none of us can address every issue or right every wrong, we can find others who are taking a stand on some issue we're passionate about and join their efforts. The combined synergy of God's people can accomplish much more than we often think. A good example is the efforts of the Alliance Defending Freedom (ADF).

In light of sixty-one years of unconstitutional tyranny from the IRS and the Johnson Amendment, what can be done about it? No one individual is probably going to be able to turn the tide, but that's the very point – we can join a growing number of preachers/pastors who are taking a corporate stand against the Johnson Amendment through the coordinated efforts of ADF.

In 2008, ADF launched the "Pulpit Freedom Initiative," an effort designed to educate American pastors about their freedom and right to speak their consciences from their pulpits. The primary purpose of this initiative was/is to encourage pastors to defy the Johnson Amendment in order to create an opportunity for ADF attorneys to defend them in court and prove that the amendment is unconstitutional.

In 2008, I was honored to be one of the thirty-three pastors from across the country who officially participated in Pulpit Freedom Initiative's first "Pulpit Freedom Sunday" as we defied the unconstitutional Johnson Amendment. Every year since, literally hundreds of pastors have joined the effort, and standing in their pulpits with Bibles held high, have defied the government's censorship of the pulpit! To this point, the IRS has put forth no "official" response. Regardless of how many Pulpit Freedom Sundays it takes, we intend to continue to defy the unconstitutional Johnson Amendment until the IRS attempts to stop us or admits either by official statement or by their silence that the Johnson Amendment is truly unconstitutional. If the IRS continues to ignore our efforts, at some point we will declare victory and spread the news to America that preachers/pastors have the right to freely speak their minds from their pulpits without any fear of governmental interference or retribution. This is how civil disobedience works and I believe it's time for us to stand against unlawful edicts and threats from our overreaching federal government.

Much more should be said about how we can and must do this, but that discussion will have to wait for another book. Suffice it to say: pastor/preacher, you are free to speak out, loudly and boldly, without fear. You have the Lord, His Word, His people, and your unalienable rights as your weapons – formidable indeed. The fight for our independence is not over; and it never will be. Eternal vigilance is the price of liberty. So dear preacher/spiritual leader, are you ready to "fight the good fight?"

Note: For those concerned about being civilly disobedient, it is important to remember that the Apostles practiced civil disobedience. In addition, our Founders, the Black Robed Regiment preachers, and generations of Americans have always understood that a law that is unconstitutional is no law at all. Consequently, breaking an unconstitutional law is by definition not an unlawful act. Consider all of those who abhorred slavery and the "Dred Scott Decision" and practiced civil disobedience by helping to free slaves using the "underground railroad." Therefore preachers need not be concerned about "breaking the law" when defying the Johnson Amendment since we believe it to be unconstitutional and therefore "not a law" in the first place.

Chapter 17

WHERE IS TODAY'S BLACK ROBED REGIMENT?

"When the political institutions of our fathers cease to be animated by their spirit and virtues, the forms only will remain, monuments of their wisdom, and not less of our folly."[591] Historian John Wingate Thornton, 1860

In chapter two we discussed how Pastor Peter Muhlenberg traded his clerical robe for a colonel's uniform. But Peter was not the only Lutheran preacher in his family – in addition to his father, Henry, his brother, Frederick Augustus, was also a Lutheran preacher. In 1774, Frederick became the pastor of Christ's Church, first known as the Old Swamp Church, in New York City.

Unlike his brother Peter who left his pulpit to lead the 8th Virginia Regiment against the British, Frederick was much like many of today's pastors, believing that a preacher should not get involved in politics and war. He had even written to his brother rebuking him for his political involvement: "You have become too involved in matters with which, as a preacher, you have nothing whatsoever to do and which do not belong to your office."[592] But as we saw, John sent a stinging response back to Frederick emphatically declaring that a Christian could not help but get involved – it was the Lord's own work.

As this heated exchange between the brothers took place, a mighty storm was brewing; a storm that ultimately would break upon Frederick and his church in a mighty cataclysm when the British invaded New York City. In May 1776, perceiving this invasion as imminent, Frederick sent his wife, Cathy, who was pregnant at the time, and their two children to stay with her parents in Philadelphia, while he remained in New York City to continue ministering to his shrinking congregation. But when rumors began to circulate that the British were planning on hanging Frederick if they caught him, his church urged him to flee for his own safety.[593] On July 2, 1776, Frederick Muhlenberg left New York City "looking over his shoulder at a city soon to be paralyzed by war."[594] Just hours later, General Howe landed on Staten Island and the British occupation of New York City had begun. As the Redcoats entered New York City, they came burning and pillaging along the way – burning and desecrating churches as well.

It was a greatly changed Frederick Muhlenberg who arrived in Philadelphia to join his refugee family. Practically destitute, with no church, no house, and no way to support his family, Frederick began to rethink his position on pastors being involved in politics and war. On March 2, 1779, Frederick Muhlenberg, the preacher who insisted that preachers should not get involved in such things, became a member of the Continental Congress. One year later, he became a member of the Pennsylvania General Assembly (House of Representatives) where he served from 1780 to 1783, serving as the Speaker the entire time. Later Frederick served as the president of the Pennsylvania Constitutional Convention where he pushed for the ratification of the U.S. Constitution. Significantly, he is one of only two people who signed the Bill of Rights. He served as a member of the U.S. House of Representatives from 1789-1797, and the preacher who said that preachers should not get entangled in such "secular" pursuits became the first Speaker of the House of Representatives of the United States of America.

Quite a change of heart wouldn't you say? So what changed Frederick's mind about preachers and politics? Simple: he was "pinched" – pinched hard enough that it hurt. Though he may not have seen the light initially, he definitely felt the heat in the end. The question is how hard will today's preachers have to be "pinched" before they will speak out? Will they, like Frederick Muhlenberg, have to lose practically everything before they are willing to stand up and speak out?

ETERNAL VIGILANCE IS THE PRICE OF LIBERTY

In the waning days of 1783, Americans were ecstatic with joy – and with good reason, they had just won a brutal, painful, and costly eight-year war. Having defeated the most powerful army in the world, they were now breathing the fresh air of freedom. On December 11, 1783, George Duffield preached the following in the Third Presbyterian Church of Philadelphia on a day of thanksgiving to God:

> "Here has our God erected a banner of civil and religious liberty: And prepared an asylum for the poor and oppressed from every part of the earth. Here, if wisdom guide our affairs, shall a happy equality reign; and joyous freedom bless the inhabitants wide and far, from age to age. ... Justice and truth shall here yet meet together, and righteousness and peace embrace each other: And the wilderness blossom as the rose, and the desert rejoice and sing."[595]

As is evident from Duffield's message, Americans believed their prospects for a happy and prosperous future were bright as they expected great things. But they also knew that liberty and independence, as wonderful as they were, could not be taken for granted. They knew the fight for liberty was not over – and it never would be. Enemies still lurked in the darkness that, if given the opportunity, would snatch away their new won freedom in a moment. The Black Regiment was not about to let that happen. They had fought hard to earn their freedom and they were prepared to fight just as hard to keep it.

In a speech in Dublin, Ireland in 1790, John Philpot Curran, Irish orator and politician, perfectly articulated what it took to preserve liberty:

> "It is the common fate of the indolent to see their rights become a prey to the active. The condition upon which God hath given liberty to man is eternal vigilance; which condition if he break, servitude is at once the consequence of his crime and the punishment of his guilt." [596]

Later Curran's words were morphed into the now famous phrase, "Eternal vigilance is the price of liberty" – a quote often erroneously attributed to Thomas Jefferson. Even though Jefferson was not the origin of that statement, he did write in a November 13, 1787 letter to William S. Smith that, "The tree of liberty must be refreshed from time to time, with the blood of patriots and tyrants. It is its natural manure." [597] Both Curran and Jefferson were articulating a fact that the patriot preachers knew well: freedom is not free; it comes at a high price, and once purchased, must forever be guarded and defended.

If history had taught the preachers anything, it had taught them that wherever good men were enjoying their God-given liberty, there were always bad men who wanted to steal it away. They also knew that this problem reached all of the way back to the Garden of Eden, where, because of Adam's fall, envy, strife, conquest, and death had become the dominant theme in the sad story of mankind. The patriot preachers taught that, short of a right relationship with God, man was lost in an endless quest to satisfy his insatiable spiritual hunger by grabbing for more power, popularity, and things.

St. Augustine had articulated this dilemma way back in the late 4th century, when he said, "Thou hast made us for Thyself, O Lord, and our hearts are restless until they rest in Thee."[598] Almost thirteen hundred years later, Blaise Pascal, the Christian Frenchman, scientist, and writer, expanded upon Augustine's declaration:

"What else does this craving, and this helplessness, proclaim but that there was once in man a true happiness, of which all that now remains is the empty print and trace? This he tries in vain to fill with everything around him, seeking in things that are not there the help he cannot find in those that are, though none can help, since this infinite abyss can be filled only with an infinite and unchangeable object; in other words by God himself."[599]

Now that they had won the war, the patriot preachers renewed their efforts to deliver this message to America. While helping build the new union they had just helped to birth, the preachers reminded Americans of their need to find satisfaction in Christ, not in success and material prosperity – things that could, if allowed, become an even greater enemy to all they had accomplished than the Redcoats themselves.

AN ENEMY MORE DANGEROUS THAN THE REDCOATS

On January 27, 1838, just fifty-five years after the War of Independence, Abraham Lincoln warned a Springfield, Illinois crowd that the greatest threat to Americans' liberty was internal:

"At what point then, is the approach of danger to be expected? I answer that if it ever reach us, it must spring from amongst us; it cannot come from abroad. If destruction be our lot, we ourselves must be the authors and finishers. As a nation of free men, we must live through our times or die by suicide."[600]

What Lincoln was articulating in the middle of the 19th century, the patriot preachers had been articulating almost one hundred years earlier in the 18th century. They knew that the greatest enemy to liberty was not the British regulars; it was a loss of a strong reliance upon God, and they intended to prevent that from taking place if they were able.

When they were in the midst of the war, the colonists had fervently and openly sought God's aid. But once the war was over and He had granted them victory and peace, the prosperity that had come began to cool their spiritual passion. The patriot preachers knew that to sustain their liberty and the success of their infant republic, it was essential that they not allow the previously red-hot spiritual fervency to wane.

So for the preachers, the war was not over – only the phase that required bullets and bombs. They understood that America was not yet out of the woods. Even though evil forces from "without" posed no immediate threat, evil forces "within" did. Affluence, arrogance, and spiritual apathy were internal foes more deceptive and destructive than ones the American army had just defeated in the field of battle. Having just made incalculable sacrifices to "insure the blessings of liberty to themselves and their posterity" the patriot preachers had no intention of now allowing these enemies to destroy all they had accomplished.

Unfortunately, it did not take long before the very sins that the Black Regiment warned of began to seep back into the hearts and minds of the American people. With liberty came prosperity and with that prosperity came pride and arrogance. Americans were beginning to believe the false notion that they were self-sufficient and had no need of God's help – certainly not nearly as much as they had during the war. Knowing well the warning in Proverbs 16:18 that, "Pride goeth before destruction, and an haughty spirit before a fall," the patriot preachers began attacking the country's new enemy.

This new threat prompted Samuel Wales, pastor of the First Congregational Church in Milford, Connecticut and professor of Divinity at Yale, to remind his Connecticut audience of the tendency of men to reduce their dependence upon God once the crisis had passed:

> "In the distresses of the late war, though they were most evidently brought upon us by the instrumentality of men, we were nevertheless much more ready to impute them to the hand of God, than we now are to acknowledge the same hand in the happiness of peace, and the other rich blessings of his providence and grace. When our wants are very pressing, we are willing, or pretend to be willing to apply to God for relief. But no sooner is the relief given than we set our hearts upon the gift, and neglect the giver; or rather make use of his own bounty in order to fight against him." [601]

Next, he warned that peace and prosperity could be as fatal to a people as an armed enemy – especially to a people who owed so much to God's providential care:

> "While prosperity is dangerous to a people in general, it is peculiarly so to those who are elevated above the common walks of life. Honor, power and wealth are attended with strong temptations, temptations which in most instances have proved too powerful for man. ... Is it not a sad truth, that since the commencement of the late war, and especially since the restoration of peace, the holy religion of Jesus, ... is, by many less regarded than it was before?

Wales concluded by reminding his audience that the loss of "true" patriotism would endanger the country:

> "Another particular evil by which we are endangered, is the want of true patriotism. By true patriotism I mean a real concern for the welfare of our whole country in general.

This patriotism is a branch of that extensive benevolence which is highly recommended by our holy religion, ... While the war lasted our patriotism was eminent and produced the most happy effects. ... The practice of religion must therefore be considered as absolutely essential to the best state of public prosperity, ... So, although we have gained that for which we most ardently wished, an happy period to the late war, yet we can by no means be certain but that some far greater evils are now before us. We may be over-run and ruined both for time and eternity by a torrent of vice and licentiousness, with their never-failing attendants, infidelity and atheism. ... Never, never, can we be secure but in the practice of true virtue and in the favor of God."[602]

THE WAR FOR INDEPENDENCE IS NOT OVER

In 1833, *The American Quarterly Register*, in writing about the patriot preachers of the Revolution, said, "As a body of men, the clergy were preeminent in their attachment to liberty. The pulpits of the land rang with the notes of freedom."[603] Would to God that today's pulpits rang with the notes of freedom!

To be a good citizen in a republic like ours requires keeping a vigilant watch over our God-given liberties and remaining active in the political process. We must remember that eternal vigilance truly is the price of freedom. Long before he was President, Ronald Reagan commented on this responsibility:

"Freedom is never more than one generation away from extinction. We didn't pass it on to our children in the bloodstream. It must be fought for, protected, and handed on ..."[604]

On July 5, 1802, although a theological liberal and a Unitarian, William Emerson, pastor of the First Church of Boston, appropriately warned Americans of the terrible consequences the country would face if it ever strayed from its founding principles:

"Should the rulers of our country, ... deviate from the course prescribed by their wise predecessors, incautiously pulling down what had been carefully built; ... instead of adhering to principles of certain utility; and should they despise the religion and customs of our progenitors, setting an example of impiety and dissipation, deplorable will be the consequences. ... disease will extend to the utmost extremities of the political body. As well may you arrest the flight of time, or entice the moon from her orbit, as preserve your freedom under atheistical rulers, ... Libertinism and lethargy, anarchy and misrule will deform our once happy republic; and its liberties will receive an incurable wound. The soil of America will remain; but the name and glory of the United States will have perished forever. This lovely peninsula will continue inhabited; but "the feelings, manners, and principles" of those Bostonians, who nobly resisted the various acts of British aggression, will be utterly changed. The streams of Concord will flow as formerly, and the hills of Charlestown grow verdant with each return of spring; but the character of the men, who mingled their blood with those waters, and who eternized those heights, will be sought for, but shall not be found."[605]

Although the patriot preachers did not live to see Emerson's fears realized, unfortunately, we in the 21st century have. We are experiencing the horror of watching America do the very things the Black Regiment warned early Americans to avoid. Having become arrogant in our prosperity and comfort, we no longer honor the Lord who gave us the very liberties we abuse, and "true patriotism" which seeks the welfare of the county by seeking the will of God is becoming a rare commodity. Thinking we are too sophisticated for a religion as archaic and exclusive as

Christianity, we have expelled God from the public square and are in the process of vilifying Christianity altogether.

Although won some two hundred and thirty years ago, our War of Independence is obviously not over – it is being waged with ever increasing intensity as we draw nearer to the return of Christ. Never before have the forces marshaled to destroy America seemed so formidable. Never before has America seemed closer to the brink of disaster than today. Never before have the stakes seemed higher.

Unfortunately, never before has America been more godless and defenseless. Never before has the American church appeared less prepared for battle. Anemic, worldly, disengaged, and silent, the church seems completely satisfied with things the way they are. Rather than "fighting the good fight" as Paul admonished, many modern Christians appear consumed with "success" and are demanding that God give them "their best lives now!" Rather than heeding Jesus' command not to "lay up treasures on earth," today's church seems intent on accumulating as much earthly treasure as possible. Like Nero, will it fiddle while their country goes up in flames?

There is hope. The church is sufficient to fight against these dark forces – but only if it is prepared for the struggle. Unfortunately, one of its deficiencies is that there are too few leaders who see and understand the real enemy. There are, of course, plenty of preachers/pastors/spiritual leaders in the church. But so far, most have been unwilling to engage in the fight for religious liberty. Whatever their reasons, they have chosen to desert their country in its present crisis. They desperately need to hear again the words of Black Regiment preacher William Smith when he said:

> "[W]e know that our civil and religious rights are linked together in one indissoluble bond, we neither have, nor seek to have, any interest separate from that of our country; nor can we advise a desertion of its cause.

Religion and liberty must flourish or fall together in America. We pray that both may be perpetual."[606]

As the American church sits idly by, it is becoming increasingly soft and fat. Choosing to ignore the determined and highly organized enemy closing in around us, we believers seem convinced we are safe within the walls of our churches. We know well what the Scriptures teach about spiritual warfare. We know we are called to be soldiers of Jesus Christ. We know that we have sufficient spiritual armor for the battle. Most importantly, we know that the Lord has promised us the victory. The only thing we seem not to know is the location of the battlefield.

But even though we know so much, we seem to have forgotten a good number of things. For example, many American pastors appear to have forgotten, or maybe never learned the lesson of the pastors in Germany in the years prior to WWII. As Hitler rose to power, he was friendly with the pastors and feigned alliances with them. As he spun his web with talk of peace and cooperation, he was busy working behind the scenes building his military machine that would eventually entrap these spiritually blind pastors and launch one of the worst wars in history. Few pastors saw through the ruse. A small number did, they spoke out, and it cost some of them their lives.

One of those pastors was Dietrich Bonheoffer. Bonheoffer, a Lutheran pastor, was a powerful preacher and prolific writer. Books of his such as *The Cost of Discipleship* and *Life Together* are still widely read by believers today. Bonheoffer staunchly resisted the work of the Nazis, even going as far as to participate in an attempt to assassinate Hitler. Consequently, he was eventually arrested by the Gestapo on April 5, 1943, imprisoned at the Tegel military prison, and finally executed on April 9, 1945, just days before American forces liberated the prison. During his courageous stand against Nazi tyranny, Bonheoffer famously said, "Silence in the face of evil is itself evil: God will not hold us guiltless. Not to speak is to speak. Not to act is to act."[607]

In stark contrast, today's pastors seem to believe that by being silent, they are steering clear of the fray. For those who do, they need to hear Bonheoffer's warning again. Like British Prime Minister Neville Chamberlain who declared in 1938 there would be "peace in our time" while Adolph Hitler was preparing to conquer the world, many modern American preachers/Christians have become "Chamberlainesque," naïvely consoling themselves with the hollow hope of "peace in our time." American preachers/pastors must not allow what happened in Germany to happen in America – they must speak loudly and act boldly!

WHERE HAVE ALL THE WARRIORS GONE?

Our country exists because previous generations were willing to *give* more than they *got*. The founding generation was willing to sacrifice their "fortunes, their lives, and their sacred honor" to gain something greater, something nobler – liberty, both spiritual and civil. John F. Kennedy's January 20, 1961 challenge, "Ask not what your country can do for you, ask what you can do for your country," seems to be more relevant than ever. Conversely, many of today's Americans, including Christians, seem more interested in what they can *get* than what they can *give* to their country.

How strange that a people who have historically been so willing to sacrifice so much to liberate so many is now so willing to sell its liberties and soul for so little. Are we now willing to passively accept the chains of socialism and slavery? "Is life so dear, or peace so sweet, as to be purchased at the prices of chains and slavery?" Forbid it, Almighty God! Are there any today who will stand up and carry the torch that Patrick Henry and his compatriots carried so faithfully so long ago? Are there any "truth warriors" left in America?

Ezekiel, the Jewish prophet, lived in the late sixth century B.C. during a time when truth warriors were in short supply in Israel. In Ezekiel 22:23-31, the prophet wrote:

"And the word of the Lord came unto me, saying, [24]"Son of man, say unto her, Thou art the land that is not cleansed, nor rained upon in the day of indignation. [25]There is a conspiracy of her prophets in the midst thereof, like a roaring lion ravening the prey; they have devoured souls; they have taken the treasure and precious things; they have made her many widows in the midst thereof. [26]Her priests have violated my law, and have profaned mine holy things: they have put no difference between the holy and profane, neither have they showed difference between the unclean and the clean, and have hid their eyes from my sabbaths, and I am profaned among them. [27]Her princes in the midst thereof are like wolves ravening the prey, to shed blood, and to destroy souls, to get dishonest gain. [28]And her prophets have daubed them with untempered mortar, seeing vanity, and divining lies unto them, saying, Thus saith the Lord God, when the Lord hath not spoken. [29]The people of the land have used oppression, and exercised robbery, and have vexed the poor and needy: yea, they have oppressed the stranger wrongfully. [30]And I sought for a man among them, that should make up the hedge, and stand in the gap before me for the land, that I should not destroy it: but I found none. [31]Therefore have I poured out mine indignation upon them; I have consumed them with the fire of my wrath: their own way have I recompensed upon their heads, saith the Lord God.'"

Sound familiar? God blamed Israel's spiritual leaders for the nation's deplorable condition. Even though the Jews deserved judgment, as a beautiful expression of His grace, God was searching for a reason to withhold that judgment. Take special note of verse 30 of that passage where God said through Ezekiel, "And I sought for a man among them, that should make up the hedge, and stand in the gap before me for the land, that I should not destroy it: but I found none."

In this passage, there are at least five points that American Christians, especially church leaders, must see:

1. The Search: God was searching for a reason not to judge Israel.

2. The Subject: God was looking for a man to stand up for what was right.

3. The Situation: It was a dark time for Israel and the absence of strong leaders had created a gap in the "hedge of protection" around the nation – a gap that God was about to allow Israel's enemies to exploit.

4. The Sorrow: Sadly, God found no one who would stand.

5. The Sentence: God would judge Israel accordingly.

I believe our present predicament is eerily similar to that of Ezekiel's day. Many of our spiritual leaders have failed miserably. Today's church is filled with compromise and liberalism. Churches that actually believe that the Bible is God's inerrant, unchanging Word are becoming a minority. Even among these churches, many are led by pastors who have lost their will to defend religious liberty. Unlike their patriot preacher ancestors, for the fear of being labeled political, these pastors seem willing to allow their country to go down the tubes. Consequently, the old adage, "as goes the church, so goes the country," has been validated right before our very eyes. Our culture slides further down the slippery slope of socialism as the church slips deeper into self-centeredness, spiritual compromise, and apathy. We need truth warriors now more than ever. As God searches for those who are willing to "stand in the gap" for our culture, is He finding anyone? Will anyone boldly stand and say, "Here am I; send me?"

WHAT YOU CAN DO

Remembering the words of Samuel Adams: "If ever a time should come, when vain and aspiring men shall possess the highest seats in Government, our country will stand in need of its experienced patriots to prevent its ruin," it appears that the time he warned of is NOW!

But many say, "What can I do, I'm only one person?" In the Boston Public Garden stands a statue of Edward Everett Hale and on its base is engraved a quote attributed to him addressing this very question:

"I am only one, but I am still one; I cannot do everything, but still I can do something; and because I cannot do everything I will not refuse to do the something that I can do."

Even though you are just one and although you may "feel" powerless, there are, in fact, some very powerful things you can do right now. Let me suggest a few:

1. Do not despair.

2. Get your own life in order – physically *and* spiritually.

3. Support a church that preaches the "whole counsel" of God.

4. Assess your own gifts/talents and enlist them immediately.

5. Become a serious student of Scripture, history, and current events.

6. Help educate family and friends.

7. Actively participate in ministries like our "Bringing Back the Black Robed Regiment," the Alliance Defending Freedom, etc.

8. Begin to "seek" opportunities to influence public policy.

9. Pray about running for a local position such as the school board, city council, etc.

10. If not, then help recruit and support those who will.

11. Pray about running for a county/statewide position.

12. If not, then help recruit and support those who will.

13. Pray that God will give you a "never say die" heart.

14. Pray that God will have mercy on our country and send a third great awakening.

BRINGING BACK THE BLACK ROBED REGIMENT

Although I am certainly not advocating for war, in the midst of this moral meltdown, one question screams out for an answer: "Where is today's Black Robed Regiment?" Sadly, most of them are missing from action. In chapter 4, I discussed how the Black Regiment preachers saw themselves as "watchmen on the wall," guarding against the approach of the enemy. Unfortunately, today's preachers/watchmen have left their posts. The prophet Isaiah encountered the same type of spiritual leaders in his day. Commenting on how God's watchmen were failing, the prophet wrote:

> "His watchmen are blind: they are all ignorant, they are all dumb dogs, they cannot bark; sleeping, lying down, loving to slumber. [11]Yea, they are greedy dogs which can never have enough, and they are shepherds that cannot understand: they all look to their own way, every one for his gain, from his quarter." Isaiah 56:10-11

If we aim to restore full liberty to our country, we will need the same commitment from modern preachers as that of Jacob Trout, John Rosbrugh, Peter Muhlenberg, James Caldwell, and the other patriot preachers you've read about in this book. If we ever needed the spirit of the Black Regiment, we need it now. Christians must beseech God to move in the hearts of His preachers/pastors to raise up a new generation of patriot preachers or we are most probably going to lose the liberties passed down to us. Scripture teaches that a steward must be faithful. We have not been faithful. I simply do not know how to state it more clearly than that.

If Daniel Webster was correct when he said that good Christians make good citizens, then for the past one hundred years or so, based upon their dismal performance as citizens, American churchgoers must not be very good Christians. Consequently, without the purifying/preserving effect of their witness in government, our culture is now experiencing a severe moral/spiritual crisis and appears to be in imminent danger of a cataclysmic socio/economic meltdown.

Interestingly, Scripture declares that when a culture finds itself in such a state, it is because God's people have failed in their responsibility to engage that culture. Although originally written to the nation of Israel almost 2500 years ago, I believe the basic principles of 2 Chronicles 7:14 apply to any people in any land. In that passage, God said:

> "If my people, which are called by my name, shall humble themselves, and pray, and seek my face, and turn from their wicked ways; then will I hear from heaven, and will forgive their sin, and will heal their land."

Notice Scripture declares that the future blessings on any people who have an understanding of God and His principles are dependent upon the repentance of *His people, the church*. God does not blame unbelievers for the deplorable state of a culture familiar with His Word, nor does He require their repentance before He brings healing to that broken culture – He blames believers and withholds healing until *His people* repent. He does not blame the White House, the courthouse, the State House, or the schoolhouse – He blames the *church house*. The Apostle Peter confirmed this Old Testament concept when he wrote:

"For the time is come that judgment must begin at the house of God: and if it first begin at us, what shall the end be of them that obey not the gospel of God?" 1 Peter 4:17

If America has any hope, it is to be found in the church. Christians must repent of their worldliness and rise up in the power of God's Spirit and take the salt and light back into every area of their culture – including the political arena. This is what the patriot preachers of the 18th century believed, and partly because they were willing to speak loudly and act boldly, America came to be. Now, in the 21st century, we are approaching a moment similar to the one our ancestors faced in the 1760s and 70s. As many preachers and their congregations played a significant role then, today's preachers must follow their bold example and do the same if we have any chance of sustaining the liberty our founding generation fought and died to provide and protect.

The good news: the American church can change our culture. The bad news: most of its leaders are AWOL and there are presently too few commanders to lead it. If the preachers, God's leaders, would do their duty and lead – a mighty army of faithful Christians could be awakened, informed, and mobilized to turn our culture back to the faith of its forefathers.

Unfortunately, many of our pastors today are more concerned about the size of their congregations, their church budgets, and their paychecks than they are in the fate of their country. Not long ago, Christian pollster George Barna conducted a study to determine why modern preachers seem reluctant to address the social issues of our time. Interestingly, he found that among the reasons they remain silent, church attendance, the amount given to the church, and the size of the church's facilities are at the top of the list.[608] Responding to these findings, Barna commented that although those things are important in their proper place, there's only one thing wrong – "Jesus didn't die for any of them."[609]

Terrified of taking a controversial stand, many preachers are consumed with keeping everyone happy and not offending their big tithers. The last thing these pastors want is controversy and conflict, and they will do almost anything to avoid it, including avoiding the truth. *For this reason, the story of the Black Robed Regiment must be retold.* The patriot preachers of the late 1700s fanned the flames of liberty and truth and when the time came, bravely led their men to fight to secure them. The modern church must rediscover their history and recapture their spirit. Like those men of God from long ago, modern preachers must once again "connect the religious and political dots" for their congregations if we hope to save our culture from certain disaster. Today's preachers must return to their posts as watchmen on the wall and keep a "sober and vigilant" watch. Without the return of this kind of spiritual leadership, America is destined to continue wandering blindly in the fog of "political correctness" and godless humanism – and, ultimately, to its doom. It was from this perspective that the patriot preachers fired the first volleys at British tyranny from their pulpits.

BUT WHAT IF YOUR PASTOR REFUSES TO SPEAK OUT

"But my pastor refuses to get involved and speak out on cultural issues, claiming he cannot preach politics in the pulpit. What should I do?" I regularly have believers tearfully ask me this question.

Before giving my answer, let me say that I am well acquainted with the immense demands and pressures of pastoring a church – I have been a pastor for thirty-four years. I know that most pastors are pulled in multiple directions by their congregations and are often expected to address or solve every problem. Believers must remember this and always be respectful when approaching their pastor – especially when it comes to politics. He most probably has had the myth of "separation of church and state" beaten into his head for most, if not all, of his life and will need encouragement to go against that taboo.

Having said this, congregations must encourage, challenge, and pressure (if necessary) their pastors to lead the way and engage believers in the struggle. It is imperative that we do this before our opportunity has passed and our liberties are lost forever.

When some pastor does have the courage to speak out, believers should immediately show their support and help defend him against the attacks that will inevitably come. He will desperately need to know that there are those in his church who agree with him and he will need their *visible* and *vocal* support. A simple "I'm praying for you, brother" or "they needed to hear that" will not suffice – you will have to come in from the sidelines and join him in the fight.

For those who find themselves in a church where their pastor simply refuses to engage in the debate, the options are much more difficult. These believers must lovingly and humbly remind their pastor that he has a responsibility to preach the "whole counsel of God" and address every area of life. They must assure him that they will be there with their support and defense in the event he is willing to take on the challenge. In the end, if he refuses to do so, then they should respectfully leave that church, find one where the pastor will address these issues from the pulpit and join him in his efforts. Believe me, he needs your help!

WHAT REALLY MATTERS IN THE END

On April 19, 1781, Henry Cumings offered a prayer in his sermon that needs to be prayed again in America:

> "O thou supreme Governor of the world, whose arm hath done great things for us, establish the foundations of this commonwealth, and evermore defend it with the saving strength of thy right hand! Grant that here the divine constitutions of Jesus thy Son may ever be honored and

maintained! Grant that it may be the residence of all private and patriotic virtues, of all that enlightens and supports, all that sweetens and adorns human society, till the states and kingdoms of this world shall be swallowed up in thine own kingdom: In that, which alone is immortal, may we obtain a perfect citizenship, and enjoy in its completion, 'the glorious Liberty of the Sons of God!' And let all the people say, Amen!"[610]

As we struggle to defend and restore liberty in our country, we must keep the right priorities. Though we must fight to the last ounce of our courage, we must remember that countries and governments pass away. People and places pass and change. Histories fade into the distant past. But through it all, God is eternal. Even if we are successful in saving all, or parts, of our country, eventually, they too, will pass away. In contrast, God's kingdom will, thankfully, endure forever. Therefore, the only thing in life that will remain is what we have done in obedience to Him and in the furtherance of His kingdom. Evangelist C.T. Studd perfectly expressed this truth in his famous poem, "Only One Life" when he wrote, "Only one life, 'twill soon be past, only what's done for Christ will last."[611]

Only one life, and that life is short at its longest. In John 9:4, Jesus said, "I must work the works of him that sent me, while it is day: the night cometh, when no man can work." The same applies to us; we only have the small window of a lifetime in which to do what God has called us to do. It's time to get busy!

The 18th century patriot preachers and their churches presided over the *sunrise* of liberty in North America. If things do not change and our modern preachers/Christians do not wake up and reengage, the 21st century preachers and their churches could very well and most probably preside over the *sunset* of liberty in North America.

In the end, what we are fighting for is the opportunity to freely and openly live and share the Gospel of Jesus Christ with a lost and dying world. In his Massachusetts election sermon on May 31, 1780, Simeon Howard said it well:

"But let every one remember that, whatever others may do, and however it may fare with our country, it shall surely be well with the righteous; and when all the mighty states and empires of this world shall be dissolved, and pass away 'like the baseless fabric of a vision,' they shall enter into the kingdom of their Father, which cannot be moved, and, in the enjoyment and exercise of perfect peace, liberty, and love, shine forth as the sun forever and ever."[612]

Until then, let us heed the 1776 challenge of Black Robed Regiment preacher William Gordon:

"May heaven influence every one of us to contribute our best abilities, according to our several stations and relations, to the defense and support of the common weal [good]."[613]

… And let us pray that God will *Bring Back the Black Robed Regiment!*"

God prosper the cause! Amen.

Endnotes

1   Thornton, J. (1860). *The pulpit of the American revolution: Or, The political sermons of the period of 1776 With a historical introduction, notes, and illustrations* (Boston: Gould and Lincoln), 304-05.

2   Sandoz, E. (1998). Political sermons of the American founding era, 1730-1805 (2nd ed., Vol. 1). (Indianapolis, IN: Liberty Fund), Vol. 1. Chapter: 19: Abraham Keteltas, GOD ARISING AND PLEADING HIS PEOPLE'S CAUSE. Accessed from: http://oll.libertyfund.org/title/816/69274

3   Ibid. Vol. 1. Chapter: 31: Elizur Goodrich, THE PRINCIPLES OF CIVIL UNION AND HAPPINESS CONSIDERED AND RECOMMENDED Accessed November 4, 2012 http://oll.libertyfund.org/title/816/69311

4   Thornton, 249-50.

5   Moore, Frank. *The Patriot Preachers of the American Revolution with Biographical Sketches, 1766-1783* (New York: Charles T. Evans, 1862),184.

6   Cooper, Samuel. *A Sermon Preached before His Excellency John Hancock, Esq ; Governour, the Honourable the Senate, and House of Representatives of the Commonwealth of Massachusetts, October 25, 1780 Being the Day of the Commencement of the Constitution, and Inauguration O.* Boston] Commonwealth of Massachusetts: Printed by T. and J. Fleet, and J. Gill, 1780. Accessed November 3, 2012: www.belcherfoundation.org/samuel%20cooper%20sermon%20on%20constitution.pdf

7   Bunce, Oliver Bell. *The Romance of the Revolution Being a History of the Personal Adventures, Romantic Incidents, and Exploits Incidental to the War of Independence* ... (Philadelphia: Porter & Coates, 1858), 440-444. Accessed April 5, 2013: https://archive.org/stream/romanceofrevolut02bunc#page/440/mode/2up,

8   Revolutionary War Archives, http://www.revolutionarywararchives.org/life-times-link/161-a-blessing-on-american-arms-at-brandywine.

9   Headley, J. T. *The Chaplains and Clergy of the Revolution*. (New York: C. Scribner, 1864),14-15.

10   Thornton, XXXVIII.

11   Adams, James L. *Yankee Doodle Went to Church* (Old Tappan, N.J.: F.H. Revell, 1989), 39.

12   Oliver, Peter. *Peter Oliver's Origin & Progress of the American Rebellion a Tory View*. Edited by Adair & John A. Schultz (Stanford, Calif: Stanford University Press, 1967), 91, Accessed on August 21, 2015: https://archive. org/texts/flipbook/flippy.php?id=originandprogres011156mbp,

13   Ibid., 93.

14   Ibid., 29, 63-64.

15   Headley, 358.

16   Baldwin, Alice M. *The New England Clergy and the American Revolution*. (New York: F. Ungar Pub., 1958), 97 (footnote #42).

17   Fea, John. *Why Study History?: Reflecting on the Importance of the past* (Grand Rapids, MI: Baker Academic, 2013), 3, 15.

18   Fea, 30.

19   Longfield, Bradley J. *Presbyterians and American Culture a History* (Louisville, KY: Westminster John Knox Press, 2013), 37

20   Letter to James Warren, October 24, 1780, Letter 199, http://web.archive. org/web/20110114145815/http://etext.lib.virginia.edu/etcbin/toccer-new2?id=DelVol16.xml&images=images/modeng&data=/texts/english/ modeng/parsed&tag=public&part=199&division=div1

21   Baldwin, Chapter 11, p. 40.

22   Louthan, Henry Thompson. *The American Baptist Pulpit at the Beginning of the Twentieth Century* (Williamsburg, Va.: Published by the Editor, 1903), 13.

23   Headley, Chapter XIV, p. 160.

24   Clyde, John Cunningham. *Rosbrugh, a Tale of the Revolution; Or, Life, Labors and Death of Rev. John Rosbrugh ... Chaplain in the Continental Army; Clerical Martyr of the Revolution, Killed by Hessians, in the Battle of*

Assumpink, at Trenton, New Jersey, Jan. 2d, 1777 (Founded up. Easton, 1880), 4-24

25   Ibid., 25-26.

26   Ibid., 25

27   Ibid., 34-35.

28   Ibid., 38-40.

29   Ibid., 40.

30   Sprague, William B. *Annals of the American Pulpit: Or, Commemorative Notices of Distinguished American Clergymen of Various Denominations : From the Early Settlement of the Country to the Close of the Year Eighteen Hundred and Fifty-five : With Historical Introductions* (New York: Robert Carter & Bros., 1858), 254-257. Accessed April 22, 2015: https://archive. org/stream/00839292.1353.emory.edu/00839292_1353#page/n281/ mode/2up

31   Clyde, 42.

32   Ibid., 43.

33   Ibid., 43-44.

34   Sinatra, Jon. "WASHINGTON'S MILITIA UNIT TACTICS AT TRENTON & PRINCETON." Colorado Society–Sons of the American Revolution. 2005. Accessed August 20, 2015. http://www.cossar.us/images/ CHRISTMAS_CAMPAIGN_1776_76.pdf.

35   Clyde, 45.

36   Headley, 163, and Clyde, 55.

37   Clyde, 58-59.

38   Headley, 161.

39   Clyde, 59.

40   Headley, 162.

41   Ibid., 162-63.

42   Ibid., 163.

43   Clyde, 2.

44   Moore, 353-354.

45   Niles, Hezekiah. *Principles and Acts of the Revolution in America: Or, An Attempt to Collect and Preserve Some of the Speeches, Orations, & Proceedings, with Sketches and Remarks on Men and Things, and Other Fugitive or Neglected Pieces, Belonging to the Men of the Revolution* (Baltimore: Printed and Pub. for the Editor, by W.O. Niles, 1822), 189. Accessed: https://archive.org/details/principlesactsof00nile.

46   Murray, D.D., Nicholas. *A Memoir of the Rev. James Caldwell of Elizabethtown.* Vol. III. (Newark, N. J.: Printed at the Office of the Daily Advertiser, 1848), 89.

47   Moore, Preface, p. III.

48   Adams, James, *Yankee Doodle Went To Church* (New Jersey: Fleming H. Revell Company Old Tappan, 1989), p. 28.

49   Muhlenberg, Henry A. *The Life of Major-General Peter Muhlenberg of the Revolutionary Army* (Philadelphia: Carey and Hart, 1849), 50-54,

50   Bellesiles, M. Muhlenberg, John Peter Gabriel. In H. E. Selesky (Ed.), *Encyclopedia of the American Revolution: Library of Military History* (Detroit: Charles Scribner's Sons, 2006) Vol. 2, 760-761). Accessed from: http://go.galegroup.com.ezproxy.lib.ou.edu/ps/i.do?id=GALE%7CCX3454901084&v=2.1&u=norm94900&it=r&p=GVRL&sw=w&asid=5b3cef57d4b4fbe9f307bb0873f1b9f6

51   Headley, 122.

52   Wallace, Paul A. W. *The Muhlenbergs of Pennsylvania* (Philadelphia: University of Pennsylvania Press, 1950),120-121.

53   Henry, Patrick, "Give Me Liberty Or Give Me Death," speech delivered on March 23, 1775 at St. John's Episcopal Church, Richmond, VA. Accessed April 27, 2015: http://avalon.law.yale.edu/18th_century/patrick.asp

54   Muhlenberg, 50.

55   Wallace, 117.

56   Ibid., 225.

57   Ibid., 128,133.

58   Ibid., 129.

59   Ibid., 129.

60   Ryun, Jim, *Heroes Among Us* (Shippensburg, PA: Destiny Image Publishers, Inc., 2002), 208.

61   Muhlenberg, 30, Frick, William Keller, *Henry Melchior Muhlenberg, "Patriarch of the Lutheran Church in America"* (Philadelphia: Lutheran Publication Society, 1902), p. 178. Accessed on December 16, 2012: https://archive.org/stream/henrymelchiormuh00fric#page/178/mode/2up

62   "The Battle of Brandywine." Pennsylvania Historical and Museum Commission. 1992. Accessed August 3, 2015. http://www.portal.state.pa.us/portal/server.pt/community/events/4279/battle_of_brandywine/473340.

63   Paine, Thomas. "The American Crisis: PHILADELPHIA, Sept. 12, 1777." Ushistory.org. Accessed August 3, 2015.

64   Wallace, 144.

65   Ibid., 167.

66   Hocker, Edward W., *The fighting parson of the American revolution; a biography of General Peter Muhlenberg, Lutheran clergyman, military chieftain, and political leader,* (Philadelphia, PA, Published by Author, 1936), 108

67   *Writings of George Washington,* (Cong.), XIX, pp. 203-05, cited in Wallace, 195-96.

68   Thomas Jefferson to George Washington, *Writings of George Washington,* (Cong.), XIX, cited in Wallace, 194-196, 196.

69   Peter Muhlenberg to George Washington, August 24, 1780: Correspondence of George Washington (Officers), Library of Congress, Wallace, 200.

70   Correspondence of George Washington (Officers), Library of Congress, Wallace, 200.

71   General Gates to Peter Muhlenberg, July 21, 1780: Gates papers, Box 19, N.Y.H.S.; Henry A. Muhlenberg, *Peter Muhlenberg*, p. 368, cited in Wallace, 200.

72   General Gates to Peter Muhlenberg, October 12, 1780: Gates papers, Box 19, N.Y.H.S.; Henry A. Muhlenberg, *Peter Muhlenberg*, p. 368, cited in Wallace, 201.

73   Ward, Harry M, *For Virginia and for Independence: Twenty-Eight Revolutionary War Soldiers from the Old Dominion* (September 15, 2011, McFarland Publishers), 113. Accessed May 5, 2015 https://goo.gl/ZJpQzG

74   Theobald, Mary, *"Whatever Happened to Benedict Arnold"* (Colonial Williamsburg Journal, Summer 2001) Accessed May 5, 2015: http://www. history.org/foundation/journal/Summer01/BenedictArnold.cfm

75   Decker, Michael McMillen, *Baron Von Steuben and the military forces in Virginia during the British invasions of 1780-1781* (University of Richmond UR Scholarship Repository) 16-30. Accessed May 5, 2015 http://scholarship. richmond.edu/cgi/viewcontent.cgi?article=1437&context=masters-theses

76   MacMaster, Robert K Honyman, Robert (News of the Yorktown Campaign: The Journal of Dr. Robert Honyman, April 17-November 25, 1781), The Virginia Magazine of History and Biography, pp. 393-394 Accessed May 5, 2015 from University of Oklahoma Library, http://www.jstor.org.ezproxy. lib.ou.edu/stable/4247677?seq=8#page_scan_tab_contents

77   Muhlenberg, 249-50, https://archive.org/stream/ lifemajorgenera01muhlgoog#page/n260/mode/2up.

78   Muhlenberg, 251, Gen. Baron von Steuben's General Orders.

79   Muhlenberg, 251, Gen. Baron von Steuben's Official Report to Congress.

80   Muhlenberg, 252, Gen. Nathaniel Greene's response to Gen. Von Steuben, Steuben Papers, N.Y. Historical Society.

81   Rogers, Thomas J., *Remembrance of the Departed Heroes, Sages, and Statesmen of America*, 1824, cited in Muhlenberg, 275-76.

82   Muhlenberg, 275.

83   Adams, Charles Francis, *Familiar Letters Of John Adams And His Wife Abigail Adams, During the Revolution: With A Memoir Of Mrs. Adams* (Boston & New York: Houghton Mifflin Company, 1875), 265. Accessed from: https://archive.org/stream/familiarletterso00adamuoft#page/264/ mode/2up.

84   Morris, B. F., *The Christian Life and Character of the Civil Institutions of the United States* (Philadelphia: George W. Childs, 1864), 334. Accessed from: https://archive.org/stream/

ChristianLifeAndCharacterOfTheCivilInstitutionsOfTheUnitedStates/
Christian_Life_and_Character_of_the_Civi#page/n337/mode/2up.

85   *The American Quarterly Register*, American Education Society, conducted by B. B. Edwards (Boston: Perkins & Marvin, 1833), Vol. V, 217, Accessed from: https://archive.org/stream/americanquarterlv5amer#page/216/mode/2up.

86   Thornton, 307-10.

87   Baldwin, Chapter 11, p. 37.

88   Ibid.

89   Ibid.

90   Ibid, Chapter 11, 39.

91   Headley, 78-80, Adams, 20-21.

92   Nichipor, M.A. (2002), "The Road Was Bloody," Cobblestone, 23(7), 25. Accessed May 1, 2015.

93   Baldwin, Chapter 11, 45.

94   Ibid, 46.

95   Ibid, 46

96   Answering the Call: The Story of Joab Houghton, http://www.hopewellvalleyhistory.org/Stories-Joab-Houghton.html. *The American Baptist Pulpit at the Beginning of the Twentieth Century*, Henry Thompson Louthan, editor (Williamsburg, VA: published by editor, 1903), Foreword, p. 13, Accessed from https://archive.org/stream/americanbaptist04unkngoog#page/n18/mode/2up.

97   Headley, 290-91.

98   Baldwin, Chapter 11, p. 41

99   Ibid, 42.

100   The Journals of Each Provincial Congress of Massachusetts in 1774 and 1775,. 283-284. Accessec May 1, 2015, https://goo.gl/UilqkZ.

101   Sandoz, Vol. 1. p. 26: Accessed from http://lf-oll.s3.amazonaws.com/titles/816/Sandoz_0018-01_EBk_v6.0.pdf

102   Headley, 287-99, Baldwin, Chapter 11, 32, 48.

103   Baldwin, Chapter 11, p. 44.

104   Ibid., 47.

105   The Connecticut Magazine: An Illustrated Monthly, Vol. 11, pp. 609-610. Accessed May 1, 2015 https://goo.gl/o5bd83.

106   Baldwin, Chapter 11, p. 33.

107   Ibid., 34.

108   Ibid., 52.

109   Headley, 128-57, *The History of Pittsfield Massachusetts,* Vol. I, Compiled and written under the general direction of a committee by J.E.A. Smith (Boston: Published by Lee and Shepard, 149 Washington Street, 1869)

110   Headley, 89-106.

111   Ibid., 121-26.

112   Ibid., 158-63

113   Ibid., 175-98.

114   Ibid., 199-204.

115   Ibid., 217-32.

116   Ibid., 233-38.

117   Ibid., 239-44.

118   Ibid., 245-49.

119   Ibid., 250-72.

120   Ibid., 276-79.

121   Ibid., 280-86.

122   Ibid., 69

123   Ibid., 71-72

124   Ibid., 72

125   Ibid., 69

126   Baldwin, Chapter. 11, 55.

127   Thayer, Christopher T., *An Address Delivered in the First Parish, Beverly, October 2, 1867, on the Two-Hundredth Anniversary of its Formation.*

(Boston: Nichols and Noyes, 1868) cited in Joseph Willard, 1738-1804, Sermons, 1775-1777, The Cambridge Historical Society. Accessed from www.cambridgehistory.org/library/willard.

128 Presbyterian Heritage Center, www.phcmontreat.org/bios/Bios-C.htm. Accessed December 27, 2011.

129 *Dorchester, Daniel. Christianity in the United States from the First Settlement down to the Present Time (New York: Hunt & Eaton ;, 1890), 265.*

130 Headley, 331-40.

131 Ibid., 300-04.

132 Ibid.

133 Ibid., 67.

134 Baldwin, Chapter. 11, 49.

135 Ibid., Chapter 11, 50.

136 History of Brunswick, Topsham, and Harpswell: Part II, Chapter 26: Military History of the Three Towns p. 680. Accessed August 8, 2015 from http://community.curtislibrary.com/CML/wheeler/ww_pt2_ch26.html. Headley, 110-114.

137 Baldwin, Chapter 11, 53.

138 Sandoz, Vol. 1. Chapter 26: http://oll.libertyfund.org/title/816/69301.

139 Sandoz, Vol.1. Chapter12: http://oll.libertyfund.org/title/816/69251.

140 Headley, Chapter 5, 60.

141 Sandoz, Political Vol. 1. Chapter:15: http://oll.libertyfund.org/title/816/69260.

142 McCabe, James Dabney, *A Comprehensive View of Our Country and Its Resources ... Giving a brief history of the birth and growth of the nation and each state separately ... and following with graphic descriptions of the rivers, lakes, mountains, cities, soil, climate, productions, minerals, manufactures, internal improvements, commerce, finances, government, schools, religious denominations, etc.,* pp. 300-301. Accessed May 1, 2015, http://name.umdl.umich.edu/ABK4794.0001.001.

143 The New England Chronicle; or, The Essex Gazette, July 13, 1775, 4. Accessed May 1, 2015, http://www.masshist.org/dorr/volume/4/sequence/851.

144 Relatively Fiction. "A Book About John Cleaveland's World – Take Two (Second Post). Accessed May 1, 2015, http://relativelyfiction.blogspot.com/2009/07/book-about-john-cleavelands-world.html

145 Headley, p. 67.

146 Ibid, Chapter 5, pp. 67-68.

147 *History of Reading*, www.historyofredding.com/HRbartlett.htm, cited 2/10/12.

148 Baldwin, Chapter 11, p.165, Headley, p. 67

149 Baldwin, Chapter 11, p.

150 Sandoz, Vol. 1. Chapter: 15: http://oll.libertyfund.org/title/816/69260.

151 Ibid

152 Robinson, Blackwell, P, "Caldwell, David" NCPedia.org. Accessed August 10, 2015 http://ncpedia.org/biography/caldwell-david.

153 Schenck, Elizabeth Hubbell Godfrey, "The History of Fairfield, Fairfield County, Connecticut, from the Settlement from 1700 to 1800," 460. Accessed August 10, 2015 https://goo.gl/Kx8Azj .

154 Medford Historical Society Papers, Volume 16. Accessed May 1, 2015   http://www.perseus.tufts.edu/hopper/text?doc=Perseus%3Atext%2A2005.05.0016

155 Headley, Chapter 1, 15-16.

156 George Washington, The Writings of George Washington, collected and edited by Worthington Chauncey Ford (New York and London: G. P. Putnam's Sons, 1889). Vol. III (1775-1776). 8/10/2015. Accessed August 10, 2015 from http://oll.libertyfund.org/titles/2378#lf1450-03_footnote_nt269_ref

157 George Washington, The Writings of George Washington, collected and edited by Worthington Chauncey Ford (New York and London: G. P. Putnam's Sons, 1889). Vol. III (1775-1776). Accessed August 10, 2015 from http://oll.libertyfund.org/titles/2378#Washington_1450-03_775

158   George Washington, *The Writings of George Washington*, collected and edited by Worthington Chauncey Ford (New York and London: G. P. Putnam's Sons, 1889). Vol. III (1775-1776). Accessed August 10, 2015 from http://oll.libertyfund.org/titles/2378#lf1450-03_footnote_nt334.

159   Washington, George, *General Orders July 4, 1775,* Accessed May 2, 2015 from http://memory.loc.gov/cgi-bin/query/r?ammem/mgw:@field(DOCID+@lit(gw030221))

160   *The Letters of Horace Walpole, Fourth Earl of Oxford,* Peter Cunningham, editor, (London: Richard Bently and Son, 1861), Vol. VI, 234, https://play.google.com/books/reader?id=LYU1AAAAMAAJ&printsec=frontcover&output=reader&hl=en&pg=GBS.PA234, *Born Fighting: How the Scots-Irish Shaped America*, James H. Webb (Broadway Books, Random House, 2004), 162.

161   Byrd, James, "*Sacred Scripture, Sacred War: The Bible and the American Revolution*" (Oxford University Press, 198 Madison Ave, New York, New York, 10016, 2013) 31.

162   Greene, Jack P. and Pole, J. R., *A Companion to the American Revolution* (Massachusetts: Blackwell Publishing, Ltd., 2000, 2004), 63. Accessed from https://books.google.com/books?id=xK1NuzpAcH8C&pg=PA63

163   Hodge, Charles, *The Constitutional History of the Presbyterian Church* (Applewood Books, Bedford, MA, 1839), Vol. I, 484. Accessed from https://books.google.com/books?id=WbUUSUzHbp0C.

164   Extract from a letter of Captain Johann Heinrichs of the Hessian Jager Corps, written from Philadelphia, January 18, 1778 – *Pennsylvania Magazine of History and Biography*, Vol. XXII, 137. Accessed from http://archive.org/stream/pennsylvaniamaga22histuoft/pennsylvaniamaga22histuoft_djvu.txt

165   *Buckley, Edmund. Universal Religion; a Course of Lessons Historical and Scientific on the Various Faiths of the World,* (Chicago: University Association, 1897), *694.* Accessed from http://archive.org/stream/MN40146ucmf_0/MN40146ucmf_0_djvu.txt.

166   Ryerson, Egerton, *The Loyalists of America and Their Times: From 1620 to 1816* (Toronto: William Briggs, James Campbell & Son, and Willing &

Williamson, 1880), Vol. 1, Chapter 18, p. 399. Accessed from http://www.gutenberg.org/files/21012/21012-h/21012-h.htm#Footnote_336_336.

167 Headley, 58, Love, p. 335; Boston News-Letter, June 23, 1774, cited in Baldwin, Chapter 9.

168 Ferguson, Robert. *The Cambridge History of American Literature*. Edited by Sacvan Bercovitch. Cambridge: Cambridge University Press, 1994. 66.

169 Thornton, 255.

170 Baldwin, Chapter XI, p. 157.

171 Baldwin, Chapter 9, p. 122.

172 Berkin, Carol, *Jonathan Sewall, Odyssey Of An American Loyalist* (New York: Columbia University Press, 1974), p. 113, cited from *Yankee Doodle Went To Church*, James L. Adams (New Jersey: Fleming H. Revell Company Old Tappan, 1989), p. 39.

173 Headley, 107.

174 Sforza, Alfred, *Portrait of a Small Town II: Huntington, New York "In the Beginning"* (Fore Angels Press, 2001). Accessed May 4, 2015, http://www/huntingtonny.gov/filestorage/13747/13817/16499/Old_First_Presbyterian_Church.pdf.

175 "Old Burying Ground (17th Century) & Fort Golgotha (1782)," excerpted from *Portrait of a Small Town II: https://play.google.com/books/reader?id=4 00MAAAAYAAJ&printsec=frontcover&output=reader&hl=en&pg=GBS. PA109.*

176 Headley, 109.

177 Ibid, 58.

178 Inscription on plaque in front of First Presbyterian Church, Caldwell, New Jersey, Erected by the New Jersey Society, Sons of the American Revolution, November 24, 1924, a located at the intersection of Bloomfield Avenue (New Jersey Route 507) and Roseland Avenue (County Route 527).

179 Headley, Chapter 5, pp. 67-68.

180 Benjamin Rush letter to John Adams, July 20, 1811. Accessed from Bennett, William J., *Our Country's Founders* (New York: Aladdin Paperbacks, Simon & Schuster, 2001), pp. 9-10, OETA, "Freedom: A History of Us," Segment

1, "July 4, 1776," www.pbs.org/wnet/historyofus/web01/segment1.html, *Founding Brothers: The Revolutionary Generation*, Joseph J. Ellis (New York: Vintage Books, 2000), 4-5. Accessed August 12, 2012 books.google.com, cited 8/8/12.

181 Rush letter to Adams

182 Ibid

183 Byrd, 101

184 Franklin, Benjamin, 1776 in the Continental Congress as they prepared to sign the Declaration of Independence, www.nps.gov/revwar/unfinished_revolution/treason.htm

185 Adams, John and Adams, Charles Francis, *Papers of John Adams, Second President of the United States* (Boston: Charles C. Little & James Brown, 1850), Vol. II p. 154. Accessed from http://oll.libertyfund.org/titles/adams-the-works-of-john-adams-vol-2-diary-notes-of-debates-autobiography.

186 Fleming, Thomas J. *1776* (New York: New Word City, 2014).

187 Tocqueville, Alexis de, *Democracy in America*, Vol. II, http://www.gutenberg.org/files/816/816-h/816-h.htm.

188 Bridenbaugh, Carl, *Miter and Sceptre:* Transatlantic Faiths, Ideas, Personalities, and Politics 1689-1775 (Oxford University Press, 1962). Accessed from http://archive.org/stream/mitreandsceptret000806mbp/mitreandsceptret000806mbp_djvu.txt.

189 Adams, Chapter, p. 14.

190 Headley, 14-17.

191 Ibid, p. 1.

192 Thornton, Preface, Pp. XXXV-XXXVI,

193 Baldwin, Chapter 1, p. 4.

194 Thornton, Preface, pp. XXXVII-XXXVIII.

195 Baldwin, 12.

196 Baldwin, Conclusion, 171-72.

197 Adams, 72.

198 Thornton, Preface, 43.

199   Thornton, Preface, 51

200   Baldwin, 86.

201   Miller, Samuel, *Memoir of the Rev. John Rodgers, D.D.*, (Philadelphia: Presbyterian Board of Publication, abridged from the original edition of 1813), 191. Accessed from https://archive.org/stream/ memoirsrevjohnr00millgoog#page/n200/mode/2up.

202   Thornton, Introduction, pp. XXXVI-VII.

203   Ibid, Introduction, p. XII.

204   Baldwin, Chapter IV, p. 39.

205   Ibid, p. 169.

206   Ibid, p. 19.

207   Bridenbaugh, p. 3.

208   Baldwin, Chapter 4, p. 5.

209   Sandoz, Vol. 1. Chapter: 10: John Allen, AN ORATION UPON THE BEAUTIES OF LIBERTY. http://oll.libertyfund.org/title/816/69240

210   Moore, Frank, Rev. George Duffield, "Declaration of Peace," Dec. 11, 1783, pp. 353-354.

211   Thornton, 46-48.

212   Sandoz, Vol. 1. Chapter: 17: John Witherspoon, THE DOMINION OF PROVIDENCE OVER THE PASSIONS OF MEN, http://oll. libertyfund.org/title/816/69270

213   Washington, George, September 17, 1796, Farewell Address, George Washington Papers at the Library of Congress, 1741-1799: Series 2 Letterbooks, accessed from http://memory.loc.gov, cited 3/2/15.

214   Adams, John, *The Works of John Adams, Second President of the United States*, Charles Francis Adams, editor (Boston: Little, Brown, 1854), Vol. IX, p. 401, Letter to Zabdiel Adams on June 21, 1776, Vol. IX, p. 229, Message from John Adams to the Officers of the First Brigade of the Third Division of the Militia of Massachusetts October 11, 1798.

215   Franklin, Benjamin, *The Writings of Benjamin Franklin*, Jared Sparks, editor (Boston: Tappan, Whittemore and Mason, 1840), Vol. X, p. 297, April 17, 1787.

216   Moore, 129.

217   Ibid, Vol. 1. Chapter: 12: Samuel Sherwood, SCRIPTURAL INSTRUCTIONS TO CIVIL RULERS, http://oll.libertyfund.org/ title/816/69251

218   Ibid, Vol. 1. Chapter: 19: Abraham Keteltas, GOD ARISING AND PLEADING HIS PEOPLE'S CAUSE http://oll.libertyfund.org/ title/816/69274

219   Headley, 59.

220   Sandoz, Vol. 2. Chapter: 48: Timothy Dwight, THE DUTY OF AMERICANS, AT THE PRESENT CRISIS http://oll.libertyfund.org/ title/817/69452

221   Adams, 26.

222   Sandoz, Vol. 1. Chapter: 21: Samuel Cooper, A SERMON ON THE DAY OF THE COMMENCEMENT OF THE CONSTITUTION, http://oll.libertyfund.org/title/816/69278 on 2012-11-02

223   Hyneman, Charles S., *American Political Writing During the Founding Era: 1760-1805*, ed. Hyneman, Charles S. and Lutz, Donald, (Indianapolis: Liberty Fund, 1983). 2 vols. Volume 1. Chapter: [38]: Zabdiel Adams 1739-1801: "An Election Sermon," Accessed from http://oll.libertyfund. org/title/2066/188687.

224   Sandoz, *Political Sermons of the American Founding Era, 1730-1805* (Indianapolis: Liberty Fund, 1998), Vol. I, second edition, Moses Mather sermon, "America's Appeal to the Impartial World," 1775, 483.

225   Thornton, 304-05.

226   St. George, Jr., William Ross, *The Patriot: Movie Review from the Journal of American History*, vol. 87, no. 3. Accessed from http://www.studythepast. com/patriotreview.pdf

227   Red House Presbyterian Church, United States Department of Interior National Park Service, National Register of Historic Places, p. 11 Accessed May 14, 2015 http://www.hpo.ncdcr.gov/nr/CS0444.pdf

228   "Hannah Caldwell," americanrevolution.org/women/women44.html,

229   "Old South Meeting House," Accessed May 14, 2015 http://www.nps.gov/ bost/learn/historyculture/osmh.htm, cited 5/14/15.

230 Sandoz, Vol. 1. Chapter: 19: Abraham Keteltas, "God Arising and Pleading His People's Cause," http://oll.libertyfund.org/title/816/69274.

231 A sermon preached before the Honorable Council, and the Honorable House of Representatives, of the state of Massachusetts-Bay, in New-England: at Boston, May 28, 1777, being the anniversary for the election of the Honorable Council (1777), Internet Archive, Cornell University Library. Accessed February 3, 2012 www.archive.org/details/cu31924104014828

232 Moore, 330-31, 33-34.

233 Sandoz, Vol. 1. Chapter: 19: Abraham Keteltas, GOD ARISING AND PLEADING HIS PEOPLE'S CAUSE, http://oll.libertyfund.org/title/816/69274.

234 Ibid., Vol. 1. Chapter: 15: Moses Mather, AMERICA'S APPEAL TO THE IMPARTIAL WORLD. http://oll.libertyfund.org/title/816/69260.

235 Ibid., Vol. 1. Chapter: 19: Abraham Keteltas, GOD ARISING AND PLEADING HIS PEOPLE'S CAUSE, http://oll.libertyfund.org/title/816/69274.

236 Ibid., Vol. 1. Chapter: 19:

237 The American Revolution, The Transatlantic Controversy Over Creating an American Bishop, Accessed May 14, 2015 http://www.ouramericanrevolution.org/index.cfm/page/view/p0207

238 *Papers and Proceedings of the Connecticut Valley Historical Society, 1876-1881* (Springfield, Massachusetts: published by the Historical Society, 1881), 92; Trevelyan, Sir George Otto, *The American Revolution* (New York: Longmans, Green, and Co, 1899), Vol. 1, 278-279. Accessed https://archive.org/stream/americanrevoluti00trev#page/298/mode/1up; Thornton, 195.

239 Knoll, Mark A, *THE ELECTION SERMON: SITUATING RELIGION AND THE CONSTITUTION IN THE EIGHTEENTH CENTURY,* DePaul Law Review, 2009-2010 pp. 1223-1248 www.heinonline.org.ezproxy.lib.ou.edu, Kerr, Harry P, *The Election sermon: Primer for revolutionaries* (Taylor Francis Online) Accessed May 11, 2015. 2015http://www.tandfonline.com/doi/abs/10.1080/03637756209375331

240 Moore, 147-49.

241 Marina, William F., *The American Revolution and the Minority Myth* (The Independent Instuitute), January 1, 1975 Accessed May 12, 2015 http://www.independent.org/publications/article.asp?id=1398

242 Thornton, Introduction, pp. XXXVIII, Preface, p. V.

243 Galloway, Bishop Charles Betts, D.D., LL.D., *Christianity and the American Commonwealth; The Influence of Christianity In Making This Nation* (Nashville, Tenn.: Publishing House Methodist Episcopal Church, South, Barbee and Smith, Agents, 1898), 77-79. Accessed from https://archive.org/stream/christianityamer00gall#page/76/mode/2up.

244 Headley, 75-76.

245 Gilman Theodore, "Clark, Leader in Revolutionary Thought," p. 12. Accessed from http://archive.org/stream/revjonasclark00gilmrich/revjonasclark00gilmrich_djvu.txt.

246 Headley, 75.

247 Baldwin, 95.

248 Fisher, Anne G., "History of First Parish in Lexington," June 1975, Revised by Bill Britton and Anne Collins 2001. Accessed from fpc.lexington.ma.us/index.php/history.

249 Headley, 76-77.

250 Gilman, pp. 8-9

251 Ibid., 11-12.

252 Ibid., 14,18.

253 Clark, Jonas, "A Brief Narrative of the Principal Transactions of That Day," appended to a sermon preached by him in Lexington, April 19, 1776 (Lexington, Massachusetts: The Lexington Historical Society, 1901), 1-2.

254 Ibid., 1.

255 Mass Moments, Massachusetts Foundation for the Humanities, massmoments.org/moment.cfm?mid=118.

256 Headley, Chapter VI, 74-32.

257 Gilman, 14.

258 Clark, 3-5.

259   "Today in History: July 13," Library of Congress, http://memory.loc.gov/ammem/today/jul13.html, cited 10/4/2011. National Guard Heritage Painting, "Stand Your Ground," Don Troiani, http://www.history.army.mil/art/A&I/stand.htm.

260   Clark, 5-6

261   Clark, 6-8.

262   Higginbotham, R. Don, "Great Events from History: The 18th Century–Battle of Lexington and Concord," Accessed September 17, 2012 salempress.com.

263   Headley, 81.

264   Headley, 81.

265   Clark, Jonas, sermon at Lexington, Massachusetts, April 19, 1776.

266   Gilman, 16

267   Fisher, Anne. "History of First Parish in Lexington." History of First Parish in Lexington. 1975. Accessed August 8, 2015. http://fpc.lexington.ma.us/index.php/history.

268   Clark, Jonas, sermon at Lexington, Massachusetts, April 19, 1776.

269   Plaque in front of First Presbyterian Church, Caldwell, New Jersey, Erected by the New Jersey Society, Sons of the American Revolution, November 24, 1924, a located at the intersection of Bloomfield Avenue (New Jersey Route 507) and Roseland Avenue (County Route 527).

270   Finley, Robert, D. D., "Memoirs of the Reverend Robert Finley, D.D.," p. 20. Accessed from "James Caldwell: 'The Fighting Chaplain,'" Leben, A Journal of Reformation Life, 2150 River Plaza Drive, Suit 150 Sacramento, California 95833 www.leben.us/index.php/component/content/article/254-james-caldwell-the-fighting-chaplain

271   Headley, 218.

272   Sprague, William B., "Annals of the American Pulpit," p.74. Accessed from "James Caldwell: 'The Fighting Chaplain,'" www.leben.us/index.php/component/content/article/254-james-caldwell-the-fighting-chaplain.

273   www.leben.us/index.php/component/content/article/254-james-caldwell-the-fighting-chaplain, cited 12/29/12.

274   "www.leben.us/index.php/component/content/article/254-james-caldwell-the-fighting-chaplain

275   Plaque in front of First Presbyterian Church, Caldwell, New Jersey, Erected by the New Jersey Society, Sons of the American Revolution, November 24, 1924, a located at the intersection of Bloomfield Avenue (New Jersey Route 507) and Roseland Avenue (County Route 527).

276   "James Caldwell: The Fighting Chaplain A." Leben. Accessed September 15, 2015. http://www.leben.us/index.php/component/content/article/254-james-caldwell-the-fighting-chaplain.

277   Headley, 219.

278   Ibid., 219-221.

279   Murray, Nicholas, Rev., D.D., "A Memoir of the Rev. James Caldwell of Elizabethtown," read before the New Jersey Historical Society, May 25, 1848.

280   Howell, Governor Ricard, Revolutionary War Correspondence from *The Writings of George Washington from the Original Manuscript Sources, 1745-1799* John C. Fitzpatrick, Editor. Accessed May 15, 2015: http://govhowell.org/revolutionary-war-correspondence/

281   National Archives, From George Washington to John Hancock, 6 December 1776. Accessed May 15, 2015 http://founders.archives.gov/?q=Project%3A%22Washington%20Papers%22%20James%20Caldwell&s=1511311111&r=5

282   "Hannah Caldwell." Accessed September 23, 2012 americanrevolution.org/women/women44.html.

283   Brydon, Norman F., Reverend James Caldwell: Patriot 1734-1781, (Caldwell, NJ: Caldwell Bicentennial Committee, 1976), 31. Accessed December 12, 2-12 from "James Caldwell: 'The Fighting Chaplain,'" Leben, A Journal of Reformation Life; Headley, p. 220.

284   Murray, "A Memoir of the Rev. James Caldwell of Elizabethtown."

285   Brydon, 36.

286   Ferling, John E., *The First of Men: A Life of George Washington* (Knoxville: University of Tennessee Press, 1988, p. 221. Accessed May 18, 2015 https://

books.google.com/books?id=yHRbR8snrfoC&q=one+third#v=snippet&q
=one%20third&f=false.

287   Stryker, William S. *The Battles of Trenton and Princeton*. (Boston and New
      York: Houghton, Mifflin, and Co., 1898), Diary of Colonel John Fitzgerald,
      December 25, 1776, 6 p.m., p. 362. Accessed May 18, 2015 https://archive.
      org/stream/battlesoftrenton00stry#page/n9/mode/2up

288   "Archives of the State of New Jersey, Newspaper Extracts," in *Reverend
      James Caldwell: Patriot 1734-1781*, Norman F. Brydon (Caldwell, NJ:
      Caldwell Bicentennial Committee, 1976), p.37 accessed from "James
      Caldwell: 'The Fighting Chaplain,'" Leben, A Journal of Reformation Life,
      www.leben.us/index.php/component/content/article/254-james-caldwell-
      the-fighting-chaplain,

289   Brydon, 34-35.

290   Murray, 82-83.

291   Headley, 223.

292   "Hannah Caldwell," americanrevolution.org/women/women44.html,

293   Headley, 224-225.

294   americanrevolution.org/women/women44.html

295   americanrevolution.org/women/women44.html

296   americanrevolution.org/women/women44.html

297   Hon. Samuel L. Southard, at a dedication honoring the Caldwells,
      americanrevolution.org/women/women44.html .

298   *Pennsylvania Journal*, October 4, 1780, cited from "Hannah Caldwell."
      Accessed September 24, 2012 americanrevolution.org.

299   "Religion and the Founding of the American Republic," III Religion and
      the American Revolution, Library of Congress, accessed from www.loc.
      gov/exhibits/religion/rel03.html, cited 9/24/12, This Day In Presbyterian
      History, June 23: Rev. James Caldwell, "The Rebel's High Priest," www.
      thisday.pcahistory.org/2012/06/june-23-rev-james-caldwell/, cited
      9/24/12; *Annals of the American Pulpit* (New York: Robert Carter &
      Brothers, 1858), Vol. III p. 225, accessed from https://archive.org/stream/
      annalsamericanp23spragoog/annalsamericanp23spragoog_djvu.txt.

300   Headley, 227.

301   Sprague, William Buell, *Annals of the American Pulpit* (New York: Robert Carter & Brothers, 1858), Vol. III, 225-227, https://goo.gl/HK1AG2

302   Headley, 229-230.

303   "James Caldwell: 'The Fighting Chaplain,'" Leben, A Journal of Reformation Life, 2150 River Plaza Drive, Suite 150 Sacramento, California 95833. Accessed December 12, 2012 www.leben.us/index.php/component/content/article/254-james-caldwell-the-fighting-chaplain

304   Murray, 84.

305   Ibid, 85

306   Ibid, 86.

307   Ibid, "James Caldwell: 'The Fighting Chaplain,'" Leben, A Journal of Reformation Life.

308   Rev. Nicholas Murray, cited in Sprague, William Buell, *Annals of the American Pulpit*, Vol. III 227; Murray, "A Memoir of Rev. James Caldwell," Vol. III, 89. Accessed from, https://archive.org/stream/annalsamericanp23spragoog/annalsamericanp23spragoog_djvu.txt

309   *The History of Pittsfield (Berkshire County), Massachusetts*, Vol. 1, compiled and written under the general direction of a committee by J.E.A. Smith (Boston: Published by Lee and Shepard, 149 Washington Street, 1869), pp. 284, https://play.google.com/books/reader?id=RhQouzPKzPwC&printsec=frontcover&output=reader&hl=en&pg=GBS.PA285.

310   The History of Pittsfield (Berkshire County), 166-67.

311   Crocker, Henry E, Howard, R.H., *The history of New England; Historical and Descriptive Sketches*, *Vol. 1* (Boston: Crocker & Co. Publishers. 1880) p. 94. Accessed May 19, 2015: https://goo.gl/BrXKaX

312   The History of Pittsfield (Berkshire County), 341-42.

313   Ibid., 346.

314   Ibid., 167.

315   Ibid., 177.

316   Headley, 132.

317   Ibid., 132.

318   Sullivan, Brian, "Day 334: Rev. Thomas Allen," Special to "The Berkshire Eagle," Wednesday, November 30, 2011, accessed from http://www.berkshireeagle.com/ci_19437066. Accessed October 11, 2012 The Congregational Quarterly, Vol. 11 (Boston: Congregational Rooms, 40 Winter Street, 1869), p. 483. Accessed May 19, 2015 https://goo.gl/9db625

319   The History of Pittsfield (Berkshire County),177-78.

320   Headley, 130-31.

321   The History of Pittsfield (Berkshire County), 209-10, Headley, 133-35.

322   Headley, 135-36.

323   Meany, Joseph, *The Noble Train of Artillery*, pp. 1-4. Accessed May 19, 2015 http://duanesburg.org/district/news/2013_14/PDFs_news/NobleTrainofArtillery.pdf

324   Allen, Thomas, *Letter to General Pomeroy*, May 9, 1775. Accessed on May 19, 2015: http://www.forgottenbooks.com/readbook_text/A_History_of_the_Town_of_Pittsfield_in_Berkshire_County_Mass_1000263658/75

325   Headley, p. 149; Bassett, James H., *Colonial Life In New Hampshire* (Boston: Ginn & Company, The Athenaeum Press, 1899), Chapter 8. Accessed October 28, 2012 www.kellscraft.com/ColonialLifeNH/ColonialLifeNHCh08.html.

326   The History of Pittsfield (Berkshire County), 284-85.

327   Headley, 148.

328   The History of Pittsfield (Berkshire County), 295.

329   Everett, Edward, *Life of Stark*, cited from *The History of Pittsfield (Berkshire County)*, *Massachusetts*, Vol. 1, compiled and written under the general direction of a committee by J.E.A. Smith (Boston: Published by Lee and Shepard, 149 Washington Street, 1869), 297.

330   The History of Pittsfield (Berkshire County), 298; Headley, pp. 150-51.

331   Hoffman Nickerson, The Turning Point of the Revolution or Burgoyne in America, (Boston and New YorkL Houghton Mifflin Company, 1928), 252. Accessed May 19, 2015: http://babel.hathitrust.org/cgi/pt?id=mdp.39015027011082;view=1up;seq=308

332   The History of Pittsfield (Berkshire County), 298-99, Ibid, Headley, p. 151.

333   The History of Pittsfield (Berkshire County), 299.

334   Thomas Allen's account of the Battle of Bennington, VT, from the *Connecticut Courant,* August 25, 1777, cited from *The History of Pittsfield,* appendix F, 500-01.

335   Headley, 152.

336   The History of Pittsfield (Berkshire County), 399; Headley, p. 154.

337   Headley, 154-55.

338   Ibid., 156-57.

339   Ibid., 157.

340   Sprague, William B., D.D., *Annals of the American Pulpit* (New York: Robert Carter & Brothers, 1859), Vol. I, p. 481-82. Accessed October 31, 2012   books.google.com/books/about/Annals_of_the_American_pulpit. html?id=L3lUAAAAYAAJ.

341   Ibid., 480.

342   Ibid., 480.

343   Kelley, Brooks Mather, *Yale: A History* (Yale University Press, 1999), p. 74. Accessed October 30, 2012 books.google.com/books/about/Yale. html?id=B2aDRhohtx8C.

344   Rothbard, Murry N., *Conceived in Liberty* (Auburn: Ludwig von Mises Institute, 1979, 1999, 2011), p. 882, https://mises.org/sites/default/files/ Conceived%20in%20Liberty_Vol_2_2.pdf.

345   The Magazine of History with Notes and Queries, (William Abbatt, 20 Liberty Street, Poughkeepsie, N.Y.). 175 Accessed May 21, 2015 https:// goo.gl/T9TrbK

346   "Naphtali Daggett, The Sixth Rector and Second President of Yale College,The Beginning of the American Revolution, 1766 to 1777," Accessed October 30, 2012 seas.yale.edu/i-am/alumnus/yale-history-blog

347   Headley, 199.

348   Sprague, 481-82.

349   Ibid.

350   Ibid., 483-84.

351   Headley, 204.

352   Moore, *The Patriot Preachers of the American Revolution: With Biographical Sketches* (New York: Charles T. Evans, 1862), "A Declaration of Peace," sermon by George Duffield, December 11, 1783, 353-354.

353   Prowell, George Reeser, *History of York County, Pennsylvania* (Chicago: J.H. Beers & Co., 1907), Volume 1, p. 861. Accessed May 22, 2015 https://books.google.com/books?id=psc4AQAAMAAJ&pg=PA861&lpg=PA8 61&dq=george+duffield+Monaghan,+PA&source=bl&ots=CImEuK2Rs z&sig=NKOfWVGx0qZ6-I71n-T4JlOfCCY&hl=en&sa=X&ei=pE5fV YaGG4yzogTmpoDwCw&ved=0CEgQ6AEwCQ#v=onepage&q=geo rge%20duffield%20Monaghan%2C%20PA&f=false *History of York County, Pennsylvania* (Chicago: F. A. Battey Publishing Co., 1886), John Gibson, Historical Editor, 655. Accessed May 22, 2015 http://files.usgwarchives. net/pa/york/history/gibson/dillsburg-churches.txt.

354   Library of Congress, Historic American Buildings Survey. Accessed May 21, 2015 http://www.loc.gov/pictures/item/pa4136/

355   Kidd, Thomas S. The Great Awakening, (Yale University Press, September 1, 2009), 276.

356   Wing, Conway Phelps, *A History of the First Presbyterian Church of Carlisle, Pa* (Carlisle: "Valley Sentinel" Office, 1877), 102-103. Accessed May 22, 2015 https://books.google.com/books?id=d2fIAAAAMAAJ&pg=PR1& lpg=PR1&dq=Wing,+Rev.+Conway+Phelps,+D.D.,+A+history+of+the+ First+Presbyterian+church+of+Carlisle,+Pa&source=bl&ots=PoYO6d6f Bf&sig=zkuj4ny13mIHWJpEJqyHnQMxJ0g&hl=en&sa=X&ei=UlRfV fTrCtjSoATz6YCgBw&ved=0CB8Q6AEwAA#v=onepage&q=riot%20 act&f=false. "Old Pine Street Presbyterian Church." Accessed May 22, 2015 http://www.ushistory.org/tour/old-pine-presbyterian.htm.

357   Wing, Rev. Conway Phelps, D.D., *A history of the First Presbyterian church of Carlisle, Pa* (Carlisle: "Valley Sentinel" Office, 1877), pp. 102-04, Allen, Richard Howe, Editor, Old Pine Street Church, (Henry B. Ashmead, Book and Job Printer, Philadelphia, PA, May 29, 1868) p. 45

358   This Day in Presbyterian History: Feb 2. Accessed November 4, 2012 www.thisday.pcahistory.org/2012/02/february-2/.

359   "George Duffield," Presbyterian Heritage Center. Accessed November 4, 2012 www.phcmontreat.org/bios/Duffield-George.htm.

360   This Day in Presbyterian History: Feb 2: George Duffield. Accessed November 4, 2012 The First Presbyterian church of Carlisle, PA, www. firstprescarlisle.com/our-history/the-duffields/.

361   Yearbook of the Michigan Society of the Sons of the American Revolution, (John F. Eby & Co. Printer, 1898) p. 117. Accessed May 21, 2015: https:// goo.gl/CdpcfG

362   "Old Pine Street Presbyterian Church," "The Church of the Patriots," Philadelphia Independence Hall Association. Accessed November 4, 2012 www.ushistory.org/tour/old-pine-presbyterian.htm.

363   Headley, 356-57.

364   Journal of the Presbyterian Historical Society, Volume 3 (1905-1906), p. 74. Accessed May 21, 2015: https://goo.gl/ilsSJn

365   Presbyterians Caring for Chaplains and Military Personnel (PCCMP). Accessed May 21, 2015: http://pccmp.org/who-we-are/history/reverend-john-rosbrugh-presbyterian-chaplain-1714-1777/

366   Headley, 358.

367   Ibid.

368   This Day in Presbyterian History, February 2012. Accessed May 21, 2015: http://www.thisday.pcahistory.org/2012/02/february-2/

369   Headley, 359-60.

370   Norris, Edwin Mark, The story of Princeton, (Boston: Little, Brown, and Company, 1917), p. 84. Accessed May 30, 2012 books.google.com/ books?id=MmUiAAAAMAAJ&q.

371   Sandoz, Vol. 1. Chapter: 17: John Witherspoon, THE DOMINION OF PROVIDENCE OVER THE PASSIONS OF MEN, Accessed from http://oll.libertyfund.org/title/816/69270 on 2012-11-02

372   "The Faithful Servant Rewarded," sermon preached at Dr. Witherspoon's funeral by John Rogers, D.D. quoting Dr. Robertson Stiles (New York: Printed by Thomas Greenleaf, 1795), p. 23. Accessed October 1, 2012 archive.org/stream/faithfulservantr07rodg#page/n5/mode/2up.

373   Goodrich, Charles Augustus, *Lives of the Signers to the Declaration of Independence* (New York: Published by William Reed & Co., 1829), p. 211. Accessed from https://archive.org/stream/goodrichsigners00charrich#page/n223/mode/2up.

374   Headley, 280-81, "President Witherspoon of Princeton," Dan Graves, www.christianity.com/ChurchHistory/11630277/, *Lives of the Signers to the Declaration of Independence,* by Charles Augustus Goodrich (New York: Published by William Reed & Co., 1829), "John Witherspoon 1722-1794," 212-13, https://archive.org/stream/goodrichsigners00charrich#page/212/mode/2up.

375   Rogers, John, "The Faithful Servant Rewarded," 24. Accessed from https://play.google.com/books/reader?id=I6saAAAAYAAJ&printsec=frontcover&output=reader&hl=en&pg=GBS.PA24

376   "Witherspoon, John," Princeton University. Accessed October 1, 2012 etcweb.princeton.edu/CampusWWW/Companion/witherspoon_john.html,

377   Ibid

378   Ibid

379   Stohlman, M., *John Witherspoon: Parson, Politician, Patriot* (Louisville, KY: Westminster/John Knox, 1976), cited from "John Witherspoon: Preacher and Patriot," by Raymond Frey. Accessed from http://people.hofstra.edu/alan_j_singer/docket/docket/11.1.17_John_Witherspoon_Preacher_and_Patriot_by_Raymond_Frey.pdf.

380   Kimball, R., "The Forgotten founder: John Witherspoon," *New Criterion*, (2006), p. 24, cited from Frey, "John Witherspoon: Preacher and Patriot."

381   "John Witherspoon," Princeton University, accessed from etcweb.princeton.edu/CampusWWW/Companion/witherspoon_john.html

382   Rogers, 26,

383   etcweb.princeton.edu/CampusWWW/Companion/witherspoon_john.html.

384   Rogers, 27,

385   etcweb.princeton.edu/CampusWWW/Companion/witherspoon_john.html;

386   Fea, John, Dr., Review of Morrison, Jeffry H., *John Witherspoon and the Founding of the American Republic*. H-New-Jersey, H-Net Reviews. April, 2006. Accessed June 6, 2015 https://networks.h-net.org/node/14785/reviews/16350/fea-morrison-john-witherspoon-and-founding-american-republic.

387   etcweb.princeton.edu/CampusWWW/Companion/witherspoon_john. html

388   Morrison, J., *John Witherspoon and the Founding of the American Republic* (South Bend, IN: University of Notre Dame, 2005), cited from "John Witherspoon: Preacher and Patriot," by Raymond Frey, http://people.hofstra.edu/alan_j_singer/docket/docket/11.1.17_John_Witherspoon_Preacher_and_Patriot_by_Raymond_Frey.pdf.

389   Federer, Bill, American Minute, November 15, 2012. Accessed November 20, 2012 www.americanminute.com/index.php?date=11-15.

390   Norris, 84, Headley, p. 283.

391   Ibid, 83-84.

392   Ibid, 84.

393   "The Rev. John Witherspoon, D.D.," *The Presbyterian magazine*, C. Van Rensselaer, editor (Philadelphia: WM. H. Mitchell, 265 Chestnut Street, 1851), Volume 1, 1851, December, p. 576, http://babel.hathitrust.org/cgi/pt?id=mdp.39015068000382;view=1up;seq=9; Goodrich, p. 217; US Gov., "Signers of the Declaration, Biographical Sketches: John Witherspoon, New Jersey," http://www.cr.nps.gov/history/online_books/declaration/bio54.htm.

394   "The Presidents of Princeton University," www.princeton.edu.

395   Frey, Raymond, Dr. "John Witherspoon: Preacher and Patriot," accessed from http://people.hofstra.edu/alan_j_singer/docket/docket/11.1.17_John_Witherspoon_Preacher_and_Patriot_by_Raymond_Frey.pdf, cited 6/15/15, Annual Meeting and Banquet of the Pennsylvania Scotch-Irish (Philadelphia: Allen, Lane, and Scott, 1904), Volumes 13-16, February 12, 1903, by Pennsylvania Scotch-Irish Society, p. 8, accessed from https://books.google.com/books?id=9C1EAQAAMAAJ&pg=RA1-PA8&lpg=RA1-PA8&dq=king+george+called+it+a+presbyterian+rebellion&source=bl&ots=mIqfKSdYG2&sig=ueSkQIi1M0aQz2MfAp2y-gfn

jPc&hl=en&sa=X&ved=0CEAQ6AEwBWoVChMImuqUiZaTxgIVi
zasCh1PigTu#v=onepage&q=king%20george%20called%20it%20a%20
presbyterian%20rebellion&f=false, cited 6/15/15.

396   *The Letters of Horace Walpole, Fourth Earl of Orford*, Peter Cunningham,
       editor, (London: Richard Bently and Son, 1861), Vol. VI, p. 234, https://
       books.google.com/books/reader?id=LYU1AAAAMAAJ&printsec=frontc
       over&output=reade.

397   "John Witherspoon," etcweb.princeton.edu/CampusWWW/Companion/
       witherspoon_john.html

398   Morrison, Jeffrey H., John Witherspoon, Resistance, and Revolution:
       "Rebellion to Tyrants [or George III] is Obedience to God." Accessed May
       26, 2015: http://www.lsu.edu/artsci/groups/voegelin/society/2008%20
       Papers/Jeffry%20Morrison.shtml

399   Witherspoon, John, *The Works of John Witherspoon*, (Edinburgh: J. Ogle,
       Parliament-Square, 1815), Vol. IX, 220-223, https://archive.org/stream/
       worksofjohnwithe09with/worksofjohnwithe09with_djvu.txt.

400   Goodrich, 217.

401   Craven, W. Frank, *Witherspoon, John*. Accessed May 26, 2015 http://etcweb.
       princeton.edu/CampusWWW/Companion/witherspoon_john.html

402   Goodrich, 220-21.

403   Frey, Raymond, Dr. "John Witherspoon: Preacher and Patriot."
       Accessed June 15, 2015 http://people.hofstra.edu/alan_j_singer/
       docket/docket/11.1.17_John_Witherspoon_Preacher_and_Patriot_by_
       Raymond_Frey.pdf.

404   The Society of the Descendants of the Signers of the Declaration of
       Independence, John Witherspoon. Accessed May 26, 2015: http://www.
       dsdi1776.com/signers-by-state/john-witherspoon/

405   Webster, Daniel, Speech delivered to the U.S. Senate on May 7, 1834
       (Washington: Gates and Seaton, 1834), 7. Accessed July 8, 2015
       https://books.google.com/books?id=dW4sAAAAMAAJ&pg=RA1-
       PA49&lpg=RA1-PA49&dq=daniel+webster+Those+fathers+accomplish
       ed+the+Revolution+on+a+strict+question+of+principle.&source=bl&ots
       =s5Yrhfen8H&sig=2hupan8zm1cAKswq4WaXo6qrO1g&hl=en&sa=X
       &ved=0CCgQ6AEwAmoVChMI3sX_yJ7MxgIVAyOsCh31qwxd#v=on

epage&q=daniel%20webster%20Those%20fathers%20accomplished%20 the%20Revolution%20on%20a%20strict%20question%20of%20principle.&f=false

406   Ibid.

407   Moore, 83-85.

408   Sandoz, Political Sermons of the American Founding Era: 1730-1805, 2 vols, Foreword by Ellis Sandoz (2nd ed. Indianapolis: Liberty Fund, 1998). Vol. 1. Chapter: 15: Moses Mather, AMERICA'S APPEAL TO THE IMPARTIAL WORLD. Accessed from http://oll.libertyfund.org/ title/816/69260 on 2012-06-01.

409   Thornton, 234-37.

410   Ibid., 110.

411   Ibid., 256.

412   Keteltas, Abraham, God Arising and Pleading His People's Cause (University of Nebraska, Digital Commons), p. 30. Accessed June 9, 2015: http:// digitalcommons.unl.edu/cgi/viewcontent.cgi?article=1030&context=etas

413   Moore, 177-79

414   Webster, Samuel, A sermon preached before the Honorable Council, and the Honorable House of Representatives, of the state of Massachusetts-Bay, (Evans Early American Imprint Collection, University of Michigan), 44. Accessed June 9, 2015: http://name.umdl.umich.edu/N12431.0001.001

415   Hollister, Gideon Hiram, (The History of Connecticut: From the First Settlement, Vol 2) 391. Accessed June 9, 2015: https://goo.gl/9krGkF

416   Boyd, 45 Kindle version.

417   The Declaration of Independence.

418   "The Fate of Blood-Thirsty Oppressors and God's Care of His Distressed People." Accessed January 10, 2012 www.themoralliberal.com/2011/10/04/ the-fate-of-blood-thirsty-oppressors-and-gods-care-of-his-distressed-people/

419   Thornton, 237-39.

420   Sandoz, Political Sermons of the American Founding Era: 1730-1805, 2 vols, Foreword by Ellis Sandoz (2nd ed. Indianapolis: Liberty Fund,

1998). Vol. 1. Chapter: 19: Abraham Keteltas, GOD ARISING AND PLEADING HIS PEOPLE'S CAUSE, Accessed http://oll.libertyfund. org/title/816/69274 on 2012-06-12.

421   Moore, 175-77.

422   Sandoz, Political Sermons of the American Founding Era: 1730-1805, 2 vols, Foreword by Ellis Sandoz (2nd ed. Indianapolis: Liberty Fund, 1998). Vol. 1. Chapter: 22: Henry Cumings, A SERMON PREACHED AT LEXINGTON ON THE 19 th OF APRIL, Accessed from http://oll. libertyfund.org/title/816/69280 on 2012-05-31.

423   Sandoz, Political Sermons of the American Founding Era: 1730-1805, 2 vols, Foreword by Ellis Sandoz (2nd ed. Indianapolis: Liberty Fund, 1998). Vol. 1. Chapter: 15: Moses Mather, AMERICA'S APPEAL TO THE IMPARTIAL WORLD, accessed from http://oll.libertyfund.org/ title/816/69260 on 2012-06-01.

424   Baldwin, 102.

425   Ibid., 130-31.

426   Sandoz, Political Sermons of the American Founding Era: 1730-1805, 2 vols, Foreword by Ellis Sandoz (2nd ed. Indianapolis: Liberty Fund, 1998). Vol. 1. Chapter: 19: Abraham Keteltas, GOD ARISING AND PLEADING HIS PEOPLE'S CAUSE, Accessed fromhttp://oll. libertyfund.org/title/816/69274 on 2012-06-12.

427   Sandoz, Political Sermons of the American Founding Era: 1730-1805, 2 vols, Foreword by Ellis Sandoz (2nd ed. Indianapolis: Liberty Fund, 1998). Vol. 1. Chapter: 17: John Witherspoon, THE DOMINION OF PROVIDENCE OVER THE PASSIONS OF MEN Accessed from http://oll.libertyfund.org/title/816/69270 on 2012-11-03

428   Sandoz, Political Sermons of the American Founding Era: 1730-1805, 2 Vols, Foreword by Ellis Sandoz (2nd ed. Indianapolis: Liberty Fund, 1998). Vol. 1. Chapter: 22: Henry Cumings, A SERMON PREACHED AT LEXINGTON ON THE 19th OF APRIL, Accessed from http://oll. libertyfund.org/title/816/69280 on 2012-05-31.

429   Sandoz, Political Sermons of the American Founding Era: 1730-1805, 2 vols, Foreword by Ellis Sandoz (2nd ed. Indianapolis: Liberty Fund, 1998). Vol. 1. Chapter: 15: Moses Mather, AMERICA'S APPEAL TO

THE IMPARTIAL WORLD Accessed from http://oll.libertyfund.org/title/816/69260 on 2012-11-03.

430   Moore, 351-52.

431   Ibid, 234-37.

432   Sandoz, Political Sermons of the American Founding Era: 1730-1805, 2 vols, Foreword by Ellis Sandoz (2nd ed. Indianapolis: Liberty Fund, 1998). Vol. 1. Chapter: 15: Moses Mather, AMERICA'S APPEAL TO THE IMPARTIAL WORLD Accessed December 13, 2012 http://oll.libertyfund.org/title/816/69260.

433   Moore, 184.

434   Sandoz, Political Sermons of the American Founding Era: 1730-1805, 2 vols, Foreword by Ellis Sandoz (2nd ed. Indianapolis: Liberty Fund, 1998). Vol. 1. Chapter: 16: Samuel Sherwood, THE CHURCH'S FLIGHT INTO THE WILDERNESS: AN ADDRESS ON THE TIMES Accessed November 11, 2012 http://oll.libertyfund.org/title/816/69264.

435   Moore, 350-51.

436   Thornton, 234-37.

437   Sandoz, Political Sermons of the American Founding Era: 1730-1805, 2 vols, Foreword by Ellis Sandoz (2nd ed. Indianapolis: Liberty Fund, 1998). Vol. 1. Chapter: 15: Moses Mather, AMERICA'S APPEAL TO THE IMPARTIAL WORLD. Accessed June 1, 2012 http://oll.libertyfund.org/title/816/69260.

438   Thornton, 303-03

439   Moore, 275.

440   Cooper, Samuel, "A Sermon Preached Before His Excellency John Hancock, of the Commonwealth of Massachusetts," October 25, 1780, Being the Day of the Commencement of the Constitution, and Inaguration of the New Government (Commonwealth of Massachusetts [Boston]: J. Fleet and J. Gill [1780]). Accessed November 3, 2012 www.belcherfoundation.org/samuel%20cooper%20sermon%20on%20constitution.pdf.

441   Sandoz, Political Sermons of the American Founding Era: 1730-1805, 2 vols, Foreword by Ellis Sandoz (2nd ed. Indianapolis: Liberty Fund, 1998). Vol. 1. Chapter: 15: Moses Mather, AMERICA'S APPEAL TO THE

IMPARTIAL WORLD. Accessed June 1, 2012 http://oll.libertyfund.org/
title/816/69260.

442   Sandoz, Political Sermons of the American Founding Era: 1730-1805,
        2 vols, Foreword by Ellis Sandoz (2nd ed. Indianapolis: Liberty Fund,
        1998). Vol. 1. Chapter: 22: Henry Cumings, A SERMON PREACHED
        AT LEXINGTON ON THE 19 th OF APRIL. Accessed May 31, 2012
        http://oll.libertyfund.org/title/816/69280.

443   Shute, Daniel, A SERMON PREACHED TO THE ANCIENT AND
        HONORABLE ARTILLERY COMPANY IN BOSTON, NEW-
        ENGLAND, JUNE 1, 1767, p. 44. Accessed June 9, 2015: http://quod.lib.
        umich.edu/e/evans/N08418.0001.001?rgn=main;view=fulltext

444   Mather, Moses, America's appeal to the impartial world, (Hartford, Printed
        by E. Watson, digitized by Duke University Library) p. 6. Accessed June
        10, 2015: https://archive.org/details/americasappealto00math

445   www.nps.gov/mima/forteachers/upload/Provincial%20Congress.pdf,
        Accessed January 10, 2012.

446   Borneman, Walter R., American Spring: Lexington, Concord and the Road
        to Revolution. (Little, Brown and Company, 237 Park Avenue, New York,
        New York, May 2014). Accessed June 10, 2015: https://goo.gl/YYaOUk

447   Fleming, Thomas, *Battle of Menotomy – First Blood, 1775*. Accessed June 10,
        2015: http://www.historynet.com/battle-of-menotomy-first-blood-1775.
        htm

448   Ibid

449   Just War Theory. Accessed June 10, 2015: http://oregonstate.edu/instruct/
        phl201/modules/just_war_theory/criteria_intro.html

450   Cummings, Henry, A SERMON PREACHED AT LEXINGTON ON
        THE 19th OF APRIL. Accessed on June 10, 2015: http://oll.libertyfund.
        org/titles/816

451   Dwight, Timothy, *The Duty of Americans, at the Present Crisis, by Timothy
        Dwight (July 4, 1798)*. Accessed June 10, 2015: http://consource.org/
        document/the-duty-of-americans-at-the-present-crisis-by-timothy-
        dwight-1798-7-4/

452 Smith, William, Rev., A Sermon on the Present Situation of American Affairs, 4. Accessed on June 10, 2015: http://americainclass.org/sources/makingrevolution/crisis/text8/sermonsonwar.pdf

453 Rogers, John, The divine goodness displayed, in the American revolution, 26. Accessed on June 10, 2015: https://goo.gl/mSYYNm

454 Mayhew, Jonathan, The snare broken. A thanksgiving-discourse, preached at the desire of the West Church in Boston, N.E. Friday May 23, 1766. Occasioned by the repeal of the stamp-act., p. 6. Accessed June 10, 2015 http://quod.lib.umich.edu/e/evans/N08145.0001.001?rgn=main;view=fulltext

455 Just War Theory, (Internet Encyclopedia of Philosophy), Accessed June 10, 2015: http://www.iep.utm.edu/justwar/#H2

456 Clark, Jonas, *The Fate Of Bloodthirsty Oppressors, And God's Care Of His Distressed People,*. Accessed June 10, 2015: https://archive.org/stream/fateofbloodthirs00clar#page/n17/mode/2up

457 Adams, James, Yankee Doodle Went To Church, pp. 18, 25-26.

458 Ibid, 38.

459 Thornton, 306-07.

460 Ibid., 310-11, 312-13.

461 Sandoz, Political Sermons of the American Founding Era: 1730-1805, 2 Vol, Foreword by Ellis Sandoz (2nd ed. Indianapolis: Liberty Fund, 1998). Vol. 1. Chapter: 20: Jacob Cushing, DIVINE JUDGMENTS UPON TYRANTS Accessed November 4, 2012 http://oll.libertyfund.org/title/816/69276.

462 Moore, 157.

463 Sandoz, Vol. 1. Chapter: 20: Jacob Cushing, DIVINE JUDGMENTS UPON TYRANTS Accessed November 4, 2012 http://oll.libertyfund.org/title/816/69276.

464 Sandoz, Political Sermons of the American Founding Era: 1730-1805, 2 vols, Foreword by Ellis Sandoz (2nd ed. Indianapolis: Liberty Fund, 1998). Vol. 1. Chapter: 29: Joseph Lathrop, A SERMON ON A DAY APPOINTED FOR PUBLICK THANKSGIVING Accessed November 4, 2012 http://oll.libertyfund.org/title/816/69307.

465   Bogue and Bennett, *History of the Dissenters*, IV, Chapter "Independence For Church And State," 494, cited in Bridenbaugh, 340.

466   Vol. 1. Chapter: 17: John Witherspoon, THE DOMINION OF PROVIDENCE OVER THE PASSIONS OF MEN, http://oll. libertyfund.org/title/816/69270.

467   Sandoz, Vol. 1. Chapter: 22: Henry Cumings, A SERMON PREACHED AT LEXINGTON ON THE 19th OF APRIL, http://oll.libertyfund. org/title/816/69280

468   Cape Cod Magazine (Wareham, Mass.: The Cape Cod Publishing Co.), May 1915, 28, and, Thornton, The Pulpit of the American Revolution, 251-254, editorial footnotes.

469   Thornton, 249-50.

470   Sandoz, Political Sermons of the American Founding Era: 1730-1805, 2 vols, Foreword by Ellis Sandoz (2nd ed. Indianapolis: Liberty Fund, 1998). Vol. 1. Chapter: 21: Samuel Cooper, A SERMON ON THE DAY OF THE COMMENCEMENT OF THE CONSTITUTION Accessed November 2, 2012 http://oll.libertyfund.org/title/816/69278

471   Adams, James L., 11.

472   Thornton, Preface, p. III.

473   Adams, James, 11.

474   Ibid, 11.

475   Ibid, 11-12, 25-26.

476   Moore, 105.

477   Sandoz, *Political Sermons of the American Founding Era: 1730-1805*, 2 vols, Foreword by Ellis Sandoz (2nd ed. Indianapolis: Liberty Fund, 1998). Vol. 1. Chapter: 17: John Witherspoon, THE DOMINION OF PROVIDENCE OVER THE PASSIONS OF MEN, Accessed May 17, 2015 http://oll.libertyfund.org/title/816/69270.

478   Sandoz, *Political Sermons of the American Founding Era: 1730-1805*, 2 vols, Foreword by Ellis Sandoz (2nd ed. Indianapolis: Liberty Fund, 1998). Vol. 1. Chapter: 32: Samuel Langdon, THE REPUBLIC OF THE ISRAELITES AN EXAMPLE TO THE AMERICAN STATES Accessed November 2, 2012 http://oll.libertyfund.org/title/816/69313.

479   *The Complete Works Of John M. Mason, D.D.*, edited by Ebenezer Mason (New York: Baker & Scribner, 1849), pp. 560-61. Accessed March 28, 2012 from books.google.com.

480   Thornton, Preface, p. III.

481   Trivers, Howard, "Universalism In the Thought of the Founding Fathers," *The Virginia Quarterly Review*, Summer 1976, pp. 448-62. Accessed March 27, 2012 www.vqronline.org. *History of Massachusetts From 1764 To July 1775: When General Washington Took Command Of The American Army*, Alden Bradford (Boston: Richardson and Lord, 1822), 361. Accessed March 27, 2012 books.google.com, Baldwin, Alice, chapter 9, p. 123.

482   Baldwin, Chapter 9, 123.

483   Adams, James, 64.

484   Thornton, 47-48, 53.

485   Ibid, 53-54.

486   Ibid, 197.

487   Headley, 27.

488   Moore, 105.

489   Bridenbaugh, 260.

490   Sandoz, Political Sermons of the American Founding Era: 1730-1805, 2 vols, Foreword by Ellis Sandoz (2nd ed. Indianapolis: Liberty Fund, 1998). Vol. 1. Chapter: 17: John Witherspoon, THE DOMINION OF PROVIDENCE OVER THE PASSIONS OF MEN Accessed November 5, 2012 http://oll.libertyfund.org/title/816/69270.

491   Newton, Thomas, *Dissertations on the Prophecies: Which Have Remarkably Been Fulfilled and At This Time Are Fulfilling In The World* (London: Printed for J. and R. Tonson in the Strand, 1766), Vol. I, 313.

492   Thornton, 320-21.

493   Edwards, Jonathan, Jr. sermon *The Necessity Of The Belief Of Christianity By The Citizens Of The State, In Order To Our Political Prosperity*, to the General Assembly of the state of Connecticut, May 8, 1794 (Hartford: Hudson & Goodwin, 1794), 44-45. Accessed March 28, 2012 www.unz.org.

494 Smalley, Jonathan, sermon, *On The Evils Of A Weak Government*, to the General Assembly of Connecticut, May 8, 1800, pp. 46-47, 50-51. Accessed March 28, 2012 www.unz.org.

495 Sandoz, Introduction, Vol. I, p. XXI.

496 Thornton, 198, *Annals of the American Pulpit* (New York: Robert Carter & Brothers, 1857), Vol. I, p. 39. Accessed April 9, 2012 books.google.com.

497 Sandoz, Vol. I, Introduction, XX.

498 Thornton, XXII.

499 Sandoz, Political Sermons of the American Founding Era: 1730-1805, 2 vols, Foreword by Ellis Sandoz (2nd ed. Indianapolis: Liberty Fund, 1998). Vol. 1. Chapter: 17: John Witherspoon, THE DOMINION OF PROVIDENCE OVER THE PASSIONS OF MEN. Accessed November 5, 2011 http://oll.libertyfund.org/title/816/69270.

500 Thornton, 339-41.

501 Ibid., 298-88.

502 Ibid., 373-76, 393-95.

503 Ibid., 403, 439, 489, 494-95, 499-500.

504 Sandoz, Political Sermons of the American Founding Era: 1730-1805, 2 vols, Foreword by Ellis Sandoz (2nd ed. Indianapolis: Liberty Fund, 1998). Vol. 1. Chapter: 26: Samuel McClintock, A SERMON ON OCCASION OF THE COMMENCEMENT OF THE NEW-HAMPSHIRE CONSTITUTION. Accessed November 5, 2012 http://oll.libertyfund.org/title/816/69301.

505 Sandoz, Political Sermons of the American Founding Era: 1730-1805, 2 vols, Foreword by Ellis Sandoz (2nd ed. Indianapolis: Liberty Fund, 1998). Vol. 1. Chapter: 28: Samuel Wales, THE DANGERS OF OUR NATIONAL PROSPERITY; AND THE WAY TO AVOID THEM. Accessed November 5, 2012 http://oll.libertyfund.org/title/816/69305.

506 Sandoz, Political Sermons of the American Founding Era: 1730-1805, 2 vols, Foreword by Ellis Sandoz (2nd ed. Indianapolis: Liberty Fund, 1998). Vol. 1. Chapter: 29: Joseph Lathrop, A SERMON ON A DAY APPOINTED FOR PUBLICK THANKSGIVING Accessed November 5, 2012 http://oll.libertyfund.org/title/816/69307.

507   Sandoz, Political Sermons of the American Founding Era: 1730-1805, 2 vols, Foreword by Ellis Sandoz (2nd ed. Indianapolis: Liberty Fund, 1998). Vol. 1. Chapter: 32: Samuel Langdon, THE REPUBLIC OF THE ISRAELITES AN EXAMPLE TO THE AMERICAN STATES. Accessed November 5, 2012 http://oll.libertyfund.org/title/816/69313.

508   Sandoz, Political Sermons of the American Founding Era: 1730-1805, 2 vols, Foreword by Ellis Sandoz (2nd ed. Indianapolis: Liberty Fund, 1998). Vol. 2. Chapter: 45: Bishop James Madison, MANIFESTATIONS OF THE BENEFICENCE OF DIVINE PROVIDENCE TOWARDS AMERICA. Accessed November 5, 2012 http://oll.libertyfund.org/title/817/69446.

509   Moore280-84.

510   http://www.dar.org/national-society/genealogy/minority-research Accessed on June 26, 2015

511   http://www.catholiceducation.org/en/culture/history/the-catholic-church-in-the-united-states-of-america.html

512   Moore, 105.

513   Sandoz, Political Sermons of the American Founding Era: 1730-1805, 2 vols, Foreword by Ellis Sandoz (2nd ed. Indianapolis: Liberty Fund, 1998). Vol. 1. Chapter: 31: Elizur Goodrich, THE PRINCIPLES OF CIVIL UNION AND HAPPINESS CONSIDERED AND RECOMMENDED. Accessed November 4, 2012 http://oll.libertyfund.org/title/816/69311.

514   Adams, John, Novanglus and Massachusettensis (Boston: Hews & Goss, 1819), 45., Accessed March 14, 2012 books.google.com.

515   Thornton, 143-44.

516   Ibid, 143-44.

517   The Declaration of Independence, 1776.

518   Hopkinson, Francis, Esq., The Miscellaneous Essays and Occasional Writings of Francis Hopkinson, Esq. (Philadelphia: T. Dobson, No. 41 Second Street, 1792), Vol. I, p. 115-16. Accessed November 4, 2012 www.google.com/search?client=safari&rls=en&q=mdccxcii&ie=UTF-8&oe=UTF-8.

519   Adams, John Quincy, "An Address Delivered at the Request of the Committee of Arrangements for the Celebrating the Anniversary of Independence at the City of Washington on the Fourth of July 1821 upon the Occasion of Reading The Declaration of Independence." Accessed November 5, 2012. www17.us.archive.org/stream/addressdelivered00adamiala/ addressdelivered00adamiala_djvu..

520   Thornton, 199

521   Sandoz, Political Sermons of the American Founding Era: 1730-1805, 2 vols, Foreword by Ellis Sandoz (2nd ed. Indianapolis: Liberty Fund, 1998). Vol. 2. Chapter: 54: William Emerson, AN ORATION IN COMMEMORATION OF THE ANNIVERSARY OF AMERICAN INDEPENDENCE. Accessed November 5, 2012 http://oll.libertyfund. org/title/817/69467.

522   Baldwin, Chapter 8, 115-16.

523   Sandoz, Political Sermons of the American Founding Era: 1730-1805, 2 vols, Foreword by Ellis Sandoz (2nd ed. Indianapolis: Liberty Fund, 1998). Vol. 1. Chapter: 12: Samuel Sherwood, SCRIPTURAL INSTRUCTIONS TO CIVIL RULERS. Accessed November 5, 2012 http://oll.libertyfund. org/title/816/69251.

524   Moore, 70-71.

525   Baldwin, 178-79.

526   Ellis Sandoz, Political Sermons of the American Founding Era: 1730-1805, 2 vols, Foreword by Ellis Sandoz (2nd ed. Indianapolis: Liberty Fund, 1998). Vol. 1. Chapter: 15: Moses Mather, AMERICA'S APPEAL TO THE IMPARTIAL WORLD. Accessed June 1, 2012 http://oll. libertyfund.org/title/816/69260.

527   Thornton, 313.

528   Moore, 12-14, 32,39.

529   Baldwin, Chapter 12, 168-69.

530   Sandoz, Political Sermons of the American Founding Era: 1730-1805, 2 vols, Foreword by Ellis Sandoz (2nd ed. Indianapolis: Liberty Fund, 1998). Vol. 1. Chapter: 15: Moses Mather, AMERICA'S APPEAL TO

THE IMPARTIAL WORLD. Accessed November 5, 2012 http://oll. libertyfund.org/title/816/69260.

531   Sandoz, Political Sermons of the American Founding Era: 1730-1805, 2 vols, Foreword by Ellis Sandoz (2nd ed. Indianapolis: Liberty Fund, 1998). Vol. 2. Chapter: 54: William Emerson, AN ORATION IN COMMEMORATION OF THE ANNIVERSARY OF AMERICAN INDEPENDENCE. Accessed November 5, 2012 http://oll.libertyfund. org/title/817/69467.

532   Sandoz, Political Sermons of the American Founding Era: 1730-1805, 2 vols, Foreword by Ellis Sandoz (2nd ed. Indianapolis: Liberty Fund, 1998). Vol. 1. Chapter: 29: Joseph Lathrop, A SERMON ON A DAY APPOINTED FOR PUBLICK THANKSGIVING. Accessed November 5, 2012 http://oll.libertyfund.org/title/816/69307.

533   Mayhew, Jonathan, sermon, "Discourse Concerning Unlimited Submission and Non-Resistance To The Higher Powers," Jan 31, 1749-50. Accessed March 14, 2012 Internet Archive, www.archive.org.

534   Moore, 68.

535   Sandoz, Political Sermons of the American Founding Era: 1730-1805, 2 vols, Foreword by Ellis Sandoz (2nd ed. Indianapolis: Liberty Fund, 1998). Vol. 1. Chapter: 10: John Allen, AN ORATION UPON THE BEAUTIES OF LIBERTY. Accessed November 5, 2012 http://oll. libertyfund.org/title/816/69240.

536   Moore, 179-80.

537   Ward, Henry Beecher, Mar 19, 1863, *The Independent* ... "*Devoted to the Consideration of Politics, Social, and Ecom Tendencies, History, Literature, and the Arts.*"

538   Moore, Preface, p. III.

539   Finney, Charles G., "The Decay of Conscience," *The Independent,* New York, December 4, 1873. Accessed January 11, 2013 The Gospel Truth, www.gospeltruth.net/1868_75Independent/731204_conscience.htm. "Lectures On Revivals of Religion," Rev. Charles G. Finney, Lecture XV, "Hindrances to Revivals," 274-75.

540   http://www.foxnews.com/opinion/2015/07/15/shock-video-planned-parenthood-sells-dead-baby-body-parts.html

541   http://www.huffingtonpost.com/2015/07/02/sweet-cakes-by-melissa-fined-same-sex-wedding_n_7718540.html

542   http://www.foxnews.com/politics/2015/08/21/army-kicking-out-decorated-green-beret-who-stood-up-for-afghan-rape-victim/

543   Paine, Thomas, *The Crisis. A*ccessed March 11, 2012 http://libertyonline. hypermall.com/Paine/Crisis/Crisis-TOC.html.

544   U.S. Religious Landscape Survey, Religious Affiliation: Diverse and Dynamic, February 2008, Chapter 1, The Pew Forum On Religion & Public Life, Pew Research Center. Accessed January 1, 2013 Religions. pewforum.org/pdf/report-religious-landscape-study-full.pdf. "How the Faithful Voted: 2012 Preliminary Analysis, November 7, 2012, The Pew Forum on Religion & Public Life, Pew Research Center. Accessed from www.pewforum.org/Politics-and-Elections/How-the-Faithful-Voted-2012-Preliminary-Exit-Poll-Analysis.aspx. "Election 2012 Marks the End of Evangelical Dominance in Politics," Jonathan Merritt, Nov. 13, 2012, *The Atlantic,* accessed from www.theatlantic.com/politics/archive/2012/11/election-2012-marks-the-end-of-evangelical-dominance-in-politics/265139/, cited 1/11/13.

545   Ertelt, Steven, "Exit Poll: 21% of Evangelical Voters Supported Barack Obama," 11/9/12, LifeNews.com.

546   Thornton, Preface, p. III.

547   Rogers, Adrian, "Do Christians need to be involved in government?" http://www.lwf.org/site/News2?page=NewsArticle&id=5309.

548   *Jefferson's Letters*, arranged by Willson Whitman (Wisconsin: E.M. Hale & Company, 1960), p. 370, "Natural Division," Thomas Jefferson letter to Henry Lee, August 10, 1824.

549   Adams, John, *The Works of John Adams, Second President of the United States: with a Life of the Author, Notes and Illustrations*, by his Grandson Charles Francis Adams (Boston: Little, Brown and Co., 1856). 10 volumes. Vol. 9. Chapter: TO JONATHAN JACKSON. Accessed April 7, 2012 http://oll.libertyfund.org/title/2107/161386/2838845.

550   Washington, George, "Farewell Address, 1796." Accessed April 7, 2012 www.loc.gov/rr/program/bib/ourdocs/farewell.html.

551   Federalist No. 10, "The Same Subject Continued: The Union as a Safeguard Against Domestic Faction and Insurrection,"Friday, November 23, 1787, by James Madison, To the People of the State of New York. Accessed April 7, 2012 thomas.loc.gov/home/histdox/fed_10.html.

552   Sandoz, Political Sermons of the American Founding Era: 1730-1805, 2 vols, Foreword by Ellis Sandoz (2nd ed. Indianapolis: Liberty Fund, 1998). Vol. 1. Chapter: 5: Charles Chauncy, CIVIL MAGISTRATES MUST BE JUST, RULING IN THE FEAR OF GOD Accessed November 5, 2012 http://oll.libertyfund.org/title/816/69228.

553   Baldwin, Chapter 10, p. 134.

554   Balch, G. W., Esq., Historical Collections Of The Danvers Historical Society, Vol. 6, "Some Account Of Reverend Benjamin Balch," p. 88, Danvers Historical Society. Accessed April 9, 20122 www.ebooksread.com/authors-eng/danvers-historical-society/historical-collections-of-the-danvers-historical-society-volume-6-vna/page-8-historical-collections-of-the-danvers-historical-society-volume-6-vna.shtml.

555   Federer, America's God and Country: Encyclopedia of Quotations, p. 235, "Lectures On Revivals of Religion," Rev. Charles G. Finney, Lecture XV, "Hindrances to Revivals." Accessed October 5, 2011 http://saynsumthn. wordpress.com.

556   Adams, John, The Works of John Adams, Second President of the United States, Charles Francis Adams, editor (Boston: Little, Brown, and Co. 1854), Vol. IX, p. 229, October 11, 1798.

557   The Collected Works Of Abraham Lincoln, Vol. IV, Roy P. Basler, editor (Rutgers University Press, Brunswick, New Jersey, 1953), p. 20. Accessed June 13, 2012 www.archive.org/stream/collectedworksof015582mbp/ collectedworksof015582mbp_djvu.txt,.

558   Clarkson, Thomas, Memoirs of the Private and Public Life of William Penn (London: Richard Taylor and Co., 1813) Vol. I, p.303.

559   Burnett, Matthias, Pastor of the First Baptist Church in Norwalk, An Election Sermon, Preached at Hartford, on the Day of the Anniversary Election, May 12, 1803 (Hartford: Printed by Hudson & Goodwin, 1803), 27-28.

560   Garfield, James A., The Works of James Abram Garfield, Burke Hinsdale, editor (Boston: James R. Osgood and Company, 1883), Vol. II, 486, 489.

561   Daniel Webster speech at the bicentennial celebration of the landing of the Pilgrims at Plymouth Rock, Dec. 22, 1820. *The Works of Daniel Webster* (Boston: Little, Brown and Company, 1853), Vol. I, pp. 22-44.

562   Jay, John, *The Correspondence and Public Papers of John Jay*, Henry P. Johnston, ed. (New York: G.P. Putnams Sons, 1890), Vol. I, p. 161.

563   Thornton, 506.

564   C.S. Lewis, Mere Christianity, (1952), p. 70. Accessed on August 24, 2015 PDF file: https://www.dacc.edu/assets/pdfs/PCM/merechristianitylewis.pdf

565   Gordon, William, *The History of the Rise, Progress and Establishment of the United States of America, including An Account of the Late War*, 3 Vols (New York: Printed for Samuel Campbell, No. 124 Pearl-Street, by John Woods, 3rd edition 1801), vol. I, pp. 273–74.

566   Thornton, 267-297.

567   Moore, Preface, p. III.

568   Adams, James, 11.

569   Thornton, Preface, p. III.

570   Adams, James L., 12-14.

571   Rehnquist, William, Supreme Court Justice, *Wallace V. Jaffree*, 1985.

572   Tocqueville, Alexis de, *Democracy In America* (New York: Edward Walker, 114 Fulton Street: 1847), Vol. II, pp. 152, 327-337.

573   Bridenbaugh, 290,

574   *Branch Ministries v. Rossotti*, 211 F.3d 137 (D.C. Cir. 2000), accessed from "Church's Loss Of Tax Exempt Status Letter Turns Out To Be A Victory For Churches," Mathew D. Staver, 2000, www.lc.org.

575   Ibid.

576   Staver, Matthew, "Church's Loss Of Tax Exempt Status Letter Turns Out To Be A Victory For Churches," 2000, www.lc.org.

577   *Lemon v. Krutzman*, U.S. Supreme Court, 403 U.S. 602 (1971), Chief Justice Warren Burger, section V.

578 George Washington, Farewell Address, September 17, 1796, "The George Washington Papers at the Library of Congress , 1741-1799, memory.loc. gov/cgi-bin/query/d?mgw:0:./temp/~ammem_iU6y:.

579 Adams, John, *The Works of John Adams, Second President of the United* States, Charles Frances Adams, editor (Boston: Little, Brown and Company, 1854), Vol. IX, p. 229, to the Officers of the First Brigade of the Third Division of the Militia of Massachusetts on October 11, 1798, The Online Library of Liberty, Liberty Fund, Inc., oll.libertyfund.org.

580 Thornton, 23.

581 Baldwin, p. 134.

582 Coffman, Elesha, "Of Church, State, and Taxes," 2008, Christian History, Christianhistory.net, Accessed June 29, 2012 www.christianitytoday.com/ ch/news/2002/may17.html.

583 H.R. Committee on Ways and Means, *Hearings on Forty Topics Pertaining to the General Revision of the Internal Revenue Code,* 83d Congress 1576 (August 11, 1953).

584 "Churches are Tax Exempt as a Matter of Constitutional Right," accessed from www.opposingviews.com/arguments/churches-are-tax-exempt-as-a-matter-of-constitutional-right.

585 *McCulloch v. Maryland,* 17 U.S. 327 (1819).

586 Ibid.

587 Stanley, Erik, "ERIK STANLEY: Tax exemption churches' right," September 27, 2008. Accessed July 4, 2012 oldsite.alliancedefensefund. org/userdocs/2008-09-27MontgomeryAdvertiser.pdf.

588 Internal Revenue Service Tax Code, 1996, Volume I:856.

589 100 Cong. Rec. 9604 (1954).

590 Stanley

591 Thornton, 161.

592 "Old Swamp Church and the first U.S. Speaker of the House," The Bowery Boys, New York City History, January 7, 2011. Accessed December 12, 2012 theboweryboys.blogspot.com/2011/01/old-swamp-church-and-first-us-speaker.html.

593   *Luther League Review: 1914-1915, Volumes 27-28*, Vol XXVII, Dec. 1914, No. 12, 13. The Lutherans of New York, their story and their problems (New York: The Petersfield Press, 1918), George Unangst Wenner, 12,14. *The Pennsylvania-German*, Volumes 3-4, Philip Columbus Croll, Henry Addison Schuler, Howard Wiegner Kriebel, Vol. III, April 1902, No. 2, 54-55. *The Pennsylvania Magazine of History and Biography* (Philadelphia: The Historical Society of Pennsylvania, 1889), Volume 13, 189-191.

594   "Old Swamp Church and the first U.S. Speaker of the House."

595   Moore, 359-61.

596   *The Speeches Of The Right Honourable John Philpot Curran*, (Dublin: Printed by Jay Stockdale And Sons, 1808), "Speech Of John Philpot Curran, Esq.; On The Right Of Election Of Lord Mayor Of The City Of Dublin, Delivered Before The Lord Lieutenant And Privy Council Of Ireland, 1790," 5.

597   Whitman, Wilson, *Jefferson's Letters* (Eau Claire, Wisconsin: E.M. Hale and Company, 1948), Thomas Jefferson letter to William S. Smith, November 13, 1787, 83

598   Augustine, Confessions I,1,i, *The Journey Toward God In Augustine's Confessions, Books I-VI*, Carl G. Vaught (Albany: State University of New York Press, 2003), 23.

599   *Pensees 10.148*, cited from *Just A Thought ... Manna For The Mind*, Ed Cook (Woodinville, Washington: August Ink Books, 2011) 148.

600   Accessed from constitution.org/lincoln/lyceum.htm.

601   Sandoz, Political Sermons of the American Founding Era: 1730-1805, 2 vols, Foreword by Ellis Sandoz (2nd ed. Indianapolis: Liberty Fund, 1998). Vol. 1. Chapter: 28: Samuel Wales, THE DANGERS OF OUR NATIONAL PROSPERITY; AND THE WAY TO AVOID THEM. Accessed June 17, 2012 http://oll.libertyfund.org/title/816/69305.

602   Sandoz, Political Sermons of the American Founding Era: 1730-1805, 2 vols, Foreword by Ellis Sandoz (2nd ed. Indianapolis: Liberty Fund, 1998). Vol. 1. Chapter: 28: Samuel Wales, THE DANGERS OF OUR NATIONAL PROSPERITY; AND THE WAY TO AVOID THEM. Accessed June 17, 2012 http://oll.libertyfund.org/title/816/69305.

603 *The American Quarterly Register*, American Education Society, conducted by B. B. Edwards (Boston: Perkins & Marvin, 1833), Vol. V, p. 217.

604 Ronald Reagan to the annual meeting of the Phoenix Chamber of Commerce, March 30, 1961. Accessed May 26, 2012 www.starkiller-online.net/wiki/index.php?title=Encroaching_Control.

605 Sandoz, Political Sermons of the American Founding Era: 1730-1805, 2 vols, Foreword by Ellis Sandoz (2nd ed. Indianapolis: Liberty Fund, 1998). Vol. 2. Chapter: 54: William Emerson, AN ORATION IN COMMEMORATION OF THE ANNIVERSARY OF AMERICAN INDEPENDENCE. Accessed November 5, 2012 http://oll.libertyfund.org/title/817/69467 on 2012-11-05.

606 Moore, 105.

607 Metaxas, Eric, *Bonhoeffer: Pastor, Martyr, Prophet, Spy* (Thomas Nelson, Inc., 2010)

608 The Barna Group, "Barna: Many pastors wary of raising 'controversy'," Chris Woodward, OneNewsNow.com, Friday, August 01, 2014.

609 Ibid.

610 Sandoz, Political Sermons of the American Founding Era: 1730-1805, 2 vols, Foreword by Ellis Sandoz (2nd ed. Indianapolis: Liberty Fund, 1998). Vol. 1. Chapter: 22: Henry Cumings, A SERMON PREACHED AT LEXINGTON ON THE 19th OF APRIL. Accessed November 5, 2012 http://oll.libertyfund.org/title/816/69280.

611 "Only One Life," C.T. Studd.

612 Thornton, 395-96.

613 Headley, 39.

Bibliography

"To John Adams from Benjamin Rush, 20 July 1811." Founders Online. Accessed August 7, 2015. http://founders.archives.gov/documents/Adams/99-02-02-5659.

"A Man of Genius and Eloquence." This Day in Presbyterian History: February 2 : Rev. George Duffield [1732-1790]. November 4, 2012. Accessed August 20, 2015. http://www.thisday.pcahistory.org/?s=John Adams.

Adams, James L. Yankee Doodle Went to Church. Old Tappan, N.J.: F.H. Revell, 1989.

Adams, John, and Charles Francis Adams. The Works of John Adams, Second President of the United States: With a Life of the Author, Notes and Illustrations,. Boston: Little, Brown, 1850.

Adams, John, and Abigail Adams. Familiar Letters of John Adams and His Wife Abigail Adams, during the Revolution: With a Memoir of Mrs. Adams. New York: Hurd and Houghton, 1875. 265.

Adams, Samuel, and Harry Alonzo Cushing. "Samuel Adams to James Warren, October 24, 1780." In The Writings of Samuel Adams,, 213. Vol. IV. New York, London: G.P. Putnam's Sons, 1908.

Alexander, James. "John Witherspoon." The Society of the Descendants of the Signers of the Declaration of Independence. December 11, 2011. Accessed May 26, 2015. http://www.dsdi1776.com/signers-by-state/john-witherspoon/.

Allen, R. H., ed. Old Pine Street Church. Philadelphia: H.B. Ashmead, Book and Job Printer, 1868. 45.

Baldwin, Alice M. The New England Clergy and the American Revolution. New York: F. Ungar Pub., 1958.

Bennett, James, and David Bogue. "Independence For Church And State." In The History of Dissenters: From the Revolution to the Year 1808. 2d ed. Vol. IV. London: F. Westley and A.H. Davis, 1833.

Ferguson, Robert. The Cambridge History of American Literature. Edited by Sacvan Bercovitch. Cambridge: Cambridge University Press, 1994. 66.

Berkin, Carol. Jonathan Sewall; Odyssey of an American Loyalist. New York: Columbia University Press, 1974.

"Bill of Rights: Massachusetts Constitution of 1780, PT. 1." Bill of Rights: Massachusetts Constitution of 1780, PT. 1. Accessed May 19, 2015. http://press-pubs.uchicago.edu/founders/documents/bill_of_rightss6.html.

"Biography — The Reverend George Duffield (Oct. 7, 1732 - Feb. 2, 1790)." Presbyterian Heritage Center. 2007. Accessed November 4, 2012. http://www.phcmontreat.org/bios/Duffield-George.htm.

Briceland, Alan V. "Daniel McCalla, 1748-1809: New Side Revolutionary and Jeffersonian." Journal of Presbyterian History, 1978, 257-59.

Bridenbaugh, Carl. Mitre and Sceptre; Transatlantic Faiths, Ideas, Personalities, and Politics, 1689-1775. New York: Oxford University Press, 1962.

"Brigadier General John Peter Gabriel Muhlenberg." NPS.gov. Accessed August 7, 2015.

Brydon, Norman F. Reverend James Caldwell, Patriot, 1734-1781. Caldwell, N.J.: Caldwell Bicentennial Committee, 1976. 31.

Buckley, Edmund. Universal Religion; a Course of Lessons Historical and Scientific on the Various Faiths of the World,. Chicago: University Association, 1897.

Bunce, Oliver Bell. The Romance of the Revolution Being a History of the Personal Adventures, Romantic Incidents, and Exploits Incidental to the War of Independence ... Philadelphia: Porter & Coates, 1858. 440-444.

Byrd, James P. Sacred Scripture, Sacred War: The Bible and the American Revolution. New York, New York: Oxford University Press, 2013.

Clark, Jonas. Opening of the War of the Revolution A Brief Narrative of the Principal Transactions of That Day,. Lexington, Mass.: Lexington Historical Society, 1901.

Cleaveland, John. "The Annotated Newspapers of Harbottle Dorr, Jr." The Annotated Newspapers of Harbottle Dorr: The New-England Chronicle: Or, the Essex Gazette, 13 July 1775. July 13, 1775. Accessed May 1, 2015. http://www.masshist.org/dorr/volume/4/sequence/851.

Clemons, Harry. "Anecdote of an Old Time Minister." Google Books. 1899. Accessed May 1, 2015.

Clyde, John Cunningham. Rosbrugh, a Tale of the Revolution; Or, Life, Labors and Death of Rev. John Rosbrugh ... Chaplain in the Continental Army; Clerical Martyr of the Revolution, Killed by Hessians, in the Battle of Assumpink, at Trenton, New Jersey, Jan. 2d, 1777. Founded up. Easton, 1880.

Collections of the Historical Society of Pennsylvania. Vol. 1. Philadelphia: J. Pennington, 1853. 70-72.

Cooper, Samuel. A Sermon Preached before His Excellency John Hancock, Esq ; Governour, the Honourable the Senate, and House of Representatives of the Commonwealth of Massachusetts, October 25, 1780 Being the Day of the Commencement of the Constitution, and Inauguration O. Boston] Commonwealth of Massachusetts: Printed by T. and J. Fleet, and J. Gill, 1780.

Craighead, John. "Biographies -- C -- Ministers -- Presbyterian Heritage Center." Presbyterian Heritage Center. Accessed

December 27, 2011. http://www.phcmontreat.org/bios/ Bios-C.htm.

Craven, W. Frank. "Witherspoon, John." Witherspoon, John. 1978. Accessed October 1, 2012.

Cunningham, Peter. The Letters of Horace Walpole, Earl of Oxford. London: R. Bentley, 1861.

Decker, Michael McMillen. Baron Von Steuben and the Military Forces in Virginia during the British Invasions of 1780-1781. Richmond: University of Richmond UR Scholarship Repository, 1979. 16-30.

Dorchester, Daniel. Christianity in the United States from the First Settlement down to the Present Time. New York: Hunt & Eaton ;, 1890. 265.

"Duffield, George." Duffield, George. Accessed November 4, 2012. https://collections.dartmouth.edu/occom/html/ctx/ personography/pers0173.ocp.html.

Edwards, B. B. The American Quarterly Register,. Vol. 5. Boston: American Education Society. Printed by Perkins & Marvin, 1833. 217.

Ege, Ralph. "Chapter IV." In Pioneers of Old Hopewell;, 20. Hopewell, N.J.: Race & Savidge, 1908.

Everett, Edward. Life of John Stark [cited from The History of Pittsfield (Bershire County), Vol. 1compiled and Written under the General Direction of a Committee by J.E.A. Smith. Boston: Lee and Shepard, 1869.

FIRST SESSION OF THE TWENTY-SIXTH CONGRESS. Washington: Blair and Rives, Printers, 1839. 543.

Farmer, Silas, Rufus W. Clark, Louis A Arthur, Henry S. Sibley, and George W. Bates. Year-book of the Michigan Society of the Sons of the American Revolution, from 1890 to 1898. Detroit: Society, 1898.

Fassett, James Hiram. "Chapter 8." In Colonial Life in New Hampshire. Boston: Ginn &, 1899.

Fea, John. "Fea on Morrison, 'John Witherspoon and the Founding of the American Republic'" Fea on Morrison, 'John Witherspoon and the Founding of the American Republic' April 1, 2006. Accessed June 16, 2015. https://networks.h-net.org/node/14785/reviews/16350/fea-morrison-john-witherspoon-and-founding-american-republic.

Fea, John. Why Study History?: Reflecting on the Importance of the past. Grand Rapids, MI: Baker Academic, 2013. 3, 15.

"February 8: Rev. Moses Allen." This Day in Presbyterian History. February 8, 2012. Accessed August 17, 2015. http://www.thisday.pcahistory.org/2012/02/february-8-rev-moses-allen.

"Alice C. Jennings." In The Connecticut Magazine, edited by William Farrand Felch, George C. Atwell, H. Phelps Arms, and Francis Trevelyan Miller. Vol. 9. Hartford, CT: [publisher Not Identified], 1905.

Ferguson, Robert A. The American Enlightenment, 1750-1820. Cambridge, Mass.: Cambridge University Press, 1994.

Ferguson, Robert A. The American Enlightenment, 1750-1820. Edited by Sacvan Bercovitch. Vol. 1. Cambridge, Mass.: Harvard University Press, 1994.

Ferling, John E. The First of Men: A Life of George Washington. Knoxville: University of Tennessee Press, 1988. 221.

Fisher, Anne. "History of First Parish in Lexington." History of First Parish in Lexington. 1975. Accessed August 8, 2015. http://fpc.lexington.ma.us/index.php/history.

Fleming, Thomas J. 1776. New York: New Word City, 2014.

Flick, AlexanderC. "The Knox Trail - History." The Knox Trail. September 26, 1926. Accessed May 19, 2015. http://www.nysm.nysed.gov/services/KnoxTrail/index.html#top.

Folsom, Joseph Fulford. "Manuscript Light on Chaplain James Caldwells Death." In Manuscript Light on Chaplain

James Caldwell's Death. Vol. 1. New Jersey: New Jersey Historical Society, 1916.

Franklin, Benjamin. "The Writings of Benjamin Franklin." Jared Sparks (Sparks, Jared, 1789-1866). Accessed August 7, 2015. http://onlinebooks.library.upenn.edu/webbin/book/ lookupname?key=Sparks, Jared, 1789-1866.

Frey, Raymond. "John Witherspoon: Preacher and Patriot." Accessed January 17, 2011. http://people.hofstra. edu/alan_j_singer/docket/docket/11.1.17_John_ Witherspoon_Preacher_and_Patriot_by_Raymond_Frey. pdf.

Galloway, Charles B. Christianity and the American Commonwealth; Or, The Influence of Christianity in Making This Nation. Nashville, Tenn.: Publishing House Methodist Episcopal Church, South, Barbee & Smith, Agents, 1898.

Gano, John, and Stephen Gano. Biographical Memoirs of the Late Rev. John Gano, of the Frankfurt, Kentucky, Formerly of the City of New York. New-York: Printed by Southwick and Hardcastle for J. Tiebout, 1806.

Gill, Eliza M. "Distinguished Guests and Residents of Medford." Medford Historical Society Papers, Volume 16. October 21, 1912. Accessed May 1, 2015. http://www.perseus.tufts. edu/hopper/text?doc=Perseus:text:2005.05.0016.

Gillespie, Robert Goggin. "Reverend William Graham, Presbyterian Minister and Rector of Liberty Hall Academy." University of Richmond Scholarship Repository. 1970. Accessed August 7, 2015. http://scholarship.richmond. edu/cgi/viewcontent.cgi?article=1306&context=masters-thesesIbid, p. 69.

Gilman, Theodore. The Rev. Jonas Clark,. 1911.

Goodrich, Charles A. Lives of the Signers to the Declaration of Independence. New York: W. Reed &, 1829. 211.

Greene, Jack P., and J. R. Pole. A Companion to the American Revolution. Malden, Mass.: Blackwell Publishers, 2000.

Hackenbracht, Jay Steele. "John Steel 1715-1779." Jaysteeleblog. March 17, 2013. Accessed August 7, 2015. https://jaysteeleblog.wordpress.com/2013/03/17/john-steel-1715-1779/.

"Hannah Caldwell." AmericanRevolution.ORG. Accessed September 23, 2012. americanrevolution.org/women/women44.html.

Headley, J. T. The Chaplains and Clergy of the Revolution. New York: C. Scribner, 1864.

Henry, Patrick. Give Me Liberty or Give Me Death. Champaign, Ill.: Project Gutenberg, 199.

Hitchcock, Gad. A Sermon Preached before His Excellency Thomas Gage, Esq; Governor the Honorable His Majesty's Council, and the Honorable House of Representatives, of the Province of the Massachusetts-Bay in New-England, May 25th, 1774. Being the Anniversary of the Elec. Boston: New-England :, 1774.

Hocker, Edward W. The Fighting Parson of the American Revolution; a Biography of General Peter Muhlenberg, Lutheran Clergyman, Military Chieftain, and Political Leader,. Philadelphia: Pub. by the Author, 1936.

Hodge, Charles. The Constitutional History of the Presbyterian Church in the United States of America. Philadelphia: W.S. Martien, 1839.

Howard, R. H., and Henry E. Crocker. A History of New England: Containing Historical and Descriptive Sketches of the Counties, Cities and Principal Towns of the Six New England States, Including, in Its List of Contributors, More than Sixty Literary Men and Women, Representing Every County I. Vol. Vol. 1. Boston: Crocker &, 1880.

Howard, R. H., and Henry E. Crocker. A History of New England: Containing Historical and Descriptive Sketches of the Counties, Cities and Principal Towns of the Six New England States, Including, in Its List of Contributors, More than Sixty Literary Men and Women, Representing Every County I. Boston: Crocker, 1880.

Hudson, Charles. History of the Town of Lexington, Middlesex County, Massachusetts from Its First Settlement to 1868. Bi-centenary ed. Boston: Houghton Mifflin, 1913.

"Zabdiel Adams 1739-1801: "An Election Sermon,"." In American Political Writing during the Founding Era, 1760-1805, edited by Charles S. Hyneman and Donald Lutz. Vol. 1. Indianapolis: Liberty Press, 1983.

"Inspiration from John Witherspoon." Inspiration from John Witherspoon. Accessed August 17, 2015.

"James Caldwell: The Fighting Chaplain A." Leben. Accessed September 15, 2015. http://www.leben.us/index.php/component/content/article/254-james-caldwell-the-fighting-chaplain.

Kelley, Brooks Mather. Yale; a History. New Haven: Yale University Press, 1999.

Kelley, Brooks Mather. Yale; a History. New Haven: Yale University Press, 1999. 74.

Kerr, Harry P. "The Election Sermon: Primer for Revolutionaries." Taylor & Francis. June 2, 2009. Accessed May 11, 2015.

Ketchum, Richard M. Saratoga: Turning Point of America's Revolutionary War. New York: H. Holt, 1997.

Ketchum, Richard M. Saratoga: Turning Point of America's Revolutionary War. New York: H. Holt, 1997. 318.

Kidd, Thomas S. The Great Awakening: The Roots of Evangelical Christianity in Colonial America. New Haven: Yale University Press, 2009.

Kidd, Thomas S. The Great Awakening: The Roots of Evangelical Christianity in Colonial America. New Haven: Yale University Press, 2009. 276.

Kimball, Roger. "The New Criterion." The Forgotten Founder: John Witherspoon by Roger Kimball -. June 1, 2006. Accessed November 4, 2012. http://www.newcriterion. com/articles.cfm/The-forgotten-founder--John-Witherspoon-2437.

Lee, Charles, and Edward Langworthy. The Life and Memoirs of the Late Major General Lee, Second in Command to General Washington during the American Revolution, to Which Are Added His Political and Military Essays. Also, Letters to and from Many Distinguished Characters Both in Europe and Am. New York: Richard Scott, 1813.

Lincoln, Willam. The Journals of Each Provincial Congress of Massachusetts in 1774 and 1775, and of the Committee of Safety, with an Appendix, Containing the Proceedings of the County Conventions-narratives of the Events of the Nineteenth of April, 1775-papers Relating to. Boston: Dutton and Wentworth, Printers to the State, 1838. 283-284.

Loetscher, Frederick, ed. Papers of the American Society of Church History: Second Series. Vol. Vol. VI. New York: Putnam, 1921.

"Joseph Fish." In Papers of the American Society of Church History, edited by Frederick William Loetscher, 6. New York: Putnam, 1921.

Longfield, Bradley J. Presbyterians and American Culture a History. Louisville, KY: Westminster John Knox Press, 2013. 37.

Louthan, Henry Thompson. The American Baptist Pulpit at the Beginning of the Twentieth Century. Williamsburg, Va.: Published by the Editor, 1903. 13.

MacMaster, Robert K. "News of the Yorktown Campaign: The Journal of Dr. Robert Honyman, April 17-November 25, 1781." The Virginia Magazine of History and Biography

79, no. 4 (1971): 387-426. Accessed May 5, 2015. http://
www.jstor.org/stable/4247677.

Marina, William F. "The American Revolution and the Minority
Myth by William F. Marina." The Independent Institute.
1975. Accessed May 12, 2015. http://www.independent.
org/publications/article.asp?id=1398.

"Mass Moments: Smithsonian Puts Julia Child's Kitchen on
Display." Mass Moments: Smithsonian Puts Julia Child's
Kitchen on Display. Accessed May 7, 2015. http://www.
massmoments.org/.

Maxey, David. "The American Revolution." National Parks
Service. Accessed August 7, 2015. http://www.nps.gov/
revwar/unfinished_revolution/treason.htm.

McCabe, James D. A Comprehensive View of Our Country
and Its Resources Giving a Brief Outline of the Birth
and Growth of the Nation and Each State Separately
... Descriptions of the Rivers, Lakes, Mountains, Cities,
Soil, Climate ... Etc. ... Intersperced with Many Exciti.
Philadelphia [etc.: Hubbard Bros., 1876.

McCabe, James D. A Comprehensive View of Our Country
and Its Resources Giving a Brief Outline of the Birth
and Growth of the Nation and Each State Separately
... Descriptions of the Rivers, Lakes, Mountains, Cities,
Soil, Climate ... Etc. ... Intersperced with Many Exciti.
Philadelphia [etc.: Hubbard Bros., 1876.

Meany, Joseph. "The Noble Train of Artillery." Duanesburg
Central School District. Accessed May 19, 2015.

Miller, Samuel. Memoir of the Rev. John Rodgers, D.D., Late
Pastor of the Wall-street and Brick Churches, in the City
of New York. Abridged from the Original ed. Philadelphia:
Presbyterian Board of Publication, 1840.

Moore, Frank. The Patriot Preachers of the American Revolution
with Biographical Sketches, 1766-1783. New York:
Charles T. Evans, 1862.

Morris, B. F. The Christian Life and Character of the Civil Institutions of the United States. 2nd ed. Powder Springs, GA: American Vision, 2007.

Morrison, Jeffry H. John Witherspoon and the Founding of the American Republic. Notre Dame: University of Notre Dame Press, 2005.

Muhlenberg, Henry A. The Life of Major-General Peter Muhlenberg of the Revolutionary Army. Philadelphia: Carey and Hart, 1849.

Murray, D.D., Nicholas. A Memoir of the Rev. James Caldwell of Elizabethtown. Vol. III. Newark, N. J.: Printed at the Office of the Daily Advertiser, 1848.

"Naphtali Daggett The Sixth Rector and Second President of Yale College The Beginning of the American Revolution 1766 to 1777." Yale History Blog. January 6, 2012. Accessed October 30, 2012. http://seas.yale.edu/i-am/alumnus/yale-history-blog.

Nichipor, Mark A. "The Road Was Bloody." Cobblestone 23, no. 7 (2002): 25. Accessed May 1, 2015. MAS Ultra - School Edition, EBSCOhost.

Nickerson, Hoffman. The Turning Point of the Revolution, Or, Burgoyne in America. Port Washington, N.Y.: Houghton Mifflin Company, 1928.

Nickerson, Hoffman. The Turning Point of the Revolution, Or, Burgoyne in America. Boston and New York: Riverside Press Cambridge, 1928. 252.

Niles, Hezekiah. Principles and Acts of the Revolution in America: Or, An Attempt to Collect and Preserve Some of the Speeches, Orations, & Proceedings, with Sketches and Remarks on Men and Things, and Other Fugitive or Neglected Pieces, Belonging to the Men of the Revolu. Baltimore: Printed and Pub. for the Editor, by W.O. Niles, 1822.

Noll, Mark. "The Election Sermon: Situating Religion and the Constitution in the Eighteenth Century." DePaul Law Review 59, no. 4 (2009): 1223-248. Accessed May 7, 2015. http://www.heinonline.org.ezproxy.lib. ou.edu/HOL/Page?page=1223&handle=hein.journals/ deplr59&id=1231.

Norris, Edwin Mark. The Story of Princeton,. Boston: Little, Brown, and Company, 1917.

"Old Burying Ground (17th Century) & Fort Golgotha (1782)." Accessed August 17, 2015.

"Old Pine Street Presbyterian Church Cemetery, 412 Pine Street, Philadelphia, Philadelphia County, PA." Old Pine Street Presbyterian Church Cemetery, 412 Pine Street, Philadelphia, Philadelphia County, PA. 2000. Accessed May 21, 2015.

Oliver, Peter. Peter Oliver's Origin & Progress of the American Rebellion a Tory View. Edited by Adair & John A. Schultz. Stanford, Calif: Stanford University Press, 1967.

"PENN BIOGRAPHIES: James Latta (1732-1801)."University of Pennsylvania University Archives. Accessed August 7, 2015. http://www.archives.upenn.edu/people/1700s/ latta_james.html.

Paine, Thomas. "The American Crisis: PHILADELPHIA, Sept. 12, 1777." Ushistory.org. July 4, 1995. Accessed August 3, 2015.

Taylor, S. H. Bibliotheca Sacra and American Biblical Repository. Edited by E. A. Park. Vol. XIII. New York: John Wiley, 1856. 193.

Parker, Captain John. "Today in History." July 13. Accessed August 19, 2015.

Peckham, George. The Magazine of History with Notes and Queries. Vol. XX. Tarrytown, N.Y.: Reprinted, W. Abbatt, 1915.

Potaski, Michael. "Uxbridge's Samuel Spring: Revolutionary War Chaplain (Page 5)." Blackstone Valley Tribune. December 8, 2008. Accessed August 7, 2015. http://www.blackstonevalleytribune.com/pdf/BLA.2008.12.05.pdf.

Powell, John. Great Events from History: The 18th Century : 1701 -1800. Pasadena, Calif.: Salem Press, 2006.

Prowell, George Reeser. History of York County, Pennsylvania,. Chicago: J.H. Beers, 1907.

Quint, Alonzo H., Christopher Cushing, Isaac P. Langworthy, and Samuel Burnham, eds. The Congregational Quarterly. Vol. XI. Boston: University Press: Welch, Bugelow, &, 1869.

"RELATIVELY FICTION: A Book About John Cleaveland's World." Relatively Fiction. July 14, 2009. Accessed May 1, 2015. http://relativelyfiction.blogspot.com/2009/07/book-about-john-cleavelands-world.html.

"REVOLUTIONARY WAR SITES IN CALDWELL, NEW JERSEY." Caldwell, New Jersey Revolutionary War Sites. Accessed August 7, 2015. http://www.revolutionarywarnewjersey.com/new_jersey_revolutionary_war_sites/towns/caldwell_nj_revolutionary_war_sites.htm.

"Red House Presbyterian Church." NORTH CAROLINA STATE HISTORIC PRESERVATION OFFICE. May 1, 2001. Accessed May 14, 2015. http://www.hpo.ncdcr.gov/nr/CS0444.pdf.

"The Rev. John Witherspoon, D.D." In The Presbyterian Magazine, edited by C. Van Rennselaer, 576. Vol. 1. Philadelphia: WM. H. Mitchell, 1851.

"Reverend John Rosbrugh (1714-1777)." Presbyterians Caring for Chaplains and Military. Accessed August 7, 2015. http://pccmp.org/who-we-are/history/reverend-john-rosbrugh-presbyterian-chaplain-1714-1777/.

"Revolutionary War Correspondence; Note 40." Governor Richard Howell. February 3, 2015. Accessed May 15, 2015. http://govhowell.org/revolutionary-war-correspondence/.

Robinson, Blackwell P. "Caldwell, David." NCPEDIA. Accessed August 17, 2015. http://ncpedia.org/biography/caldwell-david.

"Rockland County Journal, Number 21, 26 June 1852." HRVH Historical Newspapers. June 26, 1852. Accessed April 5, 2013. http://news.hrvh.org/veridian/cgi-bin/senylrc/?a=d &d=rocklandctyjournal18520626.2.4&e=-------en-20-- 1-----txt-txIN-------#.

Rodgers, John. The Faithful Servant Rewarded a Sermon, Delivered at Princeton, before the Board of Trustees of the College of New Jersey, May 6, 1795, Occasioned by the Death of the Rev. John Witherspoon, D.D.L.L.D. President of Said College. New York: Printed by Thomas Greenleaf., 1795.

Rothbard, Murray N., and Leonard P. Liggio. Conceived in Liberty. Auburn: Ludwig Von Mises Institute, 1979. 882.

Ryerson, Egerton. The Loyalists of America and Their times from 1620-1816. Toronto: W. Briggs; James Campbell & Son, and Willing & Williamson, 1880.

Ryerson, Egerton. The Loyalists of America and Their times from 1620-1816. Vol. 1. Toronto: W. Briggs ;, 1880.

Sandoz, Ellis. "John Allen, AN ORATION UPON THE BEAUTIES OF LIBERTY." In Political Sermons of the American Founding Era, 1730-1805. Vol. 1. Indianapolis: LibertyPress, 1991.

Sandoz, Ellis. Political Sermons of the American Founding Era, 1730-1805. 2nd ed. Vol. 1. Indianapolis, IN: Liberty Fund, 1998.

Sawyer, William. "The Oneida Nation in the American Revolution." National Park Service. Accessed August 7,

2015. http://www.nps.gov/fost/learn/historyculture/the-oneida-nation-in-the-american-revolution.htm.

Schenck, Elizabeth Hubbell. "Rev. Hezekiah Ripley." In The History of Fairfield, Fairfield County, Connecticut, from the Settlement from 1700 to 1800,, 460. Vol. II. New York: Author, 1905.

Schiff, Judith Ann. "Manuscript Light on Chaplain James Caldwells Death." Yale Alumni Magazine: Old Yale (July/Aug 2006). July 1, 2006. Accessed August 7, 2015. http://archives.yalealumnimagazine.com/issues/2006_07/old_yale.html.

Bellesiles, M,. Encyclopedia of the American Revolution: Library of Military History. Edited by Harold E. Selesky. 2nd ed. Vol. 2. Detroit: Charles Scribner's Sons, 2006. 760-761.

Selesky, Harold E., ed. Encyclopedia of the American Revolution: Library of Military History. 2nd ed. Vol. 3. Detroit: Charles Scribner's Sons, 2006. 760-761.

Sforza, Alfred V. Portrait of a Small Town II: Huntington, New York "in the Beginning": A Personal and Pictorial History of the Geology, First Americans, Government, Law Enforcement, and Places of Worship That Influenced the Development of Huntington. United States?: Fore Angels Press, 2001.

"Signers of the Declaration, Biographical Sketches: John Witherspoon." National Parks Service. July 4, 2004. Accessed May 20, 2015. http://www.nps.gov/parkhistory/online_books/declaration/bio54.htm.

Sinatra, Jon. "WASHINGTON'S MILITIA UNIT TACTICS AT TRENTON & PRINCETON." Colorado Society - Sons of the American Revolution. 2005. Accessed August 20, 2015. http://www.cossar.us/images/CHRISTMAS_CAMPAIGN_1776_76.pdf.

Snow, Kurt. "James Caldwell: 'The Fighting Chaplain,'"." Leben, A Journal of Reformation Life. 2008. Accessed May 1, 2012. file:///C:/Users/Mark/Downloads/Leben V4 I2.pdf.

Sprague, William B. Annals of the American Pulpit: Or, Commemorative Notices of Distinguished American Clergymen of Various Denominations : From the Early Settlement of the Country to the Close of the Year Eighteen Hundred and Fifty-five : With Historical Introductions. New York: Robert Carter & Bros., 1858.

Springfield, Mass. Papers and Proceedings of the Connecticut Valley Historical Society: 1876-1881. Springfield, Mass.: Published by the Society, 1881.

St. George, Jr., William Ross. "The Patriot: Movie Review from the Journal of American History." Study the Past. Accessed August 7, 2015.

Stohlman, Martha Lou Lemmon. John Witherspoon: Parson, Politician, Patriot. Philadelphia: Westminster Press, 1976.

Stohlman, Martha Lou Lemmon. John Witherspoon: Parson, Politician, Patriot. Louisville: Westminster Press, 1976.

Stryker, William S. The Battles of Trenton and Princeton. Boston: Houghton, Mifflin, 1898.

Stryker, William S. The Battles of Trenton and Princeton. Boston: Houghton, Mifflin, 1898. 362.

Stuart, Margaret Elizabeth Dunbar. History of the Ely Re-union, Held at Lyme, Conn., July 10th, 1878 .. New York: Styles & Cash, Steam Printers and Stationers, 1879. 106-108.

Sullivan, Brian. "Day 334: Rev. Thomas Allen." Berkshire Eagle Online. November 30, 2011. Accessed October 11, 2012. http://www.berkshireeagle.com/ci_19437066.

Thayer, Christopher T. An Address Delivered in the First Parish, Beverly, October 2, 1867 on the Two-hundredth Anniversary of Its Formation. Boston: Nichols and Noyes, 1868.

"The Battle of Brandywine." Pennsylvania Historical and Museum Commission. 1992. Accessed August 3, 2015. http://www.portal.state.pa.us/portal/server.pt/community/events/4279/battle_of_brandywine/473340.

"The Battle of Brandywine." The Pennsylvania Historical and Museum Commission. 1992. Accessed August 21, 2015. http://www.portal.state.pa.us/portal/server.pt/community/events/4279/battle_of_brandywine/473340.

"The Historical Collections of the Historical Society of Pennsylvania." Collections of the Historical Society of Pennsylvania. 1853. Accessed August 16, 2015. https://archive.org/stream/collectionshist00penngoog#page/n84/mode/2up.

"Extract from a Letter of Captain Johann Heinrichs of the Hessioan Jager Corps, Written from Philadelphia, January 18, 1778." In The Pennsylvania Magazine of History and Biography., 137. Vol. XXII. Philadelphia: Historical Society of Pennsylvania, 1898.

"The Religious Affiliation of John Witherspoon a Signer of the American Declaration of Independence." John Witherspoon, Signer of Declaration of Independence. Accessed October 1, 2012. http://www.adherents.com/people/pw/John_Witherspoon.html.

"The Transatlantic Controversy Over Creating an American Bishop." The American Revolution. Accessed May 14, 2015. http://www.ouramericanrevolution.org/index.cfm/page/view/p0207.

Theobald, Mary. "Whatever Happened to Benedict Arnold?" Benedict Arnold : The Colonial Williamsburg Official History & Citizenship Site. 2001. Accessed May 5, 2015. http://www.history.org/foundation/journal/summer01/benedictarnold.cfm.

Thorne, John Calvin. A Monograph on the Rev. Israel Evans, A.M., Chaplain in the American Army ... 1775-1783:

The Second Settled Ministry of Concord, N.H. Concord, N.H.?: [The Author], 1902. 16-18.

Thornton, John Wingate. The Pulpit of the American Revolution: Or, The Political Sermons of the Period of 1776 With a Historical Introduction, Notes, and Illustrations. Boston: Gould and Lincoln;, 1860. XXXVIII.

Tocqueville, Alexis De, and Henry Reeve. Democracy in America. Vol. II.

Tomlinson, Abraham. The Military Journals of Two Private Soldiers, 1758-1755. Poughkeepsie: A. Tomlinson, 1855. 50.

Trevelyan, George Otto. The American Revolution. New York: Longmans, Green, and, 1899.

Trout, Joab, John Penington, and Henry C. Baird. "Chapter IX - A Sermon Preached on the Eve of the Battle of Brandywine (September 10, 1777), by the Rev. Joab Trout, to a Large Portion of the American Army." In Collections of the Historical Society of Pennsylvania. Philadelphia: J. Pennington, 1853.

United States. National Park Service. "Old South Meeting House." National Parks Service. August 16, 2015. Accessed May 14, 2015. http://www.nps.gov/bost/learn/historyculture/osmh.htm.

University, Princeton. "John Witherspoon." Princeton University. November 26, 2013. Accessed May 20, 2015.

Walker, Paul K. Engineers of Independence: A Documentary History of the Army Engineers in the American Revolution, 1775-1783. Washington, D.C.: Historical Division, Office of Administrative Services, Office of the Chief of Engineers :, 1981.

Walker, Paul K. Engineers of Independence: A Documentary History of the Army Engineers in the American Revolution, 1775-1783. Washington, D.C.: Historical

Division, Office of Administrative Services, Office of the Chief of Engineers :, 1981. 85.

Wallace, Paul A. W. The Muhlenbergs of Pennsylvania. Philadelphia: University of Pennsylvania Press, 1950.

Walpole, Horace. The Letters of Horace Walpole: Fourth Earl of Orford, VI. Edited by Peter Cunningham. Vol. VI. London: Henry G. Bohn, 1861.

Ward, Harry M. For Virginia and for Independence Twenty-Eight Revolutionary War Soldiers from the Old Dominion. Jefferson: McFarland &, Publishers, 2011.

"Washington's Farewell Address 1796." Avalon Project. Accessed August 7, 2015. http://avalon.law.yale.edu/18th_century/washing.asp.

Washington, George. The Writings Of... Collected and Edited by Worthington Chaurcey Ford. Vol. I-XIV 1749-99. New York: G. P. Putnam's Sons, 1889.

Webster, Samuel. A Sermon Preached before the Honorable Council, and the Honorable House of Representatives of the State of Massachusetts-Bay, in New-England. At Boston, May 28, 1777. Being the Anniversary for the Election of the Honorable Council. By Samuel Webster, A.M. Boston: Printed by Edes & Gill, in Queen-Street, 1777.

Wesley, John. A Calm Address to Our American Colonies. London: Printed by R. Hawes, 1775. 19.

West, Timothy. "Hall, James." Hall, James. 1988. Accessed August 7, 2015. http://ncpedia.org/biography/hall-james.

Wheeler, George Augustus. "MILITARY HISTORY OF THE THREE TOWNS." In History of Brunswick, Topsham, and Harpswell, Maine: Part II, 680. Boston: A. Mudge & Sons, Printers, 1878.

"William J Federer's American Minute for November 15th." William J Federer's American Minute for November 15th.

November 15, 2012. Accessed November 20, 2012. http://www.americanminute.com/index.php?date=11-15.

Wing, Conway P. A History of the First Presbyterian Church of Carlisle, Pa.,. Carlisle: "Valley Sentinel" Office, 1877.

Witherspoon, John. The Works of John Witherspoon: Containing Essays, Sermons, &c., on Important Subjects ... Together with His Lectures on Moral Philosophy Eloquence and Divinity, His Speeches in the American Congress, and Many Other Valuable Pieces, Never before Published. Vol. IX. Edinburgh: Printed for J. Ogle, 1815. 220-223.

Yadav, Alok. "Historical Outline of Restoration and 18th-Century British Literature." Whig and Tory--Historical Outline. December 3, 2011. Accessed May 19, 2015. http://mason.gmu.edu/~ayadav/historical outline/whig and tory.htm.

Chicago formatting by BibMe.org.